Henry Drummond

Speeches in Parliament

And some Miscellaneous Pamphlets of the late Henry Drummond, ESQ (Volume 2)

Henry Drummond

Speeches in Parliament
And some Miscellaneous Pamphlets of the late Henry Drummond, ESQ (Volume 2)

ISBN/EAN: 9783744746960

Printed in Europe, USA, Canada, Australia, Japan

Cover: Foto ©Suzi / pixelio.de

More available books at **www.hansebooks.com**

SPEECHES IN PARLIAMENT

AND SOME

MISCELLANEOUS PAMPHLETS

OF THE LATE

HENRY DRUMMOND, ESQ.

EDITED BY LORD LOVAINE

In Two Volumes

VOL. II.

LONDON

BOSWORTH & HARRISON, 215 REGENT STREET

1860

CONTENTS

OF

THE SECOND VOLUME.

— ✦ —

OCCASIONAL PAMPHLETS.

	Page
ELEMENTARY PROPOSITIONS ON THE CURRENCY	1
A LETTER TO THE KING AGAINST THE REPEAL OF THE TEST ACT BY A TORY OF THE OLD SCHOOL.—1829	39
DIALOGUE BETWEEN A SCEPTICAL PHYSICIAN AND HIS CHRISTIAN PATIENT.—1829	61
REFORM, NOT A NEW CONSTITUTION.—1831	77
AN ADDRESS TO THE PEOPLE OCCASIONED BY "A LETTER TO THE QUEEN" FROM "A FRIEND OF THE PEOPLE" BY ONE OF THEMSELVES.—1839	119
JUSTICE TO CORN-GROWERS AND TO CORN-EATERS.—1830 .	141
CAUSES WHICH LEAD TO A BANK RESTRICTION BILL.—1830 .	157
LETTER TO THOMAS PHILLIPS, ESQ., R.A., ON THE CONNECTION BETWEEN THE FINE ARTS AND RELIGION AND THE MEANS OF THEIR REVIVAL.—1840	169
REMARKS ON THE CHURCHES OF ROME AND ENGLAND RESPECTFULLY ADDRESSED TO THE RIGHT REV. DR. WISEMAN AND THE REV. WILLIAM PALMER.—1841	197
REASONS WHEREFORE A CLERGYMAN OF THE CHURCH OF ENGLAND SHOULD NOT BECOME A ROMAN CATHOLIC, IN REPLY TO REV. R. W. SIBTHORP.—1842	219
ON GOVERNMENT BY THE QUEEN AND ATTEMPTED GOVERNMENT FROM THE PEOPLE	253

Page

LETTER TO SIR ROBERT H. INGLIS, BART., M.P., ON THE PAYMENT
    OF THE ROMAN CATHOLIC CLERGY.—1845 330

REASONS FOR REJECTING THE CLAIMS OF ROMISH PRIESTS.—LETTER
    TO J. W. FRESHFIELD, ESQ., HIGH SHERIFF OF THE COUNTY
    OF SURREY.—1851   375

SUBSTANCE OF THE SPEECH OF HENRY DRUMMOND, ESQ., DELIVERED
    AT A MEETING OF THE ELECTORS OF WEST SURREY.—1852   . 381

OCCASIONAL PAMPHLETS.

ELEMENTARY PROPOSITIONS

on

THE CURRENCY

THE CURRENCY.*

PRELIMINARY OBSERVATIONS.

WHEN the following Propositions were first drawn up, they were thought to be so self-evident to every one who would consider the subject, that it would be superfluous to publish them. Experience, however, has shown that the public requires much more instruction in the mere elements of every branch of Political Economy; and that, until it is more enlightened, the correct principles generally entertained by His Majesty's present ministers are liable to be perpetually thwarted.

Although merchants and bankers are not ultimately more affected by the state of the currency than any other class of the community, yet they are the first to be influenced, either by any sudden extension or sudden contraction of its amount: the manufacturers and their labourers follow next; and the landlords and agricultural population feel it the last; and these, ordinarily, not until the merchants and bankers have ceased to suffer from it: but every class feels its consequences, sooner or later, and therefore are equally interested in understanding its operations. If

> "Paper credit, that worst, tho' last supply,
> Which lent corruption lighter wings to fly,"

had never been in existence, nothing would have been more simple than all the offices of a circulating medium of barter; but paper-money has not only put the whole system, in old and highly civilised and extensively commercial states, out of joint, but has introduced so many discordant terms of credit, exchange,

---

* This treatise was originally published in the year 1819, — and republished with additional matter in its present form in 1826.

B 2

par, mint price, bullion price, &c. &c., that many persons are
deterred from an examination of the subject, by the unintelligible jargon of the language in which it is expressed.

But there is encouragement to persevere. Above two hundred years ago, Lord Bacon pointed out defects in our statute
law, and urged the amendment and consolidation of it. His
complaints and his arguments have been re-echoed ineffectually
at various subsequent periods; but it is only now, that Mr.
Peel, to his immortal credit, has begun to rectify them. In
1713, the London Merchants unanimously (Mac. An. Com. vol.
iii. p. 31) declared the trade with France a nuisance, because
it produced an annual export of bullion to that country: a
position, which the most stubborn opponent of the principles of
free-trade would hardly venture to maintain in any public
assembly at the present day. The Navigation Laws which were
first passed by the Revolutionary Parliament, for the avowed
purpose of destroying the commercial prosperity of the Dutch
(a purpose, indeed, which Sir J. Child had the sense to see
these laws did not effect), are happily at an end. The excise
scheme of Sir Robert Walpole was founded upon the same principle as the warehousing system which was introduced by the
present administration; but Sir Robert was so opposed by the
merchants, whose knavery would have been checked, and by
the factious violence of the opponents to his ministry, that he
was compelled to abandon it. In 1803, Sir Robert's principles,
under the auspices of George Rose, were triumphant.

> " Et tibi vel Betty, tibi vel nitidissima Letty
> Gloria factorum temeré conceditur horum."

Fifty years ago, Adam Smith proved the monopoly of the
Bank of England was a nuisance to the country; but Mr.
Robinson has been the first Chancellor of the Exchequer who
has comprehended his reasoning, and been able to act upon it.
In 1810, the few bankers and merchants, who ventured to maintain, in opposition to the bank directors, that a piece of paper
and a silver shilling were not equal to a golden guinea, were
looked upon by their brethren as visionary theorists; but we
have lived to see those, who at that time denied the depreciation of bank notes, heartily ashamed of that celebrated resolution, which still disgraces the Journals of the House of
Commons.

A great change of opinion, however, yet remains to be effected. To determine the laws which regulate the value of the currency, its uses, and its operation upon all the employments of civilised society, is the most important branch of economical science. Upon the *fixedness* of the value of the currency depends, whether every part of internal and foreign commerce shall be lucrative or otherwise. Unless the value of the currency be *fixed*, the landlord is at one time defrauded of his due proportion of the produce of his soil, while at another time, the tenant is robbed of his capital : the manufacturer and merchant binds himself to obligations, which it becomes impossible for him to discharge ; and the labourer finds every fluctuation alike deprive him of some farther portion of his scanty earnings.*

Political Economy is the science which teaches us how to procure the greatest quantity of conveniences at the least expense of time and labour : and, although it is the want and not the science of mankind which has ever been the parent of invention, yet it is the science alone that has taught us to explain the causes of obvious phenomena, and thereby enabled us to direct them to our own advantage. But it requires some labour to reason, and to reflect ; and since ease is the first of animal gratifications, as few men like mental as bodily exertion. Hence they invent all kinds of pretexts to excuse themselves from the trouble of examining into subjects, which they are conscious it is their duty to understand. Nothing can be more indisputable, than that it is the duty of men to study the principles by which their actions ought to be governed ; yet when in 1810, the committee on bullion excited the public attention to the nature of currency (a subject which had been lost sight of for some years), they, who supported the principles therein developed, were assailed as visionaries and theorists by those, who, assuming to themselves the title of " practical men," proved themselves, at the same time, utterly ignorant of any rule by which to regulate their own conduct : so that, to every one of the assailants it might be justly said,

"Nescis, quo valeat nummus, quem præbeat usum."

---

* " The object of every description of currency should be to make the value of property as steady, and as little variable as possible. The truth lay there ; and he who solved that problem, would certainly come to the wisest conclusion."— *Lord Liverpool's Speech, Times, Feb.* 17, 1826.

A merchant or banker, who does not understand the principles of currency, is a mere automaton; he might as well be made of cast iron, and sign his name by steam: and to hear men in those stations ridiculing all study of these principles as matters of mere theory, the truth or falsehood of which is immaterial for any practical purpose, is as reprehensible as it would be in a physician to ridicule anatomy and chemistry, as theories with which the art of healing had no immediate connection.

There are some persons, who, having investigated the truth of this department of economical science, perceive, that they cannot by any legitimate reasoning contravene its positions; but who, being bred up in the trammels of old habits, and the contracted sphere of a counting-house, either cannot apply general views to their own little employment, or apprehend that the adoption of them, if universally acted on, would interfere with their particular gains. The objections of such persons are *, "that these positions, although undeniably true, and such as would be excellent, if they were to be applied to a new country, or to one in which opposite maxims had not long been acted upon, are dangerous to be adopted in this country, burdened with so heavy a debt, and so oppressed by taxation: that we have thriven well under a contrary system, and that these views would make great inroads upon our financial and commercial arrangements; that, however true upon paper, the wisdom of statesmen is shown in knowing when to depart from and modify principles, which might be too rigidly followed up; and that, above all, this is not the time." It is waste of words to argue with such objectors: no time would ever arrive in which they could be brought to confess it was right to act upon principles which they could not overthrow. These objectors are like the slave-owners, who, under the mask of arguing against the present being the time for the abolition of slavery, secretly intend to keep their fellow-creatures for ever in their inhuman fangs. The utmost that can be allowed to them is, that in those cases in which large capitals have been embarked in pernicious monopolies, sufficient time should be granted for the capitals to be withdrawn, and invested in some other employment: but the more time it is

---

* See, for an example, the debates on the Silk Trade.

necessary to grant for this purpose, the more indispensable it is not to delay an hour in taking the first step.

They, who plume themselves upon being what they please to term "practical men," are fond of bringing forward insulated facts, from whence they draw unwarrantable conclusions; and when these facts are shown to be irrelevant, and the conclusions false, abuse as theories the arguments by which they are exposed. A collection of facts, however extensive, is perfectly useless for every practical purpose; that is, as a guide for future conduct, until it has enabled us to frame a theory which explains the causes and the consequences of those facts; and so far is it from being true, that a mere practical man (that is, a man who has no theory on the subject which he is handling) is a person to be relied on for facts, as some people erroneously suppose, no man is competent to observe and note a fact, who is not conversant with the theory of the subject to which the fact relates; for the observation of Cullen is perfectly correct, that there are many more false facts than false theories in the world. Neither is it true, that correct principles of currency can be departed from with impunity, and are of no practical importance; for a wrong apprehension of them has led to more direct ruin of individuals, and classes, than any other error in government. It is painful to speak of the directors of the Bank of England, because they are most amiable and honourable men*; but it is indisputable,

---

* These are not words of unmeaning compliment; and I fully subscribe to the following observations of Mr. John Smith: "I would defy any man to show, in the history of the commercial world, a more strict personal integrity than is to be found in the conduct of the Governors of the Bank of England, in the whole of their money transactions with the public. I will take, for instance, the period of 1816, when the Bank was deriving enormous profits; how acquired, I will not stop to consider. At this period, when they divided the immense sum of 25l. per cent. upon the capital stock (a circumstance, the previous knowledge of which would have made the fortune of any individual), yet, on examining the books, not a single director was found to have availed himself of his private knowledge, or to have possessed one shilling more of stock than was necessary to his being constituted a director, according to the charter."—*Debate on Small Note Bill, Feb.* 1826. Notwithstanding this testimony to the personal character of the directors, it is not inconsistent to contend with Hardcastle (p. 62), "That no greater evil can be imagined, than that an establishment should have the power (not by means of its capital, but by the expansion or contraction of its issues of mere paper), either to raise or lower the money-value of all property, both real and personal; and, according to its good will and pleasure, to influence and regulate the transactions of every member of the community."

that their conduct has been directly at variance with the principles developed in the following Propositions; and that, consequently, their practice has been erroneous, and has aggravated
the evil, arising from fluctuations in the value of the currency,
which has occurred. Nor can they on that account be justly
blamed: they declared their conviction of the truth of opposite
maxims in their evidence before repeated committees of Parliament: they asserted in their own court, on Sept. 22, 1825,
that the fluctuations in the money market had not been occasioned by them. They would, with their views, have been
wrong if they had acted otherwise than in the way they have;
it is owing to their ignorance of the power they possessed that
they have done so little harm: the fault has been with Government, which, in the report presented previously to the introduction of Mr. Peel's bill, admitted the principle here contended
for, and yet left the power of creating unlimited paper money
in the hands of various irresponsible individuals all over the
kingdom.

If the principles of currency had been well understood, not a
particle of the distresses, which have so often occurred, could
have been experienced. We should not have heard at one time
of the ruin of the country being threatened by a drain of gold
from the bank, nor of a bank restriction bill as a remedy for so
visionary an evil. We should not have had the effects of a
sudden and violent return from depreciated paper to a metallic
currency, ascribed to a transition state from war to peace, nor to
too great a remission of taxes; to over-population, nor to over-
production; to over-trading, nor to over-farming: neither should
we have had a rapid rise in the prices of all the productions of
industry cited as a proof of solid and permanent commercial
prosperity.*

The ordinary refuge for wilful ignorance on this question is
the alleged discrepancy between writers on political economy.
As long as the minds of men are of varied powers, so long must

---

* "There never was a period in the history of this country, when all the great
interests of the nation were at the same time in so thriving a condition."—*King's
Speech, Feb.* 1825.

"There are persons who imagine our prosperity is not permanent; but the
House, I am sure, will concur with me in opinion, that it rests on the most solid
foundation."—*Chancellor of the Exchequer, March,* 1825.

the portion of truth which each can perceive, on any given subject, vary in a corresponding degree. If the objection on that ground be made against the study of all sciences, and that of political economy be only included with the rest, the assertion at least has the merit of impartiality, although it scarcely merits serious refutation. But if it be meant to insinuate, that the diversity of sentiment is greater among political economists, than amongst writers upon any other science, the charge has not a vestige of truth to rest upon. Let the charge, however, be granted; it proves nothing but the anxiety of the objector to receive the dictum of some great name as the article of his faith, without giving himself the trouble to investigate the foundation upon which it stands. The greater the ignorance, the greater the difficulty of reconciling apparent contradictions on any subject. If a person, unskilled in medicine, read two or three medical treatises consecutively, he will rise from them with his mind in a state of complete confusion, and the last read work will appear to be at variance with all the preceding; yet the bases on which medical science is supported are as fixed as the nature of the subjects on which it treats will permit, although not more fixed than those of political economy. Even in those arts which are merely mechanical, variations perpetually take place; yet it would be in the highest degree absurd to say, that the art itself were useless, or its principles unfixed, because certain anomalies presented themselves to a superficial observer. In agriculture, for example, no point can be more settled than the advantage of an alternation of crops: yet the longer a pasture has been unbroken, the more productive with due care it becomes: does the discordance of these two facts prove, that there are no fixed principles in agriculture, or that there is no agreement of opinions amongst farmers? that it is immaterial whether the seed be thrown into the ground at one season or at another? and that the principles which direct the alternation and course of cropping are matters of mere theory, and of no practical importance? Unless every transaction, of whatever business a man carries on, be conducted upon fixed principles, it never can be carried on securely, nor stand the storms and tempests which must agitate, at one time or other, every portion of human society.

I recommend to those who affect to justify their own want of

steady principles by the alleged discrepancy in the statements
of Smith, Ricardo, M'Culloch, Mills, and Malthus *, to attend
to the following extract from the London Magazine, on the discordance of physicians: the reasoning is quite as logical, and the
humour much greater: —

" The history of small-pox is as well known to the people as
to physicians. It was the fashion to keep the patients as warm
as possible ; in warm rooms, warm blankets, with warm fires, and
so on ; fresh air was esteemed poison ; cold air death. And if
this was a fashion, it was one not without its philosophy and its
good reasons. The eruption was 'better out than in :' it might
be checked ; and, therefore, also, cordial and hot drinks formed
part of the fashion. But times at last revolved, though old
women, here and there, still hold to the old doctrines and
fashions; and it is not very likely that the fashion will retro-
grade again.

" A rational physician knows, that cold has the same virtues
in measles and scarlet fever as in small-pox ; but it is still the
fashion to keep the measles warm, for the same reason, or lest
the eruption should be repelled ; and should the reverse be
attempted, all the women, and nine-tenths of the apothecaries,
would be up in arms."

What a series of apparent absurdities bewilder the tyro who
dabbles with practical chemistry ! He finds that water is made
of the most combustible materials ; that earth is no earth,
but a metal ; that instead of but one air, there are a score ;
that diamonds are only charcoal, and charcoal diamonds ; that
there are substances of immense power which he can neither
see nor weigh ; that he himself has been all his life a plus or
minus electrifying machine ; and that if he were distilled he
would be found to contain little but azote and carbon.

But it is not with the sciences of medicine and chemistry
alone that political economy will bear the strictest comparison.
Let us take at once the sublimest of all sciences, astronomy, and
it will be found, that the conclusions of political economy are
drawn from premises as susceptible of proof, are as much in
agreement with each other, and are as little affected by the
differences of writers who have treated it, as those of astronomy

---

* See Debates in the House of Commons, Feb. 24, 1826.

itself. Every astronomer knows, that by far the larger portion of that which he believes to be true concerning it, rests entirely upon hypothesis; and that "the highest degree of certainty to which he can arrive is an ascertained and tangible analogy, and . that, consequently, it admits of more abstract argument, and allows a greater play of the imagination than any other of the sciences." The proportion of the magnitudes of the heavenly bodies to each other rests purely upon hypothesis. The annual and diurnal revolution of the earth, directly opposed to the daily sensations and eyes of the *practical* ploughboy, are founded on hypothesis. So absurd, indeed, did this revolution appear to all sober *practical* men when it was first demonstrated, that Copernicus dared not mention it for many years: the *practical* men in Italy constrained the pope reluctantly to put Galileo in prison, and made him learn penitential psalms by heart to purge away his philosophy; and when Jacquier and Le Sieur published at Rome, so late as 1742, the theories of that speculative heretic, Sir Isaac Newton, upon the same subject, they wisely inserted in a preface, that they did not presume to believe that which they had proved to be true, unless that *practical* man, the pope, should happen to be of the same opinion.

The great misfortune is, that the "practical" men, that is, those who act without the guide of reason or reflection, are always the most numerous, and the most powerful. Dr. Harvey, the author of the most important discovery that ever was made in physiology, complains in a letter to his friend, that he was no longer consulted as a physician by the "practical" men of his day: he was a theorist in their eyes, and therefore considered unsafe to be trusted. There is scarcely an instance in the history of human merit to be found, of a man conferring a benefit on his fellow-creatures by the superior powers of his head or heart, who has not been feared, hated, and slandered by his "practical" contemporaries; and at this present time we daily find attacks made upon the personal characters and motives of the more enlightened members of the king's government, when all efforts to defeat their arguments have proved unavailing. "Calumny is the tax paid for celebrity," and an increase of information is never made by the generation in which it is first promulgated; for, as Locke observes, few men after fifty acquire a new idea.

It is to merchants and bankers particularly, that correct views of the principle of currency are indispensable. This has been generally felt of late years, and there are many merchants and bankers who have consequently made themselves perfect masters of the subject. In 1793, one hundred banking houses in various parts˙ of the country were annihilated.* In 1825, nearly as many more were destroyed†; and it is not too much to assert that not one such failure could have taken place, if the managers of these houses had understood and acted upon a correct rationale of their business. If there be one part of the empire, in which just views. require to be more rigidly adhered to than another, it is in this metropolis. Here the common language of every day is calculated to delude : I refer particularly to that which points to the price of the public funds as the sole criterion of financial and commercial prosperity. In the language of the Stock Exchange, the word " better" is made to mean, that the funds are rising; although, by so doing, interest is falling; and it is universally admitted, that a country is advancing in wealth in proportion as the rate of interest is high.‡ All causes of the rise of the funds are totally left out of consideration; if they have risen they must be "better;" the rise may have taken place from causes the most ruinous in their ultimate consequences: it may have taken place, as it almost always has§, from a progressive depreciation of the currency, which must in its reaction produce the ruin of thousands; it is of no consequence; stocks are rising, and, therefore, in the cant of the Stock Exchange, "things are better." On the other hand, no consideration is ever paid to the causes of the fall of stocks : this fall may arise from enlightened ministers removing shackles from commerce, and thereby rendering trade more advantageous for the investment of money than the public funds: it may arise from greater activity in men leading them to prefer employing their

* Macpherson's Annals, p. 266.

† Tooke, p. 38 ; Lord Liverpool, Debate, Feb. 17, 1826.

‡ " From a decline in the public funds (not proceeding from political causes), we must infer a rise in the rate of interest; and as the rate of interest is governed by the rate of profit on the employment of capital, and that an increasing rate of profit is highly favourable to the acquisition and accumulation of capital; so does it argue a much sounder state of things, that the rate of interest should be gradually advancing, than that it should gradually recede."—*Hardcastle*, p. 69.

§ See Mushet.

money in some business, wherein, by the addition of their personal superintendence, they may gain a larger income than they can by leaving it idly in the Government annuities; such considerations never alter the phraseology of the stockjobbers, which is still the same to denote falling stocks, namely, "things are worse."

I once heard a young man, who spent his nights at a gaming table, say, that he liked to have some money in the funds, because it was pleasant to him, when he went to bed in the morning, to think, that his money was still playing, although he could not personally play with it. Whatever else may be thought of the sentiment, it is at least to be allowed that this worthy personage had correct views of the nature of the Stock Exchange. It is little better than a great gaming house; and it is as absurd to suppose, that a high price of the funds is an infallible test of public prosperity, as it would be to quote the bets at Tattersall's for the same purpose. Although some honourable and respectable men are to be found there, yet many of the habitual frequenters of the Stock Exchange exist solely by gaming in the funds, and do not hesitate to propagate any falsehood by which their interest may be served. Let the following extract, from the Morning Chronicle of Feb. 24, 1826, serve as an example:—

" The *extraordinary excitation,* which was produced in the city on Wednesday, *by the propagation of rumours as malicious as they were unfounded,* had yesterday subsided, and a strong feeling of indignation was expressed, not only towards those persons who were the *inventors of the calumnies,* but *those who assisted in giving them greater publicity.* There appears to have been no ground whatever for the suspicion that two London Houses would fail, and it is now pretty evident that all these *alarms were spread by a gang of organised conspirators, whose interests were to be promoted in producing a fall in the market, so as to relieve them from the effect of the rise which had taken place, on the approaching settling-day.*"

I have already observed, that, of all the subdivisions into which the science of political economy may be separated, there is not one of so much importance as the laws which regulate the currency. It is on this account that I have endeavoured to condense the subject into the shortest possible space in the fol-

lowing propositions, hoping thereby to overcome the reluctance
of some persons to their consideration. It might be admitted,
that the subject is dry; but the elements of every subject are
always dry; all grammar is dry; mere technicology must be
dry; but *ignoratus sermo, ignorata et ars;* and as it is a point
upon which the property of every individual, from the king to
the peasant, turns, there is no one, whether landlord, farmer,
labourer, manufacturer, merchant, or banker, who is not deeply
interested, not only in understanding the subject himself, but
in assisting others to understand it likewise.

ELEMENTARY PROPOSITIONS,

ETC. ETC.

1. TRADE is the exchange of one commodity for another.
2. The *intrinsic* value of a commodity is the quantum of
skill and labour required for its production: the *marketable*
value is as the supply and demand.
3. As simple barter is inconvenient, a common representative
of all commodities has been chosen to facilitate exchange.
4. This common representative is the precious metals.
5. The precious metals are less liable to waste than most
things; they are also little likely to be suddenly increased or
diminished in any considerable quantity; they are therefore the
best representative that can be found.
6. Being the representative, they are consequently the
standard measure of the values of the represented commodities;
and if they could be as fixed a measure of value as a foot rule
is of space, it would be so much the better; they are only the
best that can be found.
7. Coining is the state's warranty of the metal's weight and
purity. *

* It is necessary for a state to fix the number of parts into which it will divide
a given portion of metal for its currency, and this fixed number of parts is called

8. All commodities are said to be dear or cheap as they require more or less of this representative to be given for them; which expressions can have no meaning but in reference to the standard (6) by which the commodities are measured.*

9. If there be a smaller quantity of metal in a country at one period than another, the price of other commodities (their quantities and intrinsic value remaining the same) is said to have fallen: i. e. a smaller quantity of metal must represent the same quantity of commodities, and *vice versâ.*†

10. A country must always contain that quantity of metal which is necessary for its trade : for if the quantity of metal in it were so *small* that commodities had greatly *fallen* in price, they would be sent out of the country to be exchanged for metal to be brought back. If the quantity of metal in it were so *great* that commodities had greatly *risen* in price, the metal would be exported rather than the commodities, and foreign commodities brought back instead.

11. Thus a country must keep that quantity of metal which is necessary to facilitate its barter, and no more.

12. As trading by means of the precious metals is more convenient than simple barter (3, 4), so paper is more convenient than metal; but paper is deficient in all the other qualities that metal possesses ; *1st*, it is very liable to waste ; *2dly*, It may be suddenly increased or diminished in any quantity; it wants, therefore, all the necessary qualifications which ought to constitute a standard (6).‡

the mint price of the metal : i. e. if a pound of gold is coined into 40 equal parts, each called a sovereign, the mint price of a pound of gold is said to be 40 sovereigns. The mint should coin any bullion that is brought to it, either gratis, or at a very low price.

* As the precious metals are the standard by which all other commodities are measured, to say that they are dear or cheap, is a contradiction in terms.

† If there be a joint currency of metal and paper, and any circumstances should cause an export of the metal, it will be necessary for the issuers of that paper to diminish its quantity in order that the paper, becoming smaller in quantity, may rise in value in proportion as the metal rises. At the time of the Bank Restriction Bill, paper ought to have been withdrawn, and the Bill immediately repealed: and had the true principles of currency been understood, it would never have been passed.

‡ The precious metals are of great intrinsic value ; paper is of very low intrinsic value ; so that a greater quantity of unproductive capital is locked up in a metallic than in a paper circulation, which is an advantage in favour of paper.

13. Paper then is an equivalent for the precious metals, only inasmuch as it is convertible into them at the will of the holder, paper being the representative of an equivalent.

14. The coined metal, or paper, used in the internal trade of a country as its representative, is called the currency of that country.

15. A given portion of paper *currency* is said to be worth a given portion of metal (not according to its intrinsic, nor to its marketable value), (2) but, because it is convertible into that quantity of metal which it professes to be.

16. It has been (10) shown, that the necessary quantity of metal is preserved in a country by its free import and export: if paper be substituted for metal, besides the other defects mentioned (12), this is superadded, viz. that it cannot be exported, because it is useless everywhere but in the country in which it was first issued: the same methods, therefore, which regulate the due quantity of metal in a country, cannot regulate the due quantity of paper.

17. If the currency of a country be composed partly of metal and partly of paper, and if, from too great a quantity of metal being imported and coined, or from too great a quantity of paper being issued, the currency become redundant, as the paper cannot be exported to rectify it (16), the metal will (10); and if the paper be convertible into metal, so much will be so converted, and the metal exported, as will reduce the quantity of currency to the same amount as if there had been no paper at all.

18. As long therefore as the paper currency be convertible into a metallic one, the *joint quantity* of the two will never be greater nor less than it would be if there were no paper at all, and therefore the paper will be as efficient a representative as the metal.

19. The *relative quantities* of the two at any given period will vary from any other given period, according to the convenience of traders, and are immaterial, as the *joint quantity* is the essential circumstance.

20. If the paper be not convertible; if the quantity of currency become redundant; and if the redundancy be greater than the export of metal can correct (10, 16), the remaining paper currency will be depreciated: i. e. will not be worth so much as

it professes to be (15), and the prices of all other commodities will rise (9).

21. It has been shown (9) that the smaller the quantity of currency in a country at any one given time, the lower must be the prices of all other commodities at that time; and that if the metallic part of that currency be exported, it is because there is a redundancy of currency; if this redundancy were to be relieved by any other means, the same effect would be produced as if the metal were exported.

22. It has been shown also, that as soon as the redundancy is reduced, no farther export of metal can take place; consequently if the redundancy were relieved by any other means, no export at all would take place.

23. As the metal is exported because the *joint* currency is in excess (17), and as, if this excess be removed by any other means, the *metallic* part would not be exported (22); were a sufficient part of the paper withdrawn from circulation, no export of metal would take place.*

24. It follows, therefore, that wherever metal has disappeared from a circulation composed partly of paper and partly of metal, it is because the paper is in excess; and that no measure can be effectual to make metal return to a country from whence it has disappeared but the withdrawing part of its paper currency from circulation, and making the remainder convertible into metal, *ad libitum*.

———————

THE country has recently been involved in what has been unanimously described by His Majesty's ministers, and by all the merchants and bankers in the House of Commons, to be a state of " unexampled distress." It is necessary to inquire what was the cause of this distress; because if the same cause exists now, no one will venture to deny, that similar causes must produce similar results: and that it is our bounden duty to

* Other circumstances besides the quantity of paper can cause a variation in the supply of bullion, but nothing can permanently exclude it, nor permanently maintain it as currency, but the regulation of the paper which circulates together with it.

provide a remedy, or to warn the public to be prepared for the result.

The currency of Great Britain is computed to consist of 60,000,000*l.*, of which 20,000,000*l.* is said to be in the precious metals; 20,000,000*l.* in Bank of England paper, 12,000,000*l.* in country bankers' paper, and 8,000,000*l.* private bills.

If the whole of this currency were to be made of the precious metals, it would cause 40,000,000*l.* of the capital of the country to be immediately sunk in forming it; and it would cost a farther sum of 2,000,000*l.* annually, to supply the wear and tear of the coins, expense of assaying, coining, &c., and the loss of interest on the whole additional 40,000,000*l.*

But as the withdrawing of the paper from circulation would lead to a great demand for metals from abroad, producing a scarcity, and consequently a rise in their value elsewhere, it is probable that paper, of private traders, would be more resorted to than it is at present; and thus less currency would answer the purposes of trade, and that 20,000,000*l.* of metallic currency would suffice, in addition to the 20,000,000*l.* already existing.

A currency of 40,000,000*l.* of gold would, however, not only be a currency of higher value than the present, in the proportion of two to three, causing, consequently, the reduction of the price of all commodities to that extent, but it would be as much higher than the value of the present currency as the proportion of gold in this country, as compared with the rest of the world at that time, would be greater than the proportion of metal now in this country, as compared with the rest of the world at this time; so that the effect of resorting to a metallic currency *might be* to lower the price of all commodities nearly one-half.

This would of itself be immaterial : but another effect would be to double the amount of the taxes; to double the amount of debts, mortgages, annuities, &c.; to double the salaries of the public servants, pensioners, soldiers, sailors, &c.; causing a pressure upon the people which would probably produce some ruinous convulsion.

If, therefore, any bill, which enacts that we shall return to a metallic currency, were to be carried into full effect, it would be absolutely necessary to make some regulation upon the points specified in the last paragraph; otherwise, such a bill cannot be carried into effect; and merely to enact, that this country shall return to a metallic currency, without accompanying that measure by others, is absurd, because it is not possible, *simpliciter*, to adopt it. There would besides be a flagrant injustice in doing so; for it would compel us to pay the fundholder in a currency of a higher value than he lent; or, in other words, to pay him more than we borrowed.

There are two modes, however, by which it may be partially adopted: the one is by avowedly depreciating the coin; that is, enacting that one sovereign should pass for two (a measure for which much might be said, which is here passed by); the other mode is, and it is in fact the same as the former, only in a more circuitous, and therefore less obvious way, by keeping up, as we are doing at present, the largest possible amount of paper, with the smallest possible amount of metal.

This mode being the one now actually in operation, is certainly the better one to continue to adopt; but it is absolutely absurd to enact, that any body or bodies, be they Bank of England or others holding this paper, shall, on any sudden emergency, no matter from what cause arising, be called upon for the payment of a debt in one description, and one value of currency, which was contracted in another description, and another value; whilst, on the other hand, there is no preservative against an over-issue of paper, and consequent depreciation of the currency to any amount, except the convertibility of that paper, under some form or other, into the precious metals, at the will of the holder.

To meet the first branch of this dilemma, it is indispensable that paper, the existence of which is sanctioned by the legislature, should be a legal tender; and for this reason, I doubt the propriety of there being more than one chartered bank, which should be the bank of the state, and its paper alone the legal tender. But however this may be, all in substance that I contend for is, that if we are to have a paper currency authorised by law, that paper shall be made available to us at the time we want it most, and not only at the times when we want it least; that it shall be of use to us in times of sudden panics, when it is physically impossible to procure gold to give in exchange to the holder of paper, and not of use only when it is as easy to procure gold as paper. To meet the other branch of the dilemma, it is necessary to enact that paper shall be legal tender for no sum

c 2

above the value of 100 ounces of gold bullion ; and, in order to save the delay and expense of useless coining, that bullion, stamped at the Mint, shall be given instead of coin, according to the plan of Mr. Ricardo.

Recent events have shown, that the mere convertibility of paper into metal is not sufficient to constitute a safe currency, without there be a farther control upon the issue of paper. For it appears, that the public is not aware sufficiently early of the depreciation that is going on, to check it before it gets to so great a height, that the difference between its greatest amount (i. e. the highest price of commodities) and its lowest amount, which ensues in consequence of the reaction by the contraction of the paper (i.e. the lowest price of commodities) is so great as to cause enormous loss to, if not the ruin of, all men who have engaged to make payments, at the time of the latter state of the currency, for commodities which were contracted for in the former. The rise in the price of every production during the year 1824 and beginning of 1825 showed, to all persons who understood the principles of currency, that there was a depreciation of the currency going on, although it was impossible to ascertain the amount of it, nor precisely the quarter whence it originated.* It has subsequently appeared to have arisen partly

* The following comparative statement of the prices of different articles is taken from Mr. Tooke, p. 196 : —

ARTICLES.	Price, 1823.	Price, 1825.
Cochineal, Spanish .	24	26
Cotton, Bowed Georgia .	10½	18½
Bengal, Surat .	8¼	13½
Indigo, East India .	12	16
Iron, British .	7	13
Lead, ditto .	23½	30½
Spices, Cinnamon .	8¼	13½
Mace .	6¼	18
Nutmegs .	3½	12
Pepper, black .	7¼	9½
Sugar, B. P. Gaz. average	38	45
Havannah, white .	48	57
Silk, Reggio .	16	17
China, raw .	22	28
Speltre .	30½	41¾
Tallow, St. Petersburgh, yellow, common	37	43
Tobacco, Virginia, ordinary and middling	3¼	6½
Wool, German, fine	8½	9½
Wheat (Torrens, p. 274)	51½	66
Three per cent. Consols (March)	73½	94

from the issue of Bank of England, but chiefly from the issue of country paper. The convertibility of the paper into gold prevented the depreciation going farther than it did, and caused its being again diminished in quantity; but the suddenness of its contraction produced the ruin of thousands, which many of the sufferers, such as labourers and tradesmen, could not prevent by any management, however prudent. It has been said in the House of Commons, that the ignorance of the Bank Directors of sound principles of currency prevented their taking such steps as would have obviated much of the evil; but as there is no reason to suppose that any mode of appointing Directors of the Bank would ensure the election of more intelligent men (and more honest and conscientious cannot be found) than are there at present, it ought not to be left in their power to produce the ruin of any individual, far less of any large class of the king's subjects.

It is true that the mere convertibility of the paper is sufficient to prevent its ultimate depreciation, and to make the currency right itself *; so that at the end of one hundred years, the paper, *upon the average*, during that period, will not have been depreciated. But the mere convertibility is not sufficient to prevent ruinous vacillations, ebbs and flows to an immense amount, so that it may be doubtful whether as much capital would not have been destroyed at the conclusion of one hundred years, as would have been, by at once returning to a complete metallic currency, and depreciating the coin one-half. It is the more necessary to dwell upon this subject, because Mr. Maberly, in a speech

Whilst currency is becoming redundant, interest continues falling, and men endeavour to employ the capital so created in any way which seems to promise a higher rate than they make in their ordinary business. Hence a variety of disturbing causes are immediately put into operation; otherwise, the rise of prices would be exactly commensurate with the fall in the currency; but such is not the case in all instances; for a small *artificial* fall in the value of currency, causes a very great *artificial* and *unequal* rise in the prices of all commodities.

* " There was one point to which he would advert, because he thought the doctrine contained in it was most erroneous. On that doctrine the country bank-note circulation had been principally defended, and that was, that there was nothing better than a paper circulation convertible into gold. Now, that doctrine was true only to a certain extent, namely, that wherever a paper circulation was convertible into coin, its evils would, in the end, cure themselves. That cure, however, could only be carried into effect at the expense of the ruin of hundreds of thousands of persons; and a cure with such consequences was almost as bad as the endurance of the evil itself."—*Lord Liverpool's Speech, Feb.* 17, 1826.

much commended by Mr. Huskisson, erroneously contended, that the foreign exchanges immediately indicated the depreciation of the currency the very moment that it occurred; whereas, the bare fact of the coin being exported is proof sufficient of the currency being in excess, whether the exchanges indicate it or not.

That the mere convertibility of the paper cannot check depreciation until it has proceeded great lengths, will be obvious from considering the rise and progress of the evil. An issuer of paper lends an extra quantity of paper, say 10,000l. to a manufacturer of cloth, who causes therewith so much extra cloth to be produced. This is exported, in the usual course of trade, by the merchant, and as much cochineal as was heretofore equivalent, and which would have remained equivalent, if the currencies had remained the same, is imported in its stead. But it is not until the adjustment of the account, between the merchants in this country and the merchants to whom the cloth is remitted, and who have remitted the cochineal in exchange for it, that it is discovered whether the balance be in favour of one party or the other, and whether a further export of commodities or of bullion must be sent out in return for what has been received.* If the cloth cost 10,000l. here, it should sell for 10,000l. there also. But as the extra issue of paper here made currency more plentiful, more of it was given for the making of the cloth; and the real value of the cloth, when measured by the currency of the country to which it was

---

* A small extra issue of Bank of England paper may facilitate a much greater extra issue of country paper, and the two together will facilitate and produce an extra quantity of private bills, acceptances, &c., to a greater amount of this latter than can be well ascertained. A large proportion of the transactions which caused the rise of prices was done by means of acceptances and transfer of joint stock companies' shares. The amount of these shares, which were transferred for commodities, was considerable; and it is said by some very inquisitive and intelligent men, that the excess of these acceptances exceeded by many times the amount of the excess of bank and country notes. On this subject, a gentleman of great accuracy wrote to me as follows: "The issues of paper-money were aided to a monstrous extent by acceptances. I know three men in one connection, and five in another (I do not mean as partners), who contrived to get out, and to keep out, nearly half a million of their notes; and it appears, that they only wanted a little more time to make the large businesses, in which they embarked, and supported, profitable. They have all failed but one, and have put upwards of 300 persons out of employment. Such things as these were carried on to a monstrous extent."

sent, and from whence the cochineal was returned, was found
to be only 9,000*l.* More cloth, therefore, must be sent, or
bullion to the amount of another 1,000*l.*; and as the same
process that had raised the cloth, which was really only worth
9,000*l.*, to the apparent value of 10,000*l.*, had been performing
the same operation upon all other manufactures, bullion would
be the cheapest commodity in the country, and would be sent
out to make up for the deficient value of the cloth.

The time of the adjustment of this account will vary according
to the place to which the productions have been sent.   An adjustment with China, obviously cannot take place so soon as an
adjustment with France; and although the currency was in
point of fact in excess, the moment the notes were paid out of
the hands of the issuer into those of the manufacturer, it is
probably a year or eighteen months, at the soonest, that the
depreciation can be suspected.

If this were an insulated transaction, the evil would be soon
remedied; but, unfortunately, *vires acquirit eundo.*   The first
operation is an extra demand for labour, and, consequently, of
all the things consumed by the labourers; extra demand for
their goods causes more manufacturers to seek for assistance to
manufacture more goods by applying for notes, which they
erroneously believe to be solid money: the more prices rise, the
more notes are demanded; and the more notes are lent, the
more prices rise.   The country bankers, one and all, avow, that
the more prices rise, the more notes they issue; so that before
the adjustment of the first transaction of over-issue, the whole
country has become inundated with a false currency, which
suddenly reveals itself, by the public hearing that all the gold
has gone out of the country, at which the people are seized
with amazement and alarm.   The evil also will be severer or
lighter, according to whether a large stock of the extra commodities shall have been accumulated at home, before they were
sent abroad ; for as long as the employment of the notes, and
the labour they have set in motion, be *confined to this country,*
it is impossible for any variation to take place in the *foreign*
exchanges.

As soon as the public becomes alarmed, the poorest members
of it very wisely endeavour to convert all the paper in their
possession into gold.   Their doing so, however, increases the

embarrassment; and it is now proposed in Parliament, to take from them the power of aggravating such an evil, by suppressing all notes under the value of 5*l.* If the country bankers have lent upon mortgage, or locked up, in any similar way, the funds deposited with them, this measure will cause many of them to break. This, however, may be called only a temporary evil, and as such justified. The permanent effect of the measure will be to cause a considerable loss to the capital of the country, diminishing the power of employing labour, produce a great fall in prices, dismissal and starvation of labourers, and increase of the taxes and salaries of the public servants; because it will raise the value of the currency. But since the breaking of the country banks affects principally the labouring classes, whose wages are exclusively paid in such notes, producing the greatest misery and distress amongst them, it is a lesser evil that the capital should be sunk, than that the labourers be so much robbed. At all events, this measure ought to be resorted to until some plan be found out adequate to give us a secure paper currency. At the same time it is to be remembered, that this measure is not an absolute preservative against the effects of panic, because the largest run that ever was made upon the Bank of England was made at a period when no small notes were in existence; and farther, that the chance of forging coin successfully is much greater than that of forging country paper; and if the punishment of death were taken away altogether for forgery, the issuers of paper would readily find means of preventing its successful imitation.

The only effectual preservative against over issues of paper, is to take from all persons, who have a personal interest in depreciating the currency, the power to do so. It is idle to contend, that laws to regulate the issue of notes, payable on demand, is an uncalled for interference of government with the freedom of trade. Issuing notes is not trading, but coining money: a power which no sovereign but that of England ever suffered to depart from his own hands, and which never can be safely lodged in any other. If it is deemed necessary to continue the punishment of death as the penalty for putting into circulation worthless coin, it is passing strange that no penalty whatever should be affixed to putting into circulation worthless paper. It would puzzle a whole college of Jesuits to explain the moral difference between the two offences, and the evil to the community must be acknowledged equal in both cases. No promissory notes, payable on demand, ought to be issued by any company or individual but the bank of the state; and an account of its affairs ought to be regularly published every quarter, together with the amount of bullion purchased, imported, exported, and coined, that the public may always know exactly how it stands, and upon what principles its conduct is regulated; at the same time means should be found to prevent its being a mere tool of the executive, as the Bank of England has often been hitherto.

As we cannot dispense with a paper currency, paper must be made a legal tender; for if it be not, great ruin must ensue at particular periods, whenever a sudden and general demand for gold shall be made upon the banks which issue the paper. It is obvious, that it is physically impossible for 20,000,000*l.* of coin to satisfy the demanders of it in exchange for 40,000,000*l.* of paper. On the other hand, if all paper be made legal tender, there is an end to its convertibility into gold, and consequently to all prevention of an over-issue of it. This is a dilemma necessarily arising out of a large paper currency, the fluctuations in the value of which must be commensurate with the proportion that the paper shall exceed the coin; and the best remedy is to make one paper only legal tender, and this paper should be one over which Parliament can exercise a control.

There is one other mode by which fluctuations in the value of the currency might be prevented, that is, by fixing the amount of paper which shall be issued, by law. Suppose, for instance, that the commerce of the country requires a currency of 60,000,000*l.*; let a law authorise the issue (if by the Treasury*, so much the better) of 40,000,000*l.* of paper; this of course to be the only paper payable on demand in the country, legal tender, &c., and let the remainder of the currency be made up of coin. The state of trade could never be such as to make 40,000,000*l.* of paper excessive, and the fluctuations in *quantity* of currency would take place in the coin alone, by which the *value* of the currency would remain fixed.

A plan has been recommended for giving increased solidity

---

* The political objections to this I purposely pass by.

to the system of country banking, which is to increase the number of their partners, and ensure these partners being men of considerable property.   But no number of partners, nor no extent of property can prevent men from over-issuing their paper, when it is their interest to do so.   It must never be lost sight of, that the root of all the distresses which have occurred ever since 1793, is to be found in an over-issue of paper.   The partners in the Bank of England are numerous and opulent, but no country bank is more desirous of forcing its paper into circulation than is the Bank of England.   The measure is no doubt a wise one, for other reasons*; that is, the law which limits the number of partners is very absurd and mischievous, and therefore it is a good thing to repeal it; but as to being a cure, or even the smallest prevention against the recurrence of evils similar to those which we are at this moment experiencing, it will not, and cannot have the remotest influence.   It is farther proposed, that all issuers of notes should deposit a security for the notes which they issue; but this is as futile as the former part of the plan.   Suppose a man with an estate or stock worth 50,000*l.* deposits this security, and obtains leave to issue 50,000*l.* notes; he then, with these, buys more land, to the amount of 10,000*l.*, deposits this, and issues again so many more notes. Thus he would proceed upon a system precisely analogous to that which the country bankers at present pursue; namely, increasing their issues in proportion to the rise in prices.

As it has been contended by Lord Liverpool, in a speech of great length†, "that the principal source of the recent distress

---

* "The present system of law, as to banks, must now be altered in one way or other.   It was the most absurd, the most inefficient; it had not one recommendation to stand upon.   The present system was one of the fullest liberty as to what was rotten and bad; but of the most complete restriction, as to all that was good. By it, a cobbler or a cheesemonger, without any proof of his ability to meet them, might issue his notes, unrestricted by any check whatever; while, on the other hand, more than six persons, however respectable, were not permitted to become partners in a bank, with whose notes the whole business of a country might be transacted.   Altogether, this system was one so absurd, both in theory and practice, that it would not appear to deserve the slightest support, if it was attentively considered, even for a single moment."—*Lord Liverpool's Speech*, 17th. *Feb.* 1826.

Is it not astonishing, after this speech, that Lord Liverpool has left the cobbler and cheesemonger the power still to *issue his notes unrestricted by any check whatever*?

† "Their lordships would recollect, that on a former occasion a noble lord had referred to an expression of his on the first day of the present session; referring

is to be found in the rash spirit of speculation, which has pervaded the country for some time," and as such a position is most alarming, as it proves the utter ignorance of the Government as to the real cause of these evils, and as it will be likely to divert attention from the only true source of the recent distress, namely, the over-issue of paper, it is of importance shortly to refute that position.   No over-trading nor over-speculation can produce injury or inconvenience to any one but to those who

also, as their lordships would recollect, to what had passed last session, that *such a crisis as that now existing was not unforeseen by himself and others.*   The noble lord, their lordships would recollect, had not on that occasion repeated his whole declaration, and had said that he (Lord Liverpool) had not connected the great speculation in the country (to which he had referred) with country banks.   Now it was distinctly in his own recollection, and their lorships would find, on referring to those floating records, which, however loose, generally gave an account of what passed before their lordships undoubtedly correct in substance, that he had, in some respects, gone out of his way to give notice to those embarked in the speculations of that period; and had then stated, that *those speculations*, which he foresaw would *bring on distress and ruin*, and which induced him then to make the declaration, were not confined to this town, but had spread much more widely, and had extended through the whole of the country, through the medium of the country banks.   Government had received intelligence of this, and numerous individuals knew of it as well as government.   When he referred to this declaration, he did it out of no view of laying claim, he could assure their lordships, to any prophetic spirit, beyond that possessed by any other noble lords, who in the course of business had directed their attention to questions of that nature.   Their lordships must say, when they recollected the numerous speculations of the last year, the mining speculations, the loans to foreign countries, the various extravagant projects which were on foot, that it was impossible but sooner or later a re-action must take place.   In discussing the proposed measures, he should first endeavour to ascertain the causes of the present distress.   *And he had no difficulty in stating, that he agreed with those who had ascribed the principal part of the evil to those extraordinary and extravagant speculations which were afloat in this country during the last year, and which undoubtedly had their origin in the then great prosperity of the country."—Lord Liverpool's Speech, 17th. Feb. 1826.*

That is, speculation has brought on distress and ruin: The great prosperity of the country has brought on speculation : *Ergo*, Great prosperity has brought on distress and ruin !

It is impossible, therefore, that his lordship can have given any warning, for it is obvious that he is even now in error as to the cause of the recent distress; and moreover, he represented, in the king's speech at the close of the session of 1825, as did also his colleague, the Chancellor of the Exchequer, the high prices as founded upon and being a proof of solid and durable prosperity; whereas, they were a proof of nothing but an over-issue of worthless paper.   I presume, therefore, that this report of his speech is incorrect.   Messrs. Cobbett, Hardcastle, and Attwood foretold in print, as clearly as language could express, everything that has taken place.

over-trade, and who over-speculate. In "the recent distress,"
ruin came upon thousands who did neither the one nor the
other. Supposing a man to over-trade, that is, to buy up, or
cause to be manufactured, commodities to the amount of 100,000*l.*
more than he can obtain an equivalent for, he will lose to that
amount, but no more. The commodity which he has bought
up will have become dearer, but some other must have become
cheaper; for the 100,000*l.* which he invested in the commodity
in which he was speculating, must have been withdrawn from
some other commodity *, which must have become cheaper in a
corresponding degree. It is said that over-trading and over-
speculating, has been carried on to the extent of 17,000,000*l.*;
that is, people have invested 17,000,000*l.* in the purchase or
manufacture of more commodities than they had previously.
But where did these 17,000,000*l.* come from? They did not
coin it; neither did 17,000,000*l.* fall into their pockets, like
aerolites, from the moon. They did not sell out of the public
funds to that amount in order to invest the produce in the
objects of their speculations; for if such had been the case, the
public funds must have fallen, instead of continuing to rise, as
they actually did, as fast as all other commodities; and unless
some source can be pointed out, whence these 17,000,000*l.* were
derived, it is absurd to say that over-trading caused a rise in
the price of any other commodities than those in which the
over-trading was carried on.

The fact is, that over-trading was the necessary consequence
of an inundation of depreciated paper. Currency became so
plentiful, that the use of it, instead of being worth 5 per cent.,
was scarcely worth 2 per cent. Hence people were tempted to
invest it in any way that seemed likely to yield them a larger
profit: hence too the rise in *every* commodity, stocks, land, corn,
&c., is easily accounted for: hence there might be over-trading
to any amount, without a corresponding fall in any one, nay,
even with a rise in every one marketable commodity.

If not one shilling of the 17,000,000*l.*† which have been fool-

* He may speculate in fictitious capital.

† I subjoin here a list of the bubbles in which people have been investing, not
their property, but their depreciated paper.

Foreign Loans, Mining, and other Schemes.

The following is a list of payments made on foreign loans, mining shares, and

ishly subscribed in illusory schemes, had been so employed ; if they had remained in the pockets of the silly people who have

other undertakings, during the present year, and which amount to the sum of 17,582,773*l.*

Per cent.		£		£
35	on	1,000,000 Brazilian Loan of 1824		350,000
75	,,	2,000,000 Do. do. 1825		1,500,000
75	,,	3,500,000 Danish do.		2,625,000
56½	,,	2,000,000 Greek do.		1,130,000
25	,,	1,428,571 Guatimala do.		357,143
60	,,	400,000 Guadalajara do.		240,000
89¾	,,	3,200,000 Mexican do.		2,872,000
70	,,	2,500,000 Neapolitan do.		1,750,000
78	,,	616,000 Peruvian do.		480,480
				11,304,623

Per share.				
£25	on	10,000 Anglo-Mexican Mine shares		250,000
5	,,	15,000 Anglo-Chilian		75,000
7	,,	6,000 Arigna Iron and Coal		42,000
25	,,	500 Bolanos		12,500
3	,,	10,000 Bolivar		30,000
5	,,	10,000 Castello		50,000
5	,,	10,000 Chilian		50,000
2	,,	2,500 Cobalt and Copper		5,000
5	,,	10,000 Chili and Peru		50,000
15	,,	10,000 Cornwall and Devonshire		150,000
2	,,	2,500 Consolidated Copper		5,000
2½	,,	10,000 English Mining		25,000
2	,,	4,000 Equitable		8,000
12½	,,	1,000 Famatina		12,500
5	,,	20,000 General Mining		100,000
3	,,	1,800 Gwennappe		5,400
5	,,	10,000 Haytian		50,000
2	,,	10,000 Hibernian		20,000
3	,,	5,000 Hoomeavy		15,000
7½	,,	10,000 London United		75,000
2	,,	2,000 Manganese		4,000
5	,,	10,000 Pasco Peruvian		50,000
5	,,	20,000 Potosi		100,000
1	,,	3,000 Polbreen Tin and Copper		3,000
3½	,,	16,000 Royal Irish		56,000
330	,,	500 Real del Monte		165,000
5	,,	8,000 Royal Stannary		40,000
1	,,	5,000 Waldeck		5,000
2	,,	5,000 South Wales		10,000
3	,,	10,000 Scottish National Mining		30,000
3	,,	10,000 Tywarnhale		30,000
20	,,	1,000 Tlalpuxahua		20,000

expended them, the recent distresses would have been exactly as great, and probably greater; for these 17,000,000l. (if they were

Per share.				£
£10	„	500 Tarma	.	5,000
10	„	6,000 United Mexican Mines	.	60,000
10	„	18,000 Ditto (New)	.	180,000
15	„	10,000 Welsh Iron and Coal . . .	.	150,000
10	„	10,000 Ditto Slate, Copper, and Lead . .	.	100,000
2	„	250,000 Protector Fire Assurance . . .	.	500,000
10	„	8,000 British Gas	.	80,000
5	„	10,000 International gas	.	50,000
6	„	2,500 London Portable	.	15,000
20	„	5,000 New Imperial	.	100,000
3	„	10,000 Provincial Portable . . .	.	30,000
15	„	2,000 Independent Gas	.	30,000
5	„	9,000 Phœnix Gas	.	45,000
8	„	20,000 United General	.	160,000
2	„	10,000 Birmingham and Liverpool Railway .	.	20,000
3	„	4,000 Manchester and Liverpool . .	.	12,000
5	„	10,000 Anglo-Mexican Mint . . .	.	50,000
10	„	6,000 American and Colonial Steam .	.	60,000
2	„	10,000 Australian	.	20,000
10	„	10,000 Atlantic and Pacific . . .	.	100,000
2	„	5,000 Egyptian Trading	.	10,000
25	„	20,000 British Iron	.	500,000
6	„	50,000 British Rock and Patent Salt .	.	300,000
3	„	10,000 British and Foreign Paper . .	.	30,000
2	„	20,000 British, Irish, and Colonial Silk .	.	40,000
1	„	10,000 Bristol Ship Canal . . .	.	10,000
5	„	5,000 Steam and Packet Navigation .	.	25,000
5	„	20,000 British and Foreign Timber . .	.	100,000
1	„	5,000 British Chuan and Roman Cement .	.	5,000
5	„	10,000 Canada	.	50,000
1	„	5,000 Canal Gas Engine	.	5,000
5	„	13,000 Columbian Agricultural . . .	.	65,000
10	„	1,000 Canada and Nova Scotia . .	.	10,000
2	„	4,000 Devon Haytor Granite . . .	.	8,000
10	„	5,000 Droitwich Patent Salt . . .	.	50,000
2	„	1,000 Elbe and Weser Steam . . .	.	2,000
2	„	5,000 East London Drug	.	10,000
2	„	2,000 French Brandy	.	4,000
2½	„	20,000 General Steam	.	50,000
5	„	10,000 Gold Coast	.	50,000
6	„	8,000 Great Westminster Dairy . .	.	48,000
2	„	20,000 Guernsey and Jersey Steam . .	.	40,000
3	„	3,500 Ground Rent	.	10,500
25	„	10,000 Hibernian Stock	.	250,000
5	„	10,000 Honduras	.	50,000
1	„	20,000 Irish Manufactory	.	20,000
2	„	2,000 Imperial Plate Glass . . .	.	4,000

'sent out of the country, which I doubt) were remitted in commodities, for which, some other commodities (not, indeed of equi-

Per share.			£
£10	,,	12,000 Imperial Distillery	120,000
2	,,	5,000 Imperial Estate	10,000
1	,,	2,000 Investment Bank	2,000
3	,,	10,000 London Brick	30,000
1	,,	1,000 London and Gibraltar Steam	1,000
2	,,	1,000 Ditto Window Glass	2,000
1	,,	1,000 Lower Rhine Steam	1,000
1	,,	5,000 London Drug	5,000
1	,,	4,000 London Smelting	4,000
2	,,	1,000 London and Portsmouth Steam . . .	2,000
2	,,	2,000 Ditto and Gravesend	4,000
10	,,	10,000 Mexican Company	100,000
4	,,	6,000 Metropolitan Dairy	24,000
10	,,	2,000 Medway Lime and Coke	20,000
2⅓	,,	7,500 Netherland Patent Salt	18,750
2	,,	5,000 New Brighton	10,000
3	,,	5,000 New Corn Exchange	15,000
1	,,	10,000 National Drug and Chemical	10,000
5	,,	6,000 Patent Bricks	30,000
5	,,	4,000 Pacific Pearl Fishery	20,000 .
4	,,	15,000 Pearl and Coral Fishery	60,000
10	,,	20,000 Provincial Banks	200,000
15	,,	6,000 Patent Distillery	90,000
10	,,	5,000 Rio de la Plata	50,000
2	,,	3,500 Roman Brick and Tile	7,000
3	,,	2,500 Scarlet Dye	7,500
1	,,	4,000 Swedish Iron	4,000
3	,,	3,000 Steam Engine Machinery	9,000
2	,,	2,000 Tobacco and Snuff	4,000
3	,,	4,000 Thames and Medway Brick and Lime . .	12,000
2	,,	1,500 Ditto and Rhine Steam	3,000
1	,,	1,000 Ditto and Loire ditto	1,000
5	,,	20,000 West India Company	100,000
5	,,	20,000 United Pacific	100,000
5	,,	10,000 United Chilian	50,000
1	,,	10,000 Do. Lond. and Hib. Corn and Flour. . .	10,000
5	,,	1,000 For. Stock and Share Investment . . .	5,000
10	,,	4,000 Thames Tunnel	40,000
25	,,	1,600 Hammersmith Bridge	40,000

£17,582,773

In point of fact, I very much doubt, whether any considerable part of this sum was sent out of the country : the question is immaterial, but the following is an extract of a communication from a gentleman, upon whose accuracy the greatest reliance may be placed. "Very little of the 17,000,000*l.* was sent abroad. You can hardly imagine the extent of the roguery. I was consulted by ——— on the subject of the Chili Loan before it was contracted for, and I learned what was

valent value) will be returned; whereas, had they remained
unemployed, nothing would have been returned.   In exchange
for these 17,000,000*l.* improvidently employed, the country will
in that case be benefited to the amount of 1,000,000*l.*, and the
speculators will lose sixteen parts out of seventeen.

The cause of the present distress is exactly the same as that
which was the cause of all former similar distresses; namely, a
return from a depreciated to a sound currency.   During the last,
in 1813, it was attributed to a "transition state, from war to
peace."   Now it is attributed to "over-trading and a rash spirit
of speculation;" and men catch at any sounds that are uttered,
without ever being at the trouble of analysing the ideas which
they are intended to convey.

*A rise in the prices of all commodities can only take place
owing to a fall in the value of the currency.*   This is a rule of
universal application, and will serve as an infallible guide for
judging of the signs of a real, or of a fallacious prosperity.
Although an issue of Bank of England paper causing prices to
rise, produces a corresponding issue of the paper of other banks,
it does not follow that a contraction of Bank of England paper
will produce a corresponding contraction of the paper of country
banks; nor is the convertibility of the paper of country banks
into gold practically of any use in preventing, by timely checks,
their over-issuing; for none of their neighbours know when to
apply them, and very few dare do so, even if they knew.   The
balance of currency vibrates with so much delicacy, that its
regulation is entirely in the hands of the bullion-merchants and
bill-brokers of London : a very slight variation in the equili-
brium, when once discovered, affords a sufficient profit on the
export of gold, in small daily quantities, to these persons resident
in London, although such transactions are of too minute a nature to engage the attention of a general merchant.   I say, when
once discovered; because it must be remembered, that for a long
time after the paper part of the currency has become excessive,

intended to be done : ——— came with a letter of introduction to me, and I was
well acquainted with all that passed.   Not one shilling was sent to Peru.   Of the
Chili Loan, 750,000*l.* for a million, all that Chili received was about 100,000*l.*
Next to nothing has been sent out of the country in any projects, except to Mexico,
so that little more than a change of hands took place; and this, however much it
may inconvenience many, will not diminish our capabilities."

both the metallic part and the paper part are depreciated together, which prevents the depreciation of the paper from being immediately visible to the public eye.   When once it is apparent, by the price of the carriage of gold being less than the price of a bill of exchange, then the depreciation begins to be corrected by the export, through the persons above-mentioned; from which consideration it follows, that the consequence of an excessive issue of paper from any quarter, no matter from what, would cause a drain upon the Bank of England exclusively for gold*; when her coffers were nearly emptied, alarm would make the people fly for gold to the country bankers, who would be unable to supply them.

The probable end of the recent effects of the sudden contraction of the currency, if the Bank of England and the Government had not interfered, would have been the establishment of two prices of all commodities — a metal and a paper price; and this, perhaps, after all, would be the best and safest end to the difficulties of this question.   Besides the temporary interference (if it will be really only temporary), by the issuing of small notes, and by the advancing of more notes upon goods, a law has been passed, prohibiting the issuing of all small notes after three years. During three years, however, it gives power to the Bank of England, and country banks, to issue them or not, according to their fancies; and it gives power to the people to receive them or not, according to their fancies; so that the operation of this law depends upon two contingencies, neither of which can be accurately calculated upon.   If the effect shall be to keep out the small notes till the three years are nearly expired, then we shall have at that period the same distress, failures, &c. again, that we have lately had.   If, on the other hand, we shall have the small notes all *bonâ fide* withdrawn, we shall have stagnation of trade, manufacturers out of employ, no rents for the landlords, thousands of our fellow-creatures starved to death, and an increased pressure of taxation.   Between these two extremes, any middle state may exist, dependent upon the way in which the bill is carried into effect.   But let

* Supposing we had an exclusively metallic currency, it would be possible for a great spirit of gambling adventure to give rise to so large a quantity of bill transactions, as to produce a kind of paper currency, sufficiently extensive to cause an export of the coin.

us suppose that we have got through the operation of the bill, and that we have settled into as steady a situation as we could desire ; still the bill permits, under the most favourable view, so great a proportion of convertible paper, that it is impossible they can circulate together without producing violent and ruinous fluctuations * ; for as soon as confidence shall return, out will come paper in some form or other; prices will rise ; we shall be congratulated on our "prosperity;" away will go the gold ; and then another "pecuniary crisis," which will be much more destructive than the last, if banks shall have been formed previously with more numerous and opulent partners, all possessing the power of issuing paper, *ad libitum.*

Mr. Tooke assured us, that "the country bankers, who are supported by the power of the landed aristocracy, would spare no efforts, and leave no sophistry untried, to prevent the suppression of the notes under 5*l.*" (p. 129.) This prophecy has been realised only with respect to Scotland ; the history of the conduct of the land-owners on this subject is curious.

When the land-owners supported the series of measures usually expressed under the term of Mr. Peel's bill, they were ignorant, that by raising the value of the currency rents must fall, while mortgages, jointures, &c., would remain the same ; and accordingly they voted for the minister's plan. Agricultural produce fell, and they then began to remember, that when they had small notes it did not fall, and they teased the ministers till they passed the small note bill, of which Mr. Peel complained this year, as a measure which frittered away his plan. The necessary consequence of this measure was an over-issue of paper, and consequent re-action, such as we have just seen. Parliament met in the midst of the panic : all parties ran at the country banks (who were more sinned against than sinning, and the victims rather than the cause of the system under which they were acting), and again a bill has been passed avowedly for the purpose of suppressing notes; the land-owners evidently again not perceiving what its effects will be on the price of corn.

---

* "No fact had been more clearly established by all experience on the subject than this — that gold and paper never could be brought to circulate together. No paper would circulate where gold did, and no gold where paper circulated. There could be no common issues of both. This, he repeated, was clearly proved by all experience."--*Lord Liverpool's Speech, Feb.* 17*th*, 1826.

The Scotchmen, however, have been much keener : to the " efforts and sophistry," anticipated by Mr. Tooke, they have added declamation and menace. They have smelt out clearly enough the connection between small notes and high rents; and not an ounce of gold shall get into Scotland, nor a worthless stinking bit of dirty paper be suppressed, if they can keep it out. But if the small notes be not suppressed there as well as here, all the measures of the present session, from the king's speech down to this hour, are perfectly nugatory, as far as the public is concerned, and can only have the effect of enriching Scotch landlords and paper-money makers, at the expense of the English.

The question is, what is to be done ? Everybody, who has paid the smallest attention to the subject, however he may differ from others about the remedies to be applied, agrees, that the late distresses originated in an excessive issue of paper, and a consequent contraction of that paper ; and that, therefore, the problem to be demonstrated is, " how to render the value of the currency fixed." *

It is indispensably necessary to every plan that shall be adopted, that an immediate end should be put to the connection which has subsisted between the Government and the Bank. Whoever will be at the trouble of reading the appalling facts detailed in Messrs. Tooke's, Mushett's, Daniel Hardcastle's, and Attwood's pamphlets, will be convinced, that that connection has been hitherto productive of nothing but mischief to the country. The state of the affairs of the Bank ought to be published in the Gazette, every quarter ; the amount of its capital ; the amount of its notes† ; the amount and nature of its investments ; and

---

* " The object of every description of currency should be to make the value of property as steady and as little variable as possible. The truth lay there, and he who solved that problem, would certainly come to the wisest conclusion."—*Lord Liverpool's Speech, Feb.* 17*th*, 1826.

† Whilst these pages were in the press, a most important law has passed, which gives to issuers of paper-money, all over the kingdom, the power of compounding with the Stamp Office in such a manner as shall render it impossible for the public to know the extent of their issues. The amount of stamps was hitherto the sole criterion by which the quantity of country paper could ever be guessed, but by Mr. Sedgwick's tables, a tolerably correct appreciation could be made. It was to the amount of stamps alone that Lord Liverpool, Mr. Peel, and Mr. Huskisson appealed this year to prove the quantity of country paper in circulation, and therefore it was the sole criterion by which they had to judge. Publicity is a *sine quâ non* in any system which is to make currency steady ; yet even the little we had

the quantity of bullion in its chests.   For, whether the directors
know it or not, no one can read the above pamphlets, nor have
paid any attention to the nature of currency, without being assured that that establishment possesses a formidable power over
the properties of all its fellow-subjects; which has been, and
can be again productive of the most ruinous effects, without the
possibility of conferring one redeeming benefit.

There are three modes of attaining this desired end :

1. By having a wholly metallic currency.   The ablest advocates for this are Mr. Cobbett and Daniel Hardcastle.   To effect
this object, however, such concomitant measures would be necessary as are not likely to be adopted, and therefore it is idle here
to discuss them.

2. By having a currency partly metallic and partly paper.
This can only be done by fixing the amount of paper, and allowing this paper to be issued solely by the Government, or by the
State Bank; by which means the fluctuations will take place in
the *quantity* of coin only, and the *value* of the whole currency
will remain unimpaired.

3. By having an entire paper currency.   The ablest advocates
for this plan are Mr. Ricardo and Mr. Attwood; and the writings
of the former are, or ought to be, so well known, that it is useless to relate the details here.   This is the plan which I prefer,
because it is the cheapest; and "cheap money, if it means anything, means cheap taxes, cheap debts, and cheap burdens."

One objection has been started against this plan which must
not be passed over, and that is, an alleged facility to the crime
of forgery.

The way to obviate this objection is, to repeal the punishment
of death for that offence.   As long as the Bank of England could
hang as many forgers as it pleased, it took not the smallest
trouble to improve the construction of its paper, nor vary the

---

is now by Lord Liverpool taken away. So that every cause which facilitated over-
issues of papers last year, is in as full operation as ever, with this additional help;
and are we to believe that we shall not have another "panic?"   Very well,
Gentlemen, *vague la galère;* but when we are told that we are in the most perfect
calm, "look out for a squall," say I.   There is one comfort at any rate, which is,
that whoever will attend to the rule laid down in p. 32, and believe no one, be he
minister, or merchant, or banker, who tells him that high prices are signs of permanent prosperity, may escape the ravages of the storm.

engravings on its notes. When the disgust of the public would no longer suffer the immolation of so many human victims, it set its wits to work to find a pattern which should be absolutely inimitable; an idea as absurd as its former negligence was culpable. Let it only have the engravings of such patterns, that none but a few of the first engravers in London can make them (and it is possible to multiply the pattern upon a rose engine *ad infinitum*); and let the patterns be changed frequently, it can suffer little or no loss from forgery; certainly not more than is sustained by coining.

The public, however, must not be led to expect impossibilities from the Government, nor turn round and abuse the Executive for every consequence of its own improvidence. It is impossible (and I assert it without fear of refutation) for any legislative enactments whatever to prevent circumstances arising which shall cause vacillations in the value of the currency, fully as great as those from which the country is now suffering. Even if we had a wholly metallic currency to-morrow, causes in some degree similar might sooner or later occur. It is a necessary concomitant of old commercial countries, that the rate of interest, and consequently the rate of profits, should be progressively diminishing. One consequence of this is, that capital is sent out of the country to seek more lucrative employment : another consequence is, that a spirit is engendered in the people, if not of extravagance, at least of the opposite of saving, and a desire to embark in any scheme that promises to give a larger return of interest on their capital than their ordinary business. Payments, by means of bills of private individuals, traders, and others, are now made to an immense amount, and might be multiplied to such an extent as to drive out a considerable portion of (and why not all ?) the coin in the kingdom. During such a period prices would be rising, and all the false signs of prosperity, which have so often deceived many to their ruin, would be manifested as heretofore. No government nor laws could obviate such a course of events, nor anything but the increased intelligence on the part of the community, and thorough knowledge of the principles of currency and profits, and a manly determination to be content with diminished powers for the gratification of luxury.

In conclusion, I again repeat, that no description of currency

can be so bad as that which we have at present, because no
other could be so unfixed, and liable to so great fluctuations in
its value, without even the Government having any power over
it.   Our blindness upon this point is the more extraordinary,
because no people value so highly the advantages of security;
none have paid a higher price for the adoption of this principle;
and for this alone various iniquities, such as slavery and monopolies, are suffered to exist, rather than commit a violation
upon vested interests.   This idol, to which we shamefully sacrifice so much, viz. security of property, is tottering every day :
Bel boweth down, and Nebo stoopeth : the prosperity and peace
of the country depends upon people securely enjoying that
which they have acquired ; but repeated disappointments, and
losses of the fruit of their earnings, cannot fail to induce a
reckless spirit of improvidence and speculation, nowhere so
dangerous as among a commercial people.   And, says Mr.
Attwood (p. 36), " Our situation is a choice of difficulties, but no
human power can avoid them.   We may, perhaps, toil and
struggle on for a little longer, amidst all manner of dangers,
and all manner of sufferings and privations ; but the end of our
career is *death*.   Not *death* to the people, but to the political
system under which we live.   One important fact I ought to
mention in proof, or confirmation of this opinion.   I have never
met one single individual, who has had leisure and disposition
to turn his thoughts to the subject, who has not fully adopted
the same opinion in the end."

A Letter to the King

AGAINST

THE REPEAL OF THE TEST ACT

BY

A TORY OF THE OLD SCHOOL

1829

A

LETTER TO THE KING.

SIRE: Although there is no probability that these observations will ever fall under the eye of your Majesty, I nevertheless select this form of address, because you, sire, are more interested in the result of the following discussion than any other individual in the realm. We are told by the wisest of monarchs, that there is nothing new beneath the sun; and assuredly there will be no novelty in any thing advanced in these pages. The principles of religion and policy are not now in the old age of the world to be determined, and their mutual bounds apportioned; and any thing concerning them that would assume to be novel would be justly suspected of being for that cause alone erroneous. It is with the public as with the individual body; its remedies all lie within the narrow compass of a few general principles; and the most experienced physician can do no more than determine which is applicable to the particular circumstances of his patient. No sentiment will appear here that may not be found in the Bacons, Hookers, Cookes, Hales, and Clarendons of former times; but the wisdom of these sages has grown into desuetude, and their degenerate sons deride the maxims of their forefathers through inability to attain to the standard of their might.

Two frightful inroads are attempted to be made in the constitution of Great Britain; and as this word constitution is in the mouth of every one, for all kinds of purposes, it is necessary to define the sense in which I make use of it here. By the word constitution, then, I mean the principles which constitute the essential polity of the nation; and this essential polity I maintain to consist in the indefeasible union of divine with human

law. It would be waste of time to stop to prove this point.
The nation calls itself a Christian nation: your Majesty in every
proclamation declares that you are king " by the grace of God ; "
every national treaty is drawn " in the name of the Most Holy
Trinity ; " in like manner every subordinate functionary, as delegate of your Majesty's royal authority, is compelled to make
declaration of his Christian faith.* All the subjects of the state
are presumed to be Christians, and voluntary excommunication
must be a subsequent and overt act of any one who refuses to
be so considered. On the other hand, the church submits herself in all things to the king as supreme: she receives every
subject of the king as soon as it is born into her communion:
she teaches all her children to be subject " not merely for wrath,
but also for conscience' sake : " in short, there is no possible way
by which intimacy of union can be shown, which is not exhibited
in the relationship between the church and the state.

The first change which is contemplated is also the more complete of the two, and is to be effected under the soft and specious
term of giving relief to the aggrieved consciences of Protestant
Dissenters by the repeal of the Test Act. The Test Act required
that every person, who accepted office under the crown, should
have received the sacrament of the Lord's supper according to
the form prescribed by the Church of England. Herein two
things were required :—1. That the recipient of office should
take the sacrament. 2. That he should take it according to a
particular form. The first is the test of Christianity prescribed
by the Great Head of the church, and which no power on earth
can now alter or modify ; the latter is a point of human invention, and has varied and may vary *ad libitum.* The repeal
of the latter, therefore, is admissible ; the repeal of the former
is inconsistent with the principles of the constitution. The
principle of these restrictive statutes is clearly, that the nation
and the church are one ; and that the unity of the individual
with the nation is to be attested by his unity with the church.
This latter unity is itself attested by that sacrament, the habitual
reception of which is the only possible outward and distinguishing sign of a continued adherence to the communion of

* Mr. Brougham, who has no undue bias on his mind towards this principle, is
too sound a lawyer not to acknowledge that " the law cites as its warrant for
certain steps in every suit the injunction of the Scripture."

the church. The total and unqualified repeal, therefore, of all tests of Christianity in the office-bearers of the state implies, and does effect, the separation of the church from the state, and of religious from political duty; and thereby inculcates, that kingly government is a matter of human contrivance, and of human expediency, with which divine obligation has no concern. Hence, too, the false opinion is sanctioned, that the people, and not God, are the source of legitimate power; that power is delegated from the people to their rulers, and consequently may be resumed by the people, whenever the people shall deem such resumption to be for their benefit; whereas the true foundation of this, and of every Christian monarchy, rests upon the principle, that "the powers which be are ordained of God," and that, therefore, "whosoever resisteth the power resisteth the ordinance of God; for the king beareth not the sword in vain, because he is the minister of God, a revenger to execute wrath upon him that doeth evil:" that the king is Christ's vicegerent, and delegate of Him, who is King of kings, Lord of lords, the ONLY Ruler of princes, the representative of Him in His kingly office, even as the church is the representative of Him in His priestly office. But if all distinctions be abolished between Christian men and Atheists, it is impossible with any consistency to preserve the present established religion, which in all its formularies recognises the God of the Bible as the God of the state, after the state shall have formally renounced that God as the only one true God; after it shall have opened her highest offices to men who have no God; after it shall have separated the obligation to "honour the king," from that of "fear God;" and after it shall have avowed that men are to be subject merely "for wrath," but not "for conscience sake;" when all national protests against Atheism shall have been abandoned; when an English magistrate may be a Christian, a Deist, or an Atheist; but which of them the state will neither inquire, nor, like Gallio, care; when "the power" of such magistrates, therefore, will not be "of God" in any sense, but ultimately, as well as mediately, from your Majesty; and thus the rights of your Majesty will be placed in this predicament, that if these rights be derived from the people, they are held only on the tenure of their caprice; but if they be derived from God, and the kings are still obliged to acknowledge this at their coronation, then will our monarchs be the only laymen in their dominions who are debarred the privilege of being Atheists if they please.

Such being shortly the facts of the case, I proceed now to examine some of the arguments which have been used in recommending this most monstrous measure. It is said that hypocrites get into office at present by receiving the sacrament unworthily, and that therefore the Test is useless as a mean of excluding Atheists from office. In reply to this argument, I would ask the objector, Where is the madman who ever dreamed of doing anything which an impostor could not simulate? Do we in the ordinary concerns of life omit all precautions, because those precautions may be ultimately of no avail? Do we leave our doors open at midnight, because the robber may break in at the window? The question is not, neither ought it to be, what will be the effect of a measure, but what is our duty? This old-fashioned way of acting is indeed become obsolete; and hollow, unprincipled expediency is the only rule now adopted either in state or church. It is not correct for the advocates of the repeal to say, that persons were required to take the sacrament in order to qualify themselves for holding office; all men are required to take the sacrament in order to qualify themselves to be considered Christians; and the law only says, that unless men are Christians they shall not hold office in a Christian state. The church knows no such act as qualifying for office; she only knows the duty of communicating; it is at his own peril if the qualifier "receives unworthily, not discerning the Lord's body;" and, however deeply to be regretted, it is not in point of fact true, that only those who qualify for office receive it so. But let the extreme of the arguments of those who wish the repeal of the law be granted, and that men in order to obtain the emoluments of office will improperly receive the sacrament; that is, will falsely profess to be Christians when in secret they are infidels: — I affirm, that it is far better that infidels should be in office who have made a profession of being Christians, than that they should be in office without having made that profession: in the first case, they will be either constrained, in order to keep up their reputation for consistency, to continue to act in conformity with that profession; or the notoriety of their hypocrisy will, as in such cases it actually now does, take from their character all dangerous influence: but in the second case, as they never professed to be any thing but infidels, they acknowledge no law but the law of force, and there is therefore no pretext for finding fault with them for any crime they may commit, unless the statutes of the land shall have defined it to be an offence. The law said, and said most properly, None shall hold office in a Christian land, but members of the Christian church : the Christian church says "No one is a member of mine who does not take the holy sacrament." The new law says, " A man who worships the devil is quite as fit a magistrate as a Christian, provided only he will leave to the parsons their stalls and their tithes."

This last remark brings me to look at the declaration which is to be substituted as the condition of holding office, in lieu of the test of being a Christian. This declaration leaves totally out of the question all that was essential in the former test, namely, the religious principle, as a point of no sort of consequence ; and the only thing for which it stipulates is the immaterial, dirty money which is attached to the priestly functions. There is a baseness in this which baffles all description : the friends of the church, the high church party as it is called, the party which has so often rent the skies with its cries of " the church in danger," has now come forward with a proposition which too plainly proves what it means by church, and that if the wealth which belongs to the established church were taken from her, these her sons would as quickly leave her as rats do a sinking ship ; that it is her money alone which binds them to her, and that as far as they are concerned the withdrawing her money would as surely cause her downfall as the cutting off of the water of Euphrates produced the downfall of Babylon of old. And thus it is, Sire, with some of the loudest pretenders to loyalty and of attachment to your Majesty's person, government, and dynasty : so long as it is the fountain of power and emolument, so long will the validity of those pretensions be undiscoverable : and thence all sovereigns have been deceived : but it is they and they alone who refer their duty to their king to a still higher motive, and venerating his person not less cordially than others, reverence still more Him who established the respective relations of king and subjects, that would cheerfully take the spoiling of their goods, and follow into the most obscure circumstances the fortunes of their prince when he had neither power nor wealth to confer. This is no imaginary picture, Sire: your Majesty would know to what I am alluding, if these words were ever permitted to fall under your observation: your Majesty would remember, that there have been those who from principle lost title, honour, estate, and life, in contending against the accursed maxim, that " the people are the source of legitimate power," and *non generant aquilæ columbas.* These pretended friends of the church, however, do most miserably miscount: this will be but the first of a series of measures which will ultimately strip her as bare as she will have deserved to be stripped, if she shall not have lifted up her loudest protest against this repeal. Had she remained firm to her principles, God would have preserved to her her treasure likewise: when Solomon sought wisdom as the first thing, God superadded great wealth also. Had she sought first the kingdom of God and his righteousness, all other things should have been added unto her. She might take example from history in this matter, in the struggles of states for religious and civil liberty. In England, from the earliest times, the sovereigns and the people have contended more for religious than for political principle. Examples from Alfred, the Conqueror, Henry II., John of Gaunt, and the Reformers, might easily be adduced; and as the jewel of pure religion could only be preserved in civil liberty as its casket, God granted the latter to the people who were nobly struggling for the first. This political freedom, the consequence of the contention for religious principle, has been idolised by foreign nations, who, mistaking the effect for the cause, have, whilst unmindful of genuine religion, and immersed in popish idolatry, vainly endeavoured to gain political freedom. In every quarter they have been foiled; Sicily, Naples, France, Prussia, Spain, and Portugal, in following the shadow have passed by the substance, and England alone remains in possession of that which they have in vain attempted to retain, because she sought first that pearl which was of the greatest price.

Another plea is brought forward by some respectable persons, namely, that the requirement of a Test of Christianity is a desecration of the ordinance. This is surely one of the weakest scruples that ever entered into the imagination of pious imbecility. If these scruples had originated in a zeal according to knowledge, how comes it that they have lain dormant so long?

Nay, how comes it that they were unborn, if indeed they were ever conceived, until the Socinians and infidels engendered the idea that the rite was so desecrated? Is it not matter of notoriety, that men who pass their lives in frequenting brothels and gaming houses, have been bewailing at public meetings in various parts of Great Britain this pretended desecration? The fact of these scruples being unheard of, and of the infidels and the profligate being the persons to awaken them, is proof sufficient that this is a false colour which has been held out with the intention of deceiving the very people who have become its dupes. There is nothing in the sacrament of the Lord's Supper which sanctifies it above any other ordinance of Christ's appointment in His church. So that the question with these persons resolves itself into this: that every rite of the Christian church which a Christian state can select as a Test of Christianity in its members, becomes by that selection *ipso facto* desecrated. If this be so, then these persons must desire the complete separation of the church from the state, a point which they are by no means inclined to concede, though they would not be able to offer upon their own principles one solid argument against it. But how do they themselves act with respect to Tests of Christianity in their own private affairs? There is not one individual who makes the smallest profession of piety, who does not assemble his domestics and family to social worship morning and evening: but if a servant should refuse to attend these prayers, alleging that he does not believe in God, or in the Bible, the heads of the family would forthwith dismiss him. This their test they will not permit their servants to infringe; yet it is as great a desecration of the ordinance of prayer and praise to mock God by bending the knee in hypocritical worship for the sake of office in the house, as it is to take the sacrament for the sake of obtaining office in the state: and so obvious is this principle, and so unanswerable to any one not versed in Jesuitical quibbling, that many persons who do really and honestly entertain this opinion refuse to associate in prayer with others, of whose religious creed in every particular they feel the smallest doubt. But these pious people will debar their king from saying to his servants that which every one of them considers a point of duty to say to their own, namely, that unless their servants give the test of Christianity which such masters severally require, such servant shall serve them no

longer. It is childish to say that the king can inquire into the
creeds of all his servants: in the first place it is physically impossible for him to do so; and in the second place he individually
ought not to do so. The king of a people is a public functionary; he must look to public tests, and not to private scrutiny:
if any of his subjects conforms to the outward test which the
church appoints, he, unless in very extreme cases, is bound to
consider him fit for his service; but if, after having had such a
test, the state shall abandon it, he is left without the means of
carrying his duty into practical effect. If the word of God be
true, which says, "by me kings reign, and princes decree justice;"
if not a sparrow falls to the ground without His especial permission, a nation can only be "prospered in all its consultations, to the
advancement of His glory, the good of His church, the safety,
honour, and welfare of our sovereign and his dominions," in proportion as it shall acknowledge Him in all its ways. It is the
duty of the state to establish the Christian religion: it is the
duty of every individual to use the power and influence with
which he has been entrusted for the service of God: it is the
duty of masters, whether of few or of many servants, to say,
"Let others do as they please, but as for me and my house, we
will serve the Lord." But the parliament will now take from
its king the power to do this; it says to him, "Thou art the only
man who may not use thy power for Christ." Is this to be the
advantage of possessing power and of wielding a sceptre, that he
who does is not to be allowed to use that power for the glory of
Christ, which he has derived from Him alone? Awful prerogative of royalty!

The genuineness of these scruples arising from an alleged
sense of the desecration of the sacrament must be examined a
little closer. The new Act declares in its preamble, that *the
doctrine, discipline, and government of the churches of England
and Scotland are permanently and inviolably established;* and
in order that they may so remain, every dissenter from the said
doctrine, discipline, and government, is required by the enacting
clauses to take an oath, that he will do nothing by virtue of the
office he is to hold to *injure and weaken* the said churches, and
disturb the rights and privileges of which they are in possession.
It is obvious that a hypocrite may take this oath and mean to
break it, exactly as a man may falsely pretend to be a Christian

by taking the sacrament, and yet not be so. Here then is an oath desecrated exactly as-in the former case; and the scruples of that conscience, which is so irritable upon the subject of eating bread and wine, and so callous upon that of invoking the God of truth to the attestation of a falsehood, are of a nature that defies my powers of comprehension. But in what a situation are the dissenters placed! They are dissenters because they disapprove of the doctrine, or of the discipline, or of the government of those churches: as many of them as are Christians could not object to receive the sacrament in some form, although several might demur to the form prescribed by law. They were entitled to the respect for this demur which openness, fairness, and sincerity must always command. But if they should come forward to take an oath not to do any thing to alter that which, by their being dissenters, they *ipso facto* declare to be wrong, and ought not therefore to be *permanently and inviolably established*, they lose at once that title to our respect; their dissent then is proved not to be conscientious, but factious; and their having taken the required oath has only converted open and sincere foes into hypocritical friends, and base and insidious enemies.

They, and they only, who contend, no matter from what motive, whether they are orthodox or Socinians (or Unitarians as they deceitfully call themselves), atheists or republicans, that there ought to be a complete separation between the church and the state, are consistent in desiring the unqualified Repeal of the Test Act. A very able pamphlet upon this subject made its appearance two years ago, under the title of " Letters on the Church, by an Episcopalian:" and if the major of the author's proposition be granted, his conclusion is irresistible. The only ground upon which he can be opposed is that which I have already taken, namely, that kings are the delegates of the King of kings, and responsible only to Him. A doctrine which wicked kings have often perverted to the maintaining that God appointed them to rule, not according to His laws, but in violation of every one of them, private and social as well as divine; but which doctrine is nevertheless true, notwithstanding their perversion of it, and rebellion against Him.

It is not denied by the majority of the dissenters who have petitioned for the repeal, and it is still more unequivocally avowed by the infidel, that their object in wishing for all distinction be-

tween Christians and atheists to be abolished is, that a complete
separation between the church and·the state may be effected.
They who wish for such an effect are wise in their endeavours to
procure this repeal, for assuredly nothing will so quickly bring
it to pass.   By so doing they think to shake off one important
part by which the machinery of royal government carries on its
operations ; and they likewise imagine that the lands now in
the hands of the clergy may be applied to the relief of the
financial embarrassments of the country.   These persons would
feel indignant at being classed with ordinary revolutionists, and
plebeian radicals ; yet no revolution was ever more complete
than that which would be brought about by the adoption of their
plans.

It has been contended that the Test Act is not a national
protest against atheism, and ought not to be so considered, because it was not enacted originally with that view.   The intentions of the framers of the act have nothing to do with the
question.   But if the orthodox dissenters are willing to rest their
argument upon the conduct of their forefathers upon this matter,
the case can be shown to be completely against them.   The act
was passed with the concurrence of the dissenters at the time,
and was not intended as an exclusion to dissenters, but became
so from supervening events.   In the days of Baxter, it was considered as nothing uncommon for dissenters to take the sacrament
according to the forms of the church of England, and the fact is,
that nearly all the dissenters of that period did take the sacrament in that form.   In 1662, the Act of Uniformity was passed,
which made the operation of the Corporation Act imperative ;
since then the clause has operated in theory (but not in practice
of late years, through the annual Bill of Indemnity) to the
exclusion of all who could not take the sacrament in the form
therein prescribed.   So that with every conscientious man it was
the form, and nothing but the form, which aggrieved him.   Yet,
notwithstanding that the argument derived from the origin of
the act is against its repeal, I still maintain that the causes
which led to its enactment ought to be put wholly out of the
question in the view which I take.   Here we are in the year
1828, with a national protest upon our Statute Book declaring
that none but Christians are worthy of sharing in the royal
functions of government in a Christian land.   It matters not

a straw how it got there; any more than it does whether it was the vice or the virtue of Henry VIII. that secured the emancipation of the crown from the dominion of the pope. Here we are in covenant with God; and it is a much stronger act of rebellion to renounce that covenant and break that bond in which we find ourselves, than never to have come into that covenant at all. This is a constant principle of divine jurisprudence. In the day of awful retribution it shall be more tolerable for Sodom and Gomorrha than for Chorazin and Bethsaida; it shall be more tolerable for a heathen than for a Christian nation; more tolerable for a country which has never entered into a covenant with God, than for one which having entered in refuses so to continue. Being in possession of this national protest against atheism, I do not in the least doubt that God prepared and appointed it to us in His foreknowledge of, and reference to this very time. This is analogous to the way in which He has prepared other instruments of punishment or of blessings to nations. He makes use of obvious and visible means for this end, although the instrument is unconscious of the hand that wields it. Sennacherib being appointed to ravage Samaria, was prepared for that work and called to execute it: "howbeit he meaneth not so, neither doth his heart think so; for he saith, By the strength of my hand have I done it, and by my wisdom, for I am prudent." In like manner was Pharaoh appointed: "for this cause have I raised thee up, that I might show my power in thee." And in like manner was Cyrus called by his name two hundred years before MENE TEKEL UPHARSIN was written against the Chaldeans. Perhaps there has been no period in the history of Christendom when it would have been so necessary to be in possession of such a test as the present; for whatever may be the case with individuals, there never was a time when national religion was at so low an ebb. The proof of this would lead to greater length than is now convenient, but let the following queries serve as a criterion by which to try the justice of the charge: 1. If the form of opening each daily sitting of parliament with prayer had never been established, would that form be adopted if it were now proposed for the first time? 2. Did any people before ever attempt to establish a national university and system of education for youth, in which religion was the only thing which was deemed unnecessary to be taught in it? 3. Was

the sabbath at any former period of our history so universally
spent in idleness and vice by all ranks of society as it is now?
and the observance or violation of the sabbath is the invariable
sign throughout Scripture of a nation's acknowledgment or rejection of God. 4. Time was when every nobleman had his resident
chaplain, and in every mansion throughout the country the
family altar was raised morning and evening: where is this
duty observed now ?

I now pass on to the second inroad which has been attempted
to be made upon the constitution ; and which, although in some
respects of a different character, might be shown by analysis to
be but another manifestation of the same evil root, namely, the
amalgamation of the Popish apostasy with this essentially Protestant state.   To perceive the religious criminality of this, it
is necessary to refer to the meaning of the term " Christian
church," and also to that which constitutes the essential distinction between a true church and an apostasy.   Whoever has
the slightest acquaintance with the Holy Scriptures must know
that an apostasy is therein foretold, which shall " forbid to
marry;" " command to abstain from meats;" " sit in the temple
of God, showing himself that he is God;" " be drunk with the
blood of the martyrs " (and neither Moloch nor Juggernaut is
so drenched with human gore, both Jewish and Christian, as
Popery); together with many other points, which describe the
church of Rome so accurately, that there can be no doubt that
she and she alone is intended.   However clear this description
of the symptoms may be, still the point which constitutes the
Popish church to be THE APOSTASY is not therein mentioned, and
it must be sought elsewhere.   It will most readily be found in
referring to the declared purpose of God in establishing a visible
church amongst us Gentiles.   This we are told, in Acts xv. 14,
was—first, in order that God might " take out of the Gentiles a
people for his name."   The Jewish church had borne, and still
bears, faithful witness to the name of Jehovah; but when God
in the fulness of time had a new name to record, even the name
of Jah-Osea, or Jesus, the Christ or the anointed one, the only
intercessor, the Jewish church refused to bear witness to this
name, and therefore a church was taken out of the Gentiles for
that purpose. Secondly, as the Jewish church had a temple
service adapted to the witness which she was to bear, so the

Gentile church had its ordinance adapted to the witness it was to bear; which ordinance consisted in "the foolishness of preaching," by which it was to offer eternal salvation by means of that name alone which was recorded in her, unconditionally to every one who would receive it. Thirdly, as the chief advantage which the Jewish church had over the heathen was, that unto the former was confided "the oracles of God," so to the Gentile church also was confided the oracles of God. Fourthly, when the Gentile church was established, she was desired, by the purity of her words and works, to let her light so shine as to testify the righteousness of God before kings and people. Fifthly, she was ordered to submit to the temporal rulers of the land, even though they were Neros and Domitians.

In every one of these points the Popish church has apostatised. First, instead of bearing witness to the name of Jesus as the only way to the Father, she has raised up a host of dead men and women to the level of the Son of God as intercessors. Secondly, she denies salvation on account of Jesus alone, and mixes with His pure and spotless work the polluted works of sinful men. Thirdly, she refuses the oracles of God to man, and pretends to have other oracles than those which God has given. Fourthly, having herself violated the purposes for which a Gentile church was established, she could not bear witness for God's truth, either by the doctrine or by the lives of her members; she had need to take the beam out of her own eyes before she could see to take out the mote in the eyes of others. Fifthly, instead of submitting to the civil power, she has carried on one unceasing struggle to make both princes and people her slaves as well in mind as in body.

The struggle against this last, her unlawful assumption of power, began in England in the earliest times. When Augustine came over to preach Popery to the Saxons, the Christians then in England refused to bow to the Pope, and Augustine caused them to be inhumanly butchered. When the Pope required William the Conqueror to acknowledge that he held his kingdom of him as its lawful chief, the king answered, "Fealty I have not acknowledged, neither will I; because none did I promise, nor did any of my predecessors pay it to your predecessors." Henry II., in his celebrated Constitutions of Clarendon, endeavoured to bring the Popish priests back under the control of the

E 3

civil law. Grossetête, the Bishop of Lincoln, publicly preached against the Pope as Antichrist, and trampled his bull under his feet—a testimony continued by Wickliffe, Lord Cobham, and many others. The priest-ridden barons, indeed, who rebelled against John, and gained the famous privileges of Magna Charta for themselves, but nothing for the people, saw without the smallest compunction their king resign his crown into the hands of a Popish priest; and yet modern Papists have the matchless impudence to tell us that there was no struggle in England against Popery till the reign of Henry the Eighth. I know indeed that God made use of the vices of that wicked king, as He did of those of Alexander, Buonaparte, and thousands of others; and the end to be effected by Henry the Eighth was theseparation of this nation from the Popish apostacy, as the Protestant nation which is to stand for ever protesting against Popery; for I have shown that the Protestant church, performing every one of the duties for which a church was taken out from amongst the Gentiles, is the one true catholic and apostolic church; and that the Popish church is the apostacy, from which God has commanded every one to come out, because she is doomed to everlasting destruction.

If this country shall ever admit papists to participate in the royal functions of government, making no difference between members of the true church and those of the apostacy, from that moment God will discontinue that protection of us which preserved this nation alone, of all the original popish nations, from the effects of the French revolution. We have already gone a very improper length in paying for the instruction of popish priests at Maynooth, to be afterwards employed in spreading their poison over Ireland. It must not be supposed, however, that we need apprehend the rekindling of the fires of Smithfield. Popery, as a system of religious faith, is nearly extinct; and thence this attempt to repeal the Test Act is germane to the pushing forward the demands of the papacy: they both spring from one and the same root of infidelity, which is in church as well as in state destroying the essence of national religion, and under the mask of liberality inculcating, that there is no difference, and that there ought to be none made, "between him that feareth God, and him that feareth him not." It is of the very essence of the truth of God to make distinctions: it is of the very essence of the deceptions of Satan to level all distinctions. God put a difference between the fruits of Eden: Satan said there was none. Liberalism is this very principle of Satan in action at the present day. Every abomination that took place at the commencement of the French Revolution was admired by the lovers of liberty and philanthropists of that day in this country. When this repeal of the Test Act was mooted in the House of Commons, the ministers were taken by surprise, and carried away by the torrent of infidel liberalism which broke in upon them from without and from within. That this infidel spirit is at the bottom of the popish agitators is seen from the mode in which they habitually hold up the word of God to ridicule in their popish parliament in Dublin; although many priests are present, not one of whom expresses the slightest displeasure; and although it is a circumstance without a parallel in the history of Christendom, except in the debates of the Jacobin assemblies in France. The papists too have begun to adopt the absurd sentiment, that the people are the source of legitimate power: a maxim which is arrant nonsense, let it be uttered by whomsoever it may; whether with the formal solemnity of a Whig historian, or in the orgies of a radical election committee: but as Caliban calls himself a "thrice double ass," so is it "thrice double" nonsense in the mouth of a papist.

Having said so much upon the popish apostacy, it is necessary to put in a caveat, lest I should be imagined to vindicate the shameful persecutions to which papists have been subjected in this country, and still more in Ireland. I abhor the whole penal code against the papists; but be it remembered, that its worst parts arose at a time long posterior to the Reformation; and when men had lost sight of the scriptural character of the apostacy, and merely made use of their protestantism as a plea for the plunder of their popish fellow-subjects: but there is neither time, nor is this the proper place, to discuss this branch of the question further.

That part of the Test Act which prescribes the form in which the holy sacrament shall be received may be repealed. The mode of receiving it is immaterial, because the mode has not been enjoined. The habitual reception in both kinds, by some form, is indispensable before any one can be considered a Christian, because it has been enjoined. The pretension of the

church of England to superiority above other orthodox Protestants are absurd and unjustifiable. Neither on the other
hand let it be supposed that I am insensible to the corruptions
which exist in the Church of England, or to the perversion of
its offices and dignities to party purposes. These could not
have existed to their actual extent, except for the unequal distribution of her wealth which took place in her papal times.
Having never been reformed, the civil authorities have been
tempted to desecrate her offices·by bestowing them on persons
eminent, not for their piety, but for the favour of borough-
mongers. Had the emoluments of all bishops been equal, and
those of parsons also, and none sufficient to enable them to
emulate secular nobles in ostentation and luxury, the church
would not have fallen a victim to the seductions of power and
money. But they are miserably deficient in the history of
temptations, who suppose that the church would have run no
risk on the other side from delusions of a different character:
those arising from the power of the people would have been as
destructive as those which have arisen from the power of the
crown; and therefore the cure for her present disease is not to
be found in rushing into the opposite extreme, but in restoring
her according to the fundamental principles of her constitution;
in selecting preaching instead of unpreaching bishops to fill her
sees (the want of which bishop Latimer stated in his days was
the cause of much evil); and in taking from the heads of political factions the power to reward their adherents by appointing
them to lucrative offices in the church. This is a real desecration of holy things, in which, however, the pious express no
scruples. If all tests of Christianity be renounced, the nation
ceases to raise its national protest against Atheism. If the
sacrament in both kinds be not insisted on, the nation ceases to
exclude the popish apostacy, and to be $\kappa\alpha\tau$' $\epsilon\xi o\chi\eta\nu$, THE Protestant nation. If the repeal takes place, we may have this
anomaly; a judge sitting on the bench an avowed atheist, and
yet obliged by law to refuse the evidence of a witness who shall
declare that he does not believe in that Divine Revelation which
the judge himself may deny with impunity.

Although the Popish church brought confusion into the nations by refusing to submit to the royal authority, and by
putting a priest over the kings, she never denied the kingly

authority of Christ as supreme. This Protestant nation, by dissolving all union between church and state, and sanctioning the notion that kingly power is derived from the people, does not introduce confusion merely, as the Popish church did, but actually flies into open rebellion against the kingly supremacy of Christ altogether. Christ, as King of the nations, is as much despised at this moment as Christ the King of the Jews was eighteen hundred years ago; and as many, when they hear of the coming of this King to take upon Himself the rule, and to demand of His vicegerents and delegates an account of their stewardship in the offices in which He placed them, are as ready to exclaim in mockery, "Hail, King!" and to say, "We will not have this man to rule over us," as there were when He appeared of old in humility. But eighteen hundred years have not run in vain: the time must be near when He will come again in great power and glory, to set up that kingdom which shall never pass away; and woe be to that nation, to that prince, or to that individual, who shall not have "kissed the Son, lest He be angry, and so they shall perish from the way." Surely now is fulfilling the event spoken of by the prophet·king David: "The rulers of the earth take counsel against the Lord and against His Christ, saying, Let us break their bands asunder, and let us cast away their cords from us." The servants of Christ, they say, are no better magistrates, or judges, or counsellors, than the servants of Baal; all are alike. "He that sitteth in the heavens shall laugh; the Lord shall have them in derision; then shall He speak unto them in His wrath, and vex them in His sore displeasure."

If there was any probability of this letter meeting the eye of the august personage to whom it is addressed, I should conclude it by imploring your Majesty to reflect upon the principle upon which your royal power is held, and by which it must be maintained. I would endeavour most solemnly, whilst at the same time most respectfully, to warn your Majesty against the consequences of giving your royal assent to this measure. I am not ignorant that it is no slight matter to call upon the Sovereign of this nation to withhold his sanction from acts which his ministers advise, and the Parliament demand; but I also know that there is a power above both ministers and Parliament, to which neither of these parties ever seem to refer, and to which your Majesty is alone responsible. The responsibility of a minister may stand between the king and the people; but there is but one who can stand between any creature and the Creator, even " the King of the whole earth," whose royal prerogative the people would set aside.

I would implore your Majesty to look at this question with the eyes of a Christian statesman. Not those of a statesman only, for he might be a heathen; not those of a Christian only, for he might be nothing but a sectarian polemic; but with those becoming the Christian sovereign of a Christian people. It may be convenient, and perhaps wise on ordinary occasions, for ministers to be the real rulers, though in the name of the king; but there are times when it is fit to inform them that they are but servants; that "a breath can make them, as a breath has made," and unmake them again; and that there are cases involving the duties of the Lord's anointed, of which he, and he alone, is the fit judge.

There are thousands of your Majesty's subjects who feel for the difficulties which surround their sovereign, and who in secret pour forth daily their most fervent supplications to the throne of grace, that the all-wise and almighty Spirit, which can alone direct him, may be poured out in abundant measure upon the head of your Majesty. They are contented to be mocked and despised now; but when the time arrives that the secrets of all hearts shall be made known, they will be found to have been amongst the most loyal, as well as the most efficacious, supporters of the prince whom their God has been pleased in mercy to place over them. They are among the old-fashioned people who believe the words of the prayers which they use in the national church, though they know it is reckoned visionary and fanatical to do so; and they do not in form only but in sincerity say, " Almighty and everlasting God, we are taught by Thy holy Word that the hearts of kings are in Thy rule and governance, and that Thou dost dispose and turn them as seemeth best to Thy godly wisdom—have mercy upon the whole church, and so rule the heart of Thy chosen servant George, our King and Governor, that he, KNOWING WHOSE MINISTER HE IS, may above all things seek Thy honour and glory; and that we and all his subjects, DULY CONSIDERING WHOSE AUTHORITY HE HATH, may faithfully serve, honour, and humbly obey him, IN THEE AND FOR THEE, according to Thy blessed Word and ORDINANCE, through Jesus Christ our Lord, who with Thee and the Holy Ghost, liveth and reigneth ever one God, world without end."

I am, Sire, with every sentiment of religious devotion to the royal office, and political attachment to your Majesty's person and government,

Your Majesty's most loyal

and obedient subject and servant,

A TORY OF THE OLD SCHOOL.

Dialogue

BETWEEN

A SCEPTICAL PHYSICIAN

AND HIS

CHRISTIAN PATIENT

1829

.

DIALOGUE,

&c. &c.

PHYSICIAN.—How do you find yourself to-day?

PATIENT.—I do not know: you ought rather to tell me how I am. I remember an old choleric gentleman who flew into a great passion with the late Dr. Warren for asking him how he did, saying, "Why, Doctor, that is the very thing I sent for you to tell me!"

PH.—Tell me, then, how you feel, and I will tell you how you are.

PA.—I am in less pain, but weaker: this machine seems wearing out as perceptibly to myself as I know, in theory, it must be doing perpetually.

PH.—You have no reason to be discouraged by such sensations, for, as you observe, that is always the case, more or less. Bichat defines life to be *l'ensemble des fonctions qui resistent à la mort.*

PA.—The definition is admirable, for it exactly expresses the fact: *la mort* is king here, and sooner or later all things submit to him: it is the necessary lot of all creation.

PH.—*Pallida mors æquo pulsat pede regumque turres, et pauperum tabernas.* It is the lot, and that is sufficient for us; but I do not know why you should express yourself so largely, when you say *necessary* of *all* creatures.

PA.—First, for your quotation: I must mention a most happy translation of it by Malherbes—

> " Le pauvre en sa cabane, où le chaume le couvre,
> Est sujet à ses lois ;
> Et la garde qui veille aux barrières du Louvre
> N'en défend point nos rois."

Next, for your philosophy: if death be the universal lot of all things which have life, and that is indisputable, it is universal only because it is necessary.

Ph.—You make your statement so broad, that it will include things which I should hardly think you would be willing to admit.

Pa.—How so? I state a truth: if it be a truth, all that falls within its range must be true likewise.

Ph.—Your statement, I know, referred primarily to the decay arising from altered structure, or functionary derangement of your own body; but if you affirm that decay to be necessary, because it is invariable, your proposition must include the derangement and suffering of the moral, as well as of the physical, creation.

Pa.—Well! and what then? for this is, I suppose, the conclusion that you think I should not be willing to admit.

Ph.—Certainly; for then you are a Necessitarian and a Fatalist.

Pa.—My dear Doctor, you are a philosopher; you despise cant, superstition, and priestcraft; you are above vulgar prejudices; do not then resort to the weapons which you repudiate in others; and by affixing an opprobrious term upon me, divert your own attention, and endeavour to draw off mine, from things to words.

Ph.—But you destroy man's responsibility.

Pa.—*Caro Dottore! chi va piano va sano; chi va sano, va lontano.* We must not enter upon a new point until I have made myself clear on that with which we set out, and on which I have not had the good fortune to make myself understood.

Ph.—You affirm that moral as well as physical ill is necessary.

Pa.—If it be not necessary, then it must be arbitrary. What I mean by necessary is, that it is the result of essential properties; call it by whatever name you please, ill, evil, suffering, or by any other. Its most aggravated visible form, as well as climax, is death; and this is a necessary result of creation, or essential property in all created things.

Ph.—You are a great reader of the Bible I know; pray do you find there your opinions of necessity?

Pa.—You are not a great reader of the Bible I know, and

do not hold it in the estimation that I do: if I did not find my opinions in it, I would abandon them instantly.

PH.—Whereabouts do you find them in the Bible?

PA.—The Bible is a collection of writings which God caused certain individuals to write, in order to make Himself known to men. It is, therefore, a revelation of *the* True *One*, and *the* Good *One;* for He only is true and good. But the declaration of that abstract fact would neither instruct us nor benefit us; and the only way in which the truth can be conveyed, is by showing out the opposite, namely, that all things else but Himself are false and bad. This state does not depend upon an arbitrary decree of the uncontrollable First Cause, decreeing Himself to be good and all other things to be bad, but is essentially necessary; i. e. necessary, because constituting the essential properties of creator and creature. These opposites are therefore irreconcilable; and we are furnished with many examples of visible things which are also irreconcilable, in order to help our conception of the irreconcilable properties of invisible things, such as cold and heat, black and white, light and darkness: the total absence of any one of these produces its opposite; that is, they are essentially opposed to each other: such are their essential properties. In like manner, ill is the necessary consequence to all created things of the absence of the Creator.

PH.—Absence of the Creator! the Creator must be omnipresent.

PA.—True: He is said to be present in Hell, as well as in Heaven: but very different qualities are manifested in those two very different places: justice in punishment is only displayed in one; while justice combined with love is shown in the other.

PH.—You very much surprise me. You are quite right in saying that I hate priestcraft and imposture upon any subject, more especially upon that on which men's imaginations are so violently, and, as it appears to me, immoderately excited, I mean religion: but you have put the case in a way that I have never heard it placed in before.

PA.—I know that you do not trouble the inside of a church much, but do you never attend any place of public worship?

Ph.—Oh yes, I hear my friend Sydney Smith, whenever I can; but though a wit and a *bon-vivant*, nobody expects more theology from him than from Punch.

Pa.—But unless you go to church to hear theology, you might as well, by your own confession, sit at home and see Punch. Do you ever attend the churches where theologians do preach?

Ph.—Oh yes, I have heard most of your famous evangelicals; Daniel Wilson, and the Noels, and Cunningham, and some of the Dissenters: I have heard Hall, and Chalmers.

Pa.—Well, did you never hear theology from any of them?

Ph.—Except from the last, I can safely say that I never heard any thing but empty declamation, fit only for old women; nothing proved and made out. I sometimes, to oblige my sisters and my old mother, go with them to my parish church, and always think how lucky it is for the parson that I may not stand up and reply to him.

Pa.—I grant that the theology these men have published is miserably defective; yet it does not follow that the sermons you heard were improper for the congregations they addressed, because they were not adapted to minds like yours. But I thought I once saw you at Mr. Irving's.

Ph.—Yes, I was once there; and if the church did not lie so far away I should have gone again; for I heard a sermon which I shall never forget if I were to live a thousand years. Many things were said which I could not understand; and many more directly the reverse of what I believe to be true; but they were advanced with a power of argument that I could not despise. I think those fellows you call evangelical have far less power than the old divines whom I have sometimes dipped into, such as Hooker, Sanderson, Goodwin, and others. I wonder you did not recommend me Tremaine, which all the old ladies and dandy divines among my patients are vastly taken with.

Pa.—The author of Tremaine spends three volumes in turning an Atheist into a Deist, and thinks he has done him much service; whereas, in my opinion, he is just as far off the mark of being a Christian as when he set out.

Ph.—When you say that ill is the necessary consequence to all created things of the absence of the Creator, do you mean only when left to themselves?

PA.—I mean created things as created things; not as united to the Creator, or, as it is said, upheld by Him, which is the same thing, because then they cease to be independent creatures; but by their union, or upholding, rely upon some property not essential in, but extraneous to, themselves, and belonging to the Creator.

PH.—You infer, then, that because created matter runs into corruption, created spirit must do so likewise.

PA.—We must be somewhat more cautious here, because we are getting into regions, the language of which is beyond us. I do not deny the terms which you state; but you are aware of the difficulty of defining what spirit is, and of limiting that word to one idea.

PH.—By spirit I mean souls, if men have souls.

PA.—Do not say *if* men have souls; because you know you believe that there is a principle in man separate from, though to a certain extent influenced by, the machine commonly called his body.

PH.—Yes, I certainly admit that; and the universality of the consciousness of it is a strong fact in its favour on the one side, and the reasoning of Lawrence and the materialists decidedly false on the other.

PA.—I am glad the balance is in favour of our having souls: then, in answer to your question, I observe that I can form no idea of what spirit is; neither its form, mode of subsistence, nor consequently of the manner of its deterioration. The only light I can obtain upon the subject is from the Bible, and there I find precisely the same language used to describe the phases of it that are used to describe the changes of the body.

PH.—I am quite persuaded with Dugald Stewart, that we can receive no ideas but those which are conveyed through the medium of our external senses.

PA.—Natural philosophy likewise informs us of matter so subtle as to elude the grasp of our most delicate instruments, such as light, heat, electricity, the aroma of plants, of musk and other animals: for all which reasons I conclude that the matter of spirit or souls of men (if I may be allowed to employ such a term for want of a better) is not more different from the bodies of men than the matter of light is different from the matter of a cannon ball.

PH.—Some people would call you, from making use of the expression matter of souls, a materialist.

PA.—It is presumed that no one who is capable of entering into this question is so ignorant as to confound the doctrine here advanced with that of the materialists. I contend that the soul is a principle of life wholly independent of the body in its nature, but to the development of which a body, as a machine, is given, and which body it moves *ad libitum* within certain limits. They assert that what we call life is the product of the machine. I assert that it is the moving principle of the machine; so that we are as far as the poles asunder; as far as substituting cause for effect can place us.

PH.—I grant that there neither is nor can be any language with which to express things relating to immaterial and invisible objects, but that which is derived from the material and the visible; but why must the soul decay?

PA.—Substitute the word deteriorate for decay, and I can more easily reply to you. Created things cannot be essentially immutable: if they are mutable, and have a will, they will wish to move; and that motion will be in self-sufficiency, not in dependence on, and therefore a departure from, the Creator. If the Creator be the only good, that departure must be an ill. Decay is the expression of this essential property in physics: sin, the expression of a similarly essential property of creatureship in morals; sin being a non-conformity of the mind, or soul, to the mind or moral attributes of the Creator: sin being therefore to the soul what disease or caducity is to the body.

PH.—The decay of the visible then being an outward expression of a similar process belonging to the soul, as you do not, I presume, hold yourself responsible for not having an incorruptible body, how do you hold yourself responsible for not having an incorruptible, that is, a sinless soul? Thus I am again brought to the subject of the responsibility of man.

PA.—Concerning the responsibility of those to whom no revelation of God's will has been made I will say nothing: but it is very clear that the duty of every one in a Christian land, who must know that there is a Book which purports to contain such a revelation, is to study it: ordinary faculties are sufficient to apprehend that it is of divine origin; and the duty to take it as our guide follows as a necessary corollary. The responsibility of man, therefore, does not bring him into condemnation for not having a sinless soul; but having a sinful soul, for not believing what God has declared concerning both its sinfulness and its remedy.

PH.—Do you mean that the inclinations of the creature *could* not have been so formed by the Creator, as that it should have inclined only to Himself, and to what is good?

PA.—Certainly they might; but if they had been formed with a bias all one way, they would not have been formed with free and independent volition.

PH.—I do not think that if a creature were formed free and independent that it would necessarily depart from the Creator.

PA.—Every creature need not necessarily have volition, but only those who are responsible: they must still preserve also the other properties of creatures which are essential, such as ignorance, liability to depart from the Creator, mutability, dependency, &c.: because the want of these would constitute them not creatures, but gods.

PH.—Your argument runs hard upon proving that God created sin.

PA.—God did not create sin; nor did any one else create sin, for sin is not a thing to be created.

PH.—How so?

PA.—Sin is a condition of the creature; only give to a creature volition and free agency, and it will certainly exercise that volition in some way of its own; therefore not in conformity with the will of the Creator: this nonconformity is sin; therefore sin is a necessary condition of a creature endowed with free agency, and permitted to manifest its own innate independent will.

PH.—But still the difficulty recurs, why did God make creatures with such wills?

PA.—Nay, leave out the word *such*, and say, why did God make creatures with wills? and let me answer this question by another; how could He make beings responsible without endowing them with wills.

PH.—Suppose I grant that it was necessary, that, if beings were to be responsible, they must have wills,—then, I ask, why was it necessary to create responsible beings at all?

PA.—It is revealed that God created all things with a view

to the manifestation of Himself; and with this knowledge it seems easy to perceive, by the light of our natural reason, that if moral attributes were to be manifested, it must be by means of morally responsible beings.

Ph.—But if the Bible only declares the eternally necessary distinctions between Creator and creature, the alone goodness of the One, and consequent happiness, and the total depravity and consequent misery of every other thing, how does any benefit accrue by the study of that revelation?

Pa.—The whole force of your objective question lies in the word *only*. That which you state is not the *only* thing declared, but it is the necessary basis on which another fact rests, namely, that the Creator, knowing and seeing this to be the case, "so loved the world, that He gave His only begotten Son to come into the world, that the world through Him might be saved; that whosoever believeth on Him should not perish but have everlasting life." Now the love, wisdom, and suitableness of this entirely depend upon the former; for if the former be not true, this was not necessary; but this being done, the presumption is that it was necessary, therefore the former was true.

And now having put me to the *question forte et dure* for the last half hour, giving me a pain in my head, instead of curing one in my body, let me ask you, as an honest man, whether one great objection in your mind to the doctrine of the atonement has not arisen from a secret misgiving respecting its suitableness to your ideas of divine wisdom.

Ph.—I admit that it has. You may philosophise as long as you will, and call it Christian resignation, since you do not like the word fatalism, or any thing else you please, but in point of fact, notwithstanding the pain in your head I have now given you, you feel that you are getting better; and if you thought otherwise, you would be in just as great a fright as your neighbours.

Pa.—My dear friend, thanks be to God who has directed your skill and kind care, that I do believe myself better: but you know that the *vis vitæ* in me is very weak; and that which I am most desirous to be prepared for is, not the last interview with you on a sick-bed, but the first moment that I find myself in a state of consciousness separate from this body.

A slight spasm of the heart, or the suffusion of a drop of lymph on the brain, or a thousand other messengers from God, may effect this at any moment; or, which, perhaps, is worse still, the decay or perversion of the power of reflection. Take my creed, therefore, not from the last feverish starts of debility, but from the settled judgment of my most healthy and collected moments.

PH.—There is much of animal and nervous depression and excitement attendant on disease, which gives a decided colour to death-bed scenes. I am glad, at least, you do not make those wicked accusations of yourself and of your own sinfulness which have always disgusted me in the accounts of those who are set forth as patterns by the heralds of conventicles; for I, who have known the whole tenor of your life, should certainly set it down to stage effect, although I have a high opinion of your sincerity, and of your being incapable of imposture of any kind.

PA.—That is, my dear Doctor, you are willing to admit that I am as little of an ass and hypocrite as any one who professes to be a Christian can be. But how can you, being a philosopher, confound a principle with the manifestation or development of that principle? Wood is combustible. Would it be a sound argument in any one to dispute this, by saying that there is a chestnut beam in Westminster Hall of eight hundred years old, which has never yet burned? Men are sinners; i. e. as prone to sin as wood is to burn: whether these propensities have shown themselves, and the mode in which they have been shown, depend altogether upon external causes; as some trees are less combustible than others, and require more advantageous circumstances for the development of that property.

PH.—Surely you do not mean to confound all distinctions between degrees of criminality.

PA.—Degrees of criminality depend upon the rule by which the conduct is determined to be criminal. In England it is wrong to appear in the presence of the king with your head covered: in Turkey it is wrong to appear with it bare. Without quibbling, however, upon conventional crimes, or those which social laws alone make so, we must draw a broad distinction between what is contrary to the declared will of God,

and that which merely relates to man: yet in one sense all
crime is equal, namely, that it is opposed to the will of God,
to which, as creatures, we are bound to conform.

PH.—You place, then, the duty of man to be in perfection;
and do you mean to assert that every man is condemned who is
not perfect?

PA.—Undoubtedly I do; but now you have wheeled to the
right-about as quickly as the House of Lords, at the command
of the First Lord of the Treasury, on the Catholic question; and
you seem to be ready to find fault with me for carrying the
responsibility of man too far.

PH.—I should like to know what you understand by Hell.

PA.—It must mean both a state and place. As a state, it is
that which every creature, by continual departure from, and acts
of hostility against, God, is constantly employed in increasing
the misery of for himself; and which misery must consequently
be proportionate to the offences which he has committed against
his Creator and against his fellow-creatures, and against God's
other creatures. As a place, it is that in which God will confine
those who have consummated their enmity to Him, and hostility
to those of their fellow-creatures who have been made by His
Spirit conformable to Him; and by that confinement prevent
their annoying those whom He shall have redeemed and placed
in His future kingdom of peace, purity, and joy.

PH.—But I thought, by your saying that men were saved by
going to Christ, you meant that men were to be saved independent of any merit or demerit in them; and now you say
men make their own hell.

PA.—I take an apple-tree and plant it in my garden; the
goodness of the fruit is in proportion to the goodness of the culture. Those who go to Christ are moved so to do by the
Spirit of God; and this Holy Spirit carries on the culture of
their souls till they are ripe for their place in the mansions of
God. They who refuse the offer of salvation in Christ rebel
against God, and fit themselves more and more, by continual
acts of rebellion, for the society of the Devil, who is declared to
be the head rebel. It is obvious that the separate courses of
the two classes must produce opposite results, one of increased
conformity, the other of increased opposition to God; each its

fitness for its different ultimate destination, without being at all confounded with their original starting point, to which your question applies.

PH.—Since you mention the "Holy Spirit," let me ask you whether you can seriously maintain that absurd doctrine of the Trinity?

PA.—Why do you stigmatise the doctrine with the epithet absurd, when it is obvious that you are not competent to form a decision on the subject, since you have never examined it?

PH.—Well, I will appeal to your honesty, whilst I make a strong demand upon your justice not to betray me, when I ask you, if it is not repugnant to your common sense to be told you must believe, or be damned, that one is three, and three are one.

PA.—You need not fear my betraying you, for your confession informs me of nothing that I did not know before: you are obviously a Socinian, as every man in Christendom is, whether he avows it or not, who does not receive the truth of Scripture as it is therein declared.

PH.—As far as I have been able to examine their writings and sermons, it appears to me that the greater part of those whom you call Evangelical would be Socinians if they had brains enough to understand their own system.

PA.—That is very possible; but the doctrine of the Trinity is like every other branch of truth, not an arbitrary fact, which may or may not be according to the will of a superior, but an eternally necessary truth, without which no revelation of the Deity whatever could be made, no one of the facts connected with man's salvation take place. For self-manifestation is, as I have already observed, the ultimate end of God in creation.

PH.—You must explain this a little more minutely, if you please. What do you mean by no revelation of the Deity being able to be made, except by means of a Trinity?

PA.—That no one can see God, is a demonstrable proposition in science as well as a *dictum* of the Bible. The Father is the term employed to denote the fountain of Deity, and the essential perfection of the Divine Essence. The Son is the expression of Deity, the *express* χαρακτηρ of the Father's Person. The

Holy Spirit is the agent of Deity. Of the nature and mode of subsistence of the First Cause no created intelligence can form any adequate idea, still less express such idea in words. You must not, therefore, bind me down to the rigid meaning of the terms I employ, when I endeavour to give you an illustration of what I mean by a simile taken from natural phenomena. The second person of the Trinity, who became incarnate, is called the Sun of Righteousness : this term Sun seems to furnish me with a language from nature, by which to express the theological fact. The Sun is not the principle of light and heat, nor do we know any thing of the nature of that principle, let it be called phlogiston, combustion, or by any other word you may prefer. The Sun is that which develops, manifests, or expresses that principle. Yet if the Sun was meant to communicate to the inhabitants of this globe any of its properties, some of those properties must be brought down to them, and they must have faculties, or organs, adapted for those properties to act upon, otherwise the existence of the Sun could be of no avail to them. Here, therefore, I see an analogy to the office of the Holy Spirit, which brings down to the minds and affections of men the knowledge of the Deity, who is manifested in the incarnate Son, as the rays of light and heat bring down from the material Sun the manifestation of that principle.

PH.—If I understand you aright, your argument would lead to the denial of the possibility of seeing or knowing God but in the person of the Son.

PA.—You see the point exactly ; and, in further proof, let me add that, in order to the Father being the eternal object of worship to all His creatures, it is absolutely necessary that He should be incomprehensible.

PH.—Waving this point for the present, how does the incarnation of the Son, or of the second person of the Godhead, connect itself necessarily with the salvation of man ?

PA.—The union of Deity brought up again from destruction, or from its destroyed state, the same creature which had been destroyed. It did not stop the course of the essentially necessary property of its destructibility, for then matter would have been indestructible, i. e. eternal ; and the object is to show that there is nothing eternal; nothing that was, and is, and will be, but God alone.

Pн.—What satisfaction do you derive from the contemplation of the character of God?

Pa.—All the satisfaction which it is possible for a sinful creature to enjoy in the present state of things.

Pн.—Enter into a few particulars, if you please.

Pa.—Such as a clear perception that God is love, and that that love can only be manifested in harmony, and not at variance, with all His other attributes; that it is so manifested only in the Person and work of Jesus Christ; that there it must be infinite; that therefore, approaching Him in that way, there is nothing for any human being to apprehend, let him be ever so wicked; that as there is no happiness but in the participation and enjoyment of God Himself, that there I shall have it; that God has promised to confer it in a dispensation yet to come; and the hope of the eternal durability and gloriousness of that makes me think but lightly of all things which can happen to me here, even the crumbling to pieces of this aching body, looking forward to that which is to be revealed hereafter.

Pн.—I wish you would put upon paper the heads of this conversation, that I may think it over at leisure, for there is much that is worthy of consideration.

Pa.—I have no objection to do so, provided you, in reading what is written, will not cavil at the expressions, but get at the ideas which I mean to convey; and then if you can express my ideas in clearer language, I shall be much obliged to you.

Pн.—Perhaps you would give me leave to show it to a friend of mine, for I think it would meet some of his opinions very well.

Pa.—You had better recommend him to read some of our old divines, such as Hooker and Charnock.

Pн.— Oh, no; these old works will no more do for the present race of thinkers and reasoners, than the prescriptions we give in the hospitals will do for the hypochondriac patients of the west end of the town. A physician there must be a tolerably good cook, or at least confectioner, to get on at all: and the *Edinburgh Review* has well said that these are the days of pulp, and essence, and *consommés;* not of sirloins, and barons, and legs of mutton. So it is with the sciences; and our present conversation has contained so much in a short compass, that it is well adapted for the spirit and temper of the age.

PA.—If people will not make leisure to read, they will still less make leisure to meditate; and without meditation there can be no more health of mind, than there can be health of body without digestion.   But you may take the paper, and do with it what you please.

PH.—May I print it?

PA.—If you like.

REFORM

NOT

A NEW CONSTITUTION

1831

REFORM,

NOT

A NEW CONSTITUTION.

THE House of Commons, having refused to reform itself from within, is now, agreeably to the prediction of Lord Chatham, about to be "reformed from without with a vengeance." Reformers are on a sudden placed in a new position. Hitherto they had to contend solely against the enemies of all improvement, and the defenders of every antiquated abomination. Now they have to contend also against the enemies of the Constitution of England, who, taking advantage of our attacks on the advocates of corruption, have long deceitfully joined our ranks, in order to carry on, under our protection, their attack upon the monarchy; who are endeavouring to goad us on to our destruction, and to inveigle us into abetting their republican designs. It is, therefore, more than ever incumbent upon us to stand firm; and having resisted successfully the attacks of open opponents, to be on our guard, lest we should be entrapped by more insidious, and far more dangerous foes. We must contend against borough-mongers on one side, and constitution-mongers on the other.

"The implacable enemies of Reform," says Lord John Russell, in his address to the County of Devon, "have a new device: they are now, forsooth, for *moderate Reform.* They were asked last year—Will you transfer the elective franchise from the convicted Borough of Retford to the great town of Birmingham? No. Will you give members to Manchester, Leeds, and Birmingham? No. Will you declare that it is expedient to extend the basis of the representation of the people? No." It is, therefore, impossible to place any reliance upon those who composed

the administration of the Duke of Wellington, and we must
reject their profession for *moderate Reform*, until we see that
moderate Reform embodied in some tangible shape.   The hasty
and injudicious manner in which the present ministers have
introduced the subject furnishes their rivals with a pretext for
finding fault with this measure, and thereby aiming a blow at
all Reform.   On this side, also, we must be on our guard.
They say that, if the question had been brought forward in a
series of resolutions, several of these would have passed unanimously; and, on all such resolutions, Bills might have been
framed and introduced which would have received universal
concurrence.   Although this would certainly have been a more
judicious mode of introducing so great and important a measure,
and might be a fair ground of complaint, if made by Reformers,
the objections come with a very bad grace from the opponents
of all Reform ; for on the 2nd of June, 1829, the Marquis of
Blandford moved the following resolution :—

"That there exists a class or description of boroughs, commonly
called close or decayed, in which the returns of members to Parliament
are notoriously capable of being effected by the payment of money, in
the way of purchase, and frequently are so effected ; and also another
class of boroughs, in which the elective franchise is vested in so few
electors, that the returns are capable of being effected by the payment
of money, in the way of bribes to individual electors, and frequently
are so effected."

Upon the motion of Mr. Secretary Peel, the House decided
by a majority of 114 to 40, that *no such boroughs existed.*
See *Speech of Marquis of Blandford*, p. 4.

Thus Reformers can place no reliance whatever upon the
declaration of such persons, that they are willing to introduce a
moderate Reform ; and we are driven, for the present at least,
to rely upon the Whigs as our only resource.

The essentials of Reform consist in the following particulars.

1. The extension of the right of voting for the representatives of some one place to every person of property resident
therein.

It is scarcely necessary to defend this position, because it has
not been attacked.   The present Reform Bill stops with those
who rent a house of 10*l.* value per annum ; no reason is assigned
for this ; and it, therefore, appears to be both capricious and

absurd. Some cavilling might be raised upon what is, or is not, *property;* but let the definition be taken where it might, no principle would be involved, nor any bad result in practice would ensue.

2. The disfranchisement of non-resident voters. There are many boroughs in which the majority of the corporation, being the private friends of some neighbouring gentleman, have been induced to elect into their own body persons recommended by him. These persons are generally his relations or connections, residing all over the kingdom, and ready to pour into the borough at his bidding to vote for its representative, or for any other job in which his personal interest is concerned. Thus, a material principle is violated, which is set forth in a writ of 47 Edward III. ; where it is laid down, as a necessary qualification, that borough representatives should have a suitable knowledge of local interests. This writ required the sheriffs to return " *de quolibet burgo duos burgenses qui in navigio, et exercitio mercandisarum notitiam habeant meliorem.*" It is not necessary to contend for the literal adherence to this injunction, in order to maintain, that at least total strangers to the borough should not have the power of setting at defiance the wishes and interests of the resident inhabitants.

3. The expense of elections is an evil, because it prevents any but the very richest persons in the community from becoming candidates : hence the people have not so extensive a choice of persons for representatives as they would have otherwise. Besides the expense, the money which is expended goes mostly into the pockets of attorneys and publicans, and promotes drunkenness, riot, and debauchery in the electors. Much of this expense arises from being obliged to convey the non-resident electors to the boroughs in which they have votes; or, supposing the non-residents to be disfranchised, in the conveyance of free-holders to one spot in the county. This would be obviated by taking the votes in each parish by the churchwardens; by which method also a large portion of the subsequent litigation, owing to disputed votes, would be avoided; since the parish officers, especially if a registry be kept, would have the best means of information. For these reasons, also, it is better to take the votes in parishes, than in districts or in hundreds, where there is no constituted authority to make the return.

4. Shortening the duration of Parliaments from seven to three years. The essence of reform, as contrasted with revolution, consists in reverting to former practices wherever they have been departed from; and, where that is impossible, in shaping our reformation according to ancient principles. This latter plan has been followed in the extension of the right of suffrage to all persons of property, because all persons, possessed of that which constituted property formerly, enjoyed that right at its original institution. The same may be said of diminishing the expense of elections, and disfranchising non-resident voters. On the same principle it is proposed to shorten the duration of Parliaments. But since this point is the most important of all, we must consider it more in detail.

The most defective part of the House of Commons, and that which creates the greatest clamour, is the close, or, as Lord Chatham called them, the rotten boroughs. The questions which arise are, 1st, How do they constitute this defect? 2ndly, Whence has it arisen? 3rdly, How is it to be remedied?

In 1812, the sale of seats in Parliament was declared by Speaker Abbott to be as notorious as the sun at noonday: yet Mr. Hallam says, in his Constitutional History of England, ii. 656, that he cannot find any mention of a seat in Parliament being sold before the year 1760, although bribery began to be manifested in 1747. Since that period, however, seats in the House of Commons have been regularly sold in the market, and great abuses have thence arisen. At one time, an East India sovereign had several paid traitors in the House. Subsequently, the West India men-stealers have had hired defenders there by the same means; and whenever a monopoly, whether in trade, like that of the East India Company, or in paper money, like that of the Bank of England, was in danger, advocates for continual robbery on the public have gained admittance within those walls by money payments. It is a maxim of common sense and experience, as well as of law, Edward VI. cap. 5, 6, that no public office should be sold, under pain of disability to dispose of, or hold it. For the law presumes, as Blackstone observes, that he who buys an office, will, by bribery, extortion, or other unlawful means, make his purchase good, to the manifest detriment of the public.

It cannot admit of a doubt, that the purchase of seats in the

House of Commons, although sometimes for the mere gratification of vanity, is, in the majority of instances, for an improper purpose, and, therefore, some check ought to be put to it; and in inquiring how this political profligacy has arisen, it becomes us to observe, whether any and what change took place in the House of Commons, that can account for it. A very important change took place, namely, the lengthening the duration of time from three to seven years, for which members might remain without accounting to their constituents. A man, who bought his seat, calculated on an average of five years, during which, by flattering the ministers at one time, and threatening them at another, and by the constant access to official ears which he could nightly gain, and which he could not gain in any other way, he might succeed in bothering them into granting him a place of an annual value, more than equivalent to the price he paid for a seat.

" Long sessions, and a long continuance of the same Parliament, have an inevitable tendency to generate a systematic opposition to the measures of the Crown, which it requires all vigilance and management to hinder from becoming too powerful." (Hallam, ii. 218.) If this remark be true, as I have no doubt it is, it accounts for the increased corruption of the House of Commons having grown out of the repeal of the Triennial Bill: since it became necessary for the ministers to bribe the members, in order to carry on the public business; and not only on the score of putting an end to that corruption, but also for the purpose of preventing the House of Commons becoming too powerful, it is of great importance to shorten the duration of Parliaments. The people are clamorous for short Parliaments —take them at their word. If the duration of Parliaments was again limited to three years, the power of effecting this jobbing would be materially diminished; and if the members of the House of Commons had honestly disfranchised every borough which so acted, instead of justifying or palliating the abuse, and throwing every possible shield over the delinquency, the evil would have been cured long ago, or rather would never have existed.

It is obvious, that where there is a purchaser, there must be a seller; and that many of these boroughs, having made their privilege a matter of bargain and sale, have committed a high crime and misdemeanour against the State, and deserve to be

disfranchised: accordingly, a fit and competent tribunal ought
to be formed for the investigation of such cases, and all convicted
delinquents should be dealt with accordingly. In some cases,
also, the whole of the inhabitants have disappeared, as in the
cases of Gatton, and Old Sarum; and here the charters having
necessarily died out, the King should be advised not to send
writs to them again. On the other hand, places which were
formerly obscure, have grown into importance in latter years,
from the opulence which has been collected in them, and on
these should be conferred the privilege of sending resident persons
from among themselves, to represent their interests in Parliament; — such as Birmingham, Merthyr-Tydvil, Leeds, Manchester, Frome, &c. The sending writs to such towns as these
might run *pari passu* with the disfranchisement of defunct or
guilty boroughs; and if there were a slight variation in numbers
on either side it would be immaterial.

I subjoin two examples of the delinquent Boroughs. In the
case of East Grinstead, it appears that —

" None of the voters had ever *paid the quitrents* to the Lord of the
Borough in respect of their burgages; but that the rents of such as
were a part of Lord Sackville's estate had been regularly paid by his
steward to the Duchess of Dorset; that none of the voters *ever paid the
land tax;* but that, in the assessment, the names of the Duchess of
Dorset, or Lord Sackville, were found as the owners or proprietors of
all these tenements; and that they were in the receipt of the profits,
and were at the expense of repairing and maintaining the buildings,
&c. In the case of the burgages conveyed by the trustees of the
Duchess of Dorset, *no consideration was paid;* but the grantees, when
they accepted the conveyance, *signed a declaration of trust, as trustees
for the Duchess.* None of the grantees had the possession of their
deeds, except Mr. Gilbert, and Mr. Roper; the former the steward, and
the latter deputy-steward of the estate. *The deeds were brought in a
bag to the place of election by the agents of the Duchess of Dorset and
Lord Sackville, and carried back by them in the same manner.*"

The internal machinery, by which corruption and profligacy
in boroughs was worked, is well shown in the following memo-
randum, dated the 22nd of November, 1758, of the Corporation
of Rye:—

" We, James Lamb, Chiswell Slade, William Davis, Thomas Lamb, and Nudler Chamberlain Watson, all of the Corporation of Rye, in the county of Sussex, do hereby promise and agree to and with each other, in manner following, (viz.) Imprimis. That we, and each of us, will, to the utmost of our power, exert ourselves for the benefit of each other, for the good and advantage of this Corporation.

" Item. That no application, directly, or indirectly, shall be made by any or either of us, for any place or office, exercised within this Corporation, which is in the gift of Government, without the privity and consent of all of us.

" Item. That any, or either of us, shall not, nor will, at any time, hereafter propose, put in election, make interest for, or vote for any person or persons whatsoever, to represent this Corporation in Parliament, without the knowledge and approbation of us all.

" Item. That previous to the election of either of us, from time to time, to the office of Mayor of this Corporation, all of us shall be advised with and consulted, who, each of us, when Mayor, shall nominate, and call to his assistance as Jurats ; and who, each of us, when Mayor, shall make his annual freemen.

" Item. That all of us will, to the utmost of our power, oppose the electing and choosing any person or persons whatsoever by votes, to be a freeman or freemen of this Corporation, unless such person or persons are liked, and approved by all of us.

" Item. That we, and each and every of us, will use our interest and best endeavours, that the said Chiswell Slade shall be the next Mayor of this Corporation ; the said Thomas Lamb the next Mayor to the said Chiswell Slade ; the said William Davis the next Mayor to the said Thomas Lamb ; the said James Lamb the next Mayor to the said William Davis ; and the said Nudler Chamberlain Watson the next Mayor to the said James Lamb, unless altered by all of us.

" Item. That when the said Chiswell Slade, William Davis, and Nudler Chamberlain Watson, or either of them, is, or are elected Mayor of this Corporation, he, of them three, who from time to time is Mayor, will choose and appoint one of them, the said Thomas Lamb, and James Lamb, to be his Deputy in that office; and whenever the said Thomas Lamb, and James Lamb, or either of them, is, or are elected Mayor of this Corporation, he, of them two, who, from time to time is Mayor, will choose and appoint any one of the said Chiswell Slade, William Davis, and Nudler Chamberlain Watson, to be his Deputy in that office.

" Item. We, the said James Lamb, and Chiswell Slade, do hereby agree, equally to share and divide between us two, all profits and advantages arising, or at any time or times hereafter to arise, by the present or any future Collector or Collectors of the Customs of Rye aforesaid, hiring or making use of our warehouses, storehouses, ships, lighters, boats, or vessels; a fifth part of the sum or sums, from time to time agreed to be paid for the hire of the warehouses or storehouses, being first deducted by and allowed to the owner or owners thereof, for the rent of such warehouses or storehouses; and the usual hire, paid by other persons, being first deducted by and allowed to the owner or owners of such ships, lighters, boats, or vessels, so from time to time to be hired, or made use of by such Collector.

"Item. The said James Lamb and Chiswell Slade do hereby further agree, that if either of us two, at any time or times hereafter, shall so directly, or indirectly, by ourselves, or any other person or persons whatsoever, contract, or agree, to do any work, or find, sell, or provide any materials, goods, or merchandises, to or for the Corporation, or the Commissioners of Rye Harbour, that then the other of us shall have the liberty (upon the same terms as contracted or agreed for) of doing half such work, or finding, selling, or providing half such materials, goods, or merchandises, so from time to time to be contracted or agreed for. And we two do further agree, to submit all breaches, or non-performances, of this, and the above item, to a majority of the subscribing parties; and all the subscribing parties do agree, that any breaches, or non-performance of the two items, by the said James Lamb, and Chiswell Slade, shall in no wise affect or be a breach of any other of the preceding items. And lastly, that all the above items and agreements shall be secret; and that we, or any, or either of us, will not divulge, disclose, or make known the same to any person or persons whatsoever.

"Witness our hands, J. Lamb, C. Slade, William Davis, T. Lamb, N. C. Watson."

Nothing can be more disgraceful than the conduct of the House of Commons in its continued endeavours to screen such conclusive frauds. Speaking of the committees which decide on cases of complained-of boroughs, Lord Glenbervie says:

" In a country where justice is dispensed with a degree of wisdom, purity, and consistency unparalleled in other ages or nations, there existed the most imperfect, partial, and inconsistent tribunal which, perhaps, was ever known in any civilised Government."

Mr. Hatsell speaks of a shameful mode of trial for deciding controverted elections, in which every principle of decency and justice were notoriously and openly prostituted. Mr. Grenville, in proposing his bill to mend this tribunal, says:

" How often, while the merits of a contested election have been trying within these walls, have the benches been almost empty during the whole examination : but the moment the question approached, how have you seen the Members crowd eagerly to their seats, and then confidently pronounce upon a subject on which they have not heard a syllable, except from the parties themselves."

The wise course, therefore, is to revert to the ancient practice of triennial parliaments, when these abuses were unheard of; and therefore it may be justly presumed that they are remediable by these means.

In the above four points lay the essentials of Reform; that is, the cure of such defects as time has introduced, effected by recurrence to ancient practices, founded upon, and being nothing more than, an extended application of ancient principles. There is nothing in this plan, the effect and working of which cannot be foreseen; and nothing which could so materially disorganise the established institutions of the country, as to make it impossible to retrace our steps, should any unforeseen casualty occur. This Reform would be as efficacious and extensive as any which has ever been proposed by Mr. Pitt; by Lord Grey, when Mr. Grey; by Lord John Russell; by Lord Brougham, when Mr. Brougham; and by the Marquis of Blandford: and if it had been proposed at any moment prior to the formation of this insane project of Lord Durham, would have received the cordial approbation of them all.

There is one other point, however, upon which some persons feel very anxious at the present moment, and that is voting by ballot. It seems as if both the advocates and the opponents of this measure overrate the advantages and disadvantages which they respectively anticipate. It would certainly prevent much open intimidation, whether by powerful friends or by turbulent mobs; it would not impede bribery in the smallest degree; and it would generate less openness and plain dealing in the expression of political opinion. Probably the better way would be to leave it optional with the inhabitants of any town or county to vote by ballot, or not, as they pleased; at least, such a plan might safely be tried, until it were seen how it would work.

Proof upon proof might be multiplied, to show that seats have
been sold; and the law declares that they who have sold their
privilege ought to lose it. On this point all Reformers are
agreed; and further, that the elective franchise ought to be
conferred on certain opulent towns. It would seem, therefore,
that there could not be much room for difference upon the mode
by which these two objects should be accomplished; yet it is
possible to do a right thing in a way so wrong, that the whole
merit of the measure is as nothing to the demerit of the method,
and such is exactly the character of this part of the bill which
Lord Durham has had the perverse ingenuity to devise; for
although Lord John Russell was the organ of the administration
in proposing this bill to the House of Commons, yet it contains
principles diametrically opposite to that noble lord's published
sentiments; and since Lord Grey and Lord Brougham, the
only two other authors of plans of Reform in the cabinet, have
avowed that they wish for another and different Reform; and
since this is universally attributed to Lord Durham, who came
forward as its principal defender on Lord Wharncliffe's motion,
there can be no propriety in discussing the measure, otherwise
than that of Lord Durham, and of Lord Durham alone. It is,
no doubt, very right that felons should be put to death: but it
by no means follows, as a necessary consequence, that his lordship should be permitted to walk up and down the town with a
loaded pistol in his hand, and shoot them without the interven-
tion of judge or jury. Most housebreakers are little men; but
what would be thought of the Solon, who should therefore conclude all men under five feet high to be housebreakers, and
proceed against them accordingly? Yet such is precisely the
character of Lord Durham's bill. Some small boroughs have
been guilty of selling their franchise; *argal*, says Lord Durham,
disfranchise all boroughs which are below the standard of 2000
inhabitants. In the plans of all former Reformers the difficulty
has been to know what to do with these boroughs, because the
House of Commons had so grossly misconducted itself, that it
seemed to be hopeless to accuse and try them before that tribunal. Some, therefore, proposed to purchase up the franchise
from those who might be willing to sell; some proposed one
mode, and some another; but it remained for Lord Durham to
hit upon the device, equally novel, ingenious, and honest, of

plundering them according to their helpless incapacity of resistance.

Many of these boroughs send members by virtue of grants, or charters, from various former Kings of England. These charters Lord Durham deals with as things of no consequence, and which can be treated without the smallest ceremony, and with perfect impunity. I deny that there is any power in the Constitution of England to touch these charters. It is miserable sophistry to answer that an Act of Parliament can do anything. It is not the Act of Parliament, but the executive — that power which commands the bayonets, let it reside where it may—that can do any thing. An Act of Parliament may take away Lord Grey's or Lord Durham's patent of nobility, neither of them of very remote antiquity, provided the soldiers will obey the Parliament: but an Act of Parliament has no constitutional power to do so, although neither Lord Durham, nor Lord Grey could in such case obtain any redress. On this point the language of Junius, in his letter to Wilkes, 7th September, 1771, is decisive :—

"As to cutting away the rotten boroughs, I am as much offended as any man at seeing so many of them under the direct influence of the Crown, or at the disposal of private persons ; yet I own I have both doubts and apprehensions in regard to the remedy you propose. I shall be charged, perhaps, with an unusual want of political intrepidity, when I honestly confess to you that I am startled at the idea of so extensive an amputation. In the first place, *I question the power*, de jure, *of the legislature to disfranchise a number of boroughs*, upon the general ground of improving the constitution. There cannot be a doctrine more fatal to the liberty and property we are contending for, than that which confounds the idea of a supreme and an arbitrary legislature. I need not point out to you the fatal purposes to which it has been and may be applied. *If we are sincere in the political creed we profess, there are many things which we ought to affirm cannot be done by Kings, Lords, and Commons. Amongst these I reckon disfranchising of boroughs, with a general view to improvement.* I consider it as equivalent to *robbing the parties concerned* of their freehold, or their birth-right. I say that, although this birth-right may be forfeited, or the exercise of it suspended in particular cases, it cannot be taken away by a general law for any real or pretended purpose of improving the Constitution. Supposing the attempt made, I am persuaded you cannot mean that either King or Lords should take an active part in it. A Bill which only touches the representation of the people must originate in the House of Commons : in the formation and mode of passing it, the exclusive right of the Commons must be asserted as scrupulously as in the case of a money bill.   Now, Sir, I should be glad to know by what kind of reasoning it can be proved that there is a power vested in the representative to destroy his immediate constituent.   From whence could he possibly derive it ?   It is no answer to me to say, that the Bill, when it passes the House of Commons, is the act of the majority, and not the representatives of the particular boroughs concerned.   If the majority can disfranchise ten boroughs, why not twenty ?   Why not the whole kingdom ?   Why should they not make their own seats in Parliament for life ?

"For argument's sake, I will now suppose that the expediency of the means and the power of Parliament are unquestionable ; still you will find an insurmountable difficulty in the execution ; when all your instruments of amputation are prepared ; when the unhappy patient lies bound at your feet, without the possibility of resistance, by what infallible rule will you direct the operation ? when you propose to cut away the rotten parts, can you tell us what parts are perfectly sound ? Are there any certain limits in fact or theory to inform you at what point you must stop — at what point the mortification ends ?"

Lord John Russell, or rather, that greater than Lord John Russell and Junius combined, Lord Durham, says, he has found it at the mystic number 2,000.

"The man who fairly and completely answers this argument, adds Junius, "shall have my thanks and my applause."

All historians are agreed, that it was a wicked and unconstitutional act in Charles, to rob the corporations of their charters.   Hallam, the Whig Historian, says,

"There can be nothing so destructive to the English Constitution, not even the introduction of a military force, as the exclusion of the electoral body from their franchises.   The people of this country are, by our laws and constitution, bound only to obey a Parliament duly chosen ; and this violation of charters, in the reigns of Charles and James, appears to me the great and leading justification of that event, which drove the latter from the throne."—ii. 325.

If this doctrine be correct, it follows that the innocent boroughs cannot be disfranchised ; and that any future Parliament which does not contain members sent from them, will not be "a Parliament duly chosen," and consequently one which the people will not be "bound to obey." Of the House of Commons, constituted as it always has been, even in its worst times, Lord Grey said, on the 28th of March last,

" The House of Commons has done greater good than any legislative assembly that ever existed in any country. The British House of Commons, in my opinion, is the best legislative assembly ever established in a popular government."

Then why, in the name of common sense, alter its constitution? Surely, Lord Grey never heard of the epitaph, inscribed over the tomb of a healthy man, who played with medicine till he died: *Stava ben; e per star meglio, sto qui.*

There are two great errors which are propagated in the speeches of all demagogues to all mobs, on all hustings, and greedily swallowed, without any one having the sagacity. to call them in question: the one is, that those close boroughs are modern corruptions; and the other is, that they have been constantly used against the interests of the people, as they are called, that is, of the governed, and for the private advantages of the governors. Notwithstanding the constancy with which these assertions are made, never were any more totally devoid of truth. It is not here the question, whether the existence of close boroughs, that is, of boroughs in which the preponderating influence of some one individual is so great, that he virtually appoints its representatives, be, or be not, a good thing; that is a question which shall be considered afterwards; what we have here first to settle, is the *fact.* Have close boroughs, such as I have described them, always existed, or have they not? Now it is perfectly notorious, and sometimes referred to as a proof that such boroughs ought not to exist, that several of them had their franchise conferred upon them, solely with the view of enabling certain favourites of the Crown, at different periods, to have agents in the House of Commons.

" Many ancient boroughs, undoubtedly, at no period have possessed sufficient importance to deserve the elective franchise, on the score of their riches or population; and it is more likely that some temporary interest or partiality, which cannot now be traced, first caused a writ to be addressed to them."—*Hallam*, i. 48.

Lord Brougham, indeed, ventures to dogmatise on the other

side, doubtless presuming that no one would call his assertions
in question : but his lordship's legal and constitutional knowledge, is not quite equal to his talents at invective. He says, on
April 14,

" The freemen are the usurpers of the ancient rights of the people ;
they are the select bodies which were totally unknown in the earlier
stages of the Constitution ; they are the individuals to whom that Constitution originally never intended to secure the right of voting ; and
they are the persons, who, ninety-nine times out of one hundred, all
over England, have by usurpation acquired to themselves the privilege
of an extensive monopoly, in the choice of the representatives of the
people."

And, speaking of Old Sarum, he says,

" Can it be for a moment gravely maintained, that such a place as
this should possess the invaluable right of sending members to Parliament ?   I should be ready to meet my noble friend upon this point,
and to profess myself ready to become a convert to his opinions, if
vanquished, if its innate absurdity did not render such a task wholly
and entirely unnecessary and useless."

The passage before quoted from the Whig Hallam, shows
how much reliance is to be placed on Lord Brougham's
assertions.

Corfe Castle in Dorsetshire, and Bishop's Castle in Shropshire,
were both granted the privilege of sending members to Parliament by Queen Elizabeth, at the request of Sir Christopher
Hatton, when she gave him large estates in those neighbourhoods. Shortly afterwards, another favourite, Sir George Carew,
the Queen's Marshal, asked for, and obtained the privilege
for his borough of Newport, in the Isle of Wight, to send two
burgesses to Parliament. In the 14th year of that same reign,
Dame Dorothy Packington sent two burgesses to Parliament
from Aylesbury, and ratified, under her hand and seal, that they
were her representatives. Old Sarum was never, in the whole
course of its political existence, anything but a close borough.
Many more might be cited, but it is needless, because the fact is
well known to all, and admitted on both sides of the controversy :
and yet mob orators have the effrontery to deceive the people
by talking of these things as if they were of modern invention.

Such, however, being the case, with a House of Commons full of Members sent from such places, and by such means, we have the declaration of the Whigs in 1688, in the preamble to the Bill of Rights, prepared and sanctioned by the most eminent lawyers, more of whom were alive together at that period than at any other in our history, that " the Lords spiritual and temporal, and Commons, then assembled at Westminster, did lawfully, fully, and freely represent all the estates of the people of this realm." Not only then have we conclusive proof, that, in the opinion of the ablest statesmen that have ever ruled this country, close boroughs always did exist, but also that their existence did not create a bar to the full, and lawful, and free representation of all the estates of the people of this realm: and I further assert, without possibility of contradiction, that the complaint of them, and not their existence, is altogether of modern invention; and never was made until they became matters of purchase and sale.

I now come to the other fact of their having been used against the people, as it is called; by which I suppose is meant, in favour of the governors to the prejudice of the governed. It is difficult to grapple with this objection, because it is so undefined; yet it cannot be denied that, from the year 1789 to the present hour, the Whigs have dubbed themselves *par excellence* " the friends of the people." Their *magnus Apollo*, Mr. Fox, was " the man of the people;" and, in short, Foxites have ever been the class most notoriously designated by this term. It unfortunately happens for the position which I am now combating, that this very same set of objectors did formerly maintain that all the great aristocratical families in the country were opposed to Mr. Pitt, and were followers of Mr. Fox; and the boroughs of Lord Derby, the Duke of Devonshire, the Duke of Norfolk, and many others, were universally filled by Foxites: so that a large portion of that party called " the friends of the people," were nominees for close boroughs. It is, therefore, utterly false to say that these boroughs have invariably lent their weight to the ministers and measures of the Crown. On this subject, I refer to two passages in a book written by Lord John Russell in 1823, and entitled an Essay on the History of the English Government and Constitution. Page 341, he speaks thus : —

"It is not to be denied that a body of ten thousand farmers or tradesmen will choose no man who is not known to them, either by his station in the country, or by a course of popular harangues. If then you make none but elections by large bodies, you either shut out the aristocracy of talent from your assembly, and constitute them into a body hostile to your institutions, or else you oblige them to become demagogues by profession ; things both of them very pernicious and very dangerous to the state. It is useful, therefore, to have some elections by persons who, from their station in society, are acquainted with the characters of the men of talent of the day. This may be done either by forming some elective bodies of a few persons with a high qualification, or by giving to property a commanding influence in the return of a proportion of members."

At page 344 he continues,—

"Enlightened men of every class find their way into the English House of Commons. Those who have property in land are candidates for their respective counties ; those who have made their fortune by commerce or manufactures may easily establish an interest in cities with which they have some connection, or in towns (there are many such) where, without bribery, the inhabitants require a man of fortune to support their public institutions, and give them his custom in laying out his income. There remains the aristocracy of talent, who arrive at the House of Commons by means of the close boroughs, where they are nominated by peers or commoners who have the property of these boroughs in their hands. In this manner the greater part of our distinguished statesmen have entered Parliament ; and some of them perhaps would never have found admittance by any other way. The use of such members to the House itself, and to the country, is incalculable. Their knowledge and talent give a weight to the deliberations, and inspire a respect for parliamentary discussion, which in these times it is difficult for any assembly to obtain. The speeches, too, of able and eloquent men produce an effect in the country, which is reflected back again on Parliament ; and thus the speech of one member for a close borough is often of more benefit to the cause of truth and justice than the votes of twenty silent senators.

"Some danger as well as anxiety, it may be thought, arises from the power of nomination to a seat in a representative body. Theoretically, it would be better if the members sent by single persons were elected by a body of such constituents. But in practice, it is not found that the borough proprietors combine together to sell their influence : on the contrary, they are firm to their several party connexions, and oftentimes they preserve to the House a great orator, whom the clamour of the day or a fortuitous circumstance has thrown out. Such was, on one occasion, the case with Mr. Fox."

Such also was, on one occasion, the case of Lord John Russell. Rejected by the open borough of Bedford, in 1830, he could not have been the promulgator of Lord Durham's Bill, if his father had not nominated him for his own close borough of Tavistock. Lord Grey himself, at the very time when he was most violent in his opposition to the ministers of the Crown, was rejected by the people of his own county, and returned to the House of Commons as the representative of a rotten borough; so that his whole political character, the very means by which he is now enabled to be himself a minister, is owing to the existence of rotten boroughs; and, if further authority were required, Mr. Hallam, although decidedly adverse to the existence of rotten Boroughs, declares, in his *Constitutional History*, that their influence has been in favour of popular rights, and opposed to the prerogative of the Crown.

There is in every earthly body, individual or aggregate, something which endeavours to destroy it, and which is the evil inherent in it. The nature of the evil varies with the nature of the thing in which it is found. Its form in fixed governments is anarchy; anxiety for change; discontent with the present state; disregard, from ignorance of the nature and principles, of established usages. This is the spirit in the body politic which governments are appointed for the purpose of quelling and keeping in subjection. If rulers should ever court and seek the applause of that portion of its subjects which is guided by this spirit, government must come to an end. The upholding of all compacts, laws, charters, privileges, rights, &c., is the object and labour of statesmen, as the destruction of them is the object of all turbulent agitators in every state. Mr. Cobbett, one of the warmest and most intelligent supporters of the Bill, says,—

"If antiquity, usage, charter, were to have any weight, the Bill would be all wrong, A MASS OF INJUSTICE AND VIOLENCE. But these are to have no weight; no weight they ought; and, finally, no weight they will have. The ministers are forming a NEW SPECIES OF CONSTITUENCY."—Vol. lxxii., p. 432.

I doubt whether an instance can be found in the history of

any civilised state of the ministers of the Crown deliberately
advising their master to violate the engagements which his predecessors had entered into, and committed to the safe and
honourable keeping of their successors. There is not a single
argument which can be advanced for breaking the ancient charters, and robbing the corporations to which they were granted,
that does not apply with equal force to robbing the public
creditor. It is said that " the charters are obsolete; that William
IV. is not bound to preserve inviolate all the foolish arrangements of Henry IV. and Edward IV., or even of good Queen
Bess; that times are altered, and it is for the good of the whole
community that certain corporations should be despoiled." As
to the charters having become " obsolete," that is a word quite
as difficult to define as " ancient." Horace says of an ancient
poet,

> "Est vetus atque probus centum qui perficit annus," &c.
>
> "Suppose he wants a year, will you compound?
> And shall we deem him ancient, right, and sound,
> Or damn to all eternity at once
> At ninety-nine a modern and a dunce?"

The antiquity of some of these charters is greater than the
recorded existence of any legislative assembly, let it be called
Wittena gemote, a Parliament, or by what name it may. The
antiquity of others goes no further back than the Stuart Dynasty;
yet all are to be included under the charge of " obsolete" on the
caprice of the Lord Privy Seal. If William IV. is not bound
to keep the engagements into which his predecessors entered,
neither are the people bound to keep the engagements into
which their predecessors entered. The race that incurred the
debt is nearly extinct, and becoming more " obsolete" every day :
a new race has sprung up, which is no more bound by the
promises of their fathers and grandfathers than the King is by
his. Since " obsolete" then applies to any thing of a bygone
generation that it is convenient to vote a nuisance, few will be
inclined to refuse the title of obsolete to his father's debts.

Then it is alleged that the bill does not violate the charter of
all boroughs, but only those that contain fewer than 2000 inhabitants. But the morality of the measure is not to be determined by Cocker. If it would be roguish to violate the charter

of the city of London, or of the universities, because they are populous, it is equally roguish to rob Agmondesham and Bossiney because their population is small. This argument too is equally in favour of robbing the public creditor. The total number of stockholders is but 275,000, of whom 1500 have above 1000*l.* per annum. The population of Great Britain and Ireland, independent of the colonies, is, at the lowest computation, 20,000,000; so that nearly 80 persons would be benefited for every one who would be robbed. Here is a robbery worth committing. The thief who puts his hand into another man's pocket, and takes a sixpence while he leaves a sovereign behind, is not more moral, but a greater fool than he who takes the sovereign and leaves the sixpence; yet this is precisely Lord Durham's morality in robbing the corporations and leaving the debt; and all must acknowledge that, if the debt were got rid of, no one would desire or need a more efficient Reform.

It is contended that this Bill will not *lead* to revolution. In this I fully concur: it would be a most gratuitous *lead* if it did, for the Bill itself, *ipso facto*, is revolution; that is, it converts this monarchy of England into a republic. Those who doubt this must be ignorant either of the essential distinctions which constitute monarchies and republics, or they must be ignorant of the operations of the Bill. Lord Durham seems to think that as long as the head of the state is called king, instead of president or first consul, so long shall we have a monarchy, let him play what pranks he may with every other part of the Constitution. Sydney Smith, in his speech, talks as if it were merely a question whether he is to bellow out in his orgies, "The King, with three times three!" or, "The President, with three times three!" But the essential of a monarchy is, that political power is vested in property; the essential of a republic is, that political power is vested in the people irrespective of their property. The basis of power in one is property; the basis of power in the other is numbers. The hereditary revenues and estates of the King of England, as well as the money annually voted to him, makes him the richest man in his dominions, as well as the individual in whom the greatest quantum of power resides. The whole machinery of the government has both been contrived in theory, and has been at various times modified in practice, so as to throw political power into the hands of the wealthy classes, the

very effect which the revolutionists honestly avow they wish
to destroy by means of this Bill.   Mr. Cobbett, possessing equal
penetration and more honesty than Lord Durham, candidly says
he likes the Bill, because his wish is "to take from the aristocracy every atom of influence at elections."   Soon after the
Revolution in 1688, Sir William Temple, perceiving the inevitable mischief to a monarchy, or indeed to every state, of any
class of men possessing political power without property; and
perceiving also that power in the peerage was inalienable while
the property of peers was not, proposed that all peers who had
not adequate incomes to support their titles should lay them
down until the restored fortunes of their houses should justify
them or their successors in resuming their honours.   The close
boroughs, the small boroughs, the expenses of elections, the
qualification of candidates, have all tended to place power and
property in the same hands.   It is not the question here whether
this mode of placing power in the hands of property be a good
or bad mode: such is the tendency of the system, and that is
the point now before us.   Neither is it a fair answer to show a
particular rich man like the Duke of Buccleuch, who has no
borough, and a particular poor man, who has no property at all
except his solitary close borough.   The point to be looked at is,
not individuals, but classes; and that the effect of the whole has
been to throw power into the hands of the wealthy, is further
proved by the general language of the Reformers, which says,
that power has been too much in the hands of the aristocracy.
There is, however, one class of Reformers, who say, with Sir
Francis Burdett, that the evil of the close boroughs has been
that the boroughmongers lorded it over the aristocracy, and
that, therefore, the aristocracy had not their legitimate influence;
and this was the language of the Reformers during the whole of
Mr. Pitt's administration.   This class of arguers, therefore, also
confirms the proposition with which I set out, namely, that, in
the opinion of some political persons, power ought to be, and in
the opinion of others it has been, in the hands of the aristocracy.
    Every one of these means, by which power has been preserved
in the hands of the most wealthy classes, is diminished by this
Bill; and here again let me beg the reader to remark, that I am
not now arguing upon the propriety or impropriety of so doing,
but upon the *facts*.   The expenses of elections are diminished,

and therefore poorer men can now contest counties than formerly. The most opulent tradesman, with the largest capital and premises has no more influence than the poorest who pays ten pounds rent. The wealthy yeoman who has been in hereditary possession of his lands for centuries, who has been of importance in the county because of his vote, is now reduced to the level of a dependant tenant. The close boroughs are annihilated; and although I maintain that the existence of a funded debt is so great an evil that no country can be in any other than a diseased state that possesses it, still I am not prepared to say, that, as long as it lasts, the monied interest, as it is called, ought not to have some direct means of entering the House of Commons.

Constitution-mongers have been abroad for some years, from the Abbé Sieyes and Jeremy Bentham down to Lord Durham. What these two former might have done for Utopia, I cannot say; but I must do the justice to the French, Spanish, Italian, Portuguese, and German Constitution-mongers, to acknowledge, that they all had, and have, some machinery by which power should be kept in the hands of the richest classes; and, in general, there is, in their systems, some mode by which power mounts progressively, according as the class pays direct contributions to the State. Lord Durham alone is a bright exception. He has brought forward a measure pretending to preserve, by Reform, a monarchy, which places power in the hands of numbers irrespective of property. To say that wealthy men will always influence poor men is no answer to this charge. Wealthy men always did influence poor men, that is, pay them for doing what the rich man wanted them to do, as much formerly as they will in future; but no monarchy has ever existed, simply because it cannot exist, upon such influence alone. In the ancient republics there were men as rich as any now in England and much more so; yet their influence did not prevent these republics being pure democracies. Lord Durham proceeds to disfranchise boroughs, not because they are rich or poor, but because they do not contain a certain number of inhabitants. He does not give members to places because large properties are invested in them, but because they contain a certain number of inhabitants. The magical number is 2,000, and the amount of property 10*l*.: 1,999 is fatal, as

well as 9*l*. 19*s*. 6*d*.: yet no human being can discern the merit
or demerit of these numbers. The greatest marvel is that men
like Lord Grey should· be so cajoled. Alas ! his lordship has
furnished the melancholy solution of the enigma, by telling us
that *non eadem est mens*. But let us see how the wealth of
the country is prostrated at the feet of the paupers. The total
number of houses in towns, rated above 10*l*., is under 380,000 :
of these, 260,000 are between 10*l*. and 20*l*. Two-thirds, therefore, are in the possession of the lowest class, the most
dependant and needy little shopkeepers. The shopkeepers of
Regent Street and St. James's Street will have no more
influence than the shopkeepers of St. Giles's or Monmouth
Street although their property is a hundred times greater.
A jeweller, who pays a rent of 300*l*. and possesses a capital of
half a million, has no more influence than a little green-grocer,
or old clothesman, whose rent is 10*l*. and his capital nothing.
Birmingham may serve as an example of how "the Bill, the
whole Bill, and nothing but the Bill," will work. It contains
10,000 houses rated at from 10*l*. to 20*l*., and 2,000 houses
rated above it : hence the wealth will be outvoted by the
paupers at the rate of five to one. Universal suffrage voting
in right of personal service, has some sense ; but voting for 10*l*.
and not for 9*l*. is pure unmitigated folly. So little did the
idea of population, in ancient times, form the basis of representation, that the counties of York and Rutland had, at all times,
two Members equally. Some writs also are extant wherein the
Sheriffs are required to send two or three Knights, as if the
numbers were immaterial. On the principle of this Bill there
is no pretext for stopping short of universal suffrage. On the
principle of sound constitutional reform it might be extended
to every one paying rates, without being revolutionary. So that
Lord Durham has contrived to combine the bad of both with
the good of neither. It is not every Constitution-monger that
has a right to boast of so much ingenuity.

If the former system had been preserved, the extension of the
franchise would not have disturbed the relative proportions of
the electing classes. The northern side of Oxford Street might
have been thrown into Westminster, and the parish of Newing-
ton into Southwark, without any alteration of the nature of the
constituency in either place. But by giving members alike to

Birmingham and Brighton, there is no homogeneity of principle but that of population; and if population be the basis, then it is absurd to stop at 10*l.* In Birmingham, a great interest of money and skill, of property, and of intellect is collected. In Brighton, there is a mere aggregation of dirt, or disease, brought thither to be cleaned or healed, with neither capital nor mind to represent. Mr. Cobbett observes well upon such places:

" It is not a *real* and *permanent* rental; it is not a sum arising out of the resources of the country; it arises, in great part, from the temporary and uncertain residence of persons, whose homes are elsewhere; from the influx of foreigners; from the court, and from this being the grand resort of people living upon the taxes; it is a spot for consuming and destroying, and not for creating; it is a place for dissipating the wealth of the nation, and the means of paying the rental is drawn away from its natural resting-place. It is a mere wen, doing, in its present state, infinite mischief to the country. The endless rows of new houses, stretched out in every direction, are created by the taxes, and by the taxes alone; they are not solid private property, strictly speaking; but depend upon the public contributions; it is a *fictitious* rental, occasioned by the loss of the creative millions of the country."

These remarks apply to all such places as Cheltenham, Brighton, Holborn, Deptford, Finsbury, Greenwich, Mary-le-bone, &c. &c.

Of all the Constitution-mongers who have advocated a system of representation according to population, Mr. Grote is the best, and Lord Durham the worst. The former gentleman proposes that every 10,000 adult males should send one representative; but one common error applies to his plan as well as to Lord Durham's, which is, that neither of them perceive the grand difference between representation and delegation; the basis of the former is not numbers but classes of proprietors; the basis of the latter is numbers; the effect of the former is a mixed or limited monarchy; the effect of the latter is nothing but a pure democracy. It is difficult to believe that it is not Lord Durham's wish to bring in a republic surreptitiously, and that he is not wilfully deceiving both the King and the Reformers. The Ministers say that their Bill is not revolution but reform. The revolutionists say it is not a reform but a revolution; and honestly aver, that it is for that reason they like it. The " Ex-

aminer," which is their organ as much as the "Times" is that of
Lord Brougham, says, "the settlement of the Government on
the Democratical basis is certain." I say too, it is revolution,
and not reform; and for that reason I dislike it; but since the
revolutionists agree with my view of its tendency, it follows
that I must think them more intelligent or more honest than
His Majesty's Ministers.

I hate the debt, and have endeavoured for years to show that
it is the primary cause of all our distresses; and that when
doubled by Peel's Bill, it would drive the people to madness, and
make them overthrow the Government.   I hate the Game Laws:
I hate the West India men-stealers: I hate the Corn Laws, and
all monopolies: I hate the jobbing of magistrates, brewers, and
distillers: I hate the prostitution of Church Patronage to political
purposes, and the neglect of their duty by ball-going parsons;
and have endeavoured, as far as my small means would permit,
to oppose all these several evils, and mitigate their force where
I could not destroy them.   But they are altogether independent
of the Reform Bill, be it good, bad, or indifferent; and an
attempt to mix these questions up with Reform of the House of
Commons, is one of the grossest and wickedest impostures which
ever was practised on the people.   Let those who have deceived
them, above all the anonymous writers in the newspapers, whose
names, persons, and habitations are nevertheless perfectly well
known, rest assured, that the tide of popular tumult will return
with fearful flow against them.   I have taken some pains to
learn the idea which men had in their minds, when their tongues
were uttering the word Reform, and I never yet met one who
did not annex something or other to it, with which it had no
immediate, or necessary connexion.   One said, that Slavery
would be put an end to, for which cause the Quakers have signed
a declaration in its favour, in Northamptonshire.*   Another,

---

* Northampton, May 19.
A circumstance has occurred here, which is, I think, almost unknown in political
history, and which will have great weight, although it will not operate until the
eleventh hour. I allude to a paper which some days since emanated from the
people commonly called Quakers, or "Friends." At all events, they have proved
themselves to be "the Friends" of Reform, but it is seldom that they, individually,
and never before, I believe, *collectively*, interfered with a popular election. I may
be wrong, but I mention it, in order to show that the effect of the great measure,
which has so long engrossed the mind of every patriot, has caused the *recluse* to

that rents would be lowered; another, that wages would be raised; another, that tithes would be abolished; another, that the assessed taxes would be repealed; another, that the malt tax would be taken off; the yeomen think it will make corn dear; the manufacturers that it will make corn cheap; besides a great many other equally absurd, but not more relevant. It is absolutely impossible that even if the Reform Bill did touch all or any of these points, all such parties could be satisfied: and when it is seen that it does not touch one of them, the re-action from disappointment will be tremendous.

It is impossible to deny, from the language held throughout the British Empire during the last election, that the demand of the mass of the people is for a portion of the property of the aristocracy. By the word Aristocracy, they mean all persons whose possessions have been inherited, in contradistinction from those whose property has been created by their own personal industry. If the Ministers are ignorant of this universal feeling

come forth and "buckle on the armour." Numerically speaking, the proportion of the population of this religious persuasion is not great, but their moral influence will have great weight, which I anticipate will be felt shortly by the *anti-reformers*, who opposed the "Patriot Lords."

(COPY.)

"ELECTORS OF NORTHAMPTONSHIRE.

" Unaccustomed to take an active part in political struggles, but deeply interested for our country's welfare, and considering the present a very important crisis,— We, the undersigned, of the Society of Friends, think it right to give our support to those Candidates who have pledged themselves to the great cause of Parliamentary Reform: at the same time we are anxious distinctly to state, that we do so, not from a factious and party spirit, or vindictive feelings towards any, but from a firm and deliberate conviction, that the Bill brought forward by the present Ministry, and sanctioned by our Sovereign, so far from having a tendency to produce revolution and anarchy, is a measure fraught with the most beneficial consequences, not only to the country but to the world at large—a measure which would lead to numerous and salutary important alterations in our laws—bring about a *speedy* and *effectual* abolition of Negro Slavery—and such an alteration in our Criminal Code, as would render it more consistent with the spirit of Christianity.

(Signed) "William Marshall	R. Wommersley	John Barringer
Thos. Browett	Gray Hester	Wm. Collins
James Ashby	John Thursfield	John Ashby
Thos. Barringer	James Atkins	P. Patterson
Joseph Barnes	John Blunsom	W. Stephens."
John Mould	E. Latchmore	

" 5th Month, 15th, 1831."

II 4

in the people, their ignorance is as inexcusable as that of the
Duke of Wellington respecting the wish for Reform.   If the
Ministers are not ignorant of this feeling, then their having
neither done or said any thing to counteract it, is to have encouraged it, and adds a still blacker tinge to their treachery in this
whole proceeding.   One delusion has pervaded both Tories and
Whigs alike, which is, to suppose that the cry for Reform had
any other meaning than a determination to get rid of the pressure of taxation, no matter by what means.   The taxes at this
moment press more heavily, by nearly one half, than they did at
.the close of the war: producing starvation to the labourers;
diminished profits to the tradesmen ; and double income to
placemen, soldiers, and fundholders.   The determination of all
classes is to get rid of the pressure of taxation, and they care
not a straw by what means.   The cry for Reform is simply their
expression of this determination ; and being told by ignorant
or designing men, that if the Constitution of the House of
Commons is altered, taxation will be remitted, the people say,
"Well, then, reform the House of Commons:" but unless that
reformed House do remit taxation, not the 70,000l. a year of
pensions, but 30 millions a year of debt, that Reformed House
will be as unpopular as the present House.

Among the smart and specious things which the small wits
of the day are inventing for the sake of carrying on their system
of cajolery, one is, that " poor men only sell their votes, while
rich men sell their seats :" this reminds me of Johnson's parody,
" who kills fat oxen should himself be fat," and is much like
saying, an apple-woman sells apples, while a jeweller sells diamonds.   Undoubtedly each man sells that which he has to sell,
and by which he can gain the most; and so will continue to do
as long as the world lasts.   The "Westminster Review," and others,
say, it is absolutely false to affirm, that poor men ever do or
wish to rob rich men ; while rich men always do, and have
robbed the poor.   This latter assertion is true, simply because
the rich have always had the power to rob the poor; and wherever the poor shall have by the blessing of Lord Durham's
genius power to rob the rich, they will enter upon that, their
new and pleasant vocation, right heartily.   There is nothing
in the possession or in the want of wealth, that creates a
larcenous appetite, but *l'occasion fait le larron;* power and

opportunity are the only requisites for the development of every villainy on earth.

Another fallacy they propagate, is on the employment of favourites instead of meritorious officers; they say, that a poor man, who has cut out a frigate, or stormed a fort, cannot get a regiment or a ship, because Lord Charles, the son of Lord Boroughmonger, has applied also. It is true, that because Lord Boroughmonger has had influence in the House of Commons, his *protegés* have been promoted by the government; and thus it will ever be, only, instead of the Lord Charleses having the power in the House of Commons, the Daniel Whittle Harveys, and the Hunts, and the O'Connells will have the influence; and the Master Harveys, and the Master Hunts, and the Master O'Connells will be preferred to the poor cutters-out of frigates and stormers of forts, instead of the Lord Charleses. This may be a much better arrangement for the families of Harvey, Hunt, and O'Connell; but, as far as the public is concerned, it makes no sort of difference. The House of Commons will, and must ever, contain the persons whose influence is to be gained; and if it be not had by meal, it will be obtained by malt.

Another falsehood which is generally propagated is, that if the abuses in the House of Commons had been reformed in Lord Chatham's time, the national debt would not have been incurred; and the American war, and the last war of the French Revolution, would have been ended much sooner than they were. This falsehood shows the contempt which the Whigs feel for the people; for unless they considered them the most ignorant and unlettered people in Europe, they never would venture to make assertions which are confuted by every page of history. The fact is, that all wars are popular until the bill for glory comes to be paid. During the American war there were frequent changes of ministers, some of whom were in favour of peace, and some in favour of war. Those that were for peace immediately became so unpopular that they were obliged to resign their places as soon as they tried it; and if the ministers who were for war had not been incompetent to conduct it, and thereby brought disgrace on the country, they would have been supported all through it by the people. During the French Revolution the war was so popular, that there was scarce a place of popular

representation in England in which an enemy to the war would
venture to become a candidate; and the administration of Lord
Sidmouth, which was formed on purpose to make peace, could
not stand. Moreover, Mr. Fox, and Lord Grey, and several
others, seceded from the House of Commons because, in their
opinion, it was useless to remain in it while the people were
mad in favour of war. But even let it be granted that the fact
is as the opposite party state, still the House of Lords approved
of the war; and a reformed state of the House of Commons
could not affect the former body. It is clear, therefore, that
either the assertion is false even in the real opinion of those
who make it, or that they mean to put the House of Lords aside
as a useless part of the machine of state. I do not say this to
justify those or any other wars, and still less to justify the extravagance with which they were carried on; but I recall the
facts to the recollection of the reader, to show the utter reckless-
ness of truth of which the promoters of this Bill are guilty in
order to further their designs.

It is scarcely worth the trouble of arguing that the first act
of the new Chamber of Delegates will be to put down the
Church establishment. The clergy have had the sense to perceive this, and have opposed the candidates who have pledged
themselves to "the Bill, the whole Bill, and nothing but the
Bill," in every quarter. The Dissenters, too, have laid aside the
mask and run with the eagerness of hounds who are close on
the brush, and who have not tasted blood for some time.

The clergy are supposed to have a peculiarly accurate scent
for danger to their body. The Dissenters are also accused of
being particularly alive to their own interests. Let it be granted
that both these charges are well founded; then it follows that
both the parties who are most interested in the subject and
the best judges of the effects of the Bill, agree in what
must be the result of the measure. As long as the term Dissenter signified a person of conscientious difference of opinion
on *religious* subjects, so long was he entitled to our respect;
but since the Dissenters have come forward as a political society,
to subscribe for this purely secular purpose, they have become a
mere excrescence on the political body and are an intolerable
nuisance to the state. Their object in promoting the return of
the revolutionary members can only be to encourage them to

commit the sacrilege which they themselves have already committed in their hearts, but wanted the courage to perpetrate with the hand. The most influential individuals among them are using language now which their prudent hypocrisy would have restrained but a very short time ago. One of these, very opulent, and who gives away large sums every year, could not refrain from calling out, when occupying the chair of a charitable society lately, in allusion to the national church, " Down with the hag, down with her!"

The demolition of the Church establishment, although ultimately to be effected by the House of Delegates, is owing primarily to the Popish Bill; for it is impossible to justify the payment of the ministers of one sect after having declared that all creeds are equally true in the eye of the law. Bad also as the passing of that bill was, it was nothing in comparison to the argument of Sir Robert Peel, that he believed it wrong, but conceded it to public clamour ; inasmuch as upon this plea nothing can ever be resisted again, provided only there be sufficient clamour. The disfranchisement of the poor Irish freeholders, however, for no fault of theirs, but for the fault of the Irish landlords, who had grown this crop upon their estates in order to job with it for their own private emolument at the Castle of Dublin, was an act of injustice and tyranny that precludes the perpetrators of it from taking the high ground against the spoliation of the corporations that they might otherwise have done. Thus " their iniquity has found them out."

The robbery of the corporations and the plunder of the church (long before any direct attack is made upon the funds), aided by some mild notions that will be broached by the newly-returned delegates, will give such a shake to the security of property and the general feeling of its perpetuity as nothing can ever remedy. If there be one point on which political economists are agreed more than another, it is, that the first element in national wealth is security. But it is not an overt act on one side or the other that can give or destroy this feeling of security: it is like the general character of an individual, which is formed upon the common average of his daily conduct and not upon any one specific action. A wise man may do a foolish thing and a good man a wrong thing while a fool and a rogue may do a wise or an honest thing. The great bias of this administration is to pay no respect to that which has ever been considered of the most durable nature, and this conduct will soon give a feeling of insecurity to all. Manufacturers will not make goods for which they have no immediate demand; people will take to hoarding; diminution of currency will ensue; prices will fall; taxation will thereby press more heavily; labourers and artisans will be unemployed, while the same unsettled principles which shall have deprived them of the means of subsistence will render them more indifferent about the means by which they provide for themselves. If by some act of perfect justice the debt could be liquidated in a moment's time, the change would be dangerous to the peace of the community from its rapidity alone. If we were to add to the rapidity of a change an unprincipled character also, it is impossible to calculate the effects of such a connection.

It has been by the means of the close boroughs alone that the Crown has always been able to ensure admission to the House of Commons for its Ministers. This door will be closed under the new Constitution. One of two things therefore will necessarily follow: either that a new law must be passed giving to the servants of the Crown seats *ex officio* in the House of Commons, or else that the Ministers must give way to every fancy of the people, whom they are called upon to govern. The absurdities involved in this new Constitution; the extraordinary position in which the people of England at this moment find themselves, of being actually engaged in the discussion and formation of a new theory of government; (this most thinking people, who had prided themselves on their superior intelligence; whose old Constitution has been the admiration, envy, and model of all other nations after which they have panted,) are circumstances absolutely unaccountable on any other supposition than that of a judicial infatuation, sent by God in judgment on their ingratitude for the many blessings they have hitherto enjoyed. Not the least in the catalogue of marvels is it that they are being led by the nose, not by a man whom they have been accustomed to look up to from his legal, historical, and philosophical knowledge, such as Sir James Mackintosh: not by one whose writings show him to be a statesman of consummate practical skill, like Lord Wellesley; but by Lord Durham, of whom scarcely one in a million ever heard the name, and whose opinion those who know the most never dreamed of consulting upon any one subject whatever.

It is needless to quote extracts from Paley, Fox, and a hundred other Whigs, to show, (because every one who will reflect must know it,) that there are times of popular madness when the people would destroy themselves if they were not restrained by the firmness and superior sense of their rulers. Yet in this new Constitution, the rulers will have no power to restrain the people: they will be the creatures of the mob and ever continuing dependent upon it; and consequently, the moment they attempt to use their power to control that mob, that instant they will lose that power. This constitutes the essential difference in its practical working between a system of representation and a system of delegation; and of the first element of historical knowledge, the A, B, C, of every Constitution-monger, Lord Durham shows himself utterly ignorant. How comes he never to have read in Hallam, that it is " an important constitutional principle that each member of the House of Commons is deputed to serve, not only for his constituents, but for the whole kingdom — a principle which marks the distinction between a modern English parliament and such deputations of the Estate as were assembled in several continental kingdoms — a principle to which the House of Commons is indebted for its weight and dignity as well as its beneficial efficiency, and which *none but the servile worshippers of the populace are ever found to gainsay.*" (i. 287.)

The House of Lords will have been swept away; but this the supporters of the Bill now say is a chimerical apprehension. Yet all the newspapers which support the Bill are daring the Lords to oppose the wishes of the Ministers and of the people. If the Lords pass the Bill out of deference to the madness of the Chamber of Delegates, now called a House of Commons, it will justify the assertion of the revolutionists that it is a useless incumbrance on the wheels of democracy. Yet their conduct on the Popish Bill, the general subserviency of the bishops to the Minister of the day, and the want of firm, unbending principle everywhere, allows but little to be expected from that quarter. This same argument will be always at hand; and the new-invented absurdity of " treason against the people " is a crime to be added to our penal code under the new Constitution. Hitherto the House of Lords has existed partly by its own firmness, partly by the support of the King, and partly by the first shock of collision of sentiment having been broken in the House of Commons. It is absolutely impossible for the House of Lords and House of Commons both to exist without some common link. One or other must fall; and the only safety for the people is in the rise of a military dictator who will put down both, as Cromwell did; and if " the Bill, the whole Bill, and nothing but the Bill," passes, the sooner another Protector, even though it be Lord Durham himself, comes forward the better.

There are many very intelligent men who have been for several years the chief advocates for Reform in all its extremes, and who warmly support this Bill. They acknowledge that the term " Reform " is ill applied to it; that to reform means to re-constitute in a condition in which the thing reformed existed at some prior time; that after this Bill has passed the Constitution of England will not resemble in any point the Constitution as it now is ; that it produces a revolution greater than that of 1688, or than that effected by the Reformation ; that the whole power of the State will be henceforward lodged exclusively in the House of Commons ; that, therefore, a Republic *de facto* will be established ; and though somewhat alarmed at the working of this new machine, particularly on its first launch, they have so little respect for ancient institutions, see so little advantage in the present Constitution, and are so disgusted at the abuses which they witness, that they prefer this enormous revolution to allowing things to remain as they are. These arguments I have heard in more quarters than one, *hisce auribus*. This is a different class of supporters from any which we have hitherto considered: they are pure Republicans, and because they like a Republic they support this Bill. It is needless, therefore, to remark upon what must be their opinion of the intelligence or of the honesty of Ministers, who can sanction a Bill, having such a tendency, with such a title; who can secretly intend revolution while they cry out reform ; who can undermine the monarchy under the fraudulent pretext of supporting it; who betray their master with a kiss, saluting him with " Hail, King " in mockery, while binding him in order to prostrate him at the feet of the mob. Upon urging this upon the republican supporters of the Bill their answer is justly,

" What is that to us, let the Ministers see to that; we only look to the end we gain ; we have nothing to do with the consciences of those by whom it is given." This is very true; but let no one deceive himself with the possibility of this country continuing a first-rate European Power if she becomes a republic. The example of America is nothing to the question ; it does not bear one point of true resemblance : the essential differences are, that she has a thin population, with boundless extent and fertility of territory, and all her enemies at an immense distance; we have a crowded population, poor soil, small limits, and powerful enemies close at hand. In all great struggles the advantage will be on the side of that State which has greatest unity of counsel and execution, so that, *cæteris paribus*, a republic has in the main not so good a chance of success as a monarchy. But for one republic to exist as a first-rate power, in the midst of a family of monarchies, would be an absolute impossibility. If it lay in the heart of them all like Switzerland, it might be tolerated, partly from contempt of its weakness and partly from the mutual distrust of its neighbours, as dogs sometimes sit watching one another while the bones lie between them ungnawed by either. But if England became weakened, and long before she became settled down into a republic, her soil would be the field in which Russia and France would contend for her, and even the choice of her future masters would be a boon denied her. *Quo, quo, dementes, ruitis ?* Moreover Frenchmen in their most republican days had no horror of standing armies, and there was always safety at least for that part of the population which was willing to become military. This army made her a formidable power to attack ; but English jealousy of standing armies will render it impossible for her effectually to repulse any attack upon her soil made upon a sufficiently extensive scale.

An attempt will doubtless be made to render the army odious, by raising a clamour against employing it for the preservation of the tranquillity of the country and of the property of individuals. But so far from this being an unconstitutional employment of armed force, at no period of our history has domestic peace been preserved by any other means. Let us take as an example London in the reign of Elizabeth, when the Crown had but recently become sufficiently strong to control effectually its

powerful vassals; and when, consequently, the Crown added its
jealousy to any that the people could feel against a standing
armed force.   All that we now call London did not contain in
those days above 400,000 inhabitants; whereas the same
circumference holds now five times as many.   For the police of
this mass there was a large body guard round the court.
Between St. James's and the city there were the powerful
nobles, Leicester, Sussex, Neville, Salisbury, and many others,
each with a band of armed retainers as numerous as a regiment
of modern infantry.   In the city itself was its chartered Artillery
Company, Train Bands, &c.; the whole of which together could
not amount to less than ten thousand armed men.   It is true
that many acts of lawless riot and oppression were committed
by these retainers of the nobles; that they were a very bad and
inefficient police; and the country was plundered by highway-
men and marauders of all descriptions : but still the whole
police of the country, such as it was, consisted of soldiers.
A mob of 100,000 persons is a small mob, in comparison with
the population of London and its environs now; but quite
uncontrollable, if bent upon mischief and excited by starvation
and demagogues, by any less force than 20,000 soldiers.   Lord
Brougham wrote to the persons assembled to celebrate the
French Revolution of last July that the danger most to be
apprehended was, that the government there should not be
allowed sufficient power to carry on its functions.   His lordship
need not now go so far a-field for a similar object of solicitude
Let but the ministers be weak or wicked enough to diminish the
army, and the king's crown is not worth an hour's purchase.

It is needless to encumber the question with any remarks
upon that part of the Bill which relates to Scotland, and which
is one of its best features, since nothing can be more faulty than
the actual state of the system in the Scotch boroughs.   The representation of the counties has worked well upon the whole, but
the right of voting for superiorities, as they are called, that is,
in virtue of manors and not of lands, is unjustifiable on every
ground.   On the other hand, one of the worst parts of the Bill
is that which, diminishing the number of English, increases
the number of Irish members.   The characteristics of the three
parts of the empire, England, Scotland, and Ireland, are very
distinct: the former being remarkable for the greatest portion,

and the latter for the least portion, of sound unprejudiced plain sense. The proportions of members are to be disturbed; and Lord Durham, consistently with the discretion that he has manifested throughout this Bill, proposes to diminish the number of those members who possess the most judgment, and increase the number of those who possess the least. Surely, never was a country blessed, or cursed, before, with such a legislator as this: truly he is unique; and may defy the world to produce his fellow.

The practical point now to be considered is, What is to be done? It is in vain to look up to the Tories, for they want a head. Not only has the ground been completely cut from under their pretended willingness now, in the eleventh hour, to admit a moderate Reform, but evidence is wanted of their capacity to devise and to direct it. If their repentance had been sincere, they should not have ventured to throw out the Bill on the second reading, without having another ready to introduce *instanter*; still less should they have allowed a dissolution to take place, without setting another Bill before the country. As the case has stood, the question that has been determined by the elections has been, not between Reform and Revolution, but between Revolution and no Reform: this Bill, or nothing: and instead of finding the opinion of the Duke of Wellington correct that people did not want Reform, their anxiety for it was so *outré*, that they would rather have it in the unsightly shape of Revolution, than be without it altogether. But this is not all; not only was it a *coup manqué* not to have presented another Bill to the people, but the reason assigned by Sir Robert Peel was worse than the omission. He said, that if he had brought in a Bill, or even acknowledged that he had prepared one, it would have been thought that he was anxious for place, and that he was taking advantage of such a Bill as a means of regaining power. Did ever mortal man, who aspired to the dignity of a statesman, advance such a reason as this? What, in all the wide world, could it signify what was thought of Sir Robert Peel? The idea of himself ought never to have crossed his mind. The only point to be considered was, how to save the country from consenting to a revolutionary measure proposed to it under the mask of Reform; whereas, the only point Sir Robert Peel seems to have thought of, was his own personal

reputation. But Sir Robert Peel had been a minister of the
King; still more then it was his duty to have let the King see
that His Majesty was not obliged to take Lord Durham's Bill or
no Reform; and that it was not in the power of the present
Whig faction to bully their master, as Lord Grey and the Whigs
attempted to do when they were last in power. It is a very
serious evil that there is no head to the true Reformers, equally
distinct from the perpetuators of all abuses and from the revolutionists; and in this emergency, the question is still more
important, what is now to be done? Without entering into any
details, there are two leading points which ought to be contended
for by every means. First, the number of English members
ought not to be diminished; there is not the smallest pretext
alleged for this diminution, and, therefore, it is not possible to
expose it. Secondly, every borough ought to have an impartial
hearing at the bar of the House, or before some other competent
tribunal. If it is alleged that this will be a very slow process,
I answer, so much the better; for every change that is hasty
and sudden is sure to produce mischief in a country, let it be
ever so wise : it is the soundness of this principle that has
ever given the advocates of the gradual abolition of slavery
so great an advantage; although their secret meaning was,
by the word gradual, to oppose all diminution of its evils
whatever. Let all real Reformers join as one man, and contend
for these two points; let them not be flattered by the ultras on
either side; let them adhere firmly to this principle, and they
who have no principle must give way before them. "We are
bound," said Mr. Fox, in 1781, "to promote the true interests of
the people, in preference to the dearest desires of their hearts;
and the constitution makes us the sole arbiters of those interests,
notwithstanding the imaginary infallibility of the people. Shall
we sacrifice our reason, our honour, our conscience, to the fear
of incurring the popular resentment? And while we are appointed to watch the Hesperian fruit of liberty with a dragon's
eye, be ourselves the only slaves of the community? Perhaps I
shall be told that nothing but the worst of absurdity could suspect the people of a design against their own happiness. I do
not suspect the people of any such design, but I suspect their
capacity to judge of their own happiness. I know they are
generally credulous, and generally uninformed; captivated by

appearances, while they neglect the most important essentials, and always ridiculously ready to believe that those men who have the greatest reason, from their extensive property, to be anxious for the public safety, are always concerting measures for the oppression of their own posterity. I STAND UP FOR THE CONSTITUTION, NOT FOR THE PEOPLE. IF THE PEOPLE ATTEMPT TO INVADE THE CONSTITUTION, THEY ARE THE ENEMIES OF THE NATION. Being, therefore, convinced that we are to do justice, whether it is agreeable or disagreeable, I am for maintaining the independency of Parliament, and will not be a rebel to my King, to my country, or my own heart, for the loudest huzza of an inconsiderate multitude."

It is worthy of observation, but calculated only to excite our disgust and loathing, to find so many men who have been declaiming for years, with thundering vehemence, against the power of the crown and the tyranny of its government, now exhibiting themselves the most abject slaves of the mob. Insolent pretenders to courage against the *vultus tyranni*, simply because there was no *tyrannus* to put it to the test; cowardly flatterers of the *civium ardor prava jubentium*, the only despotism really to be dreaded. Some of these, now high in office, are said to be leagued with anonymous journalists; if such there be, we may rest assured that, let their talents, and knowledge, and virtues, be what they may, they want the first requisite for rulers, that of unflinching political courage; and, however they may shine in a "keen encounter of their wits," they are to be withered into silence by continued exhibition of simplicity and principle. Political cowards are invariably cruel, and endeavour to still opposition by the severity of their measures. Many of the most savage heads of faction in France, from 1789 to 1798, were cruel from this cause, rather than from any innate blood-thirstiness of disposition. The ministers have already exhibited two faults, which are never-failing indications of incompetence; one is precipitation, and the other disingenuousness: the attempt to hurry this Bill through Parliament is proof of the first: their representing to the King that the Commons had refused the supplies is proof of the second: no honourable man would have resorted to such equivocation.

We know that the plan of Lord John Russell was nothing like this Bill of Lord Durham, and that his conversion to its prin-

ciples is quite as great a change as that of the Tories to moderate
Reform. We know, from Mr. Brougham's speeches in Yorkshire,
that his plan was wholly unlike that which has been brought
forward. Lord Grey said distinctly, on March 28th, "the FIRST
disposition of my mind certainly was, to limit the Reform
WITHIN A MUCH NARROWER COMPASS." How then is it possible to
account for the fact, that all those Members of the Administration, who formerly voted with Mr. Brougham and Lord John
Russell, as well as those who have been pertinacious opposers of
all Reform, should on a sudden abandon their former notions,
and adopt, with the proverbial zeal of new converts, this revolutionary measure ? The only solution of the question is to be
found in the fact, that the ministers having failed in every measure of Government which they brought forward, and being convicted of incompetence, and on the point of being called up to
receive sentence for the same, threw themselves, in a fit of desperation, into the hands of the revolutionists, in order to gain
an ephemeral popularity, fatal ultimately both to themselves and
to their royal master. In no other way is it possible to account
for the fact of the hurry in which the Bill has been drawn, and
which is visible in every part of it. Mr. Cobbett, its most clear-
sighted panegyrist, says, "It bears on the very face of it the
marks of hurry, as to its details; and not once out of one
thousand times is a thing done in a hurry well done; especially
if it consists of many particulars or items." A few of the
marks must be mentioned : 85 boroughs, untouched by this act,
will not be able to exercise the elective franchise, because they
do not contain 300 houses, rated at 10l. per annum, until the
Committee of the Privy Council shall have added to their limits.
In nearly half of these there are not a sufficiency of rated
houses to be found within seven miles, and in some instances
not within forty miles. In three Welsh borough districts, there
are not 300 rated houses in the whole of the counties in which
those boroughs lie: only fifteen hours are allowed for the entire
polling of the borough districts: yet, in the Tower Hamlets,
the total number of voters will be above 26,000. Leaseholders
of farms may rent 3,000 acres of land, with capitals of any
amount, and yet not possess that vote which is conceded to a
10l. renter in a town.

In 1807, the Whigs were in power, and exhibited the same

lamentable incapacity in the science of government. Under their guidance, the British arms were disgraced in every quarter of the globe. They tried to make war, and they failed: they tried to make peace, and they failed also: they tried to conciliate the people by insulting the King, and they were discarded by their master with the approving voice of the whole empire. Their political character is thus described in the Times Newspaper, of last August 21.

" As to the Whigs, we plainly, and in the face of the people of England, deny that the country looks to them as its saviours in any great emergency. The experience of nearly fifty years has proved the real character of this party — at once haughty and pusillanimous — rash and short-sighted — noisy democrats when out of place — insolent aristocrats when in — ignorant of the noble qualities of their own countrymen, and timid depreciators of their glory, while they are ever vehement, and ready to applaud and magnify the successes of foreigners. Such are the men, we are told, England is to regard with veneration and affection."

The Whigs have made a precisely similar exhibition now; but the charms of place and power, for which they have been so long striving, were not to be renounced at the first moment that they had begun to be tasted ; and it was resolved, that if it were to be a question whether the ministers should be turned out, or the King betrayed, and the country revolutionised, that these latter were but as the small dust of the balance, in comparison with the permanence of the power of Lords Durham and Brougham. Possessed of no property in boroughs themselves, and the people not having had the same estimation of their merits that they have of their own, they have ever depended upon the charity of others for their seats in the House of Commons. Since they have had no means of governing by such methods themselves, they are determined that no other person shall possess them ; and if they cannot carry on the government of the country upon their new plan, they are resolved to revel in the fiendish satisfaction, that to do so is rendered equally impossible to every future minister of the crown.

There is not a man from one end of the empire to the other, nay, throughout Europe, that has not been struck with an astonishment as great as if some sudden visible mark of divine vengeance had lighted on the land. The French journals, conducted by some of their ablest statesmen, avowing their national desire for the downfall of the power of this country, have expressed their unfeigned delight. The most violent revolutionists in England declare that they never expected, in their time, to see anything so nearly approaching the consummation of their wishes. All the most intelligent admirers of the Bill confess, that instead of its being a reform, it is a complete new constitution, and defend it on that ground. Lord Grey has been plainly told, with savage exultation, that the time is arrived when he may enjoy the distinction of "dying in a ditch for his order." For the first time in the history of any Christian state is blasphemy openly professed and inculcated, unrebuked by the sword of the civil power. Some of the ministers have confessed, that the Bill went further than they altogether desired; and these feelings in all, are mingled with that sort of apprehension, which the beholder always experiences at the sight of a wreck, an avalanche, or the irruption of a volcano, a sublime terror at the awfulness of destruction, although he himself may be secure from harm. Lord Durham, alone, is said to have no fears; then I say to him, as Cato said of Catiline, *sin in tanto omnium metu solus non timet, eo magis refert me mihi atque vobis timere.*

AN

ADDRESS

TO

THE PEOPLE

OCCASIONED BY

"A LETTER TO THE QUEEN" FROM "A FRIEND OF THE PEOPLE"

BY ONE OF THEMSELVES

1839

AN

ADDRESS TO THE PEOPLE,

&c. &c.

ALTHOUGH no one may presume to thrust himself into the presence of the Sovereign, but must wait until he be especially summoned, yet every subject has the privilege of defending the royal person from insult, and of rejecting the officious intruder.

Some one, who styles himself "the Friend of the People," has ventured to give uncalled-for counsel to the Queen, and fancies that he is qualified to perform this office from the mere circumstance of his being "well stricken in years," and "having had no little political experience." The first plea can only be available upon the supposition, that wisdom invariably accompanies age; but a person who has lived "half a century" can have but feeble penetration, if he has not discovered more people who increase with years rather in folly than in wisdom, in garrulity than in reflection. "Old men are not always wise," says the inspired penman; and "he that hath knowledge spareth his words" until they are asked for. His second plea of "a long life of political observation, no little political experience, and a diligent study continued above half a century of the most eventful period in the whole history of our species, is" not "sufficiently powerful," without some other proof to justify the arrogant assertion, that he must "needs possess a superiority over the Queen in all that constitutes practical wisdom." Arrogance and self-conceit are very questionable ingredients in "practical wisdom." Such language—and I will not sully these pages by quoting much that is still worse—from any individual to another, is insolent; from a man to a young and unoffending female, is brutal; from a subject to a sovereign, indicates a disloyal and traitorous heart, combined with a total ignorance of the relative standing and duty of him who writes, and of the royal personage who is addressed; and as there can be no practical political wisdom whatever in any one who is ignorant of these relative duties, my object in writing this address to you, is to remind you of the principles upon which these reciprocal duties are founded, lest they should haply have slipped from your memories, or at least have become torpid, as they have evidently become wholly forgotten by him.

The practical political points on which this "Friend of the People" insists are, that "the most important alteration by far that our form of government ever suffered, the largest indeed that any country ever underwent without violence," has been effected: that "the most turbulent and difficult times through which the predecessors of the Queen ever passed, were calm weather and smooth water compared with those that await Her Majesty under the new dispensation" (p. 16); that "the monarchical principle is exposed to a new and to a rude trial of its strength in the Queen's person" (p. 7); that "the revolution effected in 1831-2 is only a prelude to still greater changes; that it is wretched folly for the Reform Bill to be called a final measure" (p. 12); that the elective franchise must be given to all men; and that as this must be granted ultimately, there is neither principle nor prudence in not granting it immediately. In all these points I fully agree; and as this "Friend of the People" has stated the matter with great ability, it is unnecessary to add anything to his forcible exposition. But he states also, that the tendency to pure republican doctrine is greatly on the increase in this country: that he is friendly to the present form of government in England, because he "believes it to be better suited to our *present condition* than a republic" (p. 12); that "upon the whole, and in the present state of society in this country, he is friendly to monarchy," and that "he and all those who hold such language are and ever will be found standing by the Queen with pen, and tongue, and sword, and will cling to monarchy when it is out of season" (p. 41).

Now no one can or ought to cling to monarchy who has no better reasons for doing so than any relating to our "*present condition*," or "*present state* of society:" and as I wish that all should cling by monarchy, and defend it with pen, and tongue, and sword, I will endeavour to set before you the only grounds on which this can be done; the only principle which can make men cling to it in all "conditions," and in every "state of society," be they what they may.

The "Friend of the People" concludes with the well expressed prayer, "that the Almighty and Allwise disposer of events, He in whose hands are the hearts of men, may endow her Majesty with the wisdom" necessary to fulfil her important duties. And her Majesty will be so endowed just in proportion as she remembers "whose minister she is;" that she is the vicegerent, the *locum tenens* of the King of kings, òf the Prince of the kings of the earth; that she is under Him the minister of the blessings of rule and government to that portion of the family of men committed to her charge. And we and all her subjects will be endowed with the necessary wisdom of being obedient to her by "duly considering whose authority she hath;" by remembering the sacredness of her character; and we shall "cheerfully serve, honour, and humbly obey her, in Him and for Him," in proportion as we bear in mind that it is through her that we receive at the hands of God all those blessings of civil government which we do need.

This "Friend of the People," however, does not yield up his own wisdom in order that he may be endowed with this wisdom from above, for he speaks of the inferiority in all political wisdom of her, because she is a female, and only eighteen years of age, to him who is a man, and "well-stricken in years." He therefore does not see in her Him who is Alone Wise, but sees nothing save "a girl," whom he proudly despises. Yet still he speaks of an "Allwise Disposer of events, in whose hands are the hearts of men:" so that we are compelled to come to the conclusion, that these words in his mouth have no more meaning than the repeating of a dozen *Pater Nosters* or *Ave Marias*.

Yet truly his words are good, though he neither understands nor believes them, and I will endeavour to call to your remembrance the instruction which we have received in this matter from our mother the church, touching the method by which the Allwise God does carry on the blessing of His people by civil government.

Amongst the baptized nations, amongst those who are partakers of the Holy Ghost, and who are responsible for the use which they make of that great gift, has arisen a constitution of things unknown upon the earth before the incarnation of the Son of God, and unknown in Mahometan and heathen countries to this day. This constitution of things is expressed by the term corporation; and the peculiarity of a corporation is, that it is an abstraction, possessing properties and powers wholly independent of the individuals by whom these powers are expressed. As a familiar illustration we may take the corporation of the City of London, whose powers are exercised by the Lord Mayor, by Aldermen, and various officers and members; and daily evidence of our senses shows that these functionaries may be endowed as individuals with as little understanding as falls to the lot of mortals, while the powers of the corporation itself are by no means diminished.

In like manner, the lawyers tell us truly, that the crown is a corporation, as the church itself is a corporation; and the government of the baptized nations could take no other form, because the church could take no other form; and the life of God, even the Holy Ghost, which is in the nations as nations, blessing men by kings, the representative of Christ the king, must needs take a form corresponding and analogous to the form of life which He takes in the church, to bless men under bishops, the representatives of Christ, the great Bishop of our souls; and so far as revelation has instructed us, and so far as our powers of understanding do extend, we may venture to say, that in no other way could God himself be manifested as the doer of all things, personally the efficient guide of His people in civil, as well as in ecclesiastical matters, and yet at the same time wholly independent of and separate from the creatures in whom He dwells, the kings and priests by whom He acts. This power and quality to bless the kings receive in their coronation, and the bishops and priests in their consecration; and to show out more clearly the details of a single kingly government, it is necessary to take a previous glance at the constitution of a single particular church, as it was constituted at the beginning.

The bishop and elders under him were ordained in the beginning by the apostles, such bishops and elders having been previously designated to the office by the Holy Ghost speaking through some other channel. Thus, then, the bishop and elders were appointed directly by God, without the assent or concurrence of the people; and in addition to these, the body of the people elected a certain number of deacons as their representatives, without whose concurrence no decree could be passed. Such was the outward form and constitution of a church at the beginning, however little it can be traced in existing institutions; and England has presented a greater similarity in her kingly government to this ecclesiastical government than any other nation, inasmuch as in her are seen her king and nobles descending by legitimate succession, together with delegates chosen and sent up from the people, forming a threefold union necessary to the completion of any legislative act; but there is no European nation where the king has been without a body of nobles, who were hereditary councillors independent of him, nor without the representatives of all classes of his subjects, in some form and under some name or other, being joined with the nobles in giving counsel, and whose opinions it was necessary to gather before any law could be passed. Thus, in the coronation ceremony of the kings of England, when the king puts his crown upon his head, the peers and peeresses place their coronets upon their heads, showing that if he is king " by the grace of God," they also are nobles by the grace of God. In the coronation of the kings of France, " L'archevêque prend, à deux mains, sur l'autel, la couronne de Charlemagne; M. le Dauphin, M. le Duc d'Orleans, et M. le Duc de Bourbon, s'avancent et se placent aux côtes de Charles X. Le prélat présente la couronne au-dessus de la tête du roi, mais sans qu'elle touche. Aussitôt les princes y portent la main pour la soutenir! Admirable allégorie, qui apprend au monde que les premiers sujets de la monarchie jurent, à la face des autels, de soutenir et de defendre la couronne que la réligion vient de benir sur la tête du chef de leur race."—(*Ab. Chron. de l'Hist. de France. Herauld et Michaud*, p. 908.)

Similar customs, recognising and setting forth the same truths, might be cited from the ancient records of every kingdom in Europe ; in these it is said truly, and it is no fiction, that the king never dies, even as a corporation never can die. " Le roi est mort, vive le roi ; " whereas, in Mahometan and heathen states no such customs ever are, or ever were observed. These are pure tyrannies, for two only classes in the state are recognised, viz. the sovereign and the people ; while the European monarchies are not tyrannies, but the whole community is an organised body, each class directly or indirectly linked with the rest in one harmonious series, from the prince upon the throne down to the lowest order of the common people.

A council is the machinery by which the ruler, who is alone responsible for rule, obtains counsel. In small councils, such as those which assist the governor of a distant colony, the senti-ments of each member of it are easily obtained; but in the great councils of large nations there is no way of ascertaining the opinions of the whole but by vote. A council, however, is no part of the office of rule of the executive; it cannot control the ruler, for that would · be to depose him from the office of rule, to erect itself into that office, and to make of the ruler the mere recording clerk, or officer to carry into effect the will of the council now become ruler: whereas the responsibility of the ruler remains, after he has received counsel, just where it did before; and the light which he will get through the council will be as often to tell him what not to do, as what to do. In prac-tice, the ruler should never state his own opinion to the council, because by so doing he will stir up the contentious and vain to take the opposite side, and the obsequious and soft to flatter and coincide with him; but he should state the question as abstrac-tedly as possible, or at least as much as possible separated from anything that is collateral, and ask the opinion of the youngest member first, and then of all, by turns, up to the oldest. Yet should he not declare his own at the time, but meditate thereon and act accordingly. Bacon has set forth much light on this matter in his "Essay on Government." The larger councils, such as the Parliaments of England, have ever been trenching on the kingly office, and now, unfortunately, the power of the Crown has been traitorously conceded to them, as the "Friend of the People" doth show.

Such are the means by which God would bless the baptized nations; He has appointed the king as his own representative, and He accords to His servants, in the act of anointing by the hand of His priests, a measure of His spirit for that end which He accords to no other individual in the realm. And God gives counsel to the king by the mouths of the nobles and commons, whom He has appointed for that end, to be the representatives and organs of Him, the only wise councillor, some by regular

succession, some by delegation from the mass. Most true it is
that the baptized sovereigns have not walked in the ways in
which God would have had them ; that they have not ruled for
Him, nor thought only how they they might be channels of His
blessings to the people, but have neglected their people, and
made use of the power entrusted to them for selfish and private
ends. Most true it is that the nobles, instead of giving faithful
counsel to the king, in the fear of God, who appointed them for
that end, and for the benefit of the people, have sought only
how they could flatter the king, and cause him to act unjustly,
that themselves might profit by the unrighteousness. Thus the
people being oppressed, have in divers times risen up against
"the powers that be," which " were ordained of God," and have
frequently made their own condition worse, being unable to
accomplish anything but a change in the form of the oppression.
Many vain men have fancied themselves competent to conduct
the affairs of the state, or at least to give counsel to those who
are appointed to do so; and the poor people have listened to
these vain and presumptuous pretenders, and followed demagogue
after demagogue, till finding all their expectations falsified, they
have been goaded to desperation. But God alone is the judge
of kings, and He is shortly about to appear again upon the earth
for that end, for He judges " the kings of the earth upon the
earth." And He has long since " prepared all things for Himself, even the wicked for the day of evil ;" and He is now withdrawing by degrees His protection from the kings who have
refused to rule for Him, and from the nobles who have refused
to be faithful counsellors for Him, and is giving them over, with
all the things which He has established for blessing, into the
hands of destroyers, of radical reformers, of *la jeune France*, of
la nouvelle Europe. The guilt is common, for a wicked king
is a judgment sent of God upon a wicked people; and both
kings and people have become gradually more and more resolved
to cast off the fear and recognition of God from all their national
and public acts; and in France the king laughs at a coronation
as a *vielle niaiserie;* and the people laugh at religion as a
thing not to be endured in the affairs of the state; and they
desecrate God's Sabbath, and deny all sanctity to marriage.

The Church being the first assembly that took the corporate form, so is it therein that its abstract nature is more

clearly discernible, and in nothing so obvious as in its two greatest and principal ceremonies—the one by which new life, even the life of God, is conferred upon those who were previously without it; and the other by which that new life is continually nourished and preserved, *videlicet,* "Baptism, wherein we were made children of God and members of Christ, and inheritors of the kingdom of heaven;" and the sacrament of the Lord's Supper, wherein the flesh and blood of Christ "are verily and indeed taken and received" by those who faithfully partake of the same. For the water, and the bread, and the wine, are but "outward and visible signs of the inward and spiritual graces," which are conferred in and by the respective ceremonies; and if God does appoint the insensible creatures as the instruments of conveying to us so great blessings, surely one lesson we may learn is, that the efficacy of all things stands in their being of His appointment, and not in any quality inherent in themselves; and if this be the case of the two great sacraments of His church, it follows that the same is the case of all the other ordinances of His house. And most blessed is it that such is the case; for surely if the worth of the thing conveying had in any wise affected the value of the thing conveyed, so great has been in all times the worthlessness of the priests and the kings, that by this time God's goodness must have ceased to be communicated to us, having been obstructed in its channel by the filth and rubbish which has been accumulating for 1800 years. But God's goodness is still communicated; children are still born to Him in the waters of regeneration, and faithful souls do feed on the flesh and blood of the Son of God; and His word continues to bless, and His worship is still carried on, and the prayers of His people are offered and accepted by Him; and the same is done in all the various sects into which His church is divided, into which the body of Christ is rent and torn. Thus also it is in the kingdoms: civil government is carried on notwithstanding the unworthiness of those to whom the power is delegated; and it matters not whether it be by one individual or another, so far as that distinction depends upon the age, abilities, learning, or sex of that individual. The sole quality that makes one king better than another is, whether or no he recognise his standing under God, and seek to Him for ability to guide and to bless, and to promote the happiness of His people. But men have so grossly lost all discernment and all recognition of God, are become so entirely sensual and earthly in all their ideas, that a late writer in the "Edinburgh Review," who erected himself into being the judge of kings, presumptuously setting himself in the judgment-seat of Christ, who is alone their judge, and despising the word of God, which says, "Judge not, that ye be not judged;" this self-erected judge affected to despise the best king that has for many years sat upon the throne of Britain, and by whom God signally blessed this nation, in preserving it alone, of all the nations of Europe, from being trampled under foot by a foreign foe, because he lacked knowledge of sciences which could have been of no service to him or to his people, and possessed only those which were most beneficial. This writer says (No. cxxxvii. p. 194), that "George the Third read the history of his own country, which, we will venture to say, every prince knows almost by heart;" that "he added to this the study of the laws and constitution of England;"—"but we may be allowed to doubt whether George the Third knew more of these subjects than every king must who attends to the business of his high office; and there is no doubt that his attention to his own business was most unremitting," but that his "understanding was narrow, and no culture had enlarged it." Verily, to serve God, and to be zealous in the business of his station, is the highest praise that can be given to any man of any degree; and one might have supposed that a man of mere sense, one without a spark of spiritual light, might have perceived that such qualities were more useful, and so more popular in this utilitarian age, than knowing how to solve a quadratic or to discover the base of an alkali.

The first man began by taking his own way, and, by refusing to walk in God's ways, involved all his posterity in pain and trouble. God, in mercy, set up various institutions to control men, restraining them by their fathers in their childhood, and then by kings and masters in after-life; and men have been continually striving to break away from this control and cast their restraints from them, saying, Let us break the bonds asunder and cast away the cords of God and of His Christ from us. But God, in mercy, has continued to stretch out His arm over the people, and keep them in subjection to their rulers, as he has over the beasts to keep them also in the fear of man; till now, at length,

after six thousand years of struggle, He is about to let men take
their own way; and they will find that the consequence of their
doing so is, that there can be no such thing as government, no
such thing as protection from any excess of oppression and cruelty,
as has been already seen in a small scale in the French Revolution, when the guillotine must have soon stopped to work for lack
of victims, unless a military despot had been permitted mercifully
to seize the reins, and to establish the government of the bayonet
and of the conscription, instead of the former one of the Bastile
and of court intrigues. Similar examples are furnished by the
actual condition of Spain.

The question really at issue in all lands now is, whether the
blessings of government proceed from God or man, from heaven
or from earth, from above or from below. Now the idea of
government proceeding from the people is a pure Irish bull.
The people are the persons to be governed, and it requires as
much wisdom to submit to be governed as to govern. The community can only be blessed by every one doing his " duty in the
state of life in which it has pleased God to call him." If the
nobles take to gambling, horse-racing, or preaching in conventicles, they are equally unholy in not fulfilling the particular
duties which God has appointed for them. If garrulous old
men, " well stricken in years," take upon themselves to give
counsel to the sovereign, they will give bad counsel, for it will
not have emanated from God, but from themselves, or from the
devil. Now the wisdom and counsel which sovereigns and all
other men need is not human wisdom, but the counsel which
comes from God; and God communicates this counsel only by
certain channels, which he has ordained for this end; and even
by these channels, not all in the same measure, but a greater
measure through one than through another. Yet as there is
no baptized person, nay, nor no heathen man, since he too is
redeemed, but who contains in him some measure of truth, a
wise king may get a measure of light from every one, provided
it comes to him in a lawful way, and not in an unlawful way;
not springing from the vanity and garrulity of childhood, first
or second. And if old age and knowledge of politics were sufficient qualifications to constitute an infallible adviser, the devil
would be the best, for he is older than any of us, with far more
cunning and experience; and every man may rest assured that

in whatever he does, if he be not serving God, if he be not a channel by which God is acting, he is an agent of the devil, whatever seeming good, or piety, or even religion, there may be in the act which he is performing.

Not only then is obedience to the Sovereign a religious duty, because he is the representative of the Lord, who is our only Lord, but it also follows that it is a duty not to obey any one who does not stand to us in that relationship. All men, as mere men, are equal, and we may not be the subject and servant of an old man, because he is " well stricken in years," any more than of " a girl of eighteen, whom no one would consult except on the choice of her gown, and perhaps not even on that," which are the supercilious expressions of this " Friend of the People," by which he endeavours to decry the Queen, and to exalt himself into the office of director of our destinies at her expense. We will not obey him, because he has no mission from Him to whom alone we may bend the knee; and we will obey this " Girl of Eighteen," because the holy oil is upon her, because she reigns by the grace of God ; because she is God upon earth to us, for all matters of temporal rule, good order, and civil blessings. We bow down before Him who is invisible in his visible representative ; and we care not about the opinions of any, nor whether republican principle gain or not ; nor about " the present condition of the country ; " nor whether she sits enthroned with her brilliant diadem on her head ; nor whether she is driven to seek a livelihood by teaching young women in Switzerland or in America, our head, heart, pen, tongue, and sword are equally hers in every situation, in every vicissitude ; nay, if a preference were given, it would rather be more grateful service when she were deprived of all power to remunerate it, than whilst stars and ribbons can be dispensed from her hands, and lucrative places remain at her disposal.

As a republic is a great theological, so must it be shown out as a great political lie. Heaven is a kingdom, not a republic ; and its ordinances are monarchical, admitting of no dissenters nor schismatics. The existence of republican bodies in Europe has been a solecism ; yet even such as they have been, they are very far different from such republics as those which speculators are dreaming of in these days. Besides, they were too small to be counted amongst the nations, and such as Switzerland, the Free

Towns, &c., had no practical political importance whatever. The ancient republics were rather aristocratic; those of the Middle Ages, entirely such ; and never were the lower orders more completely excluded from all political power, insulted with more impunity, and more brutally tyrannised over than by the aristocratic pride of the Venetian, Milanese, and Florentine governments. In America we have lately seen that the government had no power to prevent a small part of its subjects from compromising their fellow-citizens, and involving the whole country in war, by assisting the rebels of a neighbouring state; and the poor governor, Van Buren, was obliged to make the humiliating confession that the sceptre of President was an idle bauble in his hands. If France were at this moment under no more powerful government than that of America, it would be impossible to prevent 100,000 men marching to the Rhine, and seizing on the Rhenish provinces. In short, no government could exist, neither for domestic security nor to prevent foreign war. Yet it is to this mockery of a form of government that all nations are hastening, or rather to universal confusion and civil war, and anarchy, such as we see in Spain, in the vain attempt to discover some better form of blessing mankind than that which God has established for the end of His blessing men Himself. And the endeavour is vain, because God cannot have two ways of effecting the same end. Men's perverseness may obstruct the one end and retard its progress, but that which God ordained must prevail, or men must go altogether without the advantage destined to accrue from it.

Now as the Church was the first corporation, as the ecclesiastical was the first form which the life of God took amongst those who were partakers of the Holy Ghost by baptism, and as the civil form was not taken for many years afterwards, so have churchmen ever been the foremost in setting the example of all that evil which has at length inundated the whole of Christendom. The priesthood set the example of schism in separating themselves from the body, and calling themselves the church, so that the phrases " the interests of the church," " the property of the church," are expressions which have come to signify, in all languages, the interests and property of the priests, in contradistinction to the interests and property of the laity. The priesthood, instead of confining themselves to their proper borders, meddled in civil matters, and tyrannised over the king and people. The civil rulers, following the pernicious example set by the churchmen, meddled in their turn with ecclesiastical affairs, appointed bishops, &c., and thus interminable confusion has been wrought. But civil and ecclesiastical things ought to be wholly distinct : civil rank ought to give no pre-eminence whatever in the church ; and ecclesiastical rank ought to give neither privilege nor exception for all civil service. But the priests claimed exemption from the jurisdiction of the civil courts, and from military service, and from taxation ; and kings and great personages in the state were received with honours n the church which were denied to others : and the priests became possessed of property as ecclesiastics, apart from their properties as individuals. The priests having got possession of civil power employed it to punish and torment, and even put to death many of their flocks. They persecuted the poor Jews, and totally exterminated by burning them alive in Spain and Portugal : they fomented most sanguinary wars against the Waldenses, &c., and persuaded the kings that all those who protested against the wicked usurpations of the priests were enemies of the state. At length whole nations rose against them, and the rulers of England, and Holland, and of great part of Germany, refused to suffer the Bishop of Rome to have any jurisdiction in those states. But unfortunately they did not stop here : this act of schism was the forerunner of other acts ; and all protestant countries are distracted by a multiplicity of contradictory and opposing sects, till at length Christendom no longer presents one Catholic or universal church, but many national or particular sects. And now there is no one point upon which men are assured : they dispute upon what is the church and what is not; whether God loves men or not ; whether His Son died for them or not ; whether he be God or not ; whether He were man or only in likeness of manhood ; whether men are saved by Him or not ; whether He is coming again to reign upon this earth, and cast out all sin and misery from it, or not ; whether certain books were written by God, or not ; in short, there is no point of the Christian religion upon which there is unity of faith or hope throughout the Christian church.

The priests have fed themselves and not the flocks, they have plundered the people, and the people have now refused to give the priests their due. God requires that every one should devote a seventh of his time to His worship, and a tenth of his goods to His use; but men spend the former in amusement, and refuse to pay the latter. And the priests connive at the former, and are afraid to claim the latter for their Master, and the seventh day is desecrated, and tithes are no longer paid, save where the civil power still compels the payment. The people can only be what the priests have made them, and if Europe is become infidel, it is because the leprosy began in the church. This state of things is remediless, and never will the whole of the baptized be again under one jurisdiction; never will there again be but one faith and one hope. Things must get worse and worse—sects must more and more be multiplied—and man's religion, ceremonies invented by man, priests elected by man, worship ordained by man, must prevail, until the Lord Jesus Christ shall Himself come in flaming vengeance upon all who have caused, or consented to the evil, and in mercy towards all who cry and sigh for the abominations that are committed in Jerusalem.

Such being the condition of things in the church, such is also the condition of things in the state. God is equally lost sight of in both; the life of God is dying out, and dissolution and putridity must consequently supervene over the whole body of Christendom, ecclesiastical and political. Since men refused to recognise any longer God in His ordinances, God withdraws from the ordinances, and men get blessed no more. Having lost the right knowledge and the right fear of Him, they cannot observe Him in His judgments more than they did in His ordinances; and the only way by which they can be made sensible of the fact, is by tasting the bitter consequences. They have despised God's church, and thought all the schismatic and dissenting churches of the sectarians quite as good as anything that He ever appointed, nay, even a great improvement upon what we have received from our fathers, and seeking only to hear a man speak, they have got what their hearts did desire, i. e. a set of talkers. They have despised God's form of government and have thought to devise better forms of government for themselves, and they must find that they are seeking a vain shadow, and that they get no government at all. They will see this only when they find all security withdrawn from their own dwellings; when civil war or universal plunder goes from village to village, from hamlet to hamlet, from cottage to cottage; then will they repent, though too late, of having followed the blind guides who sneered at "the divine right of constables," while every man "perishes by the sword of his brother," "as it was in the days of Midian."

The delinquency of the rulers in the church and in the state, and of the people is equal; yet each party busies itself in attacking the mote in the eye of the other, without perceiving the beam in its own. Truly, kings and priests have been tyrants, and not made use of the power entrusted to them for the blessing of those below them; but so has every other individual in whom power has been lodged. Men of all classes have sacrificed the feelings and happiness of the weaker sex. Husbands have been tyrants; as the hearts of their wives — chilled and blunted with unrequited affection — do testify; masters have been tyrants; and the records of West-Indian slavery have fixed an indelible stigma upon the English and Christian name; and without going so far a-field, the chimney-sweepers' apprentices and the poor maids-of-all-work in the families of English shopkeepers, will rise in judgment at the last day, as God's witnesses, against the insolence, cruelty, and hard-heartedness of the master. Nay, what scenes are not dragged occasionally into daylight of the misery inflicted by parents, even by mothers, upon their own offspring; and by the schoolmasters and guardians to whom children are confided? It is never to be forgotten, that the most long-continued and systematic bloodshed which was made to flow during the French Revolution, was not that which was shed by the rulers, but that by the hands of the people delighting in the employment. The sins of the rulers, indeed, before God are greater than the sins of the people, because they have stood in nearer relationship to Him, and are more responsible to Him for their conduct; but so far as the people are concerned, the kings have in no wise exceeded them in cruelty nor wickedness, of any description.

It is most true that the king can do no wrong, that is, the king is not amenable to the people. The king is the servant of God, and not of the people, and before his own Master must he stand or fall. God does punish kings for the faults not only of themselves but of their whole dynasties; and thus when the judgments of each succeeding race of the kings of Israel are recorded, it is always mentioned to be for the sins of the first

usurper Jeroboam, in addition to the personal offences of the
individual sufferer.   Thus also the blow fell upon Louis XVI.,
the most virtuous of his race; and it is also to be borne in mind,
that the agents of punishment are never the willing servants, but
the despisers and enemies of God.   A rebellious people is no
more serving God, when used as an instrument of the chastise-
ment of kings, than the devil is; and Cromwell, with a text of the
Bible in his mouth, had as little religion in his regicidal acts as
had Danton or Robespierre.

   Moreover, God deals with nations as one body.   It is the
whole Jewish nation that is punished to this day for the deeds
of the individuals who put to death the Lord of life and glory.
The generation which sows is not that which reaps; and error is
but truth become rank and distorted.   The right of private
judgment, which was the truth put forth against the priesthood
who refused all responsibility to man, has been pushed now so far
on the other side, that every man thinks himself competent to be
a king and priest to himself, and all respect and deference for
superiors, whether in kings or priests, is despised as superstition.
The evil which is now destroying every altar and throne in Europe,
is the fruit of seed sown at the Reformation and by the reformers of
the Church.   Nevertheless, their stand against the wickedness of
the priesthood of that day was righteous and just, and they could
not foresee all the consequences of their acts; nor, had they
foreseen them, could they have averted them.   Severe judgments were inflicted on that portion of the priesthood which has
most mixed itself in civil matters, by the French Revolution;
but all priests of all sects are more or less guilty of the same
faults: and the whole baptized community has equally departed
from and despised the original institutions which God appointed.
The whole body of Christendom, therefore, must share in the
common destruction, although different measures of punishment
may await the Greek, the Roman, the Anglican, the Scottish and
other churches.   In England, at least, our sin is common: no
class has been before or after the other.   The Catholic Relief
Bill, and the Repeal of the Test and Corporation Acts, were
called for by the people long before they were granted by the
rulers; and these were required, not that we might thereby return
more closely to God's appointed ways, but because we were all
alike indifferent to what were His ways and what were not, and

we saw no reason why one sect was not as fitting to be recognised by the State as another. It is the people who have expunged all reference to God in many public acts, especially in the bills of lading of our merchant-ships. It is the people who are most anxious for the habitual desecration of the Lord's Day; it is the people who clamour against attempts to restrain vice and immorality, even the sale of obscene and blasphemous prints and publications, by which the minds of their own children are vitiated. It is the people who are most anxious to expunge from the schools of public instruction all that is peculiar to Christianity, and permit only what is pure Deism. It is the people also who are the greatest dupes of that restless curiosity to know all things in heaven above, and in the earth beneath, and in the waters under the earth, which gives rise to the universal desire for increased instruction, which is misnamed education. Education is that which a child receives from its youth, which is communicated by the spirit of the parents unconsciously to themselves, independent of all instruction and knowledge whatever, and whether the parents give bad or good education, the children can receive none other, for no other persons can supply to them the parents' place. Instruction may be communicated by any who have a capacity to impart any branch of knowledge, and may be bought and sold by any, so far as material things are concerned; *i. e.* knowledge of liberal or mechanical arts, &c. But spiritual instruction can be conveyed by none but by God's priests, and by them only *ex cathedrâ*, each within his proper border; and every peripatetic lecturer in a lady's drawing-room, or in a country barn, is not a teacher sent from God. Thus all private studies, of what is erroneously called "natural theology;" and all the pretended religious instruction of self-elected subscribing societies; and all the schismatic teaching of men elected by the people, is mere delusion: men learn things about religion by such means, but they never can become religious; they learn things about God, but they never can serve Him: they learn all things but the one thing, which is so well described by Mr. Carlyle in his incomparable work on the French Revolution, the only thing which can make men happy in the present condition of this world, " obedience from a sense of duty."

Whilst the want of principle is necessarily sapping all the

foundations of society, men are as usual fighting about names, and one party thinks what they call Whiggism, and another what they call Toryism, to be altogether right or altogether wrong. Yet, in truth, no such parties exist any longer in the country: Toryism used to express those who upheld the principles which I have endeavoured to set forth in this address; but I scarcely know where they are now to be found. Tories have long since ceased to be anything but a band which used the power and name of Sovereign for their own selfish ends. Whiggism once meant those who maintained that the great landed and titled families ought to possess all the real power of the state, and rule it by using at one time the crown against the people, and at another the people against the crown, as seemed them good. This party neither exists any longer: the one under the name of Conservative, selfishly endeavours to keep what it has got, though it knows not how; and the other courts the revolutionists up to a certain point, gets disgusted with the vulgarity of its new and unwashed allies, and is come to its small wits' end. In the meantime nothing is triumphant, but "Overturn, overturn, overturn!" and everything shall be overturned; not one stone shall be left upon another, "until He comes whose right it is," and then shall He give to every man according to his works.

You, the body of the people, to whom this address is made, can do nothing to stem the torrent. Your understanding of the subject—your submission to the justice of God's judgment upon us, will lead you individually to confess your sin in this matter; the common sin which you share with all, and the particular sin so far as you have been each led away by the spirit of the times. Reverence your priest, whoever he may be; and stir not from beneath his ministry. The poor Irishman, who meets his priest lying drunk by the way-side, takes off his hat to his reverence, distinguishing between the degraded being before him, and the anointing which is upon him: laugh not at, despise not the superstition of the poor Irishman; there is a worse thing than Irish superstition — it is Scottish and English scepticism: dedicate the seventh of your time to rest of body and mind from your secular pursuits, and to the active worship of God, and the visiting of the afflicted. Give to your priests God's portion, namely, the tenth of your income, let that income be derived from whence it may; and let the priest use it otherwise than for his Master at his peril. See God, the doer of all things, in His church, and amongst the nations; judge no man, but observe what God is working by men: for He is working towards one final and long-declared end, according to a certain purpose, by every individual and by every public body, whether it be called a church or a nation. Be not the servant of any man, nor of any set of men, of any party, of any faction, of any set of opinions by whomsoever possessed: serve God alone, and know that you can meet him only in flesh. Serve Him in politics in your Queen; serve Him as your Master in your master, if you have one; serve Him as your Father in your father; serve Him as your Brother in all the acts of kindness which your poor brother ever needs: by serving God you are ennobled; by serving man you are debased: but you can only serve Him in the station in which it has pleased Him to place you; you cannot serve Him in any other; moreover leave not your place of your own free will, neither to ascend nor to descend. Stir up your faith that your sins are pardoned through Jesus Christ, that you may be at peace all the day long, ever ready for leaving this world by whatever messenger God shall please to send for you; and stir up your hope in the only promise of blessing which God ever gave to the world, that you may be led to pray continually, that He will "hasten His kingdom," and "accomplish speedily the number of His elect," for there is no hope for the revival of Christendom; her end is come; and no blessing can be looked for but in the new dispensation of government, the new heavens, and the new dispensation of people, the new earth, which the Lord shall establish at His appearing.

These are the only principles which can make any of us stand by the kings now in the day when the sceptical pride and malice of all men who have cast off the fear of God, are arrayed against them; which can make us reverence the ministers of the church, and uphold them by every means in our power: which can cover us with an armour that shall make us dauntless at all times, and not only when the fancies of men please to tolerate them, in wielding tongue, pen, and sword in defence of every king and of every priest; and so, in the midst of the downfall of altars and of thrones,

> "We, undismayed, shall o'er the ruins smile,
> And light our torch at nature's funeral pile."

JUSTICE TO CORN-GROWERS

AND TO

CORN-EATERS

1839

JUSTICE TO CORN-GROWERS

AND TO

CORN-EATERS.

IT has been already shown that cheap corn is best for farmers; and whether the farmers were convinced or not, they ought to hope that such is the case, for it is certainly going to be cheap, whatever may be the consequences.

Open war has at length begun between cotton and corn. The note of preparation has been sounded long — much paper has been blotted — as many protocols, in the shape of pamphlets, have been framed on this as on the Belgian question, and with no better success; the subject has been sung as well as said, and Moore and Elliott have accompanied the belligerents as bards. But the war of paper is now to be turned into one of bludgeons and brickbats, a far more serious matter to the heads as well as to the pockets of the parties. The cotton-spinners *vi et armis* will have all the corn that can be had in England, Poland, Russia, and America. The question has been discussed entirely on selfish principles; hunger on one side, backed by avarice, is opposed by avarice alone on the other; and the manufacturer, united with his operative, will certainly prevail against the landlord alone. Moreover, the former have justice and right on their side; that is, such right as is alone received as current now. The Tories have proclaimed a free trade in creeds; the Whigs a free trade in politics and morals, or rather in vice: both have united to alter the laws by which the destitute are prevented from being starved to death; all restraints upon falsehood, blasphemy, obscenity, politics, and quackery, have been removed: an unruly tongue of a free press, which

the Scripture declares to be set on fire of hell, or which will set
on fire the whole course of nature, is declared to be the best
possible public instructor, the only proper schoolmaster for the
people; and the ministers of the crown inform us that mobs
assembling to urge one another to arm, and to carry measures
by marching in uncontrollable force to overawe the Houses of
Parliament, are the proper means of eliciting the truth. Verily,
it is no wonder that neither party can urge a single reason
against free trade in corn also.

The people are plainly crying out for more food. This is
the meaning of every cry of discontent that comes from the
masses. It was the meaning of their cries for peace during the
late war; it was the meaning of their cry for reform; reform
has disappointed them, and they cry again. It is both foolish
and cruel to reply to such cries, "Oh, you are not fit judges of
the expediency of peace or war;" or, "Oh, you do not want
reform:" rulers should not stoop to chop logic with the people,
but seek out the cause of their cry, and apply the best remedy.
A poor countryman sometimes goes to a rich neighbour, and
says, "Sir, pray give me some wine, for I have pain and in-
flammation in my bowels." If the rich neighbour replies,
"You foolish fellow, wine is fatal to a man with an inflam-
mation—you have nothing the matter with you," he answers
inhumanly and ignorantly. The poor man is in pain, and that
pain should be assuaged, though the sufferer may have misstated the cause and asked for an improper remedy.

The people now demand a repeal of the corn-laws, for which
they assign many bad reasons, and their cry is rejected upon
grounds more untenable than those on which the demand is
made. A cant is raised about "the poor farmers," as if they
were a class who would suffer : the farmer, considered merely as
a farmer, would gain as much advantage as the cotton-spinner.
The farmer is a manufacturer of corn, and it is as much to his
advantage to have corn cheap as to have leather, or iron, or
timber cheap. The landowner is the only man who would suffer
a diminution of his income; and, either from false and misplaced
humility, or from a want of understanding of his true importance, almost all the landowners who write and speechify
upon the matter abdicate their true standing, and talk a spurious
sentimentalism about "poor farmers." The landowners dare

not assume their proper tone, and say boldly, "Eng*land* alone belongs to us," because no class in the country dare take their true place. The king dare not say, "I reign by the grace of God; no good government can come but by me." The peers dare not say, "We are peers by the grace of God, and no good counsel can come to the crown but through us;" and these dare not take their proper places, because the church has been the foremost in deserting her post; and the bishops dare not say, "There is but one true Catholic and apostolic church; we are God's servants in that church, and no sound teaching can come to the people but by us."

The *immediate* pecuniary loss to the landowners is far less than their fears lead them to anticipate. The average price of wheat during a series of years would never be less than ten pounds a load, if no law whatever existed to control its import; but it must be some years before the price could sink to that level. On the other hand, the *immediate* pecuniary gain to the master cotton spinner is far less than his greediness leads him to expect. He is dreaming of sending muslins, and shawls, and fine stockings to the Crimea and Poland; as some merchants, equally wise, not long ago sent out skates to the tropics. An *immediate* gain would accrue to all day-labourers, whether employed in manufacturing muslin or corn; and as the successive governments, beginning with and subsequent to that of Mr. Pitt, have created immense masses of such manufacturers, it is the duty of the present governme t to see that they be fed; or these masses will undoubtedly now proceed to acts of violence, of which no one, in the present state of the country, can foresee the issue. The only test of good government is the amount of food which the labouring class can procure. Bread, beer, and bacon are the necessaries of life to the English labourer; if these things are now consumed in greater quantities by them than formerly, the country is better governed; but as the labourers all say that they can procure less of these necessaries, the government is worse, and the people are all discontented with it, and bent upon some change in its constitution.

They who take the part of the landowners feel rightly that this is the most important class of the inhabitants of every country, the only aristocracy *de facto*. There is no real wealth but in the produce of the soil. The proprietors of land, and

those dependent on them, are alone interested in the welfare of
any country. Manufacturers and traders have no more real
interest in a country in which they happen to be located than
the merchants of the English factories at Petersburg, Leghorn,
&c., are interested in the welfare of Russia and Tuscany. This
has been seen by the ablest statesmen in all ages, and would
still be acknowledged, only that people are grown greater fools
in proportion as they have become ignorant of the principles
and departed from the practice of their forefathers, and therefore think themselves wiser. I quote again passages from
writers which I quoted formerly, for again and again I would
have this truth inculcated by the authority of names which
ought to have weight.

Cicero says (de Rep. l. 2, iv.), *est autem maritimis urbibus
etiam corruptela ac mutatio morum; importantur non merces
solum adventitiæ, sed etiam mores, ut nihil possit in patriis
institutis manere integrum. Jam qui incolunt eas urbes,
non hærent in suis sedibus, sed volucri semper spe et cogitatione rapiuntur a domo longius; atque etiam cum manent
corpore, animo tamen excurrunt, et vagantur. Nec vero ulla
res magis labefactatum diu et Carthaginem et Corinthum pervertit aliquando, quam hic error ac dissipatio civium, quod
mercandi cupiditate et navigandi, et agrorum et armorum
cultum reliquerunt.* Lord Chatham says in his speech during
the debate on the Falkland Islands, " The little I know has not
served to raise my opinion of what is vulgarly called the moneyed
interest; I mean that bloodsucker, that muck-worm, which calls
itself the friend of government, that pretends to serve this or
that administration, and may be purchased on the same terms
by any administration; that advances money to Government,
and takes especial care of its own emoluments." Mr. Canning
says, " We well know that at this moment there is scarcely a
single power that does not look for resources to the Exchequer
of our Exchange. We are all aware that our moneyed men lend
indiscriminately to all parties; and those who are now ' the
captain's captains, the true lords of Europe,' are furnishing arms
to those who are contending against each other. Therefore let
me not be told that I may look for security in the morality of
our money-lenders. No, no! let Ferdinand himself to-morrow
show signs of strength, and a determination to fit out an arma-

ment, and the troops and fleets of Spain, raised by British capital, will sail from your ports to strangle infant liberty in South America. I defy you to prevent it, and I defy you to show anything in the morality of late pecuniary transactions to ensure you against such an event." The same character, the same indifference to real national prosperity, the same disregard of the interests of their native land, if anything is to be gained by betraying them, is observed by Russell in Germany, " Frankfort," says he, " in consequence of her commercial relations, is so thoroughly under foreign influence, and so polluted by a mixture of all foreign manners, that her population can hardly be said to have a character of their own. Even the multifarious connections with all the ends of the earth, which have made her citizens, in a manner, citizens of the world, have unfitted them to be German citizens, for they judge of the happiness of mankind by the rate of exchange. Let no one hastily condemn the worthy citizens of Frankfort for thus forgetting, in the pursuits of the merchant and money speculator, the interest of their country; or at least, before pronouncing his doom on their imagined selfishness, let him study the ports of London, or Liverpool, or Bristol, and discover, if he can, a purer foundation for English mercantile patriotism." Vol. i. fo. 52. Yet it is to this class that power now has been given, while it has been taken away from those who alone ought to possess it — the landholder, *les propriétaires*, the *possidenti* of the soil. During the late war in Canada the English and .American armies were in sight of each other for a considerable time, and neither could move for want of money. The English general applied to the English merchants for some dollars, offering an enormous interest for the loan on the part of Government. The merchants demanded a still higher interest; the aide-de-camp, afraid to agree without fresh orders, rode back to the general. While he was gone, the American general offered to the English merchants the interest they required, and he obtained the money. The American army was the first in motion to attack the English, by means of the money obtained from English merchants. During the former part of the last American war, it was very well known that English money was lent to the government of the United States to carry on the war with this country.

That which constituted the thing called Parliamentary Reform

to be a real revolution was, that it in some instances totally removed, and in all effectually diminished, the power of the
landowners, and gave a preponderating power to the manufacturers over them.   The Radicals rejoiced in the Reform Bill
because they said it was revolution ; the Tories hated the Reform
Bill because they said it was revolution ; and the Whigs alone
said it was not revolution ; would not lead to revolution ; and
was a final measure.   Both Radicals and Tories united to reply
that truly it could not lead to a revolution, because it was
already a revolution, by giving power to the people to do whatever they pleased ; that as to its being a final measure, the
assertion was manifestly absurd, because it was evident that
changes would be made in the House of Lords, church, and
wherever else the people might please.   The Radicals have been
rejoicing ever since in their newly-acquired power, and have
been openly avowing the ends which they thereby mean to
attain.   The most able of the Whigs have now found out their
error, and repent of the same ; but it is too late.   The people
who supported the Whigs have found out also that having got
" the Bill," and the " whole Bill," they have got " nothing but
the Bill ; " and as they cannot dine upon the Bill, they believe
the whole to have been a cheat on the part of their rulers, are
more clamorous than ever for additional food, with tempers
irritated against all persons and all things, and with power to
carry their evil designs into effect.   The manufacturers goad
them on, and all parties in the country, except the growers of ·
corn, are determined to have that corn cheap.   It is as false
in principle to give a man political power because he possesses
a machine for making goods to be worn in France, as it would
be to give it to the owner of a ship which carries the goods, or
to the owner of a balloon.   It is the possession of a portion of
the soil of England that attaches a man to England, and not
the possession of a bladder full of gas.   What can a man who
lives by carrying cotton from the Nile to the Clyde, turns it
there into a new shape, and then carries it to the Seine, care
who possesses the lands of Egypt, Scotland, or France ? what
preference can he have more for one than for the other, since all
are equally useful to him ?   He may be able to speak no
language but that spoken in Great Britain, and on that account
may feel more at his ease there ; but that is all that his pa-

triotism rests upon. Nevertheless, by the present ruling faction in the country, the manufacturers have received power, and whenever they can be made to unite, as they can by famine, they will carry all before them. By the ancient institutions and practices of England (which alone are its constitution, and not a theory or set of propositions drawn out on paper), power was lodged alone where it ought to be, namely, in the landed aristocracy; and no one could be a legislator who did not possess property in land; nor be a voter who did not possess an exclusive interest in England's prosperity. The powerful lords in the immediate neighbourhood of the smaller towns could at all times influence the choice of their representatives, and some towns were empowered to send them on purpose to give to the peers a direct influence in the House of Commons. Moreover, all the laws and practice tended to prevent the accumulation of a greater population than the produce of the land could support. They who occupied lands for cultivation would not give it up for building cottages, so that the agricultural population could not increase. No one could carry on a trade in a town without first serving an apprenticeship to it, which, with various other similar regulations, tended to impede the increase of the population in them.

Laws which in old times were made for the protection of traders, were subsequently supposed to have been made for the protection of trade. Adam Smith showed, the most clearly of all writers on such subjects, that the best way to promote the interest of trade was to let it alone, and that a manufacturer would become rich faster by being left to himself than by any interference on the part of the government. The grand mistake of English statesmen has been in not perceiving the difference between a rich merchant or manufacturer, and a rich people: they have not understood that an overgrown limb is both sign and cause of weakness to the whole body, and not a proof of strength or vigour even in the limb itself; and they have gone on to make individuals with colossal fortunes, together with starving millions. The Italian economists have charged the English economists with cruelty and selfishness in not considering what was best for the whole body of the people, but only what was best for the rich manufacturer. The English economists reply that they have confined themselves to their own

L 3

subject, which is to show how trade and manufactures best pros-
per; and that if statesmen have not taken into consideration
the effects of increased trade upon the welfare of all the several
other classes, the fault is in the statesmen, and not in the economists.   The charge, however, of the Italians is just; the
Scotch school of economists has treated men as mere manufacturing machines, to be retained only so long as they could
labour for the advantage of their masters.   It is owing to this
school that the revolution has been produced in the laws for the
relief of the poor.   It was asserted that there was a surplus
population ; that is, that there was a greater number of people
than were needed for the cultivation of the soil and for the purposes of trade, and therefore a greater number than could
possibly find employment; and a system has been devised to
subject to harsh treatment all who did not work, although the
authors themselves declared that it was impossible for great
numbers to find work ; and as, of course, in such a condition of
things, the young, and strong, and healthy are the first to find
work, the harsh treatment falls exclusively upon the old, the
weak, and the sick.   The ancient constitution, at least from the
days of Alfred, provided means by which no man should "die for
lack of sustenance." The lay officers of the church in every parish
had this charge, and might be punished if any did die. The revolutionists have abolished this office, and men may now be starved
to death *ad libitum;* and it is decreed that one individual shall
be placed over a large district, without whose permission no
relief shall be obtained, and without whose sanction no starving
man can make application to those authorised to order him
relief : this individual may indeed order relief himself if he like,
but it is at his peril; for if he make a mistake on the side of
mercy, and give a poor wretch a small pittance more than his
well-fed superiors shall subsequently judge necessary, the pec-
cant relieving officer is made to pay out of his own pocket for
the offence.   The framers of this new law said that they saw
little difference between the old and the new machinery ; but a
poor starving man feels and knows that there is all the difference imaginable between a man who *shall* order relief, and a
man who *may* order relief; between an overseer in an imperative and an overseer in a conditional mood.   Yet even this
injustice and robbery of the poor man's rights would probably

have been insufficient to rouse the indignation of the whole body of the people, if it had not been further enacted by these revolutionists that immense new prisons should be erected in every district, out of which no relief whatever should be given, and even in which no relief shall be given except by violating the laws of God as well as of man, in separating husbands from wives, and parents from children. No exceptions nor differences are made in favour of any who have been formerly in comfort and affluence; "decayed gentlemen and decayed gentlewomen" are objects of mockery to the Scotch school of economists. They have ever dealt with men and women algebraically, and in utter ignorance of mankind, have written and spoken of them as if they had no more passions than blocks of granite; or as if, having them, they were all alike. They have dealt with the men of the north as with the men of the south; with women and children as with men; with single as with married; with parents as with those who had never had such affections drawn forth — with stomachs that can digest everything as with those that are enfeebled by age or disease: they have treated men as so many x s and y s, and truly men's feelings are unknown quantities to them.

Mr. Pitt had but one idea, which was to procure money to hire men to fight against the French. Rich manufacturers could be easily taxed, and therefore he encouraged manufactures. The whole body of the people were justly frightened at the wicked principles at that period disseminated throughout Europe by French emissaries. Mr. Pitt augmenting this fright by his declamations, induced the landowners to mortgage their estates for ages to come; for the National Debt is nothing but a rent-charge of sixty millions a year upon the land.* It was now

---

* According to the present notion of considering this debt, it is absolutely interminable, as the country never can be relieved from it, except by an operation to which all countries are hasting, namely, a sponge; and of which the first example will probably be given from necessity, in Spain, Rome, or America. The delusion consists in not looking to the meaning of words, or rather keeping to a sound instead of to a reality. The minister borrowed a pound of the landowner; land does not grow pounds, but corn, beef, hides, mutton, wool, timber, &c.; the landowner therefore gave a portion of these for a pound, which pound he gave the minister: another minister, however, changed the value of this pound so as to make it impossible for the landowner to get one without giving twice or thrice as much of the produce of his land as he originally engaged to do, whereby the landowner is cajoled out of

fancied that manufactures were wealth, and that merchants, stockjobbers, moneyed men, and traders of all kinds were of as much, nay even of more, importance to the well-being of a country than the landowners. "Indemnity for the past and security for the future," were very pretty words, containing promises which have been most painfully falsified; and the whole present artificial condition of society is the result of the measures of the last most politic, necessary, and extravagantly conducted war. Such is the fact, and it is idle to deny it. *Le monstre a diné; peuple, payé la carte.* The encouragement of the production of cotton-yarn would not have been so detrimental, however, if the same encouragement had not also caused the production of children to such an extent, that there is now an immense population created, which the produce of the land cannot feed, and which population is so wholly and exclusively linked with manufactures, that if suddenly coal were no longer to be found in England, and to be as suddenly discovered in France, Turkey, or the moon, thither would remove all the owners of the factories, with what they call their capital, that is, with their machine on their back, and thither would follow all the people employed by them.

The forced measures of Mr. Pitt caused a great demand for and employment of men for the army, navy, and merchant shipping, a depreciated currency made an immense rise in nominal prices, and large fresh districts of land were brought into cultivation, and the old very much improved, so that there is a far greater quantity of food produced now in Great Britain than there was before the war. But the number of mouths to be filled has increased much more; and as this body of manufacturing people is an extraneous, surplus, body, it must be fed by food brought from other lands. If it were possible to wall in all the cotton manufacturers and their men, there would be

---

more than he bargained for. If the value of all articles of produce be taken at the time the debt was contracted, and compared with the value of the same articles now, it will be found that the landowners have discharged their debt, principal and interest, long ago. But how is it possible to settle the question? The debt has passed into thousands of hands; the original contractors have sold their share of it; it has been divided and subdivided in such infinite fractions that anything like really equitable adjustment is utterly hopeless. But taxation, shifted as it may be, is paid wholly and solely out of the sweat of the labourer; and those classes never will be satisfied till all taxation is repealed — nor then either.

no difficulty in importing food for them without throwing the other relationships of the community into confusion; but unfortunately this is impossible. Our statesmen do not understand, and do not maintain firmly the predominance of landed proprietors above all the other classes. In the class of landed proprietors should be included all the artisans employed by them. It is a common fallacy of the Scotch economists, in espousing the side of the manufacturers, to represent the landowners and farmers only as the agricultural class, and all artisans as belonging to the manufacturing class; but the maker of a plough is as much an agriculturist as the holder of a plough; and when all such artisans are added to the agricultural class, it will be found that the proportion is very different from what they are represented in tables framed by these economists.

Manufactures are an advantage to a country only in so far as they are consumed within the country itself. So long as coats, stockings, hats, &c., are exchanged with the farmers for corn, &c. all is well. To suffer manufactures to be exported, and to say that food shall not come back in their stead, is as foolish as if a law were to declare that a clothmaker might give to a farmer a coat in exchange for some wool, but not in exchange for corn or bacon. The only possible way to remedy the present artificial and diseased condition of the English body politic, is to feed the manufacturers with the produce of foreign countries, and at the same time to take steps to get rid of the manufacturers themselves. A heavy duty on the import of cotton would be one of the best measures; and the sums so raised should not be thrown into the common stock of the revenue, but rigidly and exclusively devoted to defray the expense of emigration of all manufacturers who can be prevailed upon to depart.

The economists and the manufacturers, when threatened with a tax, always exclaim that the French will take away our manufactures. This is the raw-head and bloody-bones which they hold up to frighten political babies. But they have omitted to explain how it is possible for the French, with no coal on their coast, to manufacture so cheaply as we can. The agricultural produce of France is diminishing every day, and the population is increasing, and both these effects are produced in that country by the destruction of the landed aristocracy, through the perpetual division of land. Yet that government has erroneously

laid a duty upon home-grown sugar, in order to encourage the
sugar of the colonies; in their foolish jealousy of us they are
wishing to have as many such towns as Manchester, Birmingham,
Glasgow, Paisley, and Dundee, &c. &c., as possible.   It would be
a cruel gift to an unhappy country that has already so many
prolific seeds of combustion in it; but certainly, if the Queen
would make a present to Louis Philippe of some hundreds of
thousands of cotton-spinners, the French king would not be
the greatest gainer.

In the healthiest state in which a country can be, that is,
where there is a just balance between the amount of manufactures and agricultural produce, a system of regulation on the
import and export of corn is advantageous, in order to effect an
evenness of price.   Even if these laws help to enhance the price
of corn, which, however, they should not do, it is better to have
corn permanently high than subject to violent alternations.
Whether the present scale of the laws be the best or not, is
comparatively immaterial; but if it be meant, by the cry for the
repeal of the Corn Laws, that all scale whatever ought to be
abolished, the cry ought to be resisted.

As manufactures are erroneously supposed to constitute the
chief wealth of a country (and it has been gravely contended by
the oracles of the mobs, that if all England were one Birmingham
or Manchester, it would be the acmé of blessing for the country),
so are colonies equally highly and equally erroneously esteemed.
So far as colonies extend the territorial limits of a small mother
country, so far are they advantageous, by furnishing additional
men to defend her, and additional food for the people.   Trade
is also beneficial as a means of furnishing employment to a too
numerous population.   But this is the full amount of benefit to
be derived from colonies, even if they had been better managed
than modern colonies have ever been by any European states;
for there is no way of preserving them for these purposes, but
by incorporating the inhabitants thoroughly with those of the
mother country, and making them send deputies to the Parliament at home; and a far better use of them still would be to make
them independent kingdoms under junior members of the Royal
family at home. Colonies have made England pretty much like the
"old woman who lived in a shoe, and who had so many children
she did not know what to do." There is no dispute that can arise

in Mexico, China, the Baltic, or the Mediterranean, without some
of the children of England being on the point of bringing the
mother country into a war. The subjects of England who have
no communication with her but by sea, vastly exceed those on
her original soil. These possessions, no doubt, nourish a body
of seamen, which enables her to man her fleets on any emergency
with great facility; but this advantage is overrated. An island
must always have more and better sailors than a continental
power. The marine must always be an inferior service in
France or Austria to the military, while the smallness of
English armies must ever make English interference on land in
continental wars of very rare occurrence. Colonies, manufactures, trade, &c., all are good in their place; their disproportion
to the agriculture and domestic population makes them a source
of weakness, and not of strength. The remedy will probably be
found in the separation of the colonies; a remedy which Canada
will kindly provide very soon; for the march of all things is towards dismemberment, separation, and antipathies.

This, then, is the sum of the matter. The Government, for
many years past, by acting upon the erroneous doctrines of a
particular school of political economists, has created a greater
population than the produce of the land can support. The
people must and will be fed; food must be got where it can;
that is, the ports must be opened. But this is nothing but a
temporary, and may not be a very immediate relief; and, at all
events, can never be more than temporary; for similar causes
will produce similar results, and population will go on multiplying faster than corn can come, for it never can come at less than
£10 a load; and the population will increase until wages fall to
a penny a day; that is, wages will fall *ad infinitum*, unless the
whole of the several processes of importation, growth, and
multiplication shall have been previously cut short by general
convulsion. The economists say, let the people be educated and
they will not multiply; and if they do, let them starve. But
people will neither be so taught nor starve; and so long as an
economist has got a leg of mutton and the spinner has none, the
economist must fight for his mutton if he means to keep it.

The economists say, that if there were perfect reciprocity between all countries, as there is between all provinces of the same
country, there would be such mutual dependence upon each

other, that the probabilities of war would greatly diminish, and England might manufacture for Poland, and Poland grow corn for England, just as Lancashire manufactures for Essex, and Essex grows wheat for Lancashire. This would be the case if there were one government over the whole of those countries, as there is over the whole of the provinces of one state. It might do under an universal empire — under another Charlemagne or Napoleon — provided also there was but one language — but never can take place whilst Europe remains under several distinct governments, opposed to each other in language, habits, feelings, and laws.

The landowners should join heart and hand to open the ports; taking care, however, that no such bill is passed which is not accompanied by another to reduce all charges of mortgage, settlement, &c. one per cent. This will give them all the advantage which, as a class, they are entitled to in the present condition of the country. Should another condition hereafter arrive, it may be proper to reconsider the matter; but the thing which now presses is more food for the people.

If there is ground for apprehending scarcity of food, the best friends to the community are monopolists. Considerable relief for the moment would be given by every one who can afford to buy other food, refusing to suffer any flour to come into their houses. It does not require much ingenuity to find substitutes for flour, and also for potatoes, in rice, Italian paste, &c.; and so little would the inconvenience be felt, that such an abstinence does not merit the name of a sacrifice. England is very boastful of her charities; perhaps there is no country in Europe where so little *personal* charity is performed, and where almost all is performed by a money substitute.

CAUSES

WHICH LEAD TO A

BANK RESTRICTION BILL

1839

C A U S E S

BANK RESTRICTION BILL.

A FRIGHT is a very unpleasant thing; and equally so whether it arises from the explosion of a steam-engine or from the sight of a mouse. The greatness of the suffering is by no means commensurate with the cause, but dependent on the nervous irritability of the patient. For frights which have a cause there is no remedy but to strengthen the nervous system; but for frights which have no cause — which are chiefly dependent upon the activity of the imagination, great relief may be obtained by the terrified person simply asking himself the question, "and what then?" Autumn is a sad time for persons so sensitive: the newspaper editors are at their wits' end to find topics of excitement: some turn literary, philosophic, scientific, &c., and fill their columns with wondrous lore; but the most approved receipt is to get up a bad harvest, distress in the money-market, and a Bank Restriction Bill.

"What! is there no just cause for alarm at a Bank Restriction Bill? Is it nothing for the Bank to stop payment of its notes in gold? Would it not derange all the money transactions of the country, and bring about commercial distress?"

The Bank refusing to pay its notes in gold, or the Government's prohibiting its continuing to do so, would derange nothing, and produce nothing. Either would only show that the commercial transactions were already deranged, and when such is the case distress must follow. But the stopping of payment of notes in gold is the consequence of commercial derangement, and not the cause : the Bank so doing would be a means of making lighter that distress which must already exist before such a measure could be thought of, if the alarms and fears of the foolish and the frightened did not prevent that alleviation. The Bank's refusing to pay its notes in gold would afford the true measure of the extent to which the derangement had already gone, because it would show every article for exportation to have two prices, a paper price, and a metallic price, a home price, and a foreign price; but it would cause nothing. The crisis of a disorder is not the cause of the sickness, but the commencement of the cure ; it marks the greatest height of the disorder, but from that moment the patient begins to amend : and whenever a Bank Restriction Bill takes place, or whenever the Bank refuses to pay in specie, the public may rest assured that if such an occurrence did not take place, there would be much greater ruin of manufacturers, greater fall of prices, and greater derangement of commercial relations.

The embarrassment under which the Bank of England is now suffering arises from two causes; first, from the circumstance that there is neither a continual bearing in mind, nor a carrying out in practice, correct principles of currency ; and, secondly, from the total ignorance of these same principles amongst the greater part of those members of the House of Commons who speak upon this subject, and who have teased and goaded the Government into tolerating much that ought not to be permitted, whereby a state of things has been induced for which the Bank of England is made responsible without being able fully to control it.

It seems to be concluded by the London merchants, from whom the Directors of the Bank are chosen, that any one who has sufficient intelligence successfully to carry on his own trade, is therefore sufficiently instructed in the principle of currency to be a Governor of the Bank, and to know how to maintain an equal measure of values for the whole empire. This opinion marks a want of due estimation amongst the governors themselves, of the real importance, and of the nature of the office which is delegated to them by the Crown. They have to perform an office *sui generis*, such as no merchants in any other, and such as no king's minister in any state ever had to fulfil.

In order not to be without some fixed basis on which to reason, the following elementary principles are transcribed.*

The usual method by which paper money is increased or diminished is by raising or lowering the rate at which it is lent. There is a continual temptation to increase the quantity of paper, because the manufacturers and merchants are continually asking for present money, which they intend to repay at a future time, in order to increase their manufactures and trade. Moreover, the more paper is in circulation, the more the profits of the Bank of England increase; and the more manufacturers and traders are employed, and the more the profits of the Bank rise, the more the country is supposed to be prospering, and the cheers of the ignorant encourage the delusion. When at length bullion begins to go out of the country, the Directors of the Bank curtail their issues, the jobbers in money begin to clamour, and prices begin to fall; so that the means of repaying, by future sales of goods, the money already advanced fails, because, both by the ceasing to put out more paper and by the export of coin, the value of all goods has diminished. Nay, pity and compassion come into help; many honourable and excellent persons represent themselves as about to be irretrievably ruined if more money, that is paper, be not lent to them; so that on every side the solicitations to put forth paper are multiplied, whilst there is nothing to counterbalance these temptations but the cold knowledge of dry abstract principles of currency; the certain conviction that, however just may be the representations of particular individuals, nothing can cause bullion to disappear but too much paper having been issued, and that nothing can avert a much greater and more extensive measure of suffering but the effectual, steady, though temperate, withdrawal of the same. In the performance of this duty, the Bank Directors are sure to be assailed by all who are suffering from the change, and by all whose trade being to job in money, estimate the prosperity of the country by the abundance of money which they may obtain for their own purposes. It is the duty, therefore, of all who are well instructed to support the Bank Directors in such times, knowing that they never do contract their issues without the most urgent necessity existing for the same.

* The propositions here referred to have already been printed at page 14 of this volume.

When the preceding propositions were first published, it was said by many, " Oh, I agree to this doctrine, and think it is all very well for ordinary times, but it is impossible to apply it in times of difficulty in the money market, or of distress amongst manufacturers." This objection is a mere subterfuge; it is a fallacy to suppose that principles can be understood, which are thought to be useful only in times when they are not put to the test. What would be said of a man who should profess his admiration for a system of navigation which he would use in a dead calm, but which he thought inapplicable to a storm? what of a general who thought the principles of the art of war good in time of peace, but inapplicable to the movement of troops in a battle? People who have spoken in such terms really do not agree with the doctrines here set forth, although they say they do, and probably think so.

By those who do not understand the true principles of currency, and who will not take the trouble to learn them, it is asserted that the causes which have produced the present embarrassments of the Bank of England are, first, a scarcity, which required a large importation of corn from abroad, which corn must be paid for in bullion; secondly, that gold and not silver is our standard, so that the smaller bulk affords facilities for exporting it which silver does not possess; thirdly, that a large quantity of cotton has been sent upon speculation to this country from America; that bills have been drawn for the amount, which bullion and not goods must be sent to answer.*

If corn has been brought to England why must gold be sent out? The Poles do not eat gold nor make clothes of it. Gold it sent out because it is cheaper than any other commodity; than velveteens, or cutlery, or any other kind of goods which the Poles could use. And why is gold cheaper? Because there is

---

* The following extract from a newspaper of large circulation is one specimen of many that might be quoted: — " It is a question not very easy of solution, how it is that a balance of trade should still be in operation against us. The payments made and making for foreign grain are, it is to be presumed, much more considerable than the public are aware of; and the exportation of our manufactures are still so inconsiderable as to be hardly worthy of being taken into account at all as a medium of exchange. Last year we shipped nothing to the corn-growing districts of the continent. This year there is the same absence of orders, and we suppose it may now be fairly understood that this branch of our export trade has all but ceased."

too much currency. How is bullion to be made dearer and the currency diminished? By withdrawing paper from circulation. But this will cause all prices to fall; no doubt all prices will fall because all prices have risen. During the period, long or short, during which the currency has been becoming redundant, prices have been rising, and therefore an increased quantity of goods have been manufactured.

As to the second alleged cause, namely, the greater facility of exporting gold than silver, it is scarcely worth the trouble of remarking that any precious metal must always be more easy of export, weight for weight, than any other commodity; and that were silver substituted as our standard for gold, it would not ultimately make any difference. There are other considerations which make silver possibly preferable to gold, but the question is comparatively unimportant.

The answer to the first alleged cause is the answer to the third. Granting that there has been an extra quantity of cotton sent to England for which bills have been drawn, and which the merely ordinary and regular trade with America cannot liquidate, bullion would not be sent from hence unless bullion were cheaper than anything else. If bullion were made dearer than any other commodity, the other commodities would go out and not the bullion. By making the bullion dearer, that is, by withdrawing paper from circulation, prices would fall in the proportion in which they had been stimulated by the increasing issue of paper.

But as all these points are already answered in the preceding propositions, let us consider the second cause of the difficulties of the Bank of England, arising from the pernicious measures which have been pressed upon the Government by some members of the House of Commons.

Whilst the Bank of England is solely responsible for keeping a due amount of circulation afloat, it is not the only body to which the Crown has abdicated its prerogative of issuing money; other bodies have been permitted to do the same. Although the exchanges are mainly the criterion of the sufficiency or insufficiency of the amount of the currency, there are in practice many little circumstances which experienced men will perceive and which prudent men will act upon without waiting for the exchanges to become permanently affected; but all power of attending to these circumstances, or even of knowing them thoroughly, is taken from the Governors of the Bank of England by the permission to others of issuing paper money; moreover, great deception is practised upon them. It has been stated upon unquestionable authority that on application being made in a town where two of these establishments existed, to know the amount of paper they had in circulation, it was discovered that they returned the balance only after mutually clearing the charges they respectively had upon each other; that is to say, one having 1,200,000*l.*, and the other 1,500,000*l.* out in circulation, the amount in the hands of each being 1,000,000*l.*, they cleared that sum, and then returned the balance, viz. 700,000*l.*, as the amount in circulation, instead of 2,700,000*l.*, which was the truth.

A jealousy and envy of the prosperity of the Bank of England has given rise to much officious meddling by parties who have exhibited nothing but total ignorance of sound principles both of currency and of banking. There is a longing to participate in some supposed mysterious advantages which the power to issue paper money affords. If any individual wishes to share this advantage, he has nothing to do but to become a proprietor, which is open to all. If the Bank of England has an exclusive privilege to issue paper money, which it ought to have, it certainly ought to pay for the same. Since the Crown pleases to depute its prerogative of issuing money to others, it is not wise to do so without procuring some equivalent advantage either to itself or to its subjects. It has been proposed that the subjects should share this advantage, by giving permission to other bodies to do the same; and it has been imagined that the mere fact of the issues being compelled to pay in gold would be sufficient to prevent the over-issues of each, just as the liability to pay in gold controls the over-issues of the Bank of England. No opinion can be more fallacious. Supposing banks to exist in Birmingham, Liverpool, Bristol, York, Newcastle, Westminster, Southwark, &c., each issuing paper money, and that the exchanges were against this country, it might happen that the bullion was going out for a certain period exclusively from Liverpool, where there would be consequently a gradual demand for it, compelling a bank there to withdraw the whole of its notes, whilst at the same moment a bank at Newcastle might be increasing its issues. The bank at Liverpool might be wholly drained and ruined, mainly by the operations of some other, without a possibility not only of saving itself, but even by its own sacrifices of mending the exchanges in the remotest degree. The effect of these banks upon the mass of the country would be exactly such as it would be were the Directors of the Bank of England to be formed into various sub-committees, one of which should curtail and the other increase the amount of paper respectively under its charge. In like manner, the Bank of England may be curtailing its paper whilst some other bank is putting more out. Nay, it is almost certain that such will be the case, for the pressure felt by the manufacturers at the operations of the Bank, will cause them to make demands upon the banks in their neighbourhoods, and the Bank of England having no control over these, will be compelled, in self-defence, to refuse an advance money upon any bills which directly or indirectly belong to other banks. Yet even this measure may be insufficient, for the currency of the country is a unity, like the blood; what is put forth in Lancashire or Somersetshire, affects the whole as certainly as what is curtailed in London affects the whole. If the other banks continue to put out paper, a fearful crash will follow, which would more suddenly subvert the whole actual condition of society than any other single act could accomplish. Such will be the effect, at no very distant period, of the establishment of any companies, banking, commercial, or by whatever name they may go, who shall have the power of issuing paper money.

It would be impossible to refuse to advance money on the bills of other banks, which also issue paper, without an appearance of great harshness, and even of hostility; exhibiting a feeling against them by no means merited. They have no business to be looking to the exchanges *directly* as the reason for extending or for contracting their issues; they may look at them *indirectly, i.e.* they may perceive by them that which the Bank of England must do, and so far direct their own actions. But, *directly*, no demand can be made upon a bank in the interior of England for coin for exportation, however, it is possible that such an event might occur to a bank at an outport, such as Bristol or Liverpool. The sole business of these banks is to attend to their own affairs and the wants of their immediate neighbourhoods; and it is possible that it might be wise and the true interest of the proprietors of a bank at such places as Birmingham, Sheffield, Leeds, &c., to be issuing paper to an immense extent upon the security of lands, houses, manufactures, and other real property, whilst the Bank of England was contracting its issues in every possible way, whereby the proprietors of the country bank would become, in the general smash which would follow, the proprietors of the freeholds on which their worthless paper had been advanced; and this is no creature of the imagination; for it has been actually done in America.

The Bank of England is the only body which ought to have the power of issuing paper money, and for this privilege it ought to pay an equivalent value, by which the public would become a participator in the advantage. This amount of paper should be fixed by Parliament at whatever is supposed to have been the minimum of the circulation during the last twenty years; and for the exclusive privilege of issuing this, the Bank should pay an annual sum to the Crown. No other body in the country should be suffered to issue notes, and those notes should not be convertible. In this way the fluctuation would take place in the amount of metallic circulation only. As to what the amount of paper should be, it is not possible to judge correctly of that until after an investigation such as no private individual is competent to make. The Lords of the Treasury, with the assistance of the Bank Directors, could easily form a sufficiently accurate estimate, and it is probable that the result would be from thirty to fifty millions. Whatever the amount be, to that amount would unproductive capital now locked up in a falsely-imagined purely metallic currency be let loose, and consequently a great relief would be given to all productive industry. Whether this relief would be of a permanent or of temporary utility, would depend upon the use which was made of it.

By the declamations which were made at the time of Sir R. Peel's Bill, one would have supposed that paper money never was again to have been seen in the country. Such, however, is not the case; for, in the first place, the prohibition was only to the issue of notes below 5l.; and, in the second place, the permission of other bodies to issue notes is a proof that a wholly metallic currency is not now the object of the Government, whatever it might have been formerly.* The plan, therefore, here proposed is no departure from any principle, but simply a question of degree. The currency is at present composed of x paper and n coin, and the only point is to fix these two values.

No doubt the old refuted assertions of the greater liability to forgery, the necessity of hanging all forgers, &c. &c., will be revived, but must not be attended to. A point of some import-ance is to know what to do with the sum to be annually paid by the Bank of England for its monopoly. The object most worthy of a statesman's exertions since the peace, was how to extinguish the public debt, a point which men of all parties seem unanimously to agree not to consider. Although the people were justly impatient of taxation, because they perceived the public property shamefully squandered, they would have willingly consented to any temporary sacrifice which they saw evidently applied to the extinction of a permanent load. Even an income-tax, if the amount had not been merged in the general receipts of the Government, but had been applied to destroying the public debt, would have been assented to. It would be well to begin with any sum, and apply it specifically to this object; for by the public debt the powers of the country are effectually paralysed, and the energies of the Government are crippled in every department of the public service.

In conclusion, one word more respecting the stopping of the Bank, or the refusal to pay its notes in gold. Whenever its bullion is gone this is the step which it must take. It may apply to the Government to issue a prohibition as of old, and the Government may accede or may refuse, but the fact will remain the same; the Bank will not pay. It cannot matter in the least whether the Government do this or not; in either case the ministers will be reviled, and, as usual, without the smallest reason. Far more ruin would be produced by the groundless fright which such a measure would cause than by the subsequent adjustment of the disturbance of commercial relations. It might happen that a few pounds would make all the difference; an amount so immeasurably small, when diffused throughout the manufacturing world, as to be perfectly inappreciable; and it might happen that several millions would not adjust the

---

* In the practical working of the system, the inland banks never issue coin, but always paper of some kind, either their own or that of the Bank of England.

difference. Time only could reveal the true amount of disturbance; and every single act which could be attempted to mitigate the evil could only aggravate it, by multiplying the fears and depressing the spirits of the whole community.

A portion of the above was reprinted with the Elementary Propositions on Currency in 1848, with the following addition : —

There is now a clamour raised for free trade in banking ; the thing that is intended is free trade in issuing paper money, which is free trade in coining. Coining is the prerogative of the sovereign, and cannot be exerted beneficially but under the control of the government. The persons who advocate this free trade in coining assert that they are convinced of the necessity of all paper being convertible into gold at the will of the holder, but all their speeches demonstrate that they do not understand what they are saying.

All panics and monetary crises which have ever taken place have been preceded by a low rate of money, which has forced speculation ; and the reaction which has followed by the rise of the price of money, and consequently fall of the prices of all commodities, has ruined thousands. No monetary system whatever can prevent such an occurrence ; the sure prognostic of a coming storm is the rate of money falling to a level with that in the public funds.

In 1847, some persons said the crisis was produced by the bill of 1842 ; others said that it is owing to the necessity of buying corn for Ireland ; others that it was owing to overtrading. The last is the only reason which has a semblance of truth in it ; but this mistakes effect for cause. The cause was the same as in all other crises, namely, an over-issue of paper by the Bank, making the rate of interest fall to the level of, or even below, that of money in the public funds ; and in proportion as the trade and commerce of the country increases, so will such panics be of more frequent occurrence, and produce more extensive ruin.

LETTER

TO

THOMAS PHILLIPS, ESQ. R.A.

ON THE

CONNECTION BETWEEN THE FINE ARTS AND RELIGION

AND THE MEANS OF THEIR REVIVAL

1840

A LETTER

DEAR SIR,

You once observed to me that " we have not, like the Italians, a positive interest guiding us to think of pictures. Every day the picture of a patron saint is before them, to whom a prayer is addressed, and they become enamoured with some token of his power or of his sufferings; and the affection excited for these is not unfrequently transferred to the representation of them — the picture. Here there is nothing similar to attract. Pictures with us are generally mere costly furniture, seen as rarities; few there are who can understand their real beauty, or who know how to look for it." To these remarks I fully subscribe; and, as I think you have here pointed out the true source of the present condition of the fine arts, I publish this letter to you in the hope of calling the attention both of artists and of admirers of the arts to the true principles which should alike animate both classes.

Some of the French newspapers contain a *feuilleton,* or essay upon some literary or scientific subject. One of these (I think either the *Débats* or the *Temps*) gave an account of a solemn funeral service, which had been recently performed in commemoration of the soldiers who had been killed at the taking of Constantin; and, after stating much in commendation of the science displayed in the music, and of the brilliancy of the execution of the performers, it was added, that after all it produced no pleasing effect upon the multitude assembled to hear it, because music, like all the arts, spoke to the feelings of the people, and not to their reason; and the music fell dead upon their ears because it struck upon a people devoid of faith, and, consequently, without the faculty necessary to feel it. The remark is just, and the more worthy of observation as coming from the confession of the faithless themselves.

When a celebrated French sculptress, who resides in Florence, was asked, Why she did not work more after the models of the Apollo, Venus, Hercules, and other celebrated statues of antiquity? she replied, " If I am to seek to imbibe the spirit which produced those works of art, and not to be a mere servile copier of the outlines, I must seek it in my religion, as the authors of those statues sought it in theirs; those sculptors were full of devotion, and laboured in their vocation to serve God according to their light; their works were works of piety and of religious feeling: I can feel no devotion for Apollo, but I do for Him who is the object of my worship, and for the persons who are distinguished as having been faithful in His service." .

This is the true source of all that has been great in the arts in every period, as I will endeavour to point out to you from their history, availing myself principally of the recent work of Monsieur Rio for that purpose. The earliest paintings, since the commencement of Christianity, were in the vaults where the worship of the Christians was conducted, and where their brethren, who had been put to death for witnessing for the common faith, had been buried. These would naturally represent certain passages in the life of our Lord, or in the life of some martyr. The paintings were mostly executed in mosaic, and painting in oil was unknown. No meretricious embellishments were permitted, and it was considered a profanation to add any of the ornaments or devices of paganism. In the traditionary life of Saint Gennadius it is stated, that an artist, who was painting a head of our Lord, copied the head of Jupiter, and that his hand withered in the profane attempt. It matters not whether the story be true or not; it at least proves the current feeling of those who lived at the time to have been against taking models from paganism. Long before the worship of the Blessed Virgin had been instituted, as it has been since established in the Romish part of the Catholic Church, the spirits of the painters were aroused to a greater contemplation of her than they would probably otherwise have been, by a controversy which arose between the Greek and Latin divisions of the Roman empire, respecting the beauty of the form in which the Son of God had appeared. The former maintaining, with St. Cyril, Clemens Alexandrinus (the reference to which may be found in Burton's *Description of Rome*, ii. 197), Origen, Tertullian, St. Justin, and other Fathers, that the appearance of our Lord was most mean and contemptible; the latter maintaining, with St. John, Chrysostom, Gregory, Nazianzen, John of Damascus, and others, that he was the most beautiful of men. This dispute became at length fierce, and many Greek priests, being ultimately driven from their country, took refuge in Italy. The dispute drew, subsequently, into it some exaggerated opinions respecting the person of the Blessed Virgin also, and under her pictures may be frequently seen the declaration that she was born without sin as well as her Son. She never was represented seated on a throne however, nor with a child in her arms (see *Lanzi, Storia Pittorica*, ii. 11) before the Council of Ephesus, in A. D. 431.

Burton observes, that "the great excellence of the art of sculpture in Greece was partly owing to the deification of their heroes. If a god was to be executed in marble, he was to bear the human form; he was in every respect to be a man. But in Egypt, the imagination was not elevated and refined by contemplating the creation of a god; and even the same wish of perpetuating the likeness of a mortal did not exist, when the bodies themselves were preserved for centuries in the form of mummies. The great excellence of the Italian painters at the time of the revival of the arts may in the same manner be attributed to the great demand for religious subjects. The Virgin Mary may at least be called the patron of painters; and Roman Catholics might say that she had revenged herself upon the Protestants by not assisting them in this art."

Although it is not to be denied that the Greeks brought with them much mechanical knowledge of the art of painting, which was highly useful to the Italian artists, yet this advantage was considerably counterbalanced by introducing also an extravagant admiration for the heathen models, which greatly contributed to debase it, as the Christians were thereby induced to mingle the subjects proper to pagan worship with those relating to their own creed. The whole Christian world of art was thus so filled with the evil consequences, that the Council of Constantinople, in A.D. 691, was obliged to take notice of them, and to prohibit the faithful from mingling irreverent allegories in the sacred subjects which were to be exposed in the churches.

After the time of Constantine, when the Christians were allowed to have buildings exclusively devoted to worship, and when mosaic was the prevailing, if not the exclusive, manner of Christian painting, a majestic figure of our Lord was usually represented as placed in the pulpit with the right hand leaning on the Book of Life, on which were written in large characters the words, "I am the way, the truth, and the life." To strike the imagination of the faithful on their entry into the church by the figure of the God-man, whose mediation they were come to invoke, and to strengthen this impression by the words which briefly, but so fully, summed up the mission of the Mediator, was the object of the Christian art in its grandeur and primitive simplicity. As the knowledge of the mechanical parts of the art of painting advanced, still religion was the great principle which guided it, so that the artist, who had the consciousness of his high vocation, looked upon himself as the ally of the preacher; and in the continual struggle which mankind has to sustain against their evil inclinations he always took the side of virtue. In conformity with this principle, at a later period, Buffalmacco, speaking of himself and of his brother painters, says, "We painters do not attempt anything but to make holy men and women by means of walls and boards; and by these means to make men, in spite of the devil, more devout and better." "*Non attendiamo mai altro che a far santi e sante per le mure e per le tavole, ed a far perciò con dispetto dei demonj gli uomini più devoti e migliori.*" The synod of Arras, in 1205, sanctified, as it were, this direction of the arts, so agreeable to the popular taste, in declaring that pictures are the book of the ignorant who did not know how to read others; "*Illorum quod per scripturam non possunt intueri hoc per quædam picturæ lineamenta contemplantur.*" There are instances of bishops, and of other ecclesiastics of high rank, labouring with their own hands to cover the walls of their churches, and convents, and places of religious meeting and instruction of the people, with representations of the facts in sacred history for their edification; and this is one of the principal reasons wherefore we see the traces of this popular writing infinitely multiplied in every possible form and dimension covering so many miles of walls.

But it was not merely for the instruction of the ignorant that the painters laboured; the faithful, also, were edified by the same means. The Christian soldier was taught, and encouraged in, the mysteries of his warfare ; how it is by dying that he conquers ; that his crown, though real, is invisible ; and that he has nothing to expect in his lifetime from his fellow-creatures but ridicule, contempt, ill-treatment, and death. On the walls of a convent, the members of which were devoted to the labours of conversion amongst the heathen, we find depicted the whole life of a missionary. In the first picture, he is represented devoting himself to the calling, and putting on the habit of the order ; in the second, he is seen with his brethren praying for the conversion of sinners, and supplicating God to be permitted to go into Asia to preach to the Saracens ; in the third, is shown their departure and arrival in the dominions of the Soldan, who commands them to be tied to a stake and beaten with rods ; the executioners are seen fatigued and covered with perspiration, whilst the people listen to the word preached to them by the missionaries even after the order to hang them upon a tree had been executed : in the last, the Soldan orders their heads to be struck off, whilst they continue faithful to the death and speak still to the attentive multitude. Such was the life of a missionary, and such the method by which he was instructed in the same, in the best times of the Church, and such it is still in the Romish communion. What it is in the things called missionary societies amongst Protestants we know too well.

The first association of painters was in Florence in 1272 or 1282, which association has since grown into the Academy of Fine Arts, and has been copied in every country in Europe. Their distinct avowal was, that they did not meet to communicate to each other their mutual discoveries, nor to deliberate upon the adoption of new methods of carrying on their art, but simply " to render thanks and praises to God; *per rendere lode e grazie a Dio;* and the motto which they took showed, indeed, the exalted and sublime idea which they attached to their art and to its proper direction, "to raise our intellect from earth to heaven : " *levar di terra al ciel nostro intelletto.*

Now, can it be wondered at that the arts have declined for
many years past, when the principles which raised and animated
them at first have so wholly disappeared ? Truly the heart
sickens more at the contemplation of the change of principle
than at the view of the diminished power of execution.

The arts attained their climax in Christendom at the period
when religious feeling and enthusiasm was at its highest.   It is
needless to point out the many causes which led to what is
called the Reformation : the insolent assumption by priests of
the right to dispose of the crowns of kings ; the crimes of the
popes of the Borgia family ; the profligacy of morals in the
court of Rome ; the general ignorance of the people ; the rapacity of the clergy, and many other circumstances forced on a
final rupture of the system of unity so essential to the true
character of the Christian Church.   These evils had been of long
standing ; for many preceding centuries they had been testified
against in England and elsewhere.   At length the testimony
became universal ; and in Italy Savonarola denounced the surrounding, and almost universal, wickedness of the priesthood
with great power and effect.   Had his faithful warnings been
listened to, instead of being crushed, the disasters that followed
under Luther and Calvin would never have occurred.   Whilst
the distance from head-quarters permitted the chiefs of the de-
fection in Germany, Switzerland, and England to escape with
their lives, it was otherwise with poor Savonarola : he too not
only testified against the ecclesiastical abuses, but against the
mercenary cruelty of the money-changers of his own country, at
the head of whom were the Medicis, and who had by money-
lending amassed such wealth that they had been enabled to
seize on and retain the sovereignty of the state ; and he thereby
drew down their vengeance as well as that of the priests, so that
Savonarola was tortured and burnt as a heretic by Pope Alexander VI.   But the whole judgment as well as feelings of the
people were with him ; a medal was struck in his honour with
an inscription declaring him to be both prophet and martyr ;
pictures were painted of him with the head surrounded with a
glory ; and so great did the veneration of him continue, that
even down to the commencement of the present century the
place of his execution was annually strewed with flowers to his
memory.—*L'Osservatore Fiorentino*, ii. 3.

Some of the most celebrated painters, poets, and literary men were amongst the friends of Savonarola; the participators of his principles, and his most devoted partisans. There, perhaps, never was a single monk, without other pretensions or powers than those put forth by eminent piety, by exhortations to read the word of God, and by faithful condemnation of wickedness, who was surrounded with so brilliant a circle of philosophers, poets, artists of every kind, architects, sculptors, painters, and engravers, and who all offered themselves to him to be, in their several lines, fellow-labourers with him, and docile instruments in producing the great social reform after which he laboured. None carried their devotion to him and to his cause so far as some painters : one, Fra Benedetto, armed himself from head to foot to defend him ; another, Baccio della Porta, better known as Fra Bartolomeo, lost, after the condemnation of Savonarola, all love and zeal for the arts; the architect, Luca della Robbia, was so full of the subject that his biographer said it made him almost frantic. Now, the principal object of the sermons of Savonarola was to decry the exclusive admiration excited by the works of heathen poets; to banish their indecent writings from the schools, and to substitute for them the reading and the study of the word of God; to censure the mixture of profane, mythological, and immodest objects in pictures professing to treat of facts in Christian history; and to banish the too common practice of placing the portraits of living men on the figures representing holy subjects. His faithful friends the painters adhered to his memory after his death; and it was Raphael himself who dared under the tyrant Pope Julius II., though a Medici (but who had himself, fortunately for Raphael, been persecuted by Alexander), to immortalise the apotheosis of Savonarola, by placing him amongst the most celebrated doctors of the church in the famous fresco of the Dispute of the Holy Sacrament, still adorning the walls of the Vatican.

Never in the history of the world, not even at the period of the first coming of the Son of God, was there such an universal excitement on the subject of religion as at the beginning of the sixteenth century. The same generation that saw the Church of Christ rent by a fearful and irretrievable schism saw also the largest constellation of great men that ever existed at one time. It is foreign to my present purpose to mention more than the names of some who are eminent in the fine arts, such as Giovanni Bellini, Perugino, Fra Bartolomeo, Albert Durer, Michael Angelo, Titian, Giorgione, Raphael, Sebastiano del Piombo, Andrea del Sarto, Giulio Romano, Correggio, Caravaggio, and many more, justifying the name of the golden age which has been given to this period.

Having now seen the general scope and intention of painters from the commencement of Christianity to the time of the highest point which their art attained, and how intimately they were mixed up in all the great measures for the amelioration of mankind, let us now advert to a few details in order to confirm, by particular instances, the truth of what we have already observed in the large. The end which the painters proposed to themselves in their numerous representations of the Blessed Virgin may be best seen from the panegyrics which they bestowed upon each other. Guido said of Lippo Dalmasio, " That no artist, however aided by genius and study, had ever united in one figure such sanctity, modesty, and purity." But it was only they who venerated sanctity, modesty, and purity themselves, who could produce the representation of such a sentiment on canvass. Andrea del Sarto never could create any thing in the least degree pertaining to it, for he was a dishonest irreligious man. Raphael succeeded in this as in every other department of his art beyond all others, so long as he was a pure and holy man himself; but, as soon as he ceased to be so, his inspiration left him: he produced more beautiful pictures in all the mechanical parts of the art, but he lost the faculty of rendering them proper to excite the devotion of the beholders. In what is called his second manner, he produced his " Madonna del Gran Duca," "Del Cardellino," and many similar, in which the countenances are really more than human for purity, modesty, and holiness; but after he became the slave of lust, and the baker's wife supplied in his affections the place which sanctity had held before, he painted indeed his " Madonna della Seggiola," exceeding all others in grace, composition, and harmony of colouring: but it is merely the lively representation of a very pretty young mother delighted in the possession of a lovely boy. He was shorn of his glory by her in whose lap he reposed; he has descended from heaven to earth; he has reversed the motto of the Academy, which was " *Levar al cielo dalla terra nostro intelletto.*"

In its power of acting directly upon the feelings of mankind at large, painting takes precedence of all the arts. It is not a matter of surprise that the country in which this art arrived at its greatest perfection is not that in which the sister arts have attained to an equally undisputed preeminence. As every nation has its peculiar language formed by the ideas of the people, whose thoughts could not be expressed in any other with the same precision, so do the arts take a different form in different nations; and, without disparaging in their style the magnificence of the churches in Italy, there is no doubt that the effect of the Gothic cathedrals in the north of Europe is far more venerable and sublime. The castles, also, of Italy were of the most miserable description, and scarcely more defensible than the palaces in the cities, which latter, indeed, had as often to sustain sieges from rival factions and families, as the former had from scarcely more numerous armies. The castles in Germany and England, as well as the Saracenic in Spain and Magna Græcia, were splendid buildings, both as respects their strength and picturesque effect, although it must be confessed that the latter object was little, if at all, in the intention of the builders. It is in the architecture which is devoted to religious purposes, in the cathedrals and churches of England, that we find the real architectural superiority of this country, and not in the houses of her nobles and gentry, which are for the most part clumsy without grandeur, and poor without simplicity; and these defects are more visible in proportion as the national style has been departed from, and that of Italy imitated, as has been specially the case since the days of Inigo Jones. With respect to Italian architecture, Burton observes truly, that " if any objection is to be made to the chaste and simple models which ancient Greece has left us, it is, that there is a heaviness and want of relief in the vast masses of solid masonry. The modern Italian architects have gone into the contrary extreme; their aim seems to have been to break every portion of the building into as many parts as possible, and in the pediments of their windows they have been particularly profuse of ornament. The difference is, probably, to be traced to the fact of the ancients having had few windows in their buildings and the moderns having many."

The cause, however, of the degeneracy of architecture lies

deeper than this : and in order to ascertain it we must revert to the origin of all buildings for worship. Every false religion is but a corruption in some shape or other of the true. The first worship offered by man consisted essentially in the sacrifice of an innocent and spotless victim in order to atone for the sin of the sacrificer, and was transacted in the open air. It was a rite performed either by individuals or by separate families, for the institution of a Church or of public worship was unknown. The first building erected for the purpose of public worship was the Tabernacle, and the second was an enlargement of the same, the Temple: the former representing the dwelling-place of God, "whose house are we," in the present dispensation which is to pass away and be removed; the latter representing the Church of Christ in a dispensation which is not to pass away, but to be permanent, and was consequently constructed of the most durable materials.

The sufferings under which every human being labours, both in his individual and collective capacities, have made at all times very precious the promises of a deliverance from them during another life to be enjoyed hereafter. This hope is the one grand truth taught in all the rites of ancient Egypt, Greece, and Rome, of which the principal emblem was water. Life after death was set forth in the insect becoming, as it were, a corpse in its chrysalis state, and again in increased beauty

> " As rising on her purple wing
> The insect queen of eastern spring."

The same truth was shown by the Nile fertilising by its waters the black and arid sand; and hence the prevalence of all the productions of that river, the lotus, the scarabæus, the crocodile, &c. Again, the same truth was set forth by the pomegranate, which, out of the shapeless and apparently dead mass, shows forth the seeds which promise a future germination. The creative power coming from the East, and revivifying dead nature, in short, regeneration after death, was portrayed in every variety, gross as well as refined, which the inventive powers of an imaginative people could suggest.

All the heathen temples of the nations surrounding Judea were either direct copies or indirect imitations of the Tabernacle and Temple. (See Preface to Wilkins's *Magna Græcia*, and his

Prolusiones Architectonicæ; Bryant's *Mythology;* Christie on *Etruscan Vases.*) When the reality of the Jewish Temple was brought out in living men, by their becoming the residence of the Holy Spirit at Pentecost, the buildings for the worship of God would, of necessity, take such a form as would enable the actings of the ministry of the Spirit of Christ to be manifested according as they are declared in the New Testament, in their fourfold form of apostles, prophets, evangelists, and pastors. The first constitution of the Church consisted of twelve apostles appointed by God, and seven deacons elected by the people. Subsequently, we know that there were bishops and elders: and, as so great a stress is laid upon the propriety of everything being done with decency and in order, it is certain that different seats must have been assigned for the different ministers, not only according to their several ranks, — which marked the extent of their jurisdiction, whether in the universal Church, or only in the particular Church, as generals and colonels in an army,—but also according to the several parts which they had to sustain in the worship. But unfortunately, long before the Christian Church had become sufficiently tolerated for it to have a building appropriated properly to its use, it had fallen from its original constitution. The apostles, after being rejected by the very Churches which they had planted, had been put to death; the voice of prophets was heard no more; and preachers and priests were all the ministers that were left, who have remained until this day under the names of bishops, priests, and deacons.

The first churches, therefore, that were built had no reference to Christian worship in its perfection and original purity. They could not be adapted for the manifestation of ministries and services which no longer existed; they could only be built to serve such a condition of the Church as was at that time in being: and this they did exhibit in various ways. For example, the altar was the most conspicuous object, being that on which is transacted the mighty mystery of feeding the spirit of man with the flesh and blood of the Son of God. " The laver of regeneration," the baptismal font, without passing through which no one can become a member of Christ's body, the Church, stood at the entrance of the building. Around the altar was the bishop's throne and the seats for his assisting ministers, but upon a platform, lower than the altar itself, — for the altar was catholic, and belonged to the universal Church, being that which we all, priests and laity, have in common, whilst the jurisdiction of the bishop and his elders was local and limited; below these, on another platform, were arranged ministers of inferior degree, but who were yet employed about sacred things : and, in almost all cathedrals, the remains of these several platforms may still be observed and distinctly traced. The pulpit was not suffered to be in the part appropriated to worship, but placed in the body of the building, where the people assembled.

From the days of Constantine, however, men began to think they might make what changes seemed best to them in the forms of worship ; for, being no longer able to understand the truth which was taught by the true forms, all forms seemed nearly equally good. Men thought, as they still think, that the forms of worship are arbitrary things of human invention, instead of being things which are as fixed and immutable as God Himself, as the form in which the Son of God appeared, and no more capable of taking divers forms than is the body of Christ. Things thus necessarily got worse and worse; for whilst in the very oldest churches the forms are preserved, which were at least according to the light that was in the faithful in the days of Constantine (such as the churches of Saint Clement, Saint Lawrence without the walls, Holy Cross, all at Rome, with many others there and elsewhere), in the modern churches all truth and propriety have disappeared altogether. In St. Peter's at Rome, and in all churches since the period of its construction, no vestige of the forms to be seen in the old cathedrals exists. Even in some where they do exist, as in the cathedrals of Geneva, Lausanne, Basle, Glasgow, and Edinburgh, it is melancholy to see the perversion and profanation of all harmony, truth, and propriety. Indeed, in all the Protestant sects, in exact proportion as they have departed from the primitive faith, have they trampled down the altar and the baptismal font, because they have trampled in heart and spirit upon the sacramental rites which are transacted at the same; and they have exalted the pulpit, because being fleshly, and having lost all faith in things of God's appointment, they are only capable of receiving such as please their ears through some idol man. Thus architecture, being limited in sacred things when rightly employed to set forth the truth of forms of worship, could not advance with the art of painting, which was not bound to so strict an object : and thus it is that the newest buildings, such as the modern churches of Italy, are so far inferior to the more ancient, because they have further departed from the original intention of such structures. (See Nibby, *Dissertazione sulle forme delle Antiche Chiese.*)

From the time of the Reformation, well-founded complaints have resounded on every side respecting the decline of the arts. As their advance was commensurate with the faith and zeal of the Church, so their decay has been but the outward and visible sign of that faith and zeal being gone. It is not a paradox to say, that, whilst on the one hand the long-established abuses and corruptions of the clergy produced the explosion which ended in the renunciation of the dominion of the Bishop of Rome by the inhabitants of the north of Europe, on the other hand a great deal of personal piety and devotion had been diffused throughout the whole of Christendom. The abuses which the priests refused to correct began, however, to extinguish whatever true religious feeling existed amongst the laity. The Reformation was the witness against the Bishop and priests of Rome, that they would not renounce their evil ways, and betake themselves to penitence and amendment of life. The artists were not the authorised reformers of the morals of the people ; they were but, as we have seen, the auxiliaries in a holy work which was the peculiar duty of others, and where the principal was unfaithful the auxiliary necessarily could not succeed. Faith and devotion became extinct : in the Romish part, by a mass of wickedness, by superstitious observances, worship of dead men and women, &c. &c. ; and in the Protestant part, by the substitution of a religion of propositions for one of faith, of fatalism for duty, of self-sufficiency for obedience to God in His ordinances. Yet all were not equally bad : as England had been the foremost and longest to protest against, and to endeavour to amend, the abuses of the clergy, so did she preserve in her division a greater measure of faith and purity of doctrine than any other part of Christendom, retaining nearly all the truth which is found in the Papacy, unencumbered by the superstitions with which it is there smothered. Hither also fled whatever remained of the arts, and found a place in those quarters in which God was most honoured, namely, in the sanctuary of the domestic hearth, and in the admiration of country scenery. Perhaps you will hesitate to admit the justice of the remark, that portrait-painting is the lowest department of the art; as surely it is, if we consider the highest department of the art, and so far as respects the creative power of the painter : but such merit as does belong to it has thriven in England in a far more conspicuous manner than anywhere else, and no other country can boast such a series of portrait-painters as Holbein, Vandyke, Sir Peter Lely, Sir Joshua Reynolds, Gainsborough, and Lawrence. In country scenery, also, the genius for land-scape-gardening and landscape-painting is universal; every cottage, house, garden, and park, is more or less adorned according to the good or bad taste of the owner; and amidst the swarms of English travellers by which in the present days foreign countries are infested, a very large proportion are able to take faithful representations of the scenes they visit; whilst the immense number of landscape-paintings and drawings annually exhibited by professional artists prove the great demand for their works and the assiduity of their labours.

But never has Protestantism produced anything in the highest department of the art of painting. In vain will be sought any superhuman expression of purity, holiness, and sanctity in any Protestant painter. They may paint old men's beards and magic effects of light like Rembrandt; they may show all the knowledge of drawing and of the mechanism of colouring that Rubens could produce : yet who would ever think of looking into the faces of his *fraus,* or of his satyresses suckling their little cubs, with any feeling but that of disgust? It is in vain that the Dutchmen have laboured, as far as sentiment is sought for; though they are superior to all in their powers of finishing flowers, carrots, and cabbages, and in ruling lines to produce the effect of the interior of a church. I do not deny a merit to these painters, nor to their subjects; there is a merit in everything, even in a woman without arms who cuts out watch-papers with her toes. Yet a taste for the Dutch and Flemish schools of painting is not noble; it is the sort of taste which in dramatic writing would prefer a harlequin farce to Shakspeare.

The artists themselves, totally mistaking the nature of the disease, have ever complained in England of the want of rich patrons. Never was complaint more unfounded. It seems as if they had looked upon the profession of an art as a trade, and thought that money could command it. They have not become like the painters of the golden age of painting, because there is neither in them nor in the public the religious feeling which can alone inspire them. The history of rich men's patronage should instruct them that, in a large proportion of instances, such patronage has been detrimental rather than beneficial. In some cases the feelings of the old masters were so violated by the nature of the orders they received, that they could not give their whole soul up to the work, and either left their pictures unfinished, to be completed by others, or refused to execute them at all. It certainly did not tend to exalt the piety of the painter, that Pope Alexander VI. ordered himself to be painted in the Vatican as one of the Wise Men from the East at the feet of our Lady; and that he caused the face intended for the Blessed Virgin to be that of Julia Farnese. He gave Pinturicchio a commission to paint several rooms both in the Castle of St. Angelo and in the Pontifical Palace, in which were introduced the portraits of many members of his infamous family, not excepting Cæsar Borgia himself. In the Colonna Palace is a picture by Pietro da Cortona of the resurrection of our Lord, and also of the saints who arose with Him, in which all the persons are blasphemously painted as portraits of members of that family. Lorenzo di Medici did not add much to the enthusiasm of the artists, though he did all that in him lay to bring them back to paganism, when he required of one to paint for him the misfortunes of Vulcan; of another, the twelve labours of Hercules; of another, heathen gods and goddesses in all their accustomed nudity; and of another, repeated representations of Venus. So immediate was the degrading effect upon some of the painters themselves, that it is said of Pontormo, that when to please Cosmo de Medici he painted for his mother Donna Maria, the gods and goddesses, with corresponding allegorical figures illustrating the liberal arts, no one would have believed that this proceeded from the same pencil which had so lately before excited universal admiration. From the same period, too, may be traced an increased number of lascivious pictures under the pretext of Venuses, Danaës, Ledas, Didos, &c., until at length, towards the beginning of the last century, a total change in the morals of the people is declared by a historian in a very remarkable manner, although indeed he ascribes it to corruption by money. *È qualche cosa· di portentoso il vedere quel medesimo popolo, che pochi anni avanti era stato, al meno quanto al' esteriore, un modello di modestia, diventare in un subito il più scostumato d' Europa.* — L'Osservatore Fiorentino, i, 38.

The effect of the arts in Italy, since the period when they attained their greatest elevation, has been exactly the contrary of that produced by them up to that time. Instead of making holy men and women, *santi e sante,* they have tended to habituate the eye and taste to scenes of indecency, which is one of the causes of the open dissoluteness of Italian society. The proportion of religious subjects painted now, in comparison with the number of those of an opposite tendency, is very small indeed; and although the direct intention of the picture may not be evil, still there is nothing to exalt or ennoble the feelings.

In sculpture the demand for monuments to departed friends keeps up a continual reference to sentiments more or less religious; this art, however, has shared the fate of its sister: but it would lead this letter to an inconvenient length to enter into this subject further.

Music is less dependent for its effects upon its own intrinsic merits than upon the association of ideas which it excites. Unlike a statue or a painting, the most perfect musical composition is not the most pleasing. All variations of airs, which exhibit the skill of the composer and the performer, are unpleasing in proportion as they are learned and depart from the simplicity of the melody. National airs produce a power over the natives which no other composition can effect, and none but natives can play, for none other can feel them: a Scotch ballad is not the same thing when performed by an Englishman. Dancing is an innocent and joyous expression of hilarity in the common people of many countries, but when practised by the higher classes of English, with their grave faces and demure demeanour, is one of the silliest exhibitions that frivolity ever invented. The perfection of dancing seems to be in the south of France. A waltz in Germany is graceful and modest; in England it resembles the vulgarity, coarseness, and indecency of stable-boys romping with kitchen-maids. The mazzurka, like the national airs of Poland and Russia, is beautiful and graceful when performed by the natives of these countries, but not when performed by any other; and even a Scotch reel cannot be danced south of the Tweed. The English can no more dance than the Dutch, for it is not the form in which their joy naturally goes forth. If Italy be the mother of music, Germany is its father; and while the former country abounds in beautiful voices and sweetness of melody, the latter greatly exceeds it in instrumental execution and in harmony. The oratorios of Handel and Mozart, and the church music of England, such as chants and anthems, are far superior to anything that Italy can produce, where the music of the stage and of the church is so confounded that it is not possible to distinguish the difference. The Italians are less capable of entering into and appreciating the merits of the arts, when they take a form different from that which is found amongst themselves, than any other people; and in nothing are they so little capable of being catholic, and of ceasing to be partial, as in music.

Whilst the artists in England have erred in supposing that it was the want of money which prevented their encouragement, it is perfectly true that painting and sculpture have never been promoted here. The same absence of religious devotion, which is apparent in the works of the artists, is equally prevalent in the mass of the people, and is further apparent from the kind of pictures which mostly please them; so that if the painters produced the highest order of pictures, there would be none to appreciate them. If, as the critic on the funeral service before-mentioned said, the music did not exercise its due power because it fell upon ears without faith, so must a painting fail in its effect when it falls under a faithless eye. For the most part the English in these days seem totally incapable of estimating or of understanding the highest branches of the fine arts. The finest specimens of easel-painting are indeed to be found in England, just as the finest jewels are to be found there: the pictures are estimated according to the sum they cost; they are another means of showing forth that which every Englishman is at all times, and in every way, fond of proclaiming with ostentation, namely, how much superior his wealth is to that of his neighbours. Nothing can be more amusing nor more characteristic than to walk into the sale-room of a collection of pictures in London, and to attend to the different observations of the artists and of the collectors. The conversation of the former is always about the merits of the picture; what was the design of the painter, where he succeeded, and where he failed; the perfection of its preservation, and where its injuries had been repaired by an able or by an unskilful hand. The conversation of the latter is invariably about its authenticity: if it be modern, then they do little beside find fault, for it requires no skill to blame, but to discover beauties requires some knowledge in the critic; if it be ancient, they dispute whether it be really by the painter whose name it bears, or whether by one of the manufacturers of old pictures, with which London, as much as any other place, abounds. If it be a Flemish or Dutch picture, there will be a hundred competitors for one that would purchase a Perugino, or even an Onorio, although no painters ever produced (except Raphael) more heavenly countenances than these. It seems quite unintelligible how any one can like to have before him continually a representation of that which in the original would be disgusting. It is conceivable how in a public gallery, or in a collection as extensive as the Bridgewater, it may be desirable to possess specimens of all masters and of all periods of the arts, and that for such an object the subject is unimportant; the picture is avowedly there as a specimen of the mechanical part of the art, not of the sentiment expressed by it: for the same reason it is conceivable that it may be advantageous to a painter to possess specimens of a similar kind, which may be useful to him in his studies: but who would wish to have for ever seated in his presence an exceedingly ugly, olive-coloured, wrinkled old woman, who was a perfect stranger? and if no one would, what could induce any private gentleman to buy the portrait of Titian's mother, painted by her son? If no one would like to see a loathsome satyress with its dugs trailing on the ground, what could induce any one to buy a picture of Rubens representing such a subject, notwithstanding the magic of his colouring? If no one would like to have in his drawingroom, or even to see before its windows, a number of Dutch boors who had drunk so much as to be filthy, what could induce any one to hang upon his walls the faithful representation of such a scene by Teniers? Even in religious subjects intended to inspire devotional feelings, it often happens that the manner of treating them is calculated to excite more disgust than veneration. Yet every such painting of the Dutch and Flemish schools is preferred to any Saint's or Madonna's head that ever was painted by the first master of the Italian school, provided only that it cost more money.

It is idle to suppose that the highest department of the art of painting can ever be encouraged, whilst the taste of the public remains as it is. I do not mean to deny a certain merit to the works of Flemish and Dutch painters; but it is necessary that the due proportion of admiration should be given upon just grounds. There is a certain kind of merit in the poems of Swift, and Little, and Burns; all I contend for is, that it is inferior to that of Dante or Milton. None can read the latter without being the better, none read the former without being the worse; and Burns has effected for the operatives of Scotland what Voltaire did for the small wits of France. They who taste and feel with Dante and Milton, and they who delight in the others, are two different classes: so are they who enjoy the Italian, and those who are pleased with the Flemish, painters. There is enough of spiritual power yet in the Church of Rome, if it were but rightly put forth, to produce again works which should be worthy of its ancient greatness, notwithstanding the rubbish by which that power is oppressed: but there is not enough power in Protestantism to put forth anything better than it does, for there never was; and it never can have in its decrepitude that which it wanted in its prime.

In your remark to which I have referred at the beginning of this letter, your benevolence has furnished an excuse for the English public which it cannot with justice plead. You say that whilst the Italians have the picture of a saint continually before them, the English have no such object of attraction. Every creed has its heroes, every sect has its saints. It is true than an English Evangelical will be horrified at the idolatry of the Papists, who say their prayers before a picture of our Lady or of Saint Francis; but he will nevertheless stir up his piety by a portrait of " pious Mrs. Hannah More " and of " the great Mr. Scott." The Baptist and the Independent who will lament that Hannah and Scott were " in the bands of the Establishment," send forth their respective magazines with the effigy of some preacher of fame in their different sects. So far from this being reprehensible, the practice is most edifying and salutary. Euse-

bius expressly declares that he had in his time seen portraits of
our Saviour and of the Apostles; and there is no reason why we
too should not revere the portraits of those who have served God
in the latter, as well as in the former, generations of men. There
is just as much love of saints, and of devotion to the memory of
the departed heroes of religion, in England, as there is of love
and devotion to anything that does not flatter personal pride.
These favourite preachers are the saints of the parties to which
they belonged; and it would be just as easy to have some remarkable scene in their lives portrayed as merely their ordinary
features; and it would seem as if such scene would answer every
purpose that the portrait does (and many more besides), of exciting the admiration of the beholder for the memory of the
departed hero. Thus the same feeling which in the Popish
country calls for the historical painting of the acts of its admired
object, calls in England for nothing but the miserable head
which is supposed to adorn some obscure journal. The sect
which has shown the most violent antipathy to the fine arts is
also that which has most widely departed from primitive Christianity. The Calvinists, who despise the sacrament of baptism
as the instrument " by which we are made members of Christ,
children of God, and inheritors of the kingdom of heaven,"
and who have imputed this power to a speech made by some
favourite preacher; who trample on the sacrament of the
Eucharist as that which feeds us with the body and blood of
Jesus Christ, and declare that it is a mere symbol of Church-
fellowship; who reject the apostolic succession of the priesthood,
and have " made to themselves priests of the lowest of the
people; " who mock at the tradition of the Church, at confession,
absolution, fasting, and penance; —these are they who went forth
at the first in a brutal crusade against the consecrated houses
of God, destroying and defiling the pictures and statues with
which those houses were adorned. The Church of England has
never recovered this coarse shock from the hands of Calvin,
Knox, and Cromwell: but, as there is now the appearance of a
return to better feelings, it is to be hoped that we may see
again the places of worship adorned, as in early times, with
paintings recording the triumphs of Christianity, whether in the
actings, death, and speedily approaching return of its Divine
Founder Himself, or in those of His most eminent servants.

Let it not be supposed that all the subjects of painting from Christianity are trite, and that nothing is left for modern artists but the repetition of what has been successfully handled by their predecessors. The one great hope of the Church has been less kept in mind from the commencement of the era, than it was in the times of paganism. We have seen already how the new and happy creation which is to arise after the passing away of all things now visible was the object set forth by the rites and emblems of paganism, but we shall in vain seek to find similar representations amongst Christians. The last judgment, indeed, has been depicted with distortions and exaggerations, as if the only scene of that great drama was one of terror : our Lord has been represented as an executioner, but not as a Saviour ; every feature of horror to scare and horrify beholders has been elaborately portrayed, but not one to soothe and rejoice. Yet the Son of God arises on the morning of that day, as the Sun of Righteousness with healing on His wings ; He comes to put an end to all the sufferings of mankind ; He comes to establish an empire of peace and blessedness, in the stead of the empire of war and tyranny with which the earth has ever been oppressed. The hope of the faithful is, that he " shall be counted worthy to stand before the Son of Man, and to escape the things that are coming upon the earth ; " to be " caught up to meet the Lord in the air ; " not to see death, but to be changed without dying. The end of this dispensation has been represented for all as an object of dread, but never as an object of joy; as a thing to be feared, but not as a thing to be hoped for. It is foreign to my present purpose to examine into the cause of this, but I state a notorious and undeniable fact. No doubt the interests of venality in a corrupted priesthood have been better served by inculcating the terror than the joy, but the interests of the world at large have been sacrificed ; the pious believer has been despoiled of his hope ; and the blessing of the universe has been delayed. Here, then, is a great and untrodden field open to the aspiring artists : and contrasts of sentiment need not be wanting, for they are to be found in such passages as " two women shall be grinding at the mill, the one shall be taken, and the other left; " the clothing with light and immortality of the one, the wonder and dismay at her situation of the other. The painters have never attempted to paint the joys of heaven, although many have portrayed the torments of hell, partly because their notions of both are mystical, or taken from paganism. But heaven is only an assembly of men and women, with the Man Jesus Christ presiding over them, and they are greatly mistaken who dream that it is possible to see God otherwise than in flesh, that is, in the Lord and His Church.

The present is a favourable time for you and for other English masters of the art of painting to be up and be stirring. For the students and young painters the first thing is to be good Christians, and the second is to labour at drawing. The bane of all success is peculiarly prevalent in these days, which is to suppose that genius can supersede the necessity of study, and that genius is an excuse for idleness. Michael Angelo studied anatomy for twelve years. In Florence, old Raphael Mengs continued at seventy years of age to attend the school of drawing from the life; and I have myself seen the oldest and ablest professors employed in the same manner. Drawing is the mechanical part in which the English artists have ever been the most deficient, of which Reynolds and Lawrence are notable examples. The sketches which Raphael made for the Transfiguration are still in existence, by which it is seen that he drew first the skeletons of his figures for that picture, then the muscles, and afterwards the drapery which covers them: the more marvel that he should have forgotten a leg of St. John, if it be forgotten; and if it be not "rather we who dream," than "great Homer who nods." The next thing for artists to do is to study nature, and not masters: by a strange perverseness, whilst Raphael is unanimously acknowledged to be the first of painters, Michael Angelo is far more copied, and has been the model after which all have more or less laboured since his time. Vasari began to mislead by extravagant praise, which was natural and pardonable in a pupil of a great man. The consequence has been, that the simple attributes of nature have been abandoned for the affectation of the stage, until the imitators arrived at their climax of caricature in Fuseli and David. Modern painters seem to have gone to the stage for madonnas and saints, as French poets do for shepherds and shepherdesses.

Whilst the young are employed in judicious and laborious study, you and the other professors must set to work to teach the public in what and how to admire the works when produced.

For this purpose, it is indispensable that you and your brethren draw up an honest descriptive catalogue of all the pictures in the public collections in London, and in as many private collections as the owners of the same will bear to hear the truth. In order to be of a convenient brevity, all account of the painter himself should be omitted except what bears upon the picture in hand: but the time and circumstances under which it was painted should be mentioned; whether for a patron, or for a public building; how far influenced and how far free in the choice and treatment of his subject; the end the painter seems to have had in view; how far he has succeeded or failed; what he has sacrificed of minor points to the principal object; what the peculiar beauties and peculiar faults of the school to which he belonged, and of the individual in particular, and how the picture shows the one and the other: the state of the picture; whether all by the painter whose name it bears, or whether completed by some scholar, and the reasons for that judgment; how far the picture has been damaged, and how far improved by time; how far repaired and restored, and whether ill or well done. Such a catalogue should be made by divers committees of three painters each, for the different masters with whose style and manners they have become well acquainted by being accustomed to copy them; for none other are capable of giving internal reasons of authenticity. An artist accustomed to copy the Italian masters cannot easily be deceived in them, but he is not competent to form an accurate opinion on works of the Flemish school; and *vice versâ*. A very good English painter, remarkable for his judgment on pictures of the Dutch school, came late in life to Italy, and expressed his astonishment to an Italian painter, that he found himself often totally incapable of discerning between originals and their copies.

The catalogue should be made honestly; by which I mean, not only without any desire to flatter the owners by unmerited praise of their pictures, but with a candid avowal of the inability to pronounce whether any given picture be an original or not, where any such doubt exists. Above all, they who make it should be insensible to the clamour which the picture-dealers will raise, by whom the judgment of purchasers is always directed. They are always more or less manufacturers of self-

called old pictures. At the same time it must be remembered,
that there is nothing in which people like to be deceived by
names more than in pictures. Some painted by artists of inferior reputation are really superior to many by those of greater
fame, though much less highly valued. Moreover, there is a
fallacy in the usual comparison between a copy of a picture
and the translation of a poem: both are no doubt generally
inferior to their respective originals, but not all equally so.
Vincent Bonner's Latin translations are quite as beautiful
as the exquisitely touching little originals. Several parts of
Sotheby's *Georgics* are not inferior to Virgil's. Hudibras himself, which might have been supposed to be the most untrans-
latable of all writers into French, has lost nothing of his spirit
in Towneley's translation. Many English poems could be perfectly translated into German, which could not be rendered into
any other language. The difficulty in poetry arises from words
not being really synonymous in two different languages, but
only equivalents in a different category of ideas. It is true that
it is exceedingly difficult to copy the true sentiment in the
countenance of a Madonna by Raphael, to give the lights and
shades of Correggio, or the colour of real flesh like Guido and
Titian. But all the merit that consists in composition of form
and correctness of drawing may be quite as well conveyed by a
copy, or even by a print; and there are many painters whose
reputation has been greater by the needles of Strange, Morghen,
and Woollet, than they would have been if left to their own
intrinsic merits alone. Indeed, I have never seen any copy of
the Madonna della Seggiola, which so completely gives the sentiment of her countenance as Morghen's engraving of it; and
the same may be said of the expression of the faces in the
Cenacolo of Leonardo da Vinci.

By such a catalogue, they who wish to be directed on the
true grounds on which their judgment should be formed may
instruct themselves; and it is common to hear people who go
to see collections of pictures say, "I wish I had somebody to
explain them to me: to tell me what to admire, and why?"
The proper way, no doubt, is to learn to draw and paint themselves; for, without knowing the principles on which pictures
are painted, and how to look at all scenes with the eyes of a
painter, they never can become really good judges: for he is

the best judge who has most laboured to be a painter himself. But the persons who call themselves *amateurs* pretend that they are far better judges of the merits of paintings than painters who have been regularly instructed in the art: they think they have found a royal road to knowledge, and that though quacks and ill-taught persons in medicine, chemistry, and anatomy, are not such good guides in sickness as regularly bred physicians, apothecaries, and surgeons, yet that what is true of the sciences is not true of the arts ; and that, after all, dunces in these are wiser than the learned. Such people are full of anecdotes of the mistaken judgments which some painters have pronounced upon certain pictures ; and hence they come most logically (!) to the inference that all painters know less than themselves. If painters give rash opinions, so much the worse ; but at all events, a painter is not so likely to give a wrong opinion as a man who is not a painter. The painters who confine their judgments to the masters whom they have been accustomed to copy will not be deceived in their works, though they will be in the works of others : but as he who is no painter has never copied any pictures at all, he must be deceived in all. A certain want of freedom will betray a copy in the presence of an original, and so will many other things ; but the self-called amateurs should be plainly told, that all their opinions are pure quackery, save in so far as they are instructed in the art of painting ; that they do not know how to look at nature with a painter's eye ; that they know not true colouring from false ; true or false lights and shades ; breadth or frittering ; that they know not the principles upon which nature herself composes her pictures, and are there-fore radically incompetent to form an opinion upon any one department or particularity of the art. "There's ten that judge for one that *paints* amiss." The number of persons who really love and really estimate the highest productions in the fine arts must be very small, for they are matters of feeling, and not of logic. Raphael thought the baker's wife very beautiful ; judg-ing from all the portraits I have seen of her, I think her very plain ; and Pope Julius II. was of my opinion, and asked Raphael what he could possibly see in her ; he replied, *Ah se sua Santità potesse guardarla coi miei occhj !* to which no answer could be made. The same idea is expressed in the old Scottish song,

o 2

> "I see a form, I see a face,
> Ye weel may wi' the fairest place;
> But she wants to me the witching grace,
> The kind love that's in her ee."

No process of reasoning can demonstrate that a woman is beautiful to another who does not think so; no one can prove that one poet is good- and another bad, as the failure of Johnson's criticisms show. If a person prefers Teniers to Raphael, it cannot be helped. There are many more persons in England delighted at staring at an old woman leaning over a bit of carpet selling carrots, by Gerard Dow, than at a Holy Family by Giulio Romano. If "Moll in the Wad" is played in the streets it will attract a greater crowd than the "Stabat Mater" of Pergolesi. Even in matters of mere sense, if a man prefers haggis and whiskey-punch to French cookery and champagne, it is idle to argue with him, and there are many who think the drunken cobbler cut out of red sandstone, in Dumfriesshire, a mighty witty production. Of all such *non ragioniam di lor ma lascia e passa.* You, with the rest of your brethren, who are at the head of the profession in England, must labour at teaching those who will not be at the trouble of being painters themselves, whilst the official professors teach the regular students; and for this trouble you must be content with small thanks and little praise: but if you think that an increased feeling for the fine arts can really contribute to elevate the minds and characters of man; if you will practise the solitary virtue which raised the grandeur of the ancient Romans, namely, the sacrifice of any personal and egotistical feeling for the common advantage; and, above all, if you look to higher ends, as did the masters in the times of the early Church, partaking of the Spirit of Him "who is kind to the unthankful," and who laid down His life to make ungrateful man happy, you will be satisfied with whatever result awaits you, in the consciousness that your true reward is in the success of your endeavours, and not in the way in which others appreciate your exertions.

I am, your very faithful Servant,

HENRY DRUMMOND.

May, 1840.

REMARKS

CHURCHES OF ROME AND ENGLAND

RESPECTFULLY ADDRESSED TO

THE RIGHT REV. DR. WISEMAN

AND

THE REV. WILLIAM PALMER

1841

REMARKS,

ETC.

I⊤ is not my intention to make any observations to aggravate
the discussion which has taken place between these two learned
and respectable priests of the One Holy Catholic and Apostolic
Church : all that has been said by either in the way of charge
and recrimination has been said and resaid by members of both
communions, — the unleavened and the leavened, — many times
during the last three centuries, doubtless to the grief of the
heart of our common Father which is in heaven, and need not
to be repeated. My object is to draw the attention of the
Catholic priesthood to the common hope of all, by means of the
points at which all are at one, whether in the admission or the
denial of them.

It is a fact, which is as much a matter of grief to intelligent
and pious priests of Spain and Italy, as a matter of unholy
triumph to their enemies, that the inhabitants of those countries
are prone to superstition and idolatry. It is equally a fact that
the natives of northern latitudes are cold and phlegmatic in their
devotions; their religion consisting more in intellectual speculations than in practical usefulness to man : idolaters and deists
are the extremes to which the ill-instructed of both extremities
of Europe incline ; but certainly these effects are little attributable to the authorised standards of any Church. Dr. Wiseman
is no more an idolater than Mr. Palmer is a deist, although
idolaters are to be found at Rome, and deists in London.

It is a proof that up to a certain point the people are instructed in the Christian religion, when their superstition takes
that form rather than any other. The Scotch and the Germans
are superstitious, but their superstition is not shown through faith
in relics or saints, but in all kinds of imaginary beings in an ima-

ginary world. In Spain and Italy it is rashly concluded that
the idolatry of the people has been inculcated by the Spanish
and Italian priests, because the belief of the vulgar rests on silly
legends about pious Christian people, and that it has not been
inculcated by German priests, because the heroes of the Brocken
and of the Geisterwelt have not been fathers and martyrs in the
Christian Church. But if the charge of idolatry were justly
attributable to the priests of the Roman Catholic Church, the
same idolatry would be found equally in every portion of that
community; amongst the learned as well as the ignorant;
amongst the German and English, as well as amongst the
Spanish and Italian, population.

Since it is the common creed of the Church that there is, and
can be, but One Holy Catholic and Apostolic Church, whence
comes it that we hear so much of the Roman Church, and the
Anglican Church, and the Genevan Church, and the Scottish?
Is Christ divided? The voice of antiquity has decided against
such names: and any Church that had assumed them, would for
that cause alone have been condemned as schismatic by our
fathers.

These names are not names of love, but of discord; they are
not titles of unity, but of division; they are contradictions to
the truth maintained alike by all, "I believe in ONE Holy
Catholic and Apostolic Church." Behold how good and pleasant
a thing it is for brethren to dwell together in unity: *ecce quam
bonum et quam jucundum habitare fratres in unum.* Is this
good and pleasant sight presented by brethren to their Father
which is in heaven? All will make the same reply. Wherefore
is this? Let the Scriptures answer, and as the Church teaches:
Whence come these wars and fightings amongst you? *Unde
bella et lites in vobis? nonne hinc? ex concupiscentiis vestris
quæ militant in membris vestris?* Every one is right in his
own eyes, but God is judge; the quarrels of nations and of
Churches are as unjustifiable as the quarrels of individuals.
Neither is it of any use to seek in former ages for the justification
and causes of things that exist now. We do indeed inherit the
sins of our fathers, and commit the same, without being able to
plead in extenuation that we have their provocation.

In order to approximate, each must see not only his own case,
but feel for the position of a brother. No Roman Catholic priest

wishes a Protestant to become an idolater; it cannot be said that no Church of England priest wishes a Roman Catholic to become schismatic; and members of the Church of England must show themselves — not as individuals, but as a Church, as a body — more sensitive to the sin of schism, before they have a right to expect that their addresses to Roman Catholics can have much weight. The Roman Catholic adheres to the creed in which he has been instructed: the Church of England man invites him, as he supposes, to become a schismatic, to consult his Bible, to renounce idolatry, and to join the Church of England. The Roman Catholic feels that if he had only to choose between the Church in which he has been instructed and the Church of England, the matter would be much simplified; but how can he be assured that, so soon as he is cut adrift from the creed of his youth, he may not be wafted where neither he nor his Church of England adviser would wish him to go?

Here is the difficulty: the Lord promised to be with His Church to the end of the world; if, then, she has been suffered to err in the remotest degree in doctrine or discipline, the Roman Catholic apprehends that the promise has failed, and he can no longer trust any promise that the Scriptures contain. This maxim the Roman Catholic is prepared to carry out to every possible consequence, and to admit any conclusion that can be drawn from it: charge his Church with what you please; convict him of the truth of the charge, so that he shall not be able to escape from your reasoning, nevertheless his reply will be, " So the Church has taught, and therefore so Christ has guided her, and therefore so I believe."

Unquestionably the promise was given, and as unquestionably it has been kept: and to this day we perceive the Church existing, and at the close of eighteen hundred years, in the midst of all corruptions and evils, not more corrupt nor more evil than it was in the lifetime of the apostles who had built it. Who can read the Epistles to the Corinthians, those of James and Peter, and the addresses to the seven churches in the Apocalypse, without being convinced that every vice and every evil was existing then which is to be found now, though more developed in these days, because the number of the baptized has greatly multiplied?

The truth that the Lord Jesus Christ has been ever guiding

His Church, is not more essential to the faith of a Roman Catholic than to that of a Protestant. It is a great principle, that nothing must be allowed to contravene or shake. It is · necessary to be very accurate in examining the terms of the promise before we determine whether it has been observed or broken; and, if observed, it will be profitable to inquire by what means it has been effected. The terms of the promise are these: *data est mihi omnis potestas in cœlo et in terra: euntes ergo docete omnes gentes, baptizantes eos in nomine Patris et Filii et Spiritus Sancti; docentes eos servare omnia quæcumque mandavi vobis; et ecce ego vobiscum sum omnibus diebus, usque ad consummationem sæculi.* It is written by the evangelist Saint Matthew, " All power is given unto me in heaven and in earth; go ye therefore and teach (make disciples or Christians of) all nations, baptizing them in the name of the Father, and of the Son, and of the Holy Ghost; teaching them to observe all things whatsoever I have commanded you; and lo, I am with you alway, even unto the end of the world."

The commission given to the eleven was to teach certain observances which had been taught to them; they were "to observe all things" that the Lord had enjoined. They were not to teach certain propositions after the manner of the heathen schools of philosophy, which were, by being received, to effect a corresponding line of conduct, but they were to teach certain observances.

This point is of importance, because in these days the commission given to the eleven is quoted by the sectaries as if it were to teach certain propositions concerning justification by faith, the place of good works, the decrees of election, predestination, &c.: and it is not meant by these observations to deny that such things do in their place deserve to be taught by pastors to their flocks; but what is meant is, that such things were not the only, nor even the primary, things contained in the commission originally given, but the " observance " of certain things, and not the belief of certain propositions.

Only one amongst the things which were to be observed was mentioned at the time the commission was given by our Lord to his apostles, and that is baptism, by which men were to be made members of the church: "make disciples of all nations, baptizing them, &c.; teaching them to observe all things," &c.

The sacrament of the Eucharist had been established before. No men on earth could teach the things which our Lord had taught the eleven, except themselves, for none others knew them. They, in their turn, commissioned other teachers, some to teach one part of what they had been taught, and some other parts, as we see by the Epistles to the Corinthians and Ephesians; so that the whole teaching of the disciples was carried on by a fourfold division of ministers: *ipse dedit quosdam quidem apostolos, quosdam autem prophetas, alios verò evangelistas, alios autem pastores et docentes;* "some apostles, some prophets, some evangelists, and some pastors and teachers." These, also, were of course to teach others "to observe the things" which Christ had taught the eleven; namely, baptism, by which they were made disciples, and the celebration of the Eucharist, which they did on the first day of every week. Thus, then, the things which were observed at the beginning were Baptism and the Lord's Supper, both of which were administered by the eleven themselves, or by others commissioned by them for that end. The priesthood and the sacraments have continued until this time; by them has the Church been preserved; and however unworthily of their great privileges the majority of Christians may have conducted themselves, nevertheless the baptized nations are distinguished above all others for civilisation, humanity, and virtue. Undoubtedly, the sacraments are not now administered as they were at the first, nor precisely in the same manner in every part of Europe; but nevertheless there is sufficient in the most corrupted form of administration to identify the present with, and render them as efficacious as, the original rites. This is analogous to the manner in which God established, at the commencement, the Jewish church. He took Moses into the mount, and showed him the pattern of the tabernacle, which was accordingly built after that pattern. In like manner, after His resurrection, and before His ascension, our blessed Lord conversed with and instructed His apostles in the form and ordering of His Church, according to which they were to build it, and to set it in order: *quibus et præbuit seipsum vivum post passionem suam in multis argumentis, per dies quadraginta apparens eis, et loquens de regno Dei.* It is doubtful whether the apostles were ever able to establish the Church during their lifetime, according to the perfect plan

which had been shown them; and, however that may be, it is
very evident that the perfect form of the Church did not last
long, even if it were ever completed in any one place, as the
disorders in the Corinthian church do testify, where they almost
rejected the authority of the apostle who had planted that
Church.   St. John complains, in his letter to Gaius, who was
Paul's host in that same place, that one of their principal men
had rejected him also.   Many Protestant schismatics have attempted to construct the Church according to the original
mind and intention of God, and have vainly supposed that this
plan could be found in the Bible.   But God did not cause a
description of the plan of His Church to be written, but He
taught it *vivâ voce* to men who taught it *vivâ voce* to others, so
far as they were able to bear it; and Paul complains to the
Hebrews that they were not able to hear the things he had to
tell them, for they were carnal, as was proved by living in
contention; and it is impossible now to ascertain what the
plan was which Christ taught to the apostles, unless God
should please to raise up prophets again in the Church to
reveal it to us.

Amidst the various divisions into which the baptized are
unhappily separated, it will be found that the most spiritual
portion is that wherein most respect is paid to the priesthood
and the sacraments.   A spiritual man is not one who has notions
about spiritual things, nor even one who has made considerable
attainment in the progress of spiritual life; but he is spiritual
who apprehends his spiritual standing apart from, and in contradistinction to, his fleshly standing; who knows what it is to be
a new creature in Christ Jesus, and understands all the duties,
privileges, and responsibilities of that relationship.   In strong
contrast stand the Churches of Rome, and of Geneva or Scotland: in the former, the value of the sacraments and the
dignity of the priesthood are fully appreciated, and the mighty
power of the priests, as the instruments of God for constituting
the creatures of bread and wine to be indeed the flesh and blood
of the Son of God; in the latter, having cast off episcopal
succession, they have of necessity no priests, for priests must be
constituted by those who are higher than themselves; neither is
baptism received as God's instrument of making men disciples
of Christ, which act is attributed to the speech of the preacher,

whereby the office of the teacher is made to nullify the sacrament: neither are the spirits of men fed at all with the flesh and blood of Christ, although bread and wine is eaten and drank in commemoration of the Saviour's death: neither are any spiritual, for none know and recognise the standing into which they are brought by the giving of the Holy Ghost at Pentecost, and of which they have been made partakers in baptism.

Thus, then, it is evident, that not only is it by the priesthood and the sacraments that Christ has preserved His Church, but that, since its unhappy divisions and guilt of schism, the spirituality of each portion has remained in proportion to the respect for " the observance of these things" which has been preserved, and not lost sight of; and let us now examine what has been the condition of the teaching in these various divisions.

The character and style of the ecclesiastical teacher must ever be analogous to the style of the age and of the country in which he lives. We must, therefore, take a more catholic view of the subject of teaching than we can attain to by a mere weighing of Augustine with Hooker, Jerome with Beveridge. The matters aimed at by all are the same; namely, to inculcate faith in the remission of sins through Christ's death which is past, and hope of a share in His eternal kingdom of blessedness which is to come.

The " observances" of the early Church taught both these things: the forms of worship set them forth visibly before the eyes of the people. So far as it can be gathered from the ancient liturgies which have come down to us, the order of worship appears to have consisted in the celebration of the Eucharist by the priests daily at midday, and by the people on the first day of every week. At the first and last hours of the day there were also services, and at nine and three o'clock. In these services the people were exhorted to confess their sins, not merely as children of Adam, but as baptized persons, who had therefore sinned more than others in offending against the grace of God; the confession of sin was made in the name of the body, which body began to be constituted at the day of Pentecost, and contains all the living and the dead who have been baptized into it from that day until the day of the final close of this dispensation: hence the confession was catholic, and the sin confessed was not only personal, but that of all mankind, and specially ·of all the baptized; sin original a d transmitted, as well as actual; this, after being confessed, was pronounced by the priest to be blotted out by the blood of the Lamb; and hence was avowed daily the great truth to which subsequent polemists gave the name of original sin, of justification by faith, of God's election, &c.

During the corruptions of the dark ages, when opulent ecclesiastics were as much warriors as priests, when temporal power was their object, and when they sought to attain it by violence, gorgeous ceremonies were added to the primitive worship, which, if they did not obliterate, at least obscured the meaning of the truth still remaining, although concealed in the ritual. Morality began to be taught in schools as a science after the manner of Aristotle, and men looked rather to the acuteness of intellectual gladiators than to the quiet instructions of the parochial pastors in order to be advanced in the precepts of Christian doctrine. Subtle disputations upon every possible and impossible subject abounded throughout Europe, and still fill the pages of every system of *Theologia moralis.* At length the great schism, which, under the name of reform, began to vex the Church, afforded a new fund of questions to ingenious men, wearied with the topics which had hitherto interested them. Nothing was too sacred to be handled : the mode of the subsistence of the persons in the ever-blessed Trinity, and the unfathomable attributes and being of the invisible God, were treated with the familiarity with which men discuss questions of botany or natural history. New ways of worshipping God were devised by men; the ceremonies signified nothing, and therefore taught nothing; and men were compelled to look to sermons without, and not to the rites transacted within the holy place, in order to learn the things that belonged to their everlasting peace. Hence it is that polemics came to be substituted for worship, and the whole life of Protestantism is not peace, but war. A quiet clergyman, doing his own duty in his own parish, who neither rails at his bishop nor meddles with the flocks of his neighbours, is supposed to be dead; and one who perpetually leaves his charge in order to declaim in self-constituted societies against ancient institutions, and against those who fill them, is extolled for his zeal, and reputed to be exuberant of spiritual life.

It is very much to be doubted whether, after deducting all that is personal, local, and sectarian, the amount of catholic truth which would remain in the writings of the most celebrated in every orthodox Church is not equal. The fervent language of Augustine would, indeed, be lost on the mass of the Scottish people, whilst the abstract acuteness of northern Protestants would find little sympathy in a glowing Spanish imagination. Each class and character of mind, as well as each age and nation, must have its writers and teachers particularly adapted to it; and catholic charity, or a mind enlarged with the capacity of Christ, will approve of, because able to appreciate the merits of, each in its way, just as in the schools of painting, the florid colouring of one may please more, without causing displeasure to another, who prefers a severer and more accurate master.

The fulfilment of the promise of the Lord to be with His Church, in teaching the things which He commanded to be taught, is necessarily contingent upon the fulfilment of that condition. The eleven themselves were not exempt from the temptations to teach other things than those which they were commissioned to teach; and St. Peter, having so taught, was withstood because he was to blame, *quia reprehensibilis erat*, and required to retract and renounce them. The history is a warning to all who should, in subsequent times, teach other than what the apostles taught, and all things which they have so taught they must repent of and abandon. Moreover, in such things they must be withstood, but only by those who have authority to do so.

The most remarkable instance of things now taught and practised in the Church, which are contrary to the instruction of Christ and contrary to the instruction of the apostles, is the refusal to give to the laity the wine in the Eucharist. This abuse of the power intrusted to the rulers of the Church is so flagrant, that it has ever worked, and is now working, more hostility, however smothered, to ecclesiastical authority, than any other circumstance. To this may be added, the carrying on of public worship in a language unknown to the people; the compelling of all priests, indiscriminately, to abjure marriage; and the forcing of all persons to be subject to any interrogatories, however disgusting and offensive to delicacy, which the priests please to put, under the pretext of perfect confession. A large

body of the Roman Catholic clergy in Germany is now determined to put an end to these abuses, even at the risk of incurring much evil of a different kind; and this body of clergy
in Germany is supported by many ecclesiastics in France and
Italy. The above-mentioned abuses all relate to matters of
discipline, and not of faith, and might be easily corrected,
if the Sovereign Pontiff should be induced, by timeous interference, to save the Church from the further evil of another
extensive schism. But it requires much intrepidity to break
through the impediments which official forms and prejudices
would place in his way. For the government of the Church at
Rome is as unwieldy a machinery as the government of Austria,
and the sovereign is often prevented by that which is well
termed the *bureaucratie*, which is, in other words, the *vis
inertiæ* of the clerks and subalterns, through whose hands all
details must pass before any decree can go forth as law, and
produce any active result. Above all, it behoves the Court of
Rome to see that the application of the truth, that Christ has
ever guided His Church, is carried too far in many things, and
that the time is come when it is indispensably necessary to
curtail this doctrine within its true and proper limits.

In the faith of that which is past, namely, in the facts of
Christ's death, of the two natures of His one person, and of the
efficacy of the satisfaction for the sins of men made upon the
cross, in short, in everything that is contained in the Apostles',
Nicene, and Anathasian creeds, all are agreed; but on the present condition of the Christian Church, and on the hopes of men
for the future, it is hard to say whether there exists more error
in one communion than in another, or whether there be not as
much unity of error in what respects the present and future, as
there is of truth in what respects the past.

If the Church had ever spoken upon the passages of Holy
Scripture to which I am about to direct the attention of the
reader, I should have abstained from presuming to bring forward
what must have been considered private judgment in contradistinction to the judgment of the Church : but as she has in no
council, nor by any authority, spoken upon them, it is permis-
sible to any one to refer to them in no hidden and mysterious
sense, but in the plain, obvious, and undoubted meaning of the
terms.

The apostle refers to the seasons (Acts xvii. 26, Rom. i. 20) as the proof of God's goodness which all may understand : God's instructions are upon a great scale obvious to all. The truths which He inculcates are not wrapt up in shreds of sentences, and recondite meanings of abstruse terms : above all, to the Christian Church does He speak plainly, in having given another church and another dispensation as its example and warning : the example of His dealing, both with a faithful people, whilst walking in His ways, and the warning of His conduct to them when apostate and departed from Him.

The Church is represented in the Apocalypse under the figure of a harlot ; as one who has committed fornication with the kings of the earth : that is, mystically as one who has sought for protection, and rank, and power, and influence, and support, from secular princes, and not trusted alone to spiritual means for her success. The Protestant sects charge this character upon the Church of Rome : writers in the communion of Rome (see Decameron with Pope Gregory's sixteenth letter to the author) charge that character, and apply the figure, with equal justice, to Protestantism. Both are equally right and equally wrong, for the figure does not apply to any part, but to the whole ; and the wonder and astonishment of the seer is, that she whom he had previously had represented to him as the pure and spotless bride, should now have come into this dishonourable and filthy condition. Now it is not a sect or part of the baptized which is the bride, but the whole body of the baptized : even if it were a part, still it is the same part that is seen in the latter condition that is seen in the first : if then it be the Roman Catholic Church which is the latter, it is also she that is the first ; and *vice versâ.* It is quite obvious that since the days of Constantine the union of Church and State has been productive of serious spiritual evils to the former, whatever may have been the effect upon the latter ; and the union has ended in these days in making the Church the perfect slave of the State. Everywhere she is oppressed, and everywhere she is tempted to join the ranks of those who are destroying all the thrones of Europe, in the hopes that she may then be liberated and free to do her own work. Thus the Abbé Lammenais is urging the pope to become a revolutionist ; the Romish priests in Ireland are agitating to the same end ; and some of the Oxford associates of Mr. Palmer are calling upon their friends to *look to the people* (see Church of the Fathers) for support, rather than to regal and aristocratical power.

Under this aspect of oppression the Church is represented as still in darkness and bondage, and to her, under this view, do the writings of the prophets apply, which allude to her as now in Egypt, although they were written many ages after the literal deliverance of the Jewish Church from that literal bondage. In like manner, when the whole body of the baptized is viewed catholically in its many divisions of Greek, Roman, Gallican, Anglican, Scottish, Swiss, &c. &c., presenting, instead of unity, the confusion and contradiction of many opinions, yet unable to deliver herself, and produce unity, peace, and harmony again, no term can describe her state but that of Babylon, distinguished for its want of unity in speech and confusion of tongues, and for its being the last place of captivity into which the Jewish Church was brought.

A catholic eye sees such to be the true condition of the whole of Christendom, whilst a sectarian eye can see only these conditions as applicable to its rival, and not to itself. Yet the Jewish Church was always dealt with as an unity: the true priests considered themselves as priests of the whole body of the circumcised, and offered sacrifices for the whole. After the unhappy division into the two and the ten tribes, the priests did not divide the sacrifices, but offered them for the entire nation, and not only for that part with which they happened to be connected. A memorable instance of this occurs in the case of the restoration of the two tribes out of Babylon under Ezra: so soon as they returned to Jerusalem he offered twelve oxen, one for each of the tribes, although only two were present and had returned with him, and ten had been carried away, as judged and sentenced idolaters, into an endless captivity more than two centuries before: still for these also did he offer as well as for those present, for he knew that all the circumcised were as one, being viewed as one in Abraham, to whom all the promises were made.

In like manner God will deal with the Christian Church as an unity, and the priests of the Christian Church are priests of the whole, and not of a part; just as baptism is into the body of Christ, and not into a sect or portion of that body, and every baptized person is as certainly responsible for all the terms of the Christian Covenant, and entitled to its privileges, as was every circumcised person to those of the Jewish covenant. So the Sacrament of the body of the Lord is not confined to the assembly in the midst of which the rite is celebrated, but it is offered for, and eaten for, the whole baptized world. In like manner the priests are priests of the One, Holy, Catholic Church, or they are no priests at all; and in this view of the subject I purposely abstain from discussing who are and who are not priests; who have been rightly consecrated, and who have taken upon themselves the office without due authority; who have been rightly or imperfectly baptized : as these topics would necessarily give a narrower limit to the view than that which I am now taking, and divert the attention of the reader from the matter more immediately in hand.

Thus it is also that the term "Apostasy," which signifies "falling from a standing," is the condition into which the Church as a whole falls, and not a condition into which one part falls, and into which another does not come. The two tribes vaunted themselves greatly that they had never become idolaters ; the Pharisees, who were the most religious people of that day, were proud that they were not deists like the Sadducees; yet the Lord spake more severe things against the Pharisees than against the Sadducees or the two idolatrous tribes. The standing of the Christian Church was to have God, through the Holy Ghost, ever residing in her, guiding her through her priesthood, and governing the baptized nations through anointed kings. The blessing of the people was to recognise God in His anointed kings and priests; worshipping the Invisible through the visible, but yet apart from and above it. The apostasy or antichrist consequently is the refusal to recognise Christ in these His ordinances, the rejecting of the bands of Christ in kings and priests: and St. John tells us that that spirit *qui solvit Christum* had begun to work in his time : whilst the Apostle Paul tells us that the lawless one, *ille iniquus, ὁ ἄνομος*, should be hindered from manifesting himself completely until the heavy arm of the secular power was taken off. For the power of the secular arm, which repressed rebellion against itself, would necessarily produce indirectly a submission to all other authority also, even if it had not directly lent its power to the Church to enforce its decrees: so that although the alliance of the Church with the State produced evil in one way, it produced good in another. But now the unbridled right of private judgment, which first was proclaimed at the time of the Reformation, has produced its natural effect, and no one will submit to another; and every one will be king and priest unto himself; and God is not recognised in His kings nor in His priests; and priesthood is treated as a mere trade; and kingship is considered a merely human form of government which the will and wisdom of men may change whenever they please: for that all power proceeds from below and not from above, from the mob and not from God.

This spirit of rejecting authority as an ordinance of God has now pervaded every portion of Christendom, and every rank in society. Kings and priests themselves are not exempt from it, because a moral, like a spiritual epidemic, affects all classes alike. This " speaking evil of dignities," " casting off the bands of Christ, the Anointed," is spoken of in Psalm ii., in St. Paul's Epistle to Timothy, in the Epistles of St. Jude and of St. Peter, as the condition of things in the last days: it is a state of things which no power that is now upon the earth, and no machinery at present in existence, have sufficient force to remedy; and it is a spirit which must be the last, because it is a spirit of destruction of everything, and of building and upholding of nothing. All mankind are more or less looking to a republic, to a state of freedom from restraint, both in civil and religious matters, totally unlike anything which has yet appeared in the world. It is avowed that the world, with all its institutions, whether of kingdoms or of churches, has been only in its infancy, and that now it is arriving at that maturity of wisdom which will enable it to chalk out new plans for itself, vastly superior to all that have been hitherto seen. They who know their duty are afraid of avowing true principles. The priests in France do not reclaim for God the houses and lands which have been sacrilegiously taken from them; and neither king dare claim, nor statesman inculcate, obedience as a duty to the vicegerent of God.

It is indeed questionable whether the Church ought ever to have received lands, but there can be no doubt about the necessity of its having buildings, and that these buildings having once been given to God cannot be desecrated to any secular purpose. The support of the priests was to arise from tithes; and the tenth of every man's income as much belongs to God as the seventh of his time; and the payment of the one and the observance of the other are matters of eternal obligation, having been established long before the institution of any church either Jewish or Christian. The successive developments of God's eternal and unchangeable purpose to bless His creatures in His kingdom to come, do not abrogate anything that has been previously established. Circumcision is not abrogated to the Jews now; and every Jew who is ignorant of the hope revealed in Christ, and who knows nothing but that given to Abraham, is bound to be circumcised. The Christian ought not to be circumcised, because he has a higher and a better hope, and is partaker of better promises, of which he received the earnest in baptism; he renounces the Jewish hope and the Jewish rite, not because that is not good in its way, and in its kind, but because, having one better and infinitely superior, he stands in no need of the old.

Christians have ever laboured to convert the Jews, but they have laboured in a bad spirit and in a bad way. The denunciations of God are continued and great against all who shall misuse that people, and it is the greatest sin for which Christendom is answerable, and that which above all has need to be confessed and repented of, if we would avert God's impending and already begun judgments upon all ecclesiastic and civil institutions. In the malignity of the rage which urged the priests of past ages to torture, mangle, and burn the Jews alive, and the laity to plunder, rob, and insult them, Christians lost sight of the great truth for which the Jews have been the only faithful witnesses for God upon the earth. Indeed, although the constancy of the faith of Christians in all times amidst sufferings has been wonderful, that of the Jews, amidst the cruelties practised upon them by Christians, has not been less praiseworthy. Moreover, respecting the amount of testimony for the object of the Jewish hope, in comparison with that of the Christian, much more can be said in favour of the former than of the latter. The Fathers have taken frequent occasion to remark upon the extraordinary manner in which the two advents of Christ are mixed up in the views and writings of the prophets, in the same chapter and same verses, so that, as has been well remarked by some able critics, the Jewish prophets evidently saw the two advents as one, and perceived nothing of the condition and history of the Church which was to intervene between them. The Jews themselves, since the commencement of the Christian era, have been forced by circumstances into the idea that there are two Messiahs, the one a suffering martyr, and the other a triumphant prince. It is certain that if the passages of the Holy Scriptures, which speak of the sufferings and humiliation of Messiah were to be arranged on one side, and those which speak of His glory and dominion were to be arranged on the other, the latter would predominate tenfold. The Jews bear witness unto the death for the latter, and deny that the former have been fulfilled in the person of Jesus of Nazareth ; the Christians testify exclusively of the former, and have wholly lost sight of the latter. Thus the second advent of the Lord and Saviour has become no object of hope, but an object of terror : no idea is connected with it, even amongst the saints, but the coming of an executioner. The Christian Church has fallen lower than the ancient heathen, for they looked forward to a glorified world to come. The only hope ever held forth to the world, was from the establishment of the kingdom of God upon it. To the Thessalonians Paul writes: *Expectare Filium ejus de cœlis. . . . Nonne vos ante Dominum nostrum Jesum Christum estis (spes nostra) in adventu ejus? . . . Ad confirmanda corda vestra sine querela in sanctitate ante Deum et Patrem nostrum in adventu Domini nostri Jesu Christi cum omnibus sanctis ejus. . . . Hoc enim vobis dicimus in verbo Domini, quia nos qui vivimus, qui residui sumus in adventum Domini, non præveniemus eos qui dormierunt. Quoniam ipse Dominus, in jussu et in voce Archangeli, et in tuba Dei, descendet de cœlo, et mortui qui in Christo sunt resurgent primi : deinde nos qui vivimus, qui relinquimur, simul rapiemur cum illis in nubibus obviam Christo in aere, et sic semper cum Domino erimus. Itaque consolamini invicem in verbis istis.* Where is now the man who ever consoles himself, or any one else, with the hope of the coming of the Lord ? The Romanists scare it away with the cry of millenarianism, as the Protestant sectaries do the sacraments with the cry of popery. If the Lord were this day to come down and touch the earth, where is the church, or sect, or even individual, who would give Him welcome? where is the bride who would cry, "Come, Lord Jesus!" No: Satan has deceived the whole world, and made all men believe that his triumph, which is death, is the coming of the Lord: and thus, as no one believes or looks forward to translation without seeing death at His coming, neither does any one see the hopelessness of the present condition of the Church, but each sect is buckling on its armour for more deadly feud with its brother, as our' Lord foretold would ever be the case with those who said " the Lord delayeth His coming," *moram facit Dominus meus venire,* and Christians spend whatever religious energy they have, in beating their fellow-servants of their common Master.

Whilst the Roman Catholics are exerting themselves to draw over to their communion members from all other; whilst in some countries, such as England and Ireland, these exertions excite great opposition, and whilst societies are formed amongst Protestants to send books and emissaries to shake the faith of Roman Catholics in the things most surely believed amongst them; the attention of both parties is diverted from the real character of the evil which assails Christendom. Party warfare is ever more hot than national, sectarian more fierce than catholic. During the first years of the Reformation it was natural that the interests which pressed at the moment should absorb all other considerations; but now that matters are settled down into a fixed and determinate position, which no human power nor arguments can alter, it becomes the priests of the one Catholic Church to look to more important things than private, personal, local, individual, national or sectarian objects, and to enlarge their minds and spirits to the catholic purpose of God now about to be accomplished.

And there is ground to hope that out of the mass of the baptized a small remnant shall be gathered to bear witness, in the midst of all sects, and all churches, and all nations, who shall be prepared before their brethren for the harvest; for the harvest at the end of the age, *messis est consummatio sæculi,* consists not only of the general ingathering, but of a previous firstfruits: and even this previous firstfruits is preceded by a few green ears dried artificially before the full time, as may be seen in the second chapter of Leviticus, and in the passages in the Apocalypse which speak of these things. Moreover, it is declared in Isaiah i.

that if the Church will put away her sins, she shall receive absolution, and that her ordinances shall be restored to her as they were at the beginning, and that "afterwards she shall be called the faithful city," although she had "become a harlot," and although all "her silver had become as dross," and although she had "stained her hands with blood," so that her prayers, rites, and ceremonies, had all become an object of abomination, instead of an object pleasing to a holy God. And they who have faith in God's promises, and who will cry to Him to fulfil them, shall see these things accomplished; and they shall be prepared for His coming; and they shall be caught up "to meet Him in the air," according to the promises which He has so often given. But it is not my intention now to enter into this matter, because long extracts would be required from the Scriptures, together with reference to the writings of the Fathers, in order to show that nothing was inculcated but what was in harmony with the catholic faith.

The correction of abuses is not so easy a matter as they who are ignorant of these subjects commonly suppose. Many of the Roman Catholic clergy in Germany, and some in Italy, have been labouring at this object for many years. The sovereign Pontiff himself, both before and subsequent to his elevation to the holy see, has had it in contemplation to remedy many things, which good purpose, however, he has not been able to effect. The contrariety of opinions amongst the bishops of the Church of England would make any attempt at a unity, which is the first characteristic of the Church, and essential to its taking any step as a body, perfectly chimerical. Where, then, can we look for help, in such a miserable state of schism, but to God Himself, "from whom we have so deeply departed?" For He does hold the Christian priesthood responsible for the sins of the whole body of the baptized, and truly His judgments upon it are abroad on the earth. The wicked are the Lord's sword, and it is whetted and drawn for the slaughter of kings who have not blessed the people committed to their charge, and of priests who have not led the baptized in the ways of God; and neither throne nor altar in Christendom shall escape. God is just: it behoves us to recognise His justice; and laying our mouths in the dust before Him, cry, "Unclean, unclean!" The only part for those who are faithful is to cry and sigh for the abominations which are done in the Church: for the Lord has said, *Transi per mediam civitatem in medio Jerusalem; et signa thau super frontes virorum gementium et dolentium super cunctis abominationibus qui fiunt in medio ejus.* In these times specially He says to the priesthood, *Inter vestibulum et altare plorabunt sacerdotes ministri Domini, et dicent, Parce Domine, parce populo tuo, et ne des hæreditatem tuam in opprobrium, ut dominentur eis nationes.* This is our duty; remembering it is also written, *Diliges proximum tuum sicut teipsum; quod si invicem mordetis, et comeditis, videte ne ab invicem consumemini.* Thou shalt love thy neighbour as thyself: but if ye bite and devour one another, see that ye be not consumed one of another.

At the commencement of this dispensation was revealed the mystery of godliness, God manifest in the flesh; and now at the close of the same is revealed the mystery of iniquity, the lawlessness which refuses to recognise God in any institution amongst men, or to obey kings and priests as ministers of God, and as those in whom and by whom alone, as members of His body since the incarnation and giving of the Holy Ghost, He rules, blesses, and teaches men. Every public controversy encourages the spirit of private judgment, which is the spirit of lawlessness; and when Mr. Palmer publishes, he necessarily calls on the inferior clergy to sit in judgment on Bishop Wiseman, and, at the same time, calls on the laity of his own flock to sit in judgment on himself. Schism in the Church has produced, as a necessary consequence, the passing by every priest of the bounds of his own mission. A statement which might be useful in the hands of some, is detrimental when it falls into the hands of others, so that it is impossible for paper war to effect any good. Each has need of the support of his brother, for God is now calling His priesthood to account for all the idolatry, and all the division, as well as for all the immorality and ignorance of His ways that are found upon the earth. The priesthood was appointed to be the instructor, and the means of preventing these very evils; and if these evils are found, the priesthood has failed to effect this object, for which, amongst others, it was sent. But never can the miserable condition of the Church be mended by each division proclaiming the mote that is to be seen in the eye of the other, unmindful of the

beam that is in its own.   In order to heal others, the injunction
is to the physician first to heal himself; *ejice primum trabem
de oculo tuo, et tunc videbis ejicere festucam de oculo fratris
tui.*   It is in vain that the Church of Rome calls to the Church
of England to refuse the cup to the laity ; to conduct the worship
in an unknown tongue ; to command her priests to repudiate
their wives; to subject women to the disgusting details of the
confessional ; and to suffer the allegiance of the people to the
Queen to be contingent upon the word of a foreign bishop.   It
is equally vain for the Church of England to call upon Roman
Catholics to unite with a Church which has no government;
where the preachers are daily contradicting each other and the
standards of the Church with impunity ; and where every variety
of faith is known and avowed amongst the bishops themselves.
Nothing but an authority superior to both, such as a duly constituted œcumenical council, could possibly bring such discrepancies into union.   But each may cease from widening the
breach : and more than ever shall be now fulfilled the promise
of *beati pacifici, quia filii Dei vocabuntur.*   Blessed are the
peace-makers, for they shall be called the children of God.

REASONS

WHEREFORE

A CLERGYMAN OF THE CHURCH OF ENGLAND

SHOULD NOT BECOME

A ROMAN CATHOLIC

IN REPLY TO

REV. R. W. SIBTHORP

1842

REASONS

ETC.

Sir,

Since there is reason to suppose that many clergymen of the Church of England are in the same state of mind as that in which you were previous to the step which you have recently taken, it is an act of kindness " not to permit any of these, so far as in me lies, to conclude " your reasons " unanswerable."

In your letter you " give only some of the reasons, though confessedly such as have chief weight with you ; " and the following observations will be limited to such points as you have yourself adduced.

Whilst endeavouring to imitate the courtesy of your language, I pray you not to accuse me of holding you an offender in a word, if it be found necessary to analyse your expressions, in order to show the fallacy of the conclusion at which you arrive ; since it is requisite to do so, not so much for the sake of discovering your own meaning as for the sake of preventing others from being led away by similar incorrectness of expression, and possibly of ideas. It gives me great pleasure to find myself agreeing with you in testimony, from my own long and intimate acquaintance with Roman Catholics in almost every country in Europe, to " their apparent devotedness to religious duties, the supreme place which these seem to have in their regard ; the cheerfulness, yet earnestness of piety which mark the members of her communion." I too " have found little of these things among my Protestant acquaintance — my misfortune, doubtless, but so it is." Into the reasons of this I do not now enter, but come at once to the matter in hand.

In the very title of your pamphlet, there is at the best an ambiguity, and certainly, though perhaps not intentionally, an unfairness. You contrast the Anglican with the Catholic Church; you must know, and therefore it is the more to be regretted that you should have been unmindful that the clergy of the Church of England declare, with as perfect sincerity as the clergy of any other communion, their belief in One, Holy, Catholic, and Apostolic Church: and hence the true question is, not whether any one should leave a sect, in order that he may become Catholic, a point which no one would deny, but whether he should cease to be Anglican and become Roman; whether, the word Catholic being a common term, and therefore put out of the question on both sides, he should leave one part or section of that same common Catholic. And your mode of putting the question is doubly unfair, since the Romanists themselves lay great stress upon the addition of the word Roman to the passage in the apostles' Creed, and never in any similar dispute omit to maintain the necessary qualification of the word Catholic by that of Roman.

Whilst engaged in a series of lectures on the Levitical law and institutions (p. 5), you state that you were led to review the Jewish economy in the Church under the Old Testament dispensation. You found that they were typical of good things to come, from Israel, viewed as a nation, down to the smallest ornaments of the tabernacle, respecting which Jehovah had said, "See that thou make all things according to the pattern which was showed thee in the mount." You then endeavoured to find the accomplishment of these things in Christendom. You rejected the "frequent assertion (p. 7), that all the shadows of the old law were accomplished in Christ alone, and that it is unnecessary to look for the body or substance of them elsewhere, as hastily and ignorantly made." You show in a few words the folly of the mystics, who talk of a spiritual church without an organised body, and properly conclude that "the Church under the Old Testament was a close type of the Church under the New, and not of her Divine Head only." Proceeding under this guide, you found that the Church of the Old Testament was "a compact united body really and visibly united in all its parts; combining a number of provincial and locally separate portions in one religious nation or people; combining them in a most strict, perfect, and evident unity of faith, of worship, of laws, of discipline, of religious ordinances, and even of minute ceremonies—no variety permitted,—no departure from the oneness demanded being sanctioned in any individual. Such was the ancient Israel; and if typical of the Church, such should be the Israel of God under the New Testament." (p. 8.)

Chronology is one of the eyes of history: but this organ of light is wanting in your statement. The Jewish economy, as a whole, existed from the Exodus to the death of our Lord, that is, during a period of fifteen hundred years. Your statement is not a true description of the condition of the Jewish Church at any period, save during the lifetime of Moses and perhaps of Joshua, and of a short time under Solomon. Your theory is true both of the Jewish and of the Christian Churches; but if your statement be meant to be history, it is untrue. I admit your theory, but deny your fact: I consent to your theology, but deny your history; and of this we shall see more hereafter.

You proceed. " At the head of this body, nation, or church, was one supreme dignitary, of priestly order, invested by God with singular prerogatives, ruling in perpetual succession over Israel, until the Lord should come; in his person, offices and residence, a centre of unity to the whole nation far and near, — a representative on earth of the Divine High Priest in heaven. There was a regularly organised and consecrated tribe of two degrees, priests and Levites, &c. From the Dan to the Beer-sheba of that land, which was this ancient church's appointed heritage, there was not an Israelite that lived not in fealty and submission to the supremacy of the one high priest," &c.

Surely you have drawn largely upon your imagination for your facts, and been so dazzled by the beauty of the vision of that which God designed, as to be unable to perceive in the history the total failure of its accomplishment. " At the head of this body, nation, or church," was no "supreme dignitary of priestly order," at its first establishment, but Moses, who was over and superior to Aaron the high priest. After forty years both these died, and no " supreme dignitary of the priestly order" assumed the command, guidance, or rule, but Joshua, Moses' minister and successor: which command he continued to exercise to the day of his death. After this, notwithstanding the Israelites had a high priest, they fell entirely away from what they had been formerly. The whole nation and church became a mass of confusion; there was no possibility of exercising " one religious rite in one harmonious agreement;" partial deliverers were raised up for them in one part, and then in another part; the nation was ruled by Judges, to whom Kings succeeded, because the people had become so fleshly, so unspiritual, that they could not bear the rulers which God had hitherto given them. But the worship was not as it had been at the first, and a temple differing in many particulars from the tabernacle in its proportions, form, materials, and furniture, was builded, not by the high priest, but by the king. Even on the dedication of this it was not the " one supreme dignitary of the priestly order " who sanctified the temple, offered the sacrifice, and blessed the people, but Solomon, who was no Levite. No sooner was Solomon dead, than five sixths of the people departed from the temple and worship. Of the two tribes which, not following the usurper, remained faithful to the legitimate line of their kings and to the temple, and who did not set up another altar for themselves, the kings and high priests departed so completely from God's ways, that He was obliged to send prophets to assume the command, and give directions both to the kings and to the high priests. At length they became so hardened that they would not listen even to the voice of prophecy; and the whole nation, the royal as well as the priestly tribe, and all the people, passed under the yoke of the heathen Romans.

Such is a plain unvarnished epitome of the history of the Jewish nation, and it completely contradicts the picture which you have given of it. That which you have described is no doubt that which Moses saw in the mount, save that you have left him out of the case altogether; and that which he saw was the pattern of the house which we are, but which pattern, constructed subsequently by him, as certainly never existed beyond the lifetime of Moses himself.

You, with this correct theory in your imagination, proceeded to search for its reality in the actual condition of Christendom; of course you found no resemblance to it in the sects which boast of schism, and you instituted a comparison between the churches of England and Rome; and you seem to have concluded, that because the reality and the antitype were not to be found in the former, they must necessarily be found in the latter.

There is no doubt but that the Christian Church has been warned by God in His written word, through the medium of symbolical things and acts, of snares into which she would not have fallen if she had given heed to the warning, but it is by taking heed to all, and not only to one or two, that she would be so delivered. The 10th chapter of the first Epistle to the Corinthians is an example of this, and many other passages in the epistles. In the same class of warnings is to be reckoned the book of the Revelation given to St. John. Now, whilst fully agreeing to everything which you allege against the sects, there are nevertheless certain characteristics given of an evil condition, in which the Church shall come, which cannot possibly apply to them. The kings of the earth have never committed fornication with dissenters and schismatics; the conventicles are not clothed in purple and scarlet; they do not forbid to marry; nor command to abstain from meats; the blood of all the martyrs from the beginning is not to be found in them. Of no Protestant sect can it be said that she is a mother of harlots, although she may be daughter. These things I only bring forward, in order to show that the way to arrive at truth in the matters in hand is not by a partial and insulated, but by a catholic and large examination and reconciliation of all that is written; not by seizing hold of one part and sacrificing all other parts to it. If a parallel exists between the condition of the Jewish Church and that of the Christian, the parallel must be reciprocal; and it is just as easy, and generally much more so, to trace the type after knowing the antitype, than to find the antitype from only knowing the type; and it is obvious, from the allusions to the histories, persons, and ceremonies of the Old Testament which are made by the writers of the New, that they could not have known the meaning of any type until the antitype had been brought out; according to the well-known aphorism, *veteri testamento novum latet, novo testamento vetus patet.* It must be as easy, at least, to find an instance in the Jewish Church of the actual condition of Christendom, as it is to find an instance of the actual condition of Christendom, in the typical Jewish Church. Where, then, can be found an instance of a part of the Jewish Church calling itself exclusively the Israel of God, and cutting off the rest of the circumcised from all the hopes and promises given to Abraham; denying the circumcision of all others, and refusing to allow them their share in the inheritance of the land? This is the parallel you have to show, and being unable to show this, you may rest assured that you are not competent to interpret the lesson that is taught to Christendom by the history of the Jews.   Circumcision alone defines the border of the Israel of God : baptism alone defines the border of the Church of God.   Let the truth be granted for the moment of everything which the Romanists in all ages have written, and said against all those who have differed from them ; still the faults of the separatists from Catholic unity are as dust in the balance in comparison with the separation of the ten tribes from the two.   Yet at no time, by the most violent follower of the law of Moses, were the ten tribes counted as not of Israel; and what is still more remarkable, one hundred and fifty years after they had gone into a place of unknown captivity, lost sight of by their brethren, and become more than idolaters, still, on the return of a part of the two tribes from captivity, did the high priest offer up twelve bullocks and twelve goats for the whole house of Israel; showing that he knew that every circumcised man was of the Israel into howsoever evil condition he had fallen, and setting an example of catholicity of principle and of practice truly worthy of imitation by the Catholic united Church, and which is violated in Christendom only by Romanists and close-communion Baptists.

Such a thing was never heard of amongst the circumcised as any part presuming to call itself the House of Israel to the exclusion of the rest; and amongst the typical warnings which ought to be noticed is that against those who should presume in after times to say, "The temple of the Lord are we."   Thus you had no right from the ancient Church to expect to find amongst the baptized one portion which should claim to itself all the privileges which are the birthright of all the baptized alike.   I now come to the other thing you sought for, which was an "impressive, magnificent, and significant ritual."

Magnificence is easily furnished by gold lace and wax tapers; impressiveness is given by other as well as by religious pageantry; therefore the whole merit of these depend upon the third quality, which is the significancy.   Hence it is that the modern mushroom sects which have sprung up since the Reformation have uniformly founded a form of worship without any ceremonies whatever; and rightly, because they are utterly ignorant of the import of all, and therefore to have set up a magnificent ritual could not have been impressive because it could not be significant, and they were better altogether without any. The things to be signified in the Jewish Church are not the things to be signified in the Christian Church : each thing in the Jewish Church has no doubt its corresponding thing in the Christian Church, but still very different from the former. In order to illustrate, by an example, what is meant, I take the three great feasts of the two Churches. First, the Passover, significant of the deliverance of the children of Abraham out of Egypt, and their first constitution as a nation, before they were builded into a Church, or had any place of worship or ritual prescribed to them ; secondly, the Feast of First-fruits, expressive of their taking possession of the promised land ; and, thirdly, the Feast of Ingathering, commemorative of their final rest from all their labours. In like manner, the Christian Church has its three great feasts, commemorative of the three great events which effect it ; first, the nativity of Jesus of Nazareth, which is the coming of Godhead into flesh ; secondly, the resurrection, which is redemption from death and the taking of man up to the right hand of God ; and, thirdly, Pentecost, or God the Holy Ghost descending in order permanently to dwell in men. I say nothing of the day of atonement and that of the crucifixion, because there is more of a unity between them, and the rite which taught the one might teach also the other. But in the case of the three times when all the males were enjoined to come up to Jerusalem, and in the three great events appertaining to the Christian Church, it is obvious that the rites which taught the one could not be expressive of the other ; and whilst it is not to be doubted that every part of the worship of the Christian Church is, or ought to be, as significant as every part of the Jewish, and that it is as impossible to change it from what God would have it, and did originally appoint it, or rather intend it, it is no less equally clear that the imitation of the Jewish worship by the Church of Rome is most clumsy, and is almost exclusively confined to its garments of brocade and cloth of gold, and its candles and its incense, without having the remotest intention of inculcating anything by the same.

It is very well for you to think you have found a correspondence with the Jewish Church in the Church of Rome, because you have only in it a magnificent ritual : but this is your private opinion; you must renounce it if you remain in the Romish communion, for she founds her ritual upon no such doctrine. She rejects all example of the Jewish Church as stoutly as the most spiritualising evangelical mystic in England; she as resolutely maintains that all the Jewish economy is done away in the death of Christ, as any of the persons whose errors on this head you have so well pointed out.

I might refer you for proofs of this to the answer to Ben Ezra, by Vidal, published at Rome in 1834; but I quote a still stronger confirmation in the following extract from the last edition of Murtene, *De Antiquis Ecclesiæ ritibus*: for if there be a part of the service of the Christian Church which is more strictly in accordance with the Jewish than another, it is the division of hours and time of day at which the rites are celebrated: yet even these are not referred to Jewish practices at all, but are declared to be expressive of New Testament transactions: Jam vero si quis quærat quibus potissimum de causis adducti fuerint Apostoli virique apostolici, ut has ad precandum Deum horas potiusquam alias elegerint; respondemus mysticis præsertim rationibus motos fuisse: haud recolenda nimirum præcipua Dei beneficia istis horis hominibus aut jam collata, aut aliquando conferenda, uti videre est in variis sanctorum Patrum testimoniis a nobis jam adductis, Cypriani maxime Chrysostomi, ac constitutionibus Arabicis Concilii Nicæni; alias profert Cardinalis Bona in Tractatu de Divina Psalmodia, capite secundo, quas fuse, nec minus pietate quam eruditione plenas, suo more prosequitur. Has non sine fructu consulent legentque pii lectores, nobis interim eas referre contentis, quas ad conservandam divinæ redemptionis memoriam. Glossa in cap. 1, de celebratione Nicissarum his versiculis comprehendit:

> Hæc sunt septenis propter quæ psallimus horis.
> Matutina legat Christum, qui crimina purgat.
> Prima replet sputis.   Causam dat tertia mortis.
> Sexta cruci nectit.   Latus ejus nona bipertit.
> Vespera deponit.   Tumulo completa reponit.

Vol. ii. p. 2.

You would find it no easy task to trace the ceremonies of Rome back to those of Aaron (a position which you have been content with asserting, but have not stopped to prove) with as much clearness and precision as Middleton, in his letter from Rome, has shown many of them to have arisen from heathenism.

Not, however, that I assent to the inference which that writer has drawn from the facts which he has so plainly stated.

If you sought, and you have sought rightly, that every part of the service of the Christian Church should be expressive, you should have sought first for the things to be expressed : and, secondly, gone to the New Testament for instruction in the mode of expressing them. If you had done this, you would have found that the Church of England is greatly superior in this particular to any other sect in Christendom. You remember that the ordinances of ministry which the Lord ordained for the edification of His Church until it should arrive at the fulness of the stature of a perfect man in Christ, were apostles, prophets, evangelists, and pastors ; whilst is to be taken, combined with this, that there are but three orders of ministers, bishops, priests, and deacons. In the service of the Church of England you have an example of these four ministries : you have at the commencement of the service, an exhortation which, from the nature of the evangelist's work, as described by St. Paul, and from the examples of its performance given in the Acts, we find to be the style of address appropriate to the evangelist. Next follows the confession of the sin to which the address of the evangelist has exhorted all present, by the pastor and confessor on behalf of the people, by him into whose ears may have been poured in secret the burdens which oppress the consciences of different members of the flock. Next follows the absolution pronounced by the bishop, if he be present, or, if not, by him who rules next in the Church, fulfilling by apostolic authority the commission given to them of loosing the oppressed of their burdens, absolving them from their sins, and opening the door of reconciliation to their heavenly Father. Then follows the reading of the Scriptures from a distinct place appropriated to the same, anciently called the Ambo, marked in all ancient cathedrals by its usual outward ornament of an eagle, the emblem of St. John the last of the prophets, and so indicating that this is a prophetic office; and in the Romish Church she has still further preserved a witness against herself, in that, by causing a candle to be held to him who reads, she testifies that without other light than that which is in the mind of the reader, he cannot understand that which he reads. Thus have you in the Church of England a service significant of Christian verity per-

formed according to the four ministries given at the beginning
in the New Testament, whilst in the Romish Church you have
nothing but an imitation of dresses taken from the Jews: and
which of the two churches, in the mere fact of observances, is
most in harmony with the test which you have yourself adduced,
judge you.

You say, that when you "looked back to the ancient Church.
of England as first founded by St. Augustine, you found the
most entire agreement, and an actual, visible, professed oneness
with that apostolical Church (of Rome) as it had existed for
six centuries" (p. 13). I have already shown that you have
superficially read the history of the Jewish nation; and it now
appears that you have as superficial an acquaintance with the
ecclesiastical history of Christendom. In the first place, Christianity was not planted in England by Augustine. When he
came, he found the shores of St. George's Channel covered with
Christians: he commanded those of Banchor to acknowledge
the supremacy of the Bishop of Rome, claimed but shortly
before for the first time by Gregory; they alleged that they
never had heard of such a supremacy, and refused to submit to
it, and soon afterwards the king put them to death. I will not
dwell upon this point longer now, but only remark what an
extraordinary transaction this is for you to qualify as an example
of entire agreement between Augustine and the Church as it
had existed previously.

You say, p. 15, "Every well-established kingdom has its
central government, acting both as its effective executive, and as
that which combines together, regulates and invigorates all the
subordinate authorities, and otherwise scattered parts. It cannot exist without it, no more than the body without a heart," &c.
&c. You add a great deal more on the same subject, stated in
very forcible language, all of which is undeniable; and you conclude the paragraph (p. 6) with these words: "Be it remembered that the fundamental principle of Protestantism under
every form rejects it; setting at defiance the testimony of
nature, reason, fact, antiquity, and scripture. I fear, because
that combined testimony forbids the anarchy and self-will on
which its results are based, and not solely, as is sometimes
adduced, because the power of rule had been abused."

This reasoning is complete against anything of the name of
Protestant being exclusively the Church of Christ, but it does

not prove even negatively that the Church of Rome is. It is a matter for thankfulness to God, and of wonder also, that the Church of England has existed as a system so long without any discipline whatever; and that it has done so, has been by means of the secular rank and advantages which its ministers have enjoyed, and not by any ecclesiastical power resident in itself. But as the grand matter in hand is the question whether the sect of Rome is, amongst the body of the baptized, alone the Church of Christ, and not the merits or demerits of Protestants, we will leave this point, and proceed to the remainder of your argument.

Your next position is the assertion of the supremacy of St. Peter. Now it is unquestionable that Peter had a supremacy, if by the word supremacy you mean something distinguishing him from the rest of the apostles; but if you mean by it, as the Papists do, that he was of a higher rank than the other eleven, that he was their superior as a bishop is the superior over his priests, then there is not sufficient proof to be derived from the passages of Scripture which you bring in support of your position, and there is abundant proof to be brought from other Scriptures to negative your position. Your argument, however, is, that St. Peter was as superior to the other apostles as Aaron was to the rest of the priests; you say that the supremacy given to him of holding the keys which opened or shut the kingdom of heaven, was no more shared with the other apostles, because the same declaration is made subsequently to them, than the claim of St. John to be the beloved disciple is shared by the other apostles being also beloved apostles. The argument is unsound, because it does not treat of things of equal kinds; no one ever supposed that being the beloved disciple constituted an order in the Christian hierarchy; but you are maintaining that the words spoken to Peter placed him in a higher rank than his brethren in the ministry. Your simile of the High Priest means this or nothing. Moreover, your argument is, that unity of government must reside in one individual; that, therefore, one apostle must have been over the rest. Furthermore, you declare that (p. 18) " when he died, to whom the special promise and charge had been given, another took his position to occupy it, and continue the Church in her divinely-arranged and existing constitution, if haply the Lord should come in his days. And thus another and another have successively filled the chair of St. Peter for eighteen hundred years, on the same warrant, with the same design, and the same darkness as to the time of the Lord's return."

I have admitted that St. Peter had a distinction above the other eleven : that St. John had another : the only fact before us is the nature of that distinction.   You assert that it was a superiority of rank beyond that of other apostles, and you have in this last argument gone a step further, and declared that St. Peter's successor after his death, though no apostle, had the same rank higher than apostles which his predecessors enjoyed. St. Peter was put to death during the lifetime of some of the other apostles.   St. John survived him several years : and you assert that he who succeeded to Peter was the head of the Church, as Peter had been even during the lifetime of the other apostles : in short, the table of precedence in the christian hierarchy, after the death of Peter stood thus : 1. Peter's successor ; 2. Apostles, &c.   Now in the passage which I have already quoted from the Epistle to the Ephesians, and in the parallel passage in that to the Corinthians, we are told that the order set in the Church was first, apostles; secondly, prophets, &c.   You say, first Peter's successor, secondly, apostles.   Your theory is cut up root and branch by these two passages from the Epistles; it is altogether untenable.   You seem to be aware of the weakness of your position, for, in p. 19, you say, " It was not to be expected that in the second and third centuries there would be found, even had there been public documents, that clear perception of the designed succession to St. Peter which the ninth and tenth centuries present."   This might have been a just inference if there were not plain and direct passages, which assert the very opposite to that which you are maintaining ; but as there are such passages, the opinions of all men in the ninth and tenth centuries are rather proofs of the extent of divergence from God's ways of governing the Church to which men then had arrived, than proofs of what those ways were a thousand years before.   Silence might be interpreted any way, and therefore you had as good a right to use it on your side as an opponent on his side ; but unfortunately for the argument, there was not silence in the ages previous to the ninth and tenth centuries; supremacy was claimed, yet not on that score, and supremacy was denied ; and neither party adduced the case of Peter as an argument in favour of either.

Even if the High Priest of the Jews were a type of the Pope, it would not bear out and justify the conduct of the latter. The High Priest never dreamed of altering a stitch of a curtain, nor a peg to a board of the tabernacle which Moses had constructed: he never presumed to make the slightest alteration in the age, sex, or manner of offering any sacrifice; he never ventured to change, in the smallest particular, the rites and ceremonies which had been established. But the Pope has made perpetual changes; even the Church of England declares that a church has power to decree rites and ceremonies, whilst no such power was given to the Jewish; and the Pope has altered them continually. Moreover, in the power, right, and authority hereby claimed for the Pope, you have gone beyond what was the doctrine of the Church in England in the days of Augustine, St. Thomas, and Warham; and of the Church in Ireland, France, and Germany: the Church in these countries contended that the Pope alone had not the power ascribed to him, but that it was the Pope presiding in, and pronouncing the decree of an Œcumenical council that was this absolute and infallible declarer of the mind of God, which you declare him to be without any council, and sitting in his own private room. The Spaniards and Italians, indeed, hold the doctrine which you do, and they corroborate their doctrine from matters of fact, in these days, in a very curious manner. They say that the present condition of the Church proves that the infallible guidance resides in the Pope alone, and not in the Pope in council, since there has been no council for three hundred years; if, therefore, they say, the direction be only in the Pope and council, the Church has been without guidance for three hundred years: but the Lord's promise is, that he would be always with his Church, *ergo*, he has been with the Pope alone. Thus, with the ordinary excess of young zeal, you have run into the utmost extreme of Ultramontanism, and far beyond the doctrine of the Roman Catholics in Britain. How the French bishops would now decide cannot be said, because, since the Revolution of July, they seem to have abandoned all their former opinions respecting the rights of the Gallican Church, and in order to separate themselves more and more from the revolutionary liberals, have thrown themselves, with complete abandonment, into the arms of the court of Rome.

There is an expression concerning St. Peter's supremacy,

which shows you to have paid but very little attention to its nature. You say, " No other apostle shared his office in the formation of the Church " (p. 17). What church ? You will reply, the Christian Church. Well, but St. Paul informs us that the ministry to the circumcision was committed to Peter, and the ministry to the Gentiles committed to him. He paid no deference to Peter : if Peter were bishop of Rome, Paul had the impertinence to write a letter to Peter's flock, without making the smallest reference to Peter, or taking the slightest notice of him in it. If the Romans were Jews, then the Romanists might have some colour for pretending that Peter had presided over the converts there ; but if they were not, it is clear that Peter was not their spiritual father, but Paul.

But you are wrong in supposing that the supremacy of St. Peter was a truth in the bud, which did not expand and blow before the ninth and tenth centuries. A supremacy of one bishop over all other bishops was claimed in the third, to which I have already shortly referred ; and how was it met ? Was it by saying to him that claimed it, you are wrong because you are not the successor of Peter in Rome ? No, it was met by the bishops of Rome themselves declaring for many years that, for any bishop to assume the title of universal bishop, to assume a supremacy over his brother bishops, was to assume the character of Antichrist. The Patriarchs of Constantinople were the first to claim a jurisdiction *in* other patriarchates, and subsequently *over* other patriarchates ; this their undue assumption was re- sisted by the bishops of Rome ; until at length Gregory the Great assumed it himself, and his partisans then began to invent the figment of Peter having been bishop of Rome. It is a very remarkable circumstance that Peter is the only apostle whose authority was disputed by his brethren, he himself rebuked, and compelled to retract his errors. God, who has caused all holy Scripture to be written for our learning, has no doubt caused this history to be recorded, that we may have the incontestable authority of His written word for saying that the assertion of any such supremacy of Peter beyond other apostles, as that claimed by the Papists for him, is false. There is probably not to be found in the history of the world a lie so flagrant as this of the Romish priests ; a lie so capable of ample refutation by reference to history ; a lie for which so little positive can be brought to its support, and for which so much positive history can be brought to disprove; a lie proclaimed with such loud unblushing impudence in the face of an inquiring and intelligent universe: it is pre-eminently THE LIE of the Papacy.

The power given to Peter was given also to the rest of the apostles. The same power was exercised by Paul, to whom no such power was given by word from the Lord. Paul bound, for he gave over to Satan. Paul loosed, for he said, "I forgive in the person of Christ." It is, therefore, plain that the power belonged to the apostolic office, by whomsoever exercised, and not to Peter exclusively. The question of Peter's ever having been at Rome rests on a very faint tradition: a much better authenticated tradition speaks of Paul having been in Britain. Now Peter was not an apostle to the Gentiles, although, indeed, he was made the instrument of admitting the first Gentiles into the Church. The lineal descent from the apostles, therefore, to the bishops of the Church in England, must be from Paul and not from Peter, under both views of the case. It would seem that the original question agitated between the two apostles was continued still between the two churches, for Paul declares himself to be not a whit behind the very chiefest of the Jewish apostles, withstood Peter to the face, and blamed him, and refused all deference to him whatever in points of authority.

You proceed, in page 19, to speak of the advantages which the Papacy has been to the world, and truly the advantage has been great; but in the statement which you have made, there is nothing which is not equally true of the Greek Church. "It has guided the vessel of the Catholic Church over the agitated seas and heaving billows of eighteen hundred years of strife and tumult and warfare, and tribulation of every kind, presenting her yet a goodly vessel unwrecked, and cheeringly pursuing her onward appointed course. It has maintained holy order and discipline among her motley crew, assimilating them, though gathered from every tribe under heaven, in duties, hopes, trials, and joys; it has kept them one whom nature had divided, but grace again had united." The Greek Church has subsisted longer, and done the same.

In the condition into which the Church had come in the days of Gregory, the power claimed by the Bishop of Rome, reluctantly acquiesced in by some, but at length cordially embraced

by all, was made of God to be an instrument of great blessing
to the Church; and its advantages would be much more
apparent, were it not for two considerations; first, that as much
unity of doctrine and discipline has been preserved in the Greek
Church from Archangel to Persia, without any centre of unity,
unless the tyrannical usurpation of the emperors of Russia can
be so called; and, secondly, that the unity preserved in the
Romish Church is either an unity preserved by putting to death
all who disagree with the priests, or else it is not an unity either
of doctrine or of discipline, but simply of recognition of the
vicegerency of the Pope, as in the case of the united Greeks,
who retain all their peculiar tenets and practices, although considered in union with the Church of Rome.

This consideration suggests the only way in which an ecclesiastical union between any Protestant Churches and the see of
Rome would be possible; for the Pope for the sake of having
his supremacy acknowledged, would willingly forego, or modify,
or explain any tenets, as easily as he does those of the Greek
Church. But such union is impossible for two reasons: first,
because the Protestants do not feel the sin of schism which is
destroying them; and secondly, because the Papacy dare not
confess itself to have been in error in a single iota. These
things prevent that "first step towards the restoration of unity,
and to any effectual measures for remedying the disasters of
the sixteenth century, and placing the Christian family once
more in that position Christ left, and desires to find it " (p. 22).

P. 23. "The Church is a positive institution of Christ for
the diffusion and maintenance of his religion throughout the
whole earth, until his coming again. That religion is harmonious and immutable truth. There is *not one system or set
of truths for one age* or part of the world, and a *different one
for another.* Nor will there be another revelation of saving
truth. The Church, *as the Lord instituted it,* must be the
most wise and suitable appointment for the accomplishment of
His gracious purposes towards mankind by means of it. There
is not only all absence of proof that he either instituted or maintained *different forms of government and modes of worship,*
and a variety of discipline, but everything to warrant the certainty of a contrary conclusion; and every deviation, therefore,
from that government or form of His Church which He gave it,

and from that discipline and worship which He personally or by His apostles approved, *is a most presumptuous innovation*, and a daring disregard of the Divine will, and fraught with danger to the souls of men : for if saving truth be one, it is of consequence that all men be kept in one harmonious profession of it. Whatever has a clear and direct tendency to foster diversity of sentiment, or action, is hostile to the unity of the Spirit. And it is evident that difference of worship and church discipline, as it is called, is destructive of the bond of peace, and so affects the unity of the Spirit, &c." You further proceed to show the folly, as well as hypocrisy, of the Protestant sects which talk of unity of *fundamentals*, whilst they are not agreed on what are or are not fundamentals. In this and all similar statements, you are clear and irrefragable in your exposure of the actual condition of all Protestant sects ; but you then jump to the conclusion that, because the Protestant sects are in error, the Romish sect must hold the truth. A more accurate statement of the type of the Jewish Church would have shown you that its apostasy did not consist in one part remaining orthodox whilst the others were idolaters : the two tribes who might best have pretended to that character were they who crucified the Lord of Glory ; were they who were declared by the prophet, under the names Aholah and Aholibah, to be worse than their brethren who had altogether become idolaters ; the Jews who would have no dealings with the Samaritans were they who were denounced as worthy of more judgment than the cities of the plain. The system of government for the Church was not by a universal bishop, but by apostles, prophets, evangelists, and pastors. The system of government for a see was by a bishop with four-and-twenty priests (presbyters), canons, or prebends, under and around him, with his subordinate deacons, helps, &c. &c. Such a thing was never heard, nor dreamt of, in the Christian Church in the first ages, as of one bishop assuming jurisdiction within the see of another bishop, still less of his assuming jurisdiction over another bishop himself: and there is *not one system or set of truths for one age, and another for another;* and to have introduced such a novel *mode of government* is a *most presumptuous innovation,* which novel mode of government and presumption is more flagrant in the Papacy than elsewhere.

You assert that "Rome and Ephesus, Corinth and Philippi, Sardis and Philadelphia, were distinct churches only as to their locality — their members differing, indeed in degree of piety and of consistency of profession; but the same in every point of doctrine, discipline, and worship. They had one and the same baptism, altar, apostolic rule, episcopacy, ordained ministry, and communion with St. Peter, while he lived, and his successors in Rome after his death." The bishops of these places were united, indeed, under Peter, as one of the apostles, but less under him than under Paul, who was as specially the apostle of the Gentiles as Peter was of the Jews, and not under him at all save as an apostle — not under him at all as bishop of Rome, even if he ever held that see. "Ecclesiastical history annihilates altogether the supposition that in the primitive church existed various differing denominations, some having sacraments, some none; some government by bishops, some rejecting episcopacy; some having a form of worship, some abhorring it: some baptizing infants, some refusing to baptize them. There is not a shadow of ground for such an idea: it is absolutely incompatible with the admission of the truth of ecclesiastical history." Perfectly true: and it is as absolutely incompatible with the admission of the truth of ecclesiastical history, that some churches were under apostles, and some under bishops of other sees, for each bishop was confined to his own see, and had no jurisdiction beyond it; or that any one bishop was subject to another, or that the apostles who survived Peter were subject to Peter's successor; which is your assertion.

It is certainly true, as the Oxford divines assert, that the Church of England is such as the branch which Augustine planted, with this single difference, that it no longer recognises the supremacy of the bishop of Rome over the bishops of England: you say that on account of this difference, St. Augustine and Dr. Howley cannot be of the same mind; and therefore the church now cannot be the same church that it was then. Your statement lies open to many objections; first, the church does not stand in the opinions of Augustine and Dr. Howley, but in the priesthood and the sacraments: if Dr. Howley have as clear a descent from the apostles as St. Augustine had, he has the same authority to administer the sacraments as Augustine had, whether the bishop of Rome likes him to do so or not. Some

ignorant or dishonest papists have pretended that the genealogy
of the priesthood in the English bishops is not correct: the
more learned and more honest amongst them say that, waving
the question of the succession, still they had no mission; but
surely if they who consecrated them had a right to consecrate
them, they had an equal right to give them mission. But the
most serious defect in your argument is the convenient *petitio
principii* that St. Augustine is of one mind with the Bishop of
Rome now. For example, would St. Augustine contend at present that the Bishop of Rome has a right to absolve the Queen's
subjects from their allegiance? that kings do not hold their
authority *jure divino* as completely as the bishops hold their
authority; but that they hold their crowns at the will of the
Bishop of Rome? Now, if St. Augustine would not admit this
he would be excommunicated by the present bishop of Rome;
and if he did, Dr. Howley would be perfectly right in saying,
that, so far as his influence extends, the Bishop of Rome should
have no power or means of employing emissaries to preach such
doctrines within the realm of England. How far it might be
right to deal with it by excommunication is another question,
since it is rather a matter for the Queen's consideration: and
she would do no more than a bare act of precautionary self-pre-
servation to banish out of her kingdom all persons who should
attempt to weaken the allegiance of her subjects towards her,
by inculcating any such opinions. Your words are loose and
equivocal; you say, "While St. Augustine, St. Thomas, and
Archbishop Warham would require me to profess a hearty allegiance to the see of Rome, *in matters spiritual and ecclesiastical,* as divinely constituted to rule and consecrate the *kingdom*
of Christ on earth, Archbishop Howley would threaten me with
heavy penalties if I held the Bishop of Rome to have any jurisdiction at all in England, or any supremacy beyond his own
see." The allegiance in matters spiritual and ecclesiastical is
not the whole truth; it is in matters temporal that the chief
objection would lay with Dr. Howley, as a loyal subject and a
privy councillor. He is right, ecclesiastically, to object as much
to the interference of the Bishop of Rome with his see, as to that
of any other bishop; but he is equally right, temporally, to
object to any ecclesiastic, and above all any foreigner, interposing
between his sovereign and her subjects. To this interference,

St. Thomas and Archbishop Warham would have no objection; but whether St. Augustine would or not, is pure guessing. There is a looseness, or more than looseness, an error of expression, when you speak of Christ's *kingdom* being concentrated on earth under a bishop, or high priest of any kind, at Rome or anywhere else. If we refer to your typical nation, you will find that the nation, the kingdom, was never under the high priest, but under Moses, Joshua, the Judges, and the Kings. The assumption, therefore, of the kings of the earth being under the Bishop of Rome, is without any warrant, and directly contrary both to type and plain injunction. In the next place, although St. Thomas and Archbishop Warham were in error concerning the supremacy of the see of Rome, it does not follow that they would have agreed with the modern papists, who have gone the length, since the Council of Trent, of denying the evidence of their own senses, and declaring that there is no bodily presence of bread and wine in the Eucharist. This is your present faith; and it is extremely difficult to reason with any one who so puts his reason in abeyance, or rather extinguishes it altogether. Perhaps this paper is not paper; all its qualities are only accidents, and do not make its real substance after all: it may be a table, or a chair; the ink may be milk, for colour also is an accident. Yet this is the absurdity of absurdities, which is the real test of a papist. You may believe the real presence of the flesh and blood of Christ to be in the consecrated elements, or not, as you please; if you are not willing to declare that you believe the *modus operandi* of its presence there to be by a total withdrawing of the substance of bread and wine, although your senses of sight, taste, and smell, tell you that it is bread and wine; if you believe that there is any bread also there, you are a heretic. Now, as a man who willingly and advisedly breaks his back, makes himself unfit to exercise any function of his body, so does a man who adopts such an absurdity as this render himself mentally unfit for the exercise of his reason, or of any faculty of his intellect whatever.

These two points might be alone sufficient to make any clergyman of the Church of England refuse to join the Papacy. The ordinances of the Church were not given to destroy and annihilate, but to regulate and direct all the gifts which he had

previous to the existence of these ordinances. Priests were not
given to be masters and tyrants over thrones, which existed
before priests were ever heard of; nor to teach people not to
believe their senses, which were also given before priests. I
might run through almost the whole detail of the popish discipline, and show that instead of being a kind and loving
mother, to foster, cherish, mature, and bring into healthy exercise the faculties, she has been a cruel and tyrannical step-
mother, to crush, weigh down, and destroy the children of God ;
but I have deemed it more advisable to limit myself to such
points as you yourself adduce, and therefore I must not travel
out of the record.

There is another point in the Eucharist, which you state so
loosely as to leave entirely in the back-ground the real difficulty,
namely, where you speak of it in p. 40: "Every instructed
Catholic knows and believes it to be the proper doctrine of the
mass, that therein is a propitiatory application of the sacrifice
of Christ for the benefit of the quick and dead." This is, no
doubt, the true doctrine of the Eucharist, but it is not the
doctrine of the Romish mass. The Romanist does not eat bread,
he eats nothing but Christ Himself; and the refusal of the cup
to the laity is justified upon the ground that if the smallest
morsel of the wafer be taken, the whole of Christ is taken —
flesh, blood, soul, and divinity is eaten: *that this is really
Christ dying over again.* I know perfectly well all that you
can bring forward in support of your position, and I know also,
notwithstanding all the assertions of unity, the real disagreement
that can be shown upon this, and upon all the other sacraments,
upon the authority of the Pope, the immaculacy of the blessed
Virgin, and every other fraction of Romanism ; but if I bring
forward clear passages which prove that you have kept back or
not stated the most material part of that which the Romish
church teaches on this point, I have arrived at my Q. E. D. In
the *Theologia Moralis* of Liguori, lib. vi. tract. iii. you may
read, 305 — *Quæs: hic I. In quo consistat essentia sacrificii
missæ? Magna hæc est questio inter D. D. Plures enim adsunt sententiæ.* PRIMA *sententia dicit consistere in sola sumptione; quia in illa tantum reperitur destructio sive immolatio
victimæ; et ita tenent P. A. M. etc. etc.* SECUNDA *sententia
dicit consistere in oblatione, cum sacrificium nihil aliud sit*

quam oblatio ; ita A. G. E. etc. etc.   TERTIA sententia commu-
nior docet consistere in sola consecratione ; et ita tenent, etc. etc.
Ratio, quia in consecratione omnia adsunt requisita ad sa-
crificium, nempe oblatio quæ jam fit in actu exercito prout
Christus quoque tum in carne, tum in cruce non verbis, sed
facto Deo Patri se obtulit ; adest etiam DESTRUCTIO *seu im-*
molatio VICTIMÆ, *dum vi verborum jam corpus a sanguine*
Christi separatur.   Hæc sententia est quidam valde proba-
bilis et communis ; sed probabilior mihi videtur QUARTA *sen-*
tentia quam tenent Bell. etc. etc.   Hæc sententia dicit essentiam
eucharistæ consistere partialiter in consecratione et partialiter
in sumptione ; in consecratione enim ponitur victima, et in
sumptione consumitur.   Ratio, quia verum et reale sacrificium
veram requirit et REALEM DESTRUCTIONEM *rei oblatæ, quæ non*
habetur, nisi per sumptionem sacerdotis qua DESTRUITUR SACRA-
MENTALIS ESSENTIA CHRISTI.   *Nec obstat dicere, quod in conse-*
cratione jam habeatur mors mystica, et in tantum non habetur
MORS REALIS, *in quantum propter naturalem concomitantium,*
nequunt Christi sanguis et anima a corpore separari.   Nam
respondetur, quod si concomitantia illa naturalis IMPEDIAT
mortem, impediat etiam sacrificium, quod sine verâ ac reali
destructione non consumitur.   It is lamentable to find, after
all that has been said and written upon this blessed sacrament,
how far behind even the writers of the Romish communion are
in the true doctrine and real understanding of this wonderful
mystery of the unbloody sacrifice ; and how completely, by their
clumsy and fleshly attempts to honour it, they have taken all
mystery out of it, and lowered it into a mere useless working
of a miracle, like the changing of water into wine at the marriage
of Cana in Galilee ; so that the teaching of the Romish priests
is as wide of the truth on the one side, as that of the miserable
sectarians is on the other, who merely eat a supper in commemoration of a departed friend.   This is not the place to inquire
into the source of these errors and discrepancies in that system
which alone claims to itself the characteristic of unity ; but I
know that the discrepancy works profitably to the priests in
practice ; to one who in ordinary circumstances communicates,
and is resolved to keep possession of his common sense, they
will talk only of its *propitiatory application* of the merits of
Him who was dead and is alive for evermore ; but to a poor

broken-hearted widow weeping over the death of a husband, or a son, they will declare that his soul is enduring the pains of fire, the duration of which it is in her power to shorten by the offering of masses, for the saying of which they are to receive five francs each, wrung out of her harassed and terrified affections.

I cannot silently let the charge of change be affixed upon the Church of England, by which it is attempted to be inferred that she is no Christian Church, because she is not now as she was in the apostolic times, and in the days of St. Augustine, St. Thomas, and Warham. The Romish Church is equally, by the same reasoning, not the Christian Church: she did not in the beginning assert that she was not to be obedient to secular princes, but that secular princes were to be obedient to her; she did not teach that paying a priest to eat the Lord's Supper would deliver a dead individual from any punishment his sins had deserved, nor maintain that, in the blessed sacrament of the Eucharist, neither bread nor wine was present; she did not hold that it was necessary for all the priests to be unmarried; she did not enjoin that her services should be performed in a language unknown to her children; she did not refuse to give the wine of the Eucharist to all except the officiating priest; she did not debar the faithful from the free perusal of the word of God; she did not proclaim war upon, and extermination of, her erring children, nor urge on the civil authorities to burn them alive; she was not at the beginning ruled by a bishop presuming to call himself of higher rank than all the apostles, except Peter; she had not added to the canon of Scripture books unknown and unrecognised by the apostles, and declared them of equal authority with the words of the Lord Jesus Christ; she had not for money granted liberty to contract incestuous marriages; she had not demanded thirty thousand pounds for the canonisation of a saint *; she had not sanctioned an immoral code of action, such as Pascal has shown from the writings of the Jesuits. By these things it is seen that (p. 33) the unity of Rome is no

---

* An Italian nobleman who had been nearly ruined by the fees exacted by the priests at Rome for canonising one of his ancestors, called his sons together, and told them to be very good men, and to be very obedient to the Church, but to stop short of that extreme degree of perfection necessary to be declared a saint; for if there were any more saints made in the family, it would be utterly ruined in this world, whatever additional interest it might have in the next.

longer such an unity "as all the chief figures used in the New
Testament to set it forth; suppose, for instance, that of a vine,
a household, a family, a temple, a bride.   If the Church of Rome
from the day of Pentecost to the death of St. John, (allowing
for practical corruptions and abuses, which even in the apostolic
age had begun to prevail in different local or provincial
churches,) was a sound member of the mystical body of the
Lord — of his visible Church — the modern *Roman* establishment is an unsound one: and if the latter be sound in her
present doctrinal tenets, and her 'assertion' of the supremacy
of the pretended 'see of St. Peter,' the *Romish* Church is to be
regarded as most unsound."

P. 37. Having satisfied yourself that it was God's will in the
Jewish church that the high priest should be the head ruler of
the nation, although he never was so at any one moment, but
had always Moses or Moses's successor, Joshua, over him, and at
last the kings, you became likewise satisfied upon an equal
error, which is, that a bishop, and not an apostle, was the instrument appointed of God for the government of the Church universal; and having adopted these two fundamental errors, which
are the basis of all your reasonings, and all your acts, you then
proceeded to change your sect.   "I was once pressed with this
principle, that a person was bound to remain in that church in
which the providence of God had placed him, by his birth,
baptism, and calling into the ministry."   That which is by the
law of the land established, you passed over with the silent contempt with which every Popish and schismatic radical treats
such considerations; and proceeded to testify your abhorrence
of the Protestant principle of self-guidance, by rejecting the
counsel and authority of your diocesan, who was over you in the
Lord.   "But I do not understand the words *that Church in
which, &c.,* nor how there cannot be properly more than one
church; and if the providence of God has not placed me within
her, the express command of God requires me to give up all
consideration, and join her.   The principle referred to, assumes
what is to be proved."   You have spoken very properly of
the senseless ravings at Exeter Hall, and of the Reformation
Societies; yet, here again you have adopted their favourite
text: they say Popery is Babylon, and the command of God is
clear, to come out of her: you say all churches but that of Rome

are Babylon, and the command is clear to come out of them. You are never accurate in your use of the word Church : there is truly but one Church, which is the body of Christ, just as there is but one Jewish church: circumcision marks the one, and baptism defines the other : but it is nevertheless correct to call all congregations of baptized persons, meeting for the avowed worship of God in Christ, as churches; because St. Paul calls the assemblage of baptized Corinthians a church, although they were rejecting him, did subsequently reject St. John, were full of error and all uncleanness, both carnal and spiritual. Let us suppose the condition of the churches of Corinth and Ephesus, after the death of the apostles, both left under the guidance of their respective bishops, and that errors had crept into both: the angry disputants in each would call the other Babylon, and enjoin their opponents to quit their mother church, and join themselves to them. But what would have been gained by such a measure ? would any have been a bit less in a city of confusion by such a step ?

It sounds very fine and very disinterested to avow the " giving up of all considerations," and the taking up of the cross and following of Christ, which is the usual salvo that every schismatic makes to himself, who turns his back upon his spiritual mother, insults its ministers, quarrels with his old friends, and adopts a new set; but, instead of being an act of spiritual courage, it is, in many instances, one of moral cowardice; and in all one of spiritual delusion. Duty can only be performed in that state of life in which it has pleased God to call us. If God has given to any one light upon or insight into His ways, beyond what is vouchsafed to those around him, that light has been communicated, not for his own advantage, nor for the puffing up of himself with the conscious possession of greater wisdom than his neighbours, but for the purpose of imparting it in such a manner, and in such a measure, that it may prove not an apple of discord, but a fruit of grateful refreshment, to his fellow-travellers. If this light be upon the errors in doctrine and practice of the body to which he belongs, it is his duty to bear his share of the common burden, and not selfishly to throw it off his own shoulders, and leave others to struggle with, and under it, as they best may. The eyes of many of the Romish priests in Germany have been for a long period open to four

great abuses in the Papacy, which they are struggling hard to
get amended; these are the conducting of the worship of God
in a language unknown to the people; the compulsory celibacy
of the clergy; the indecent questions in auricular confession; and
the refusal of the cup to the laity in the blessed Eucharist.   The
Protestants all around have often urged them to leave the communion of the Church of Rome, which they with greater wisdom
have refused to do.   Had you seen, as you plainly do, the too-cer-
tain speedy dissolution of the Church of England from her want of
discipline, and want of unity amongst her bishops, the part of a
faithful and loving son would have been to have mourned over the
evil, shared her danger, and laboured to avert it.   If your testimony had been rejected; your loving remonstrances turned
to your reproach; your zeal misunderstood; and your praiseworthy efforts blamed : your witnessing martyrdom would have
proved a seed, the fruits of which should assuredly have been
reaped, though you might have never lived to taste the blessing :
yet your good work would not have gone unrewarded, and you
would have been recompensed in the kingdom of the Just One.
But to turn round and rail against her who gave you spiritual
birth, and who has nourished you hitherto to your present
stature, to uncover the nakedness of your mother, and draw
down the curse upon yourself which accompanies those who do
such things; to join with a band which prevents your continuing your undivided allegiance to your sovereign, and will suffer
you to give only an obedience contingent upon the will of a
foreign priest, — is neither the conduct of a wise man, of a
sound theologian, nor of a good citizen : and therefore it is
that I earnestly hope no clergyman of the Church of England
will be seduced from their duty to follow your example.   In
order to become a Papist, you have acted upon the most ultra-
Protestant maxim, and have chosen your own pastor, and your
own church.   You have erected yourself into a judge of both
churches upon spiritual matters: but where did you derive
the discernment necessary for such a purpose ?   You know that
the natural man discerneth not things which can only be spi-
ritually discerned; that had you been a heathen or a Jew, you
were incompetent to form a judgment upon the matter; that all
the points which you have discussed would have been as absolutely unintelligible to you, as a subtle question in English

grammar would be to a Chinese who did not know the language. You must, therefore, have been born of the Spirit; you must have had spiritual sight, a spiritual knowledge; and you can have received such only through the sacrament ordained for giving spiritual life, administered to you by a priest ordained in the church of England. Your conduct, therefore, belies your doctrine; you leave the Church, because she is no church; whilst the only possibility of your doing so arises from the fact that she is a church.

I have much, very much more that I could add, not only from the books, but from a personal knowledge of the practical working of Popery in most of the countries in Europe; but will not say more at present. In the panegyric which you pass upon it, from p. 45 to the end of your pamphlet, the ground of your approbation is personal, selfish, and uncatholic. It is what any close-communion Baptist or Wesleyan might say for his own sect. The end contemplated by you is purely your personal salvation, your personal holiness, your personal privileges, your personal feelings, your personal interests: self first, self middle, and self end. This may be a sufficient motive to account for a journey from England to Rome; for a change from Anglican to Roman: but Catholicism is a higher region than sectarianism. To be a Catholic, should be something more than this, something more than is every sectarian in Christendom, Romish, Anglican, Genevan, &c. Not one expression of a thought more large than the sect of Rome, has escaped you.

To be really Catholic, it is necessary to recognise the unity of the Church: to remember that it is by baptism men become united to it, partakers of its privileges, and liable to its penalties. It is this whole Christendom which constitutes the Israel of God; it is this whole Christendom that has become one great Babylon; it is this whole Christendom that has fallen from its original standing, so that it presents nothing now to the world of the unity it ought; nothing but a mass of quarrelling, contradictory sects, living in enmity with each other, and not in brotherly love; and all under pretence of zeal for truth. No one can essentially mend his condition by flying from one sect to another. The only thing that is possible, and which shall be productive of good, and not of evil, is, first to know the condition, and then to feel the sin of it: to look fearlessly at the extent of it, and learn how impossible it is for God to accomplish His purpose of delivering the world from the dominion of sin and misery, by the Church in her present condition; and then cry to God Himself to come to the help of His redeemed; not for their merits, but for His own glory's sake, and for the accomplishment of His own most gracious determined purposes of mercy towards man.

You are now to be rebaptized. The priests may quibble as they please, and say that your baptism, not having been rightly administered, is therefore invalid; or that although the books of the Church of England may be sound on the point, still that there is no discipline in the church to enforce what they enjoin; that a large body, called evangelicals, never mean to administer regeneration by that ordinance, but impute to their own sermons the power which God gives to baptism alone; that you may have been baptized by one of these licensed heretics, who, with a treachery unparalleled in the Christian Church, still hold rank and receive emoluments in it; and that, therefore, you are not regenerated; yet you know that you have been regenerated; and, therefore, for you to be now baptized, is for you to become an Anabaptist, as well as a Papist. Next, you did in ordination take upon yourself responsibilities from which no power on earth can absolve you; as surely as a baptized man cannot become a Jew; as surely as a Mahometan cannot become a heathen,— so surely cannot he who has been ordained become a layman; or a bishop sink back, and become a simple priest. God holds the civil sovereigns responsible for the peaceable government, freedom from evil, liberties, and happiness of the people under them; and God holds the priests responsible for the truth, ignorance, vice, superstition, and infidelity of the flocks committed to their charge. The English were committed to you; you voluntarily bound yourself to teach the doctrines enjoined in the rubric of the Church of England, and from this vow there is no power on this earth to absolve you. You will reply now, that the Church has all power; but it is a false assumption of the priests: the Church has no power to absolve subjects from allegiance to their rulers: it has no power, as the Papacy itself admits, to dissolve marriages; it has no power to decree incest to be lawful; it has no power to absolve priests from their ordination vows. That vow is upon you, and to

answer for your fulfilment of it must you appear at the judgment-seat of Christ, who is as much Lord of the English as of
the Roman vineyard. It is Protestantism alone, that Protestantism which you profess to abjure, which has taught and
teaches that which you practise, namely, that men can take up
and lay down responsibilities as they please; be priests or not,
bishops or not, worship in this or another way, be subject or
not, as each one's several fancy, which he calls his conscience,
shall please to dictate. As a clergyman of the Church of
England must you be judged.

In leaving the body of the clergy of the Church of England,
and joining the body of the clergy of the Church of Rome, you
have dissevered yourself from a corps which, compared with
that of any other church, is superior upon every point in which
comparison can be instituted. I am not saying that the English
nation is in the state in which it ought to be; that there has
not been remissness, and supineness to the spiritual necessities of those confided to the care of the pastor; but in proportion as the clergy have been efficient and have been listened to,
in that proportion are the people enlightened and moral. In
the Papacy, in proportion as the priests have been most unim-
peded in their course, there are the people most idolatrous, superstitious, and depraved. You have joined yourself now to a band
which has shed more human blood, to please its God, than ever did
the priests of Moloch or Juggernaut: a band which has trampled
on the rights of all mankind as a religious duty; not in moments
of political convulsion merely, when violent men of all sects have
given way to their personal antipathies, but a band which has
made it a rule of action, at all times and in all places, to destroy
by sword and by burning alive all who resisted its usurpations:
a band that has laboured at the extermination of all who protested against its vices, even in the meekest manner, as in the
case of Scipio de Ricci, as well as the miserable Jews in Spain,
and Portugal, and Italy: to a band which has ever excited the
hostility of the civil power by false accusations of political insubordination against those who were only disobedient to the
unwarrantable assumptions of arrogant priests, as in France,
and as there is every reason for believing they are at this
moment doing in Savoy: to a band which continues to this hour
its hard-hearted immolations of young females in convents, and

whilst obliged to skulk from public execration into obscure corners, in order to perform the deeds which will not bear the light, do still exercise in remote places cruelties, under pretence of ecclesiastical discipline, perpetrated by the priests of no other sect. These acts are the fleshly mockeries of the power of the keys, the proofs that the Church is no longer able to deliver over to Satan, and, therefore, did the priests, instead of confessing that this power is departed from her, set up the power of the stake and of the faggot, the thumbscrew and flagellations, in its stead. Should you be cajoled into the belief that the fatherly care of your new superiors will never in these days be exercised over you in some such a manner, be warned, nevertheless, how you trust yourself into any convent situated in a sequestered mountain, under pretext of enjoying a *retreat* for your soul's good; since, however that may fare, your bodily profit will be very different from what you anticipated, even if you be ever suffered to come out to tell the tale. And even if this be not so, the motto of the priesthood is *semper eadem;* all the iniquities of the priests, as a mass, — for I speak not of individuals, of Alexanders, of Johns, &c., I speak of the acts of the body,—all are assumed and maintained to be the very acts of God Himself by them : whatever the practices of the priests have been, they have never repented ; and contend, that if God has not been with them in these things, then has He suffered His Church to be without His guidance, contrary to His promise, which cannot fail. These are the things which, called by priests the exercising of a HOLY OFFICE, have aroused the indignation of all mankind, and whatever praiseworthy sufferings may have been endured by a few martyrs, they as a body, fully merited the vengeance they brought down upon themselves at the French Revolution. Husbands and fathers terribly requited the insults offered by priests in the confessional to wives and daughters. It is these things unrepented of, vindicated, palliated, or explained away, instead of being confessed, that force men in Popish countries into infidelity ; and unaccustomed to separate the precious from the vile, compelled to receive everything or nothing, they are urged to the fatal alternative of renouncing all belief in Christianity itself, and the rites of the Church, from proper disgust at the abominations which they see associated with it. While Protestants, in their indignation against the wicked cruelties of the Inquisition, attack, with indiscriminating zeal, that which is truly venerable, because found combined with them, the priests use the holy things with which the Romish Church abounds, as a shield to protect the abuses with which they have defiled her. Man's common sense can be insulted no longer, the day of reckoning of the priests is come, and every Papist will be carried away by the torrent of infidelity, who will not, or who cannot, separate the gold from the dross in his church.

It has been painful to be obliged to bring forward what has been here stated respecting the Roman Catholic Church, because she is commendable in many points of view: and it would be a more pleasing occupation to show her merits than her demerits. She contains every Christian verity of doctrine, if no of practice; an assertion which can be proved of no other division, sect, or department of the Church: the manifestation of the power and presence of the person of the Holy Ghost has been more frequently in her than anywhere else, and as it is even now said to be in the *Tre Mirabili Virgini* near Trent, of whom an account has been published in Italian by Riccardi, and in English by Lord Shrewsbury, although the priests have, of necessity, misunderstood, perverted, and misused that as every other spiritual advantage. Certainly the supremacy of a bishop over other bishops, and, above all, of a patriarch over bishops, is not so great an evil as the supremacy of lay sovereigns, writing liturgies, as in Germany, appointing to dioceses and to cures everywhere. Whatever evils may be in her, however truth may be buried, smothered, and concealed, there it still may be found; which is more than can be said for the greater part of the churches which have separated from her. The Church of Geneva scarcely holds one single sound doctrine; she denies all truth in the Trinity, Incarnation, Sacraments, and Orders. The German churches are in a very little better condition. The Church of Scotland is rent with contention within, whilst struggling for deliverance from oppression without. If any union is ever to be effected between the Church of Rome and those who have separated from her, it can only take place by pursuing a course the very opposite from that which you have followed in your pamphlet, the very opposite of that taken by all Reformation Societies. It must be by each party looking at

the faults in itself, and not at those of its rival; and looking at
the beauties of its rival, and not at its own. It is not the
Spirit of God that either caused or continues the schism, but
the spirit of the accuser of the brethren, the spirit of the railer,
the spirit of the fault-finder. What God is about to do now,
none can tell; for few can see what He is actually working
before their eyes; but there seems to be but one opinion, which
is that the end is come to all things as they now subsist; and
the fretful hurrying from sect to sect, will rather turn the mind
from the quiet consideration of and waiting for the events,
whatever they may be; for in this way have the mightiest transactions which God has wrought amongst men been unheeded, if
not despised, because their thoughts were preoccupied with their
own schemes and plans. The ordinances of God's house were
meant for defence and protection of all within, and especially of
such as are unable to conduct and defend themselves. If you
had not, in becoming a Papist, acted on the Protestant right of
private judgment, in all the lawlessness of its abuse, despising
the counsel of those over you in the Lord, you would have put
yourself under the guidance of your bishop, and God would
have given you, through him, rest and peace from your troubles.
Now, having abjured him, and taken another leader, at least
have faith in that step, and abide under the authority of the
spiritual pastor, whom you at present profess to believe to have
a better and fuller commission for your guidance.

ON

GOVERNMENT BY THE QUEEN

AND

ATTEMPTED GOVERNMENT FROM THE PEOPLE

———

L'Angleterre est de notre tems le seul pays de l'Europe où se rencontre une aristocratie qui sache et qui puisse se défendre. Si elle triomphe, le développement du principe démocratique est entravé dans tout le monde ; si elle succombe, il poursuit et précipite sa marche.

1842

GOVERNMENT BY THE QUEEN,

MANY years have passed since the king's advocate found it necessary to write against " the wicked instruments of rebellion, who endeavoured to poison the nation by persuading the people, firstly, that our monarchs derive their rights from them; secondly, that, therefore, since they derive their rights from the people, they are accountable to them for their administration, and consequently they may be suspended or deposed by them; thirdly, that the people may reform without them, and may rise in arms against them, if the monarch hinder them to reform."

The question is not abstract but practical, because men are now in action. Every one is meddling with, and trying to amend, the course of government. It is a case of absolute necessity that the people be directed where to look aright for the cause of the evil which they feel, and for the remedy which is to be applied; for on this alone depends the nature of the issue, whether in amendment and reform, or in increased misery.

Men are continually boasting that the age of delusion is at an end; that now all things are so well analysed, that nothing which will not bear accurate examination can stand. It is proposed, therefore, in accordance with so philosophic a spirit, to examine a few of the phrases which are in all mouths, and are the watchwords of the great body of those people who pride themselves in the name of Liberal. " My cousin Nicholas " asserts, that John Bull is particularly felicitous in misnomers: that when he calls a man " a soldier of fortune," he means a " soldier with no fortune; " the man who demands payment under a threat of arrest he terms a "Solicitor;" names a cinder heap in the suburbs, "Mount Pleasant;" and calls a well-known piece of water the "Serpentine River," because it is *not* a river, and because it is *not* serpentine. It would be well if there were no misnomers on more important subjects, for Bulwer says, "when the world has once got hold of a lie, it is astonishing how hard it is to get it out of the world."

The health of the body of any animal is not proportionate to the quantity of food which is swallowed, but to the quantity which is digested. A meagre, ill-nourished frame is often accompanied by a voracious appetite. A rickety, misshapen urchin is frequently produced by the ill-judged stuffings of a fond parent. It depends upon the use which is made of the food after it has been received, whether it conduces to the vigour or to the enervating of the frame.

It is the same with the mind. Men are now overgorged. They have no time for digestion, and they reflect less than ever, whilst they read more. Thus, there is a great amount of words, with very few ideas; and books which compel men to think (such, for example, as the admirable work of Mr. Carlyle on the French Revolution) are little read.

It is necessary to bear in mind that the generation which reaps is never the same generation that has sown. One sows, and another reaps. We who are alive now, are the victims of those who have gone before us. The forms of public institutions change insensibly like the form of our clothes, and of the furniture of our houses, without any one knowing by whom the change is effected. Yet still it is but forms which change; principles are unchangeable. A woollen coat is still a woollen coat, sofas are still sofas, however the form may have varied from the earliest times, and whatever new shapes they may have presented in the days of Cæsar, Louis XIV., or George IV.

But the form being an outward thing, and the principle an interior thing, men are content for the most part with considering what is obvious, and neglect the most important altogether. Lawyers who are in daily practice are fully employed in putting forth the machinery of the courts, and have no time to reflect on the principles which judges must bear in mind. Statesmen are wholly occupied in the details of business, and in managing to retain their offices, and have not leisure to consider how each measure may affect principles which perhaps they have never understood.

The Church has been made use of in latter times as an instrument by which secular government may be administered, as in former times kings and nobles were made use of by the priests as means by which they might obtain wealth and power. This mutual abuse of temporal and ecclesiastical government has at length produced a repugnance in men's minds to any union between the Church and the State, to any admixture of religion with politics. But religion is the principle of which politics are but the form: Church and State are but two actings of the one Supreme Governor of both. Yet whoever would judge of the events which took place in the sixteenth century, commonly jumbled together in the single word Reformation, only from the writings of the best secular historians of that period, such as Schiller (Der Dreissigjährige Krieg) or Fazzi (History of the Reformation in Geneva), would be inclined to believe that political motives worked that great change in Europe, and that religion was only secondarily concerned; whilst, on the other hand, all the ecclesiastical writers see nothing but the squabbles of priests about dogmas which few of them understood, which drove them on all sides into grievous acts of cruelty, and left them in a state of mutual wrath, which has continued down to the present day.

The root of all evil, as well as of all good, is in the Church, from which the fruit of political blessing or mischief is borne in the State. The principles of monarchy were sapped by the Protestant preachers, such as Calvin and Knox; the doctrines of insubordination and anarchy were broached with, if possible, more coarseness by the Roundheads, came into genuine operation at the French Revolution, and are now universally propagated by the evangelical Protestants throughout Europe, and by the Papists of Ireland. At length the statesmen have been carried away also, and anti-monarchical principles are cherished, and anti-monarchical doctrines are promulgated, by the counsellors and ministers of sovereigns. The reformers attacked the ignorance and profligacy of the priesthood, and the corruptions of the Church of Rome, by arguments which are of equal avail against all priests, and all courts. The application of these principles to civil governments was seen in Scotland, and ob-

served by Queen Elizabeth, but denied by the reformers for a
time, because they courted the protection of the temporal power,
and allied themselves with it as completely as the priests of
Rome had done before.   But a specimen of the true and legitimate effect of these doctrines was suffered to manifest itself in
the German Anabaptists of that time (the Chartists, and
Socialists, and Repealers of the sixteenth century); and the
conduct of Knox to his queen, the writings of Buchanan and
Milton, and the works of the Roundheads of England, left no
room to doubt of what are the legitimate fruits of the doctrines
which produced the Protestant Reformation.   I do not under-
value the amount of good which was in it, but into that subject
it is not my present purpose to enter.

The principles of religion were sapped by the Reformation :
not the principles of popery only, but the principles of all
religion.   Religion is a system of bindings of men to God and
to each other : it recognizes God in every institution of His
appointment; it recognizes God in families, ruling and blessing
the children, servants, and dependents, through the father and
master, and by no other means ; it recognizes God in nations,
ruling them by kings, and by no other means ; it recognizes God
in the Church, teaching the things concerning Himself, and concerning man's eternal condition, by ministers of various degrees
endowed with special gifts for that end, and by none other but
by them ; so that no priest can supply the place of the father in
the family, nor of the king in the State ; nor can any layman
supply the place of the priest as minister of the sacraments, or
as teacher in the Church.

It is most true that men have not reaped the benefit from
these institutions which they were appointed to produce; and
instead of families and nations being blessed and guided aright
by those who have been set over them, history is little but a
recital of the deeds of wickedness by which kings and priests
have perverted the gifts with the use of which they were intrusted.   The great error of those who perceive this state of
things, and there are few who do not, is, that in their endeavours
to remedy it they try to change the institutions, instead of
limiting their exertion to the amendment of the individuals who
fill them.   The institutions of families, of monarchies, and of a
Church, are as good now, and as well adapted to insure the

happiness of mankind, as they were the first day they severally issued out of the hands of the Omniscient and Omnipotent Author : and man has no right to set them aside, nor to change, nor to modify them in any way ; but Protestants have gone on devising new forms of worship, and new modes of instruction, by self-constituted teachers, and self-constituted confederacies and societies, till they have more and more departed from the instrumentality which God ordained at the first: and now, as a legitimate consequence, men are departing from monarchy in heart, and thinking that other forms for the government and conduct of nations are better adapted than that to secure the happiness of man.

As Protestantism was the name which irreligion took of old, Liberalism is the name which it gives itself now. Liberalism is the very opposite of religion ; it is a system of unloosing, of unbinding of all bonds whatever. Liberal opinions in politics signify the denial of all sacredness in obedience to kings or to other supremes ; and Paley, the great authority at Cambridge, thinks he has set that point for ever at rest by sneering at the divine right of constables : Liberalism maintains that the people's will is the *summa lex*, and ought to be obeyed, and that no force ought to be exercised over them : so that if the people revolt, and rise in insurrection, and the government repress the insurrection by firing upon the rioters, it is high treason against their majesty. Liberal opinions in religion mean that all sects are much upon a par, and that a bishop with his hereditary right from apostolic succession, and a schismatic mob-elected preacher, are equally " reverend brethren; " that all creeds are nearly equally good, for that all are problematical, and that therefore it is illiberal, narrow, bigoted, &c., to pronounce that any one is exclusively right, and all others erroneous. In short,' the most brief, and at the same time most accurate, definition of Liberalism is, that it is irreligion. *Antichristus ; qui solvit Christum.*

Liberalism has at length unsettled everything: it has destroyed the bonds of religion : it has obscured sound principles of government; it has produced a strange confusion in men's minds, so that words no longer express ideas accurately. The encyclopædists said of old, that which Talleyrand adopted, that words were made to disguise and not to express men's thoughts. The strangest notions are put forth throughout Europe under

the terms " constitution," " charter," " order," " national education," " government," &c. Effect is mistaken for cause; constitutions are supposed to be causes and not results, and men are
hunting for forms of government to be devised by their own
wits, in which the majority shall rule over the minority, and in
which there shall be neither oppression nor discontent.

All agree that the state of parties in England was never so
involved as at the present moment, and one of the ablest daily
journalists lately avowed that he did not know what the terms
Whig and Tory meant. In truth, these words have as little
signification as if the parties were to take the names of red and
white roses. It is therefore necessary to recal their real import
in times past.

Whigs are they who think that the aristocracy are the real
heads and governors of the State, and that it belongs to them to
restrain both king and people within due bounds: that the
word monarchy is improperly applied to the sovereignty of
England, because they also share the $\alpha\rho\chi\eta$, or rule; and they
effect this through the influence of their wealth and family
connexions, by which they command votes in both houses of
Parliament. Thus, from the days of Cromwell they have been
the abettors of all opposition to kingly power; they were the
enemies of the Stuarts, and the friends of the family of King
William and of the House of Hanover, so long as the latter
was contending with their legitimate kings; they were the
Orangemen of Ireland ; they became the opposers of the Hano-
verian dynasty so soon as it was firmly established without
rivals; they were the friends of the American rebellion; the
panegyrists of the French Revolution ; the palliators of the
treasons which broke out at various times during that period.
Not that the Whigs were democrats, or had any democratic
tendency, either in their political theories or in their personal
character ; but they would espouse any cause or party which
could lessen the power and influence of the Crown to such a
degree as that they should be enabled to domineer over it.

Tories are they who know that kings are the vicegerents of
God; that the ministers of state are responsible to their king
alone, and look only to him for approbation of their services;
that the houses of Parliament constitute the great national
council by which the king receives the necessary knowledge of

the wants of his people, and whose consent is requisite in order to render valid any law which is to be binding upon all; but that the king alone is the source of all executive power in every ramification. Thus the Tories were attached to their legitimate kings of the House of Stuart from the earliest times, and followed their fortunes alike in their fall as in their prosperity; and when that line became extinct in the time of George III., they served faithfully the House of Hanover which succeeded.

Thus no one but a Tory can be, in the largest, fullest, and most comprehensive sense of the word, religious, or a royalist: so that Toryism and monarchy stand and fall together. A liberal may have a very pious heart, full of benevolence and love to God and man, yet, for want of intelligence, may be doing his utmost to destroy everything which God has established.

In the present days the remains of Tories and Whigs can be discovered only by searchers for antiquities, like monuments amongst the ruins of castles and cathedrals. It is not easy to understand what a Conservative is; Whiggism has some sense in it, and is respectable; Radicalism is intelligible and detestable; but it is impossible to define Conservatism. So far as it can be made out, it seems to be a professing of Toryism, and a practising of Radicalism; a pretending to serve the Crown, but in reality looking to the favour of the people for its reward: its doctrines seem to be much like the instructions which are said to have been given by the Directors of the East India Company to Warren Hastings: "Be the father and oppressor of the people; be just and unjust, moderate and rapacious." It says, it wants to uphold monarchy, but it encourages things inconsistent with it; and it cannot do otherwise if it looks to the approbation of the people, and not exclusively to that of the crown. All parties are alike poisoned with liberalism more or less, which shows itself in one form in one party, and in another form in another. The Bill to admit Romanists into a Protestant legislature was carried by those who acknowledged it was wrong, but who still justified it through fear of civil war; thereby instructing the people that if they would clamour up to the verge of revolt, their demands should be complied with. The Roman Catholic peers have all taken an oath that they will do nothing to favour the overthrow of the Protestant Church; but the oath is not

valid in the judgment of the court of Rome, and is not binding
upon their consciences so far as they are Romanists; yet so far
as they fear God, and are honourable men, they will keep their
vows.   The reason why it is just for the Crown not to confide
in a Papist is, that a Papist can give to his king only a limited,
partial, and contingent allegiance.   The oaths which the Papists
in Parliament have taken, may be pronounced bad at any
moment by the court of Rome; and they are so far bad *ab
initio,* that they have never received the sanction of the Church;
and even if they had, they could be set aside, and they who had
taken them instructed to violate them : a doctrine founded upon
the power given to the Church to bind or loose in earth or
heaven.   It is not possible, therefore, for a king to place the
same well-grounded confidence in a Papist that he can in a
Protestant, for, the more the Popish minister is religious, the
more he will be ever ready to betray his master.   No oath nor
engagement of any Papist is worth anything, because the priests
of Rome have so annihilated his personal conscience and responsibility, that he is willing at all times to deny his own
senses, when the priests command him to do so.   Yet the party
which admitted them had great skill in government, and had
never before been deficient in moral energy and courage equal
to the occasion.   It is one thing, however, to have boldness in
battle, and another to be firm in council ; and it is easier for
some men to face a cannon than an impeachment.   But if
danger is to be incurred in these days, and risk to be run, it is
from the latter and not from the former that it will arise.
There are greater evils than civil war, great though it be.   The
dismemberment of the empire by the dissolution of the union
with Ireland is a greater evil than any civil war.   Fortunately,
as a mere question of expense, it would be more costly to keep
up such a standing army and navy as would be necessary to
preserve Ireland from becoming a province of America or France,
if it had a parliament on College Green, than it would be to rule
it by martial law; and therefore Ireland will be preserved.   But
agitation was taught by the Romish Relief Bill, and democratic
charlatanism has found out the means of making it a profitable
trade.

Two qualities must combine to make a perfect statesman ; the
one a thorough knowledge of principles towards the development

of which all his measures tend; the other, a readiness to do the best thing it is possible to do in the circumstances of each moment, as they arise. These qualities were combined in military matters in Napoleon and the Duke of Wellington; and in politics there have been examples of this happy combination in Lord Burghley, Lord Oxford, Lord Chatham, and Lord Wellesley in India. Most other ministers have had the latter talent only; and the latter talent only, whilst it is most obvious, as in Sir R. Walpole, Mr. Pitt, &c. &c., is almost sure to commit acts of irretrievable mischief. The former quality without the latter is merely inoperative; the abstraction of a political mystic; the latter is always in action, and often, whilst acting well for the moment, is laying the foundation of future ill. Thus by his mode of conducting the war, his extravagance, his contempt for aristocracy, his sacrificing the private estates of the king (a measure which ought immediately to be reversed), Mr. Pitt has been the author of as much embarrassment in the present days as he overcame in his own. To the same cause is to be attributed the indecent haste with which the revolutionary throne of Louis Philippe was fraternised by the advice of the ministers of William IV., a recognition from its haste scarcely less fatal to the monarchy of England than the Reform Bill itself. To have treated ultimately with a government *de facto* which had supplanted a government *de jure*, when we had marked by our slowness our disapprobation of the principles of its origin, was one thing; but to be the first, and within a very few hours of its birth, to rush into its arms contrary to the wise counsel of our ambassador at Paris, was uncalled for, unnecessary, and at the least indecent. Unfortunately it was worse: it was sympathising with anti-monarchical principles; it was pandering to the sordid mercantile spirit which overlooks all considerations in comparison with the gain of trade. France was a rich customer, and French people must be flattered in order to induce them to buy more cotton. The mischief done was to the throne of England as well as to the throne of France, for principles are universal, and not geographical. When the French Government countenanced the American rebels against George III., it had at least the plea that it was thereby weakening the power of an enemy, but in our act we had no such justification.

The admission of dissenting schismatics, avowedly the enemies of a hierarchy into the council of a sovereign, in which prelates holding their charges by apostolic succession sit, was an evil measure of the same nature as the admission of Romanists. For this the clergy clamoured as loudly as any others. In times when it was considered important that the king should be assured of the soundness of the religious principles of those whom he employed in high situations in the State, there was no means of ascertaining this except by the *employé* producing a certificate of his being in the communion of the Church. The clergy gave these certificates to many whom they knew not to be fit subjects. The infidels remonstrated against being compelled to participate in a ceremony to which they attached no importance, and which participation they declared was a violation of their consciences : the clergy were afraid to refuse the certificate, through fear of being prosecuted in the civil courts as the cause of preventing any one from receiving his due, and acted a very unworthy part in the whole matter : a Romanist priesthood would not have done so.

Liberalism, that is, laxity of religious principle, having effected these changes in the ecclesiastical part of the English constitution, effected shortly afterwards a corresponding change in the monarchical part. They who had made the former had no idea of the nature of the change they were working, and still less had their opponents. The lineal descendants of old Whigs, in their turn, when they came to reform the House of Commons, were equally unconscious that by that measure they were destroying the monarchy. The one admitted the enemies of the ecclesiastical, the other the enemies of the monarchical department of the State into the council of the essentially Protestant monarchy, and the necessary end of these measures must be, that neither the Church nor the monarchy can be unimpaired.

One of the present ministers, himself a member of the cabinet which prepared the Reform Bill, said to the late ministers in May, 1841, that "he feared that her Majesty's government, while seeking a popularity they did not find, were endeavouring to enrol on their banners the fatal revolutionary doctrines of number against station and property." This able statesman does not perceive that this is precisely what he himself did when he advocated the adoption of the Reform Bill. Another of the authors of the Reform Bill has told us that one portion of those who are discontented with it, consists of those "who looked upon the Reform Bill as the triumph of the liberal party, and the extinction of their adversaries:" and again, "in scanning the general scope of the Reform Bill with Lord Althorp, we always concluded that the Tory party were a party too deeply rooted in the property of the country to be thus destroyed; and that when the warmth of enthusiasm for reform should somewhat subside, they would have as fair a prospect as any party of obtaining a majority in the reformed House of Commons. We endeavoured to deprive the Tories of their undue power to overbear the opinion of the nation, not to proscribe them, should the national voice be raised in their favour." In another place Lord John Russell speaks of "the borough system" as that which was destroyed. Now the Whigs possessed a greater number of rotten boroughs than the Tories: therefore the Reform Bill did not give power to the Whigs at the expense of the Tories; but power to the liberal party at the expense of both: and it was Whiggism and not Toryism which was destroyed by it, save in so far as Toryism is identical with monarchy. Yet it is clear that the authors of the Reform Bill, so far from wishing to destroy the monarchy, could not be made to understand, by the splendid speeches of Lords Harrowby, Mansfield, and Lyndhurst, that their measures had any such tendency.

Prior to the late Reform Bill, the principle of the representation consisted in this, namely, that in one way or other, each and every class of persons in the kingdom was represented as a class, not as a mere aggregate of so many individuals. The way in which this was effected was susceptible of improvement, and the improvement of that way would have been a reform. But to change the system of representation of classes to a mere delegation of numbers, was not to reform a hitherto existing thing, but to make a new thing. The old principle was sound and monarchical, the new is false and republican. By the old, the highest aristocracy was represented, and many boroughs were originally called upon to send members to parliament expressly to give power to some great nobleman in their neighbourhood. In some places freeholders alone were represented; in others, every individual inhabitant householder; in others, freemen only of the particular place; in others, merchants only;

and the system was so far adequate to the end proposed, for the
feeling of landholders as a class is the same in one place as in
another, in Cornwall as in Yorkshire, in Scotland as in Ireland;
the feelings of merchants as a class are the same in Liverpool as
in Bristol and Dundee and Cork: the feelings of the lowest
orders are the same, whether in Westminster or in Nottingham.
Furthermore, some places were obliged to choose persons possessed of one amount and description of property, and some
another.   This system in all its parts being done away with,
there is none other that can have common sense in it but
universal suffrage.   It is quite absurd to fix a money qualification: a house of ten pounds a year value is as different in
London and in Thurso, in Kent and in Kerry, as it is possible
for things of the same name to be.   Moreover, the boundary
between ten pounds, and nine pounds nineteen and sixpence,
is so perfectly arbitrary, that no argument brought against it
can be resisted: and hence it is that the Radicals are not
satisfied, and never can be, until they obtain universal suffrage.

Every revolution of a kingdom has been effected by the kings
themselves.   In 1688, the king of England ran away and de-
serted his post: in 1789, the king of France would neither do
what was necessary to preserve his crown, his life, and his nobles,
nor would he suffer the queen, or any one else, to do it for him.
We know from the best authority that in 1830, by command of
his master, " the private secretary of the king wrote a letter to
the peers in opposition, requesting their absence from the House
of Lords, whilst a bill of the highest importance to the country
was passing through the various stages: a precedent of the
highest danger, which nothing but the respect felt by both
parties for the person of the sovereign could have induced them
to permit."   The error of Tory principles would naturally run
into viewing the will of the sovereign as superior to everything that would control it; and with this error the Whigs have
in all times, sometimes justly and sometimes unjustly, but invariably, charged them.   Liberalism, whilst professing whiggism,
did, in this instance, make use of the influence of the crown in
a manner unheard of since the days of the first Charles, and in
a manner confessed to be " far less justifiable than the creation
of peers " in sufficient numbers to insure the passing of the
measure.   It was truly said of King William by his brother

George IV., that he would at any time sacrifice his crown to obtain the huzza of a mob. The proper use for the king to have made of the opposition to the Reform Bill which he found in his hereditary councillors, was to have directed his ministers to remodel it. It has been proved above that it was not carried by the consent of the three estates of the realm: two of them overbore the third, the one by noise and brute violence, the other by wheedling and cajoling.

Few persons know the meaning of the word Commons. The ordinary use of it in popular harangues is, as if it signified the mob, or at least those who were not noble. Nothing can be more erroneous. The word, as is well observed by Sir James Lawrence, from whose work on the Nobility of British Gentry I take these observations, does not signify common people in contradistinction to the nobility, but signifies communities. The *communitas terræ*, or community of the kingdom, was anciently only the barons and tenants *in capite*. This *communitas terræ*, or *le commun de la terre*, was sometimes styled *tota nobilitas Angliæ*, or *universitas baronagii*, and signified the body of the nobility of the realm; *le corps de la noblesse*. On other occasions, the sheriff convoked the *communitas comitatûs*, or the body of freeholders, tenants *in capite*, in his county. At length, in 1265, the citizens were first summoned to parliament to represent the *communitates civitatum*, the bodies of citizens or corporations.

Communitas, like *Societas*, means people partaking the same rights, and was equally applicable to the most exalted and to the most humble classes; thus the assembly of the whole, being called the House of Commons, would not offend the dignity of the most illustrious. The assembly of the knights might possibly have been called the House of Commons (*communitates comitatum*), though the plebeians from the towns had never been summoned. At the coronation of Edward II., when the king was asked, " Do you promise to observe the laws and customs which the *community* of your kingdom shall have chosen ? " there were no citizens nor burgesses present. The community there was composed of mitred abbots, priors, earls, barons, great men, and the whole body of tenants *in capite*. A general assembly for the whole kingdom was always styled in the singular, *la communauté*, or *le commun*; but when different communities sent deputies, they were styled in the plural, *les communautés*, or *les communs*, or properly *les communes;* as is seen in Edward II., 1318: "Notre seigneur et roi par assent des prelâts, comtes, et barons, et communautés de son roiaume."

The Norman barons soon forgot the genders of words in French, and frequently made in two following lines the same word both masculine and feminine. But the French always translated the English House of Commons into *la chambre des communes* (communities), and not into *la chambre des communs* (common people). By a statute of Henry VI. none but gentlemen born, *generosus a nativitate,* were capable of sitting in parliament, and in 1460 an election was set aside because the person returned was not of gentle birth. Mr. Holland observes, that " as the knights of the shire corresponded to the inferior nobility of other feudal countries, we have less cause to be surprised that they belonged to the same branch of parliament as the barons, than at their subsequent intermixture with men so inferior in station as citizens and burgesses." A complete list of the sheriffs and knights of the shire would be one of the most distinguished *nobiliaires* in Europe.

The knights, in some respects, resembled the citizens; they appeared not on their own account, but as deputies of other tenants *in capite;* and therefore it was that they were assembled with the citizens, who were the deputies of other citizens; and though the knights condescended to sit under the same roof with citizens and burgesses, they were summoned to appear *gladio cincti,* and they always maintained the dignity of their order. The most trifling distinction suffices to destroy the idea of equality, and the distinction of the spur is still observed. The knights no longer appear in arms, but they alone may wear the spurs. Any other member who should approach the House with his spurs on is liable to be stopped by the usher, and must divest himself of this mark of knighthood.

This entire system had been wearing away until the Reform Bill put an end to it, and wrought a greater revolution than ever was effected in the history of any other country save France, for it transferred power from the higher to the lower classes. This matter is not raked up here for the purpose of making a charge against any one, but for the purpose of showing the real nature of the measure called Reform, because the Conservatives, as they call themselves, often talk as if it were now possible to carry on the government of the country as it was carried on before that measure was passed : at one moment calling it a revolution, and at the next reproaching the Queen's ministers with not acting as if the country had been unrevolutionised ; in which conduct there is neither patriotism nor common sense. If the government can be carried on as they fancy, then the Reform Bill was not a revolution ; if the Reform Bill was a revolution, then the government cannot be carried on in the same way that it formerly was. Let the intentions of different individuals have been what they may, the result is the same, and the avowed motives are only alluded to in order to corroborate the view here taken of the nature of the measure. The only true conservatism is to support any and every government ; for the question now is not between one or other government, but between any government or none. It is absurd to speak of the Reform Bill as a final measure ; it is merely an initiatory measure ; and nothing can stop its swallowing up the whole monarchy, but a series of measures which are not likely to be taken. The power of the House of Commons has increased, is increasing, and ought to be diminished. In former times the unruly tongues of members were restrained by the king's giving them occasional opportunities for reflection in the precincts of the Tower, and to claim liberty of speech was necessary for the due performance of their functions. A greater example of solemn mockery cannot be found on this earth than that of the Speaker appearing in these days at the bar of the House of Lords to request freedom for the speech of the members of his House. Whilst abolishing the ancient rights of others, it has clung pertinaciously to its own, now grown useless for any good, and productive only of evil ; and the House has gone the length of claiming the right to slander, and to propagate slander, against all its fellow-subjects, and exemption from the jurisdiction of the courts of law. " Hitherto no tyranny bu the tyranny of monarchies and aristocracies has been an object of alarm, and it is right that men should know of a worse tyranny than either, in order that they may feel the value of the corrective influence of monarchical and aristocratical institutions." If it be not controlled, the House of Commons will be a greater collective tyrant than a single dictator ; six hundred

licensed slanderers are worse than one Cromwell. I say with
the *Dict. Philosophique, Tyrannie pour tyrannie, j'aime
mieux être devoré par un gros lion que par douze cent rats
mes confrères.*

It must not be supposed that the Conservatives who opposed
the Reform Bill understood the real principles upon which it was
mischievous any better than they who promoted it, but they had
inherited certain maxims and phrases from the Tories which expressed the truth, so that when they brought these forward,
their adversaries could not answer them. For instance, the
Duke of Wellington continually inquired how, after the Reform
Bill was passed, *the king's government* could be carried on ?
The question fell powerless on the ears of the ministers, because
they had no feeling that it was the *king's government* which was
to be carried on : their feeling was that it was *their* government,
and they expected to carry it on by continually flattering the
people, and granting their demands. The Radicals knew full
well that by the bill no government of them could be carried on
either by the king, or by the aristocracy; that all power was in
their hands ; and that every argument which justified that
measure was equally valid to justify another just like it, and
another, and another.

It is quite true that a reform of the House of Commons was
necessary, because by the growth of population in some places,
and by the decay of it in others, the House of Commons did not
give that efficient counsel to the Crown which it is its office to
give. The proper way to have reformed, and not to have revolutionised it, was to have advised the king to issue writs to the
chief magistrates of such places as Leeds, Manchester, Paisley,
and to call on the householders, or payers of a certain amount
of taxes, to choose two persons to represent their interest in
parliament : to have issued no more writs to such places as Old
Sarum and Gatton, which were absolutely without an inhabitant;
to have summoned members from the Colonies ; to have called
a fresh parliament annually ; to have instituted an accurate
examination into the qualifications of all members of parliament;
to have raised it for all in proportion to the decreased value of
modern money : to have put an end to riot and debauchery and
expense, by taking votes in every parish simultaneously; and to
have permitted every voter to vote openly or in a box, as he

pleased. The House of Lords might have been improved according to the plan of Sir William Temple, by not permitting any peer to take his seat unless he had a landed income clear and proportionate to his rank, without interfering, however, with the king's power to create. Such would have been a real reform; an amendment of the actual condition of the two Houses, according to the former principles and practices; it would have been hailed with acclamation by the people; but when the heads of the Tory party resisted all reform whatever, and even went the length of saying that none was necessary, nor even desired by the people, the assertion drove men out of all bounds of reason, and they hailed and carried, with the madness of passion, "the whole bill, and nothing but the bill."

When men say that they wish to destroy the power of the Tories, they say that they wish to destroy all government by the king. They realise the character of the boy in Hogarth's caricature, who is represented sitting astride upon a post which supports the crown, and which he is cutting with a saw, unmindful that when he has succeeded in bringing down the crown, his own neck will infallibly be broken. This is not a quarrel between two factions to carry on the same kind of government: it is not a matter of indifference to the rest of the community, as if it were merely whether John or Peter should have the pre-eminence, receive a certain salary, and be the king's favourite; it is not a question of court favouritism; the question is, whether the *king's government* shall or *can*, or whether it shall not and *cannot*, be carried on at all. The office of king heads up and gathers into unity all the privileges of all the different classes in the whole kingdom: and the impairing of his power is the impairing of all the others; and the impairing of the privileges of the rest impairs his; it is the violation of the order of the whole political machine, which can no longer work as it has worked hitherto; there will be and must be continual jars, and continual jars will cause strains and bendings everywhere, even if nothing break. The question must not be evaded nor trifled with; the principles of the Tories are the principles of the monarchy, and of the whole social condition of the people under it: they are the only principles upon which it is possible for any good government to exist. It was not pretended at the time of the Reform Bill that the power of the Crown had been increasing and ought to be diminished; the attack upon it was more subtle and more formidable than by any such open declaration; it sapped the foundations of the monarchy in destroying privileged classes; it did not intend to curtail luxuriant exuberances, but to uproot the whole system.

The sovereigns have lately too much given up the reins of government into the hands of their servants; and because the ministers, and not the king, are alone responsible, i. e. may be cashiered and punished in various ways, the Crown has almost ceased to govern at all. The privy council is, however, the council of the king, and not of the councillors, and he ought always to be present when the cabinet meets: if he cannot preside in person, it has a president of his appointment, who should preside in his stead, and be the channel of transmitting *literatim* to the king all that passes. The mode of taking counsel in all cases, as Lord Bacon has shown, should be by the king submitting the matter for counsel in such a form that the king himself shall conceal his own sentiments; because all men are divided into two classes, the one desiring to flatter by agreement, the other to show their importance by differing; and as the object of the king should be to procure an unbiassed opinion, he should take care to avoid exciting those feelings which would militate against his obtaining the desired end. For the same reason he should ask the opinion of each *seriatim*, beginning with the junior as the one least likely to influence the others. Many things may be said in a council which will appear to be contradictory, but which are not really so, being only opposite sides of viewing the same subject; and some of the members, to avoid repetition, may merely utter a supplement to what has been before said by others. He who presides in the council will alone be capable of putting the whole together, so as to bring unity and light for action out of it; and it was from so doing that Queen Elizabeth was enabled to rule with the wisdom she did. Having thus obtained the unbiassed opinion of all, he should not declare his own, but having meditated upon what he has heard, direct accordingly that minister to whose department the matter belongs. No affairs, whether great or small, are well done when the master's eye is not present upon them, and the routine and detail of the public offices have been formerly much neglected.

Not many years ago, the ordinary expression was "During Sir R. Walpole's *administration*," or "During Lord Chatham's *administration*," or "During Mr. Pitt's *administration*;" more recently, however, the expression is changed to "Lord Grey's *government*," "the Duke of Wellington's *government*," "Sir Robert Peel's *government*," "Lord Melbourne's *government*." The change of expression is not accidental; the spirit of some recent discussions and documents was to consider it a *government* that was to be *formed*, not the Queen's government which was to be *administered*. More recently still, another Haji Baba unused to our ways, might have supposed from the language of public speeches and addresses to electors, that Lord John Russell and Sir Robert Peel were competitors for the crown of England, whilst the Queen was nothing but a mistress of revels, to entertain the retainers of either Rose, to preside at concerts and balls for their diversion at Buckingham Palace, and to provide pageants for the amusement of foreign ambassadors. No doubt, when the subject is thus stated, every one feels the difference, and entertains the same opinions as those here expressed; but the remark is made to show how little is left of real Tory principles, and how little all who have any talent for rule differ from Liberals, whether they happen to range on one or other side of the House of Commons. Yet the form of words would signify little; everything would depend upon the spirit in which they were uttered; whether the *feeling* be really Tory or Liberal—whether the Queen be the agent of Lord John Russell or of Sir Robert Peel to carry on their governments, which is Whiggism, or whether they are agents to carry on her government, which is Toryism.

It has been already pointed out, that we must be on our guard not only against the false interpretation which it is the custom to put upon words, but also against being seduced by the names which individuals and parties give to themselves, and to each other. A man is not "a Conservative," because he calls himself such; and as to "Tory," almost every one is afraid to take the name, and skulks and courts the mob, to avoid the obloquy with which the term is associated in low and radical minds. Two papers, calling themselves sometimes Tory and sometimes Conservative, contained in the beginning of July last the following passages: one speaks of "the traitor Bishops of

Cologne and Posen !" — traitor bishops! the sole offence alleged by the King of Prussia is, that they refuse to give the blessing of the Church to those who despise the same. The other paper writes: " Can any Protestant bishop be found faithless enough to his God and to his fellow-believers, to vote away any portion of the money which has hitherto been consecrated with such studied justice to so holy a purpose — to vote that money away, we say, for the support of infidel schools and Popish schools — schools where no Bible is seen or read, and where adulterate double translations only are used ? If so, we trust that diocesan meetings of the clergy in the diocese of every such apostate bishop will be called, and that the renegade be summoned before them ; and if he fail to appear, or, appearing, to exculpate himself, that all future communication between him and his clergy be cut off." Now this is the rankest revolutionary radicalism ; the writer may be hired to take the name of Tory, but his heart and hand are radical.

Few individuals ever profit from the experience of others ; neither does one nation from that of another; still less does one age from that of its predecessor ; otherwise we might have learnt wisdom not only from our own experience, but from the example of our neighbours. France is as ready now to run the career which made inevitable the horrors of the revolution of 1789 as she was then ; and England is taking rapid strides in the same direction.

The whole of what was called the ministerial crisis of 1839 in France, was a contest whether the ministers should be subservient to the king, or whether they should be in opposition to the king, and serve the chamber of deputies. The opposition journals, which are written by the leaders themselves, declared that they would oppose any ministers, no matter who they were or what they did, who did not oppose the king.* M. de Cormenin, who is the oracle of the opposition, says, that the king shall eat and drink, and do the honours to ambassadors, but that he shall not meddle with politics, summing up the whole

* A radical member for one of the largest manufacturing towns is (December 1841) boasting to his constituents that he will organise such an opposition as that no government can stand before it for three years. This is a true portrait of radical statesmanship, and the utmost amount of capacity for government that can be had in such quarters.

état de la question in these words; *En resumé, à toute la nation, la souveraineté; à la majorité des électeurs universels, la nomination de la chambre; à la chambre, l'omnipotence constitutionelle; au roi, les honneurs du trône, la représentation extérieure, la suprématie* nominale, *l'herédité et l'inviolabilité; aux ministres responsables, le gouvernement.* In reply to these maxims, the organ of kingly power has truly said, *l'opposition a beau parler de son dévouement absolu aux principes, ses attaques d'aujourd'hui ont un caractère purement personnel. Les choses pour elle c'est tout simplement le droit de tirer en aveugle* sur tous les gouvernemens possibles; sa nature, c'est la négation de tout principe de gouvernement. *Elle prendra successivement pour drapeau tous les hommes d'Etat qui auront echoués devant les majorités parlementaires; elle les abandonnera le jour où elle leur aura livré le pouvoir.* The cause of the personal hatred of all classes to the king is, that he alone in all France is capable of carrying on any form of government.

Hence, then, the fallacy, the fatal fallacy, of giving power to the people of England. If unlimited power be exercised by a king, he will use it according to his caprice, to oppress both the aristocracy and the people: if the aristocracy possess it, they will use it to control the crown, as formerly in Poland, and England; and also to tyrannise over the people, as in Russia and Hungary at this day, and formerly in France and England; if the people possess it, they will destroy all government everywhere. And it is for this absolute power in the people that the Liberals are contending: absolute mob power; irresistible power; uncontrolled and uncontrollable despotism; nothing short of this; nothing more and nothing less; avowing, that whenever the Lords and the Crown resist the Commons, the Lords and the Crown must be made to succumb before them.

Eventually the people will demonstrate, even to those who will not perceive it now, that it is impossible that government can proceed out of themselves; a fact which is being exhibited before our eyes in France, and which would teach us wisdom, if h ι d but sense sufficient to profit by the lesson. It was foreseen under the restoration, and declared publicly by many i ters; but these were unfortunately the defenders of all the unjust as well as of the just privileges which appertained to the lde n time, and therefore the writings of persons with so little justice were not only unheeded, but impelled the people forward in their mad opposition to privileges which are essential to the well-being of the whole mass. The privileges possessed by the aristocracy in France before the revolution of 1789, which were unjust, were, that the nobles were exempt from taxation ; that they could kill and maim their inferiors without incurring the same punishment as if they had killed or maimed an equal ; that their game might destroy the property of their neighbours, who had no redress against them ; that these unjust privileges were not confined to such as were actual peers of France, but all the younger branches of their families enjoyed them also ; these, and many more such shameful tyrannies, provoked a vengeance which, as a class, the nobles but too well deserved.

Government, whether of a nation, of an army, of a fleet, or in short of any large body of men, consists in repressing individual interests, individual passions, individual wishes, individual propensities, so as to produce one homogeneous action. It is hence of necessity oppressive to every individual freedom ; crosses throughout the country individual avarice in manufacturers and traders ; and stands in the way of individual ambitions, which are ever aspiring after rule : it is, therefore, continually and necessarily irritating all egoism, and nothing but a sense of the duty of obedience can preserve men in willing subjection to government ; and there can be no sense of duty towards men, which is not founded upon a sense of responsibility to God. Hence *point d'autel point de trône*, of which we shall see more hereafter. Government, therefore, is always the object of men's personal hatred, in proportion as they are desirous of advancing the interests of themselves, or those of the class to which they belong. The privileged classes have hitherto known and felt the truth of this, because they have felt and experienced that the lower orders would soon overpower them, were it not for the power of the rulers to defend the one, and to repress the other. The benefit of government is palpable to these, and comes directly home to them, and therefore they, more easily appreciating its advantages, are more ready to support it. But the case is widely different with the lower orders ; the blessings of rule come to them in a more diluted and secondary form, while the compression of, and opposition to, their own particular interests, by the promotion of which interests nearly all their intellectual powers are absorbed, comes direct and immediate. Thus the mass of the people has been ever ready at all times, in all countries, and under all forms of government, to rise up against those in whose hands resided the power; and yet so true it is that no government can arise out of these lowest classes, that insurrections never have succeeded, unless aid was lent by some of the nobles placing themselves at their head. The servile war in ancient Rome, the Jacquerie in France, and many similar failures, might be quoted. During the reign of Louis XVI. it was the nobles who began to lower the royal family in the estimation of the people; and all the successive leaders, Mirabeau, Talleyrand, Lafayette, and the Duke of Orleans, who prepared the way for Robespierre, were nobles. In 1830, the fighting of the people would have ended in nothing, had not Lafayette, Simonville, and other nobles, put themselves at the head of affairs. We find the revolutionists in England now continually discussing in their assemblies which nobleman they shall select for their leader; for they are perfectly conscious that the gift of rule and headship is entirely denied them. Thus every one is popular in proportion as he will be the boldest in finding fault with the rulers; and every demagogue, however popular, lasts no longer than until a more violent than he arises: and the converse is equally true, that as opposition to the government constitutes popularity, so government itself can only be, in all times and under all circumstances, more or less unpopular.

In speaking of the government of France at the beginning of 1831, M. Guizot said: *Si l'on persiste dans la voie où l'on s'est engagé, il n'y a pas de gouvernement possible—enfin l'ordre ne peut exister avec la liberté, sans que les gouvernemens soient plus ou moins impopulaires.* I am not sure whether it were he or another of the revolutionary ministers who said on the same occasion, *Que la chambre ne s'y trompe pas; par cela même qu'elle décide de la direction du gouvernement, elle est destinée désormais à n'être point populaire;* and upon this M. Lafitte, the president of the council of ministers, said, *L'orateur qui descend de la tribune* (who has just sat down) *me parait être le premier qui ait posé la véritable question.*

In the government of a country, the greater part of its concerns consists not of insulated, solitary, or even new facts and circumstances, but of things in progress from age to age, not only within its own limits, but connected with similar interests in neighbouring countries. Amongst merchants, reputation for integrity is not acquired by any particular act, but by the habitual conduct of years, and such a reputation is a necessary part of that capital with which they conduct their business. So it is with a state. The honour and reputation of a country is an essential part of its force, and it goes forth in the word of its sovereign, which he keeps inviolate. Traders are continually urging the violation of treaties, whenever some prospect of gain to their own interests is held out, which the honour of a king's word does not suffer to take place. Now a representative assembly is composed of individuals sent up as the organs of the particular interests of their respective localities. The people of Nottingham send up the man who they think will best promote the sale of stockings, caring not one straw for the fate of bark, hides, tallow, &c. The people of Bristol send up the best speechmaker for sugar colonies, perfectly reckless of the murder of negroes, or the fate of long wool, and blankets, which the West Indies do not require. Such delegates might, however, act together without much collision; but there are others who are sent by interests directly opposed to each other. Paisley sends the man who will demand, most noisily and pertinaciously, leave to send cotton cloth to Poland, and bring home corn in return; whilst Essex as certainly sends a man who will tell the Paisley man to take himself and his cotton to Poland, and eat corn there to his full, but that no Polish corn shall come up the Thames. Now these contending interests can never themselves agree upon a unity and permanence of action which are essential in the government of a country : and they cannot generate anything different from themselves. A House of Commons, a Chamber of Deputies, is not only no part of a government, and can make no part of government, but is the very antipodes to all government; it would be a nuisance so positive and intolerable, that it must be suppressed, were it not for the rulers preventing its mischief from breaking out. I speak here of the House of Commons as a pretended part of the government; not as a legislative body, nor as a part of the great national council of the king ; in both which capacities it is impossible too highly to value it ; but I speak solely of the false pretensions which are assumed for it by the terms " constitutional government," " our mixed government," " government by the three estates of the realm," &c. &c. The very element of its being, viz. its consisting of delegates from contending and irreconcilable interests, which precludes the possibility of its being in itself, or giving rise to, a government, is that which especially qualifies it to be the council which is required.

The peculiar characteristic of European, i. e. Christian nations, consists in their corporations. A corporation is an abstraction in which a power resides wholly independent of the individual members who compose it. Such things were unknown before the Christian era, and are unknown to this day in Pagan and Mahometan countries. How then came they to be found in Christian nations? Because they are Christian ; because they are builded on the model of the Church, which is the great corporation from which all the others have emanated. The power of the Church consists in its being the body of Christ, the dwelling-place of the Holy Ghost. The two principal means by which the Church acts are material, inanimate things, and thus men are taught that the efficacy cannot reside in the instrument, but in its being appointed for a certain end by God. These are water, through which, as the instrument, when blessed or made holy or sanctified by the word of the priest, a new and divine life is imparted in baptism; and bread and wine, through which, being sanctified also by the word of God spoken through the mouth of the priest, the nourishment of that new life is continually bestowed. Hence we learn that all its rites and ceremonies are equally efficacious for their destined ends, whether performed by good or wicked priests, because their efficacy resides not in the priest, who is only the administrator, but in their being the appointment of God. Even amongst men the personal merit or demerit of an ambassador from one king to another, does not affect the quality of the message which he bears ; the value resides in him whose agent he is, not in the agent. In civil society the power of each corporation of a city, or other corporate body, is irrespective of the abilities of the mayor, aldermen, or other of its functionaries, and cannot be diminished nor exceeded, though it may be greatly perverted and misapplied, by their folly or wickedness. The crown, however, is in the

State the great corporation; and its power, rights, and prerogatives are nothing affected by the talents or incapacity of him
who exercises them.   Now as the Lord Jesus Christ is He who
by His Spirit, through the ministers of His Church, regenerates
men in baptism, and feeds them at the communion table with
His own flesh and blood, so does He rule men by kings, and
protect them by the various officers placed under kings to carry
out the blessings of rule unto the remotest members of the civil
family.   And as His two offices are quite distinct, and never
can be united but in His single person, the true Melchizedek, so
must ecclesiastical persons have no rank or consideration in the
state; neither must kings, nor any who are not called to the
priesthood, meddle with things in the Church.   In order, therefore, to fulfil the ends for which men were created, redeemed,
and regenerated in Europe, it is indispensable that they should
be united in monarchies.   Monarchies are as essential to the
fulfilment of God's purpose in Christendom as the Church.

Because the effecting of all things ordained amongst men
stands not in the men themselves, but in God, who appointed
them, it must not, therefore, be concluded that men are merely
like the material natural things, accomplishing purposes in
which they have no participation.   The sun, the moon, and the
stars, the courses of the seasons, and of the rivers, the productions of creation, everywhere obey the directions and fulfil the
ends for which they were appointed.   These, however, have no
responsibilities, because they have no will, because they are not
free to use or to abuse the powers assigned to them.   Furthermore, it is not to be concluded that God, having made responsible creatures, will ever so act with them as to destroy that
responsibility, or in such a way as to bring contempt upon His
own gifts.   For whilst the sun, and moon, and rivers, and tides,
and seasons have never ceased unremittingly to bless, kings and
priests, nobles and masters, men in power, have for the most
part omitted to bless those confided to them for that end.
Natural talents, strength of body, and intellectual attainments
of various kinds, are the gifts of God, and since He has limited
Himself to act in flesh, He can only act in accordance with, and
not in violation of, natural talents and attainments.   The better
the instrument, the better will the work be performed, for here
is no question as to the capacity of the Worker.   Hence, whilst

kings and priests are God's means of guiding and teaching, the more the minds and hearts of the individuals who exercise the functions of kingship and priesthood have been duly cultivated, the more perfect and unalloyed will be the blessings which God is enabled to convey by them. As the example of this, the Church has ever taught that natural defects of any kind are bars to the fulfilling of the office of the ministry, being the outward signs of imperfection considered abstractedly, and not in the individual, although the abstraction could not be represented but in a person; hence, too, in many states, as women are ordained of God to be ruled over and not to rule, they have been debarred the right of succeeding to titles, and to all landed property.

It is not a sufficient answer to the above observations respecting monarchies, to say that the Christian Church can adapt itself to any form of temporal government, and therefore a republic can be Christian as well as a monarchy. I am speaking of the Christian Church, not as she now appears, but as she ought to be, and as an instrument for effecting that purpose of God which consists in showing forth Himself in the body of Christ; the supposed answer refers to Christianity solely as an instrument for saving individual members of the human family. In this last sense one sect of Christians may be as good as another; there may be as many souls saved in the Protestant sects as in the Churches of Rome and England, yet nothing can be more unlike the Christian Church than the Protestant sects. A clear distinction must ever be drawn between what God has ordained and would have, and what God permits. God permits sin, sickness, and suffering, but He has ordained nothing but blessing. God has permitted republics, but He has ordained monarchies. He permits schisms, but He has ordained unity in His Church. But neither sin, nor sickness, nor suffering, nor republics, nor schism, show forth the perfections of God, which He would have Christian nations to show forth. He has permitted sects to arise as a warning and a scourge to wicked priests, and republics as a warning to wicked princes and nobles, and chartists as a scourge to wicked rich men (James v. 1.), as He has disease to be the consequence of sin.

A nation is in one sense said to be Christian when all the members of it are baptized; that is, when all the people have

been brought into the responsibilities of that condition before
God. But there is much ambiguity in this expression, because
it does not state clearly the whole of that condition. When a
nation is spoken of as one, it is under the idea of a polity, and
in its corporate character, not as a confused mass of individuals.
When we speak of the English nation, a certain number of
individuals who speak English is not merely meant, but the
people who are bound together as one, under one government,
one body of laws, one set of customs, &c. In like manner a
ship's crew is not a certain number of individuals shut up in a
ship, but persons who are bound together for one object under
one commander. So a Church is not a certain number of
praying people, but an organised body. An individual man
is not a mere mass of flesh, and bones, and blood, but an
organised being. The essence of all lies in the organisation, in
the mutual dependence, and separateness of the functions of all
the parts; and without this organisation and mutual dependence,
the mere existence of the rough materials of the component parts
is useless. Thus a Christian nation is one in which its organisation is such as God has given it, according to God's rules, and
in which He is recognised as the real Worker in all the parts.
A mere portion of geographical territory covered by baptized
people, is not a Christian nation; they must have a Christian
organisation, or they are not a Christian nation, a unity.
America accordingly is not, in this sense, a Christian nation;
nor is France. All the inhabitants of America or France might
be very pious people, and yet those countries are not Christian
countries. It is exceedingly difficult to get this idea now into
men's minds, because they have lost the higher idea from which
it emanates, of the unity of the Church. The Edinburgh
Review avows itself utterly at a loss to understand the difference
between an essentially Protestant nation and essentially Protestant horsemanship. It would lead into more detail than is
necessary for the present object, to trace how the idea of the
unity of the Church was destroyed in the first instance by the
clergy separating themselves from the body of the baptized, and
calling themselves "the Church," to the exclusion of the rest, so
that in all countries the phrases, "the interests of the Church,"
"the property of the Church," "the rights of the Church," &c.,
have come to signify nothing but the interests, property, and rights

of the clergy, separate and distinct from the catholic interest, property, and rights of the whole community of the baptized. The priests set the example of rending the body of Christ, and, as things have advanced, they have become worse and worse; in all the Protestant sects, separatists have rather been applauded for their zeal than reproved for schism; and unity, an essential characteristic of the Church, is not to be found, no, not except in outward form, even in the Church of Rome.

It is in accordance with the principles here inculcated that it was said lately by an eloquent French preacher, *La France est athée*. There never was a time when there was a greater number of laborious pious clergy in that country than at the present moment; there may be also, and perhaps are, more persons truly religious in it than there has been for many years past; but the government is not based upon Divine right; education is not based upon religion; it is not in the hands of the teachers of religion; the Lord's day is not honoured; marriage is not held sacred; the nation in its corporate capacity is infidel. Now the liberals in England desire that in these points England should be as France. The larger portions of the Dissenters are extremely anxious about their own personal salvation: they believe in God; they believe more or less in the fact of an atonement having been offered by the Son of God; and they believe in a future state; but in all that constitutes God's purpose with Christendom, and the means by which He would effect that purpose, the meaning of the Christian Church and Christian Monarchies, they are as completely infidel as Mahometans. They have adopted all the absurdity as well as what is good in the *dictum* of one of their saints, Luther, namely, that justification by faith is the *articulus stantis vel cadentis ecclesiæ*. If he had said of a standing or of a falling man, he would have been right; but all men might believe this, and yet there might not be a vestige of the body of Christ discernible upon the earth. The test of a standing or falling church is faith in priesthood, and in the efficacy of sacraments administered by it, and therefore it is that the Church of Rome is so superior in many ways to all the other Christian sects. Thus a double current is running in both countries; individuals have been becoming pious, whilst the body has been becoming infidel; so during the early ages, just as the Church was departing more

and more from the purity of her original constitution, the world
abounded in eminent saints, martyrs, fathers, and confessors.

Whilst the Papists have exalted the Church and decried the
Scriptures, the Protestants have exalted the Scriptures and
decried the Church. The truth is found in uniting them
both. It is plainly written in the Scriptures, that in the
last days men shall be found fighting against the Lord
and against His Church. They seem, however, to imagine that
the fable of the giants contending against Jupiter is to be
realised, and that the Son of God will be seen sitting upon a
cloud, with men shooting or throwing stones at Him. The
Christ against which men fight in the last days, is not the
individual Jesus of Nazareth, but all men invested with His
authority and speaking in His name, namely, kings and the
Church, the mystical body of Christ, — the faithful followers
bound up in one organised society, bearing witness to God's
King and God's Church, which two together form God's Christ,
the true Melchisedec. And this is already going on whilst men
are thinking that the time is far distant when such an event is
to take place. The sectarian priests in the Church of Rome,
who have separated themselves from the body of the baptized,
and who, in times past, have assumed temporal power, and
presumed to dethrone kings, have ever despised royal authority,
save as it was subservient to them. These priests have first
taught the people to reject Christ in the king, and in this they
have been followed by many of the Protestant sects : that is to
say, they have not taught them to see and acknowledge Him in
the king, as much and as completely as they see and acknowledge Him in the priesthood; on the contrary, they have
taught that the king is inferior to the priest, and that he reigns
mediately through the priesthood, and not immediately from
God. But the Church teaches us that the Lord Himself is the
only " King of kings, the only Ruler of princes." Kings are
not responsible for their conduct to any person, or persons, or
thing upon the earth; they are not responsible to the bishop of
Rome, nor to the Church, for the use which they make of their
powers; they cannot be unkinged, nor can a priest be deprived
of his orders. This is also true of every headship : a father is
not responsible to any but God for the education of his
children; a husband is not responsible to any but God for his
conduct towards his wife; a master is not responsible to

any but God for his behaviour towards his servants: always understanding that in no case do men in these conditions interfere with the personal, but only the relative, rights of those below them.

That which has been termed "the alliance between Church and State," has been nothing but an improper interference of each with the peculiar province of the other. A separation of this improper alliance is taking place, not by the substitution of what is better, but by the denial of any reciprocal duties at all. There is also a considerable stirring up in men's minds to seek after truth in this matter. In England, many members of the Established Church, as is seen in their writings published at Oxford, and elsewhere, are going on to perfection; and within the pale of the Church of Rome, in France, and in Germany, there are many ecclesiastics, who, finding everything shaking around them, are compelled to inquire into the causes of God's displeasure with His anointed kings and priests, and out of every party and nation some will be found to be faithful witnesses that " God ruleth in the children of men."

For the last preaching to the world is the preaching of " the kingdom," and not of " the humiliation " of Christ, albeit none shall partake of the former who have not shared the latter: and it must be the last, because when men do openly, avowedly, and intelligently reject government by God through kings, they reject all possible government; and chaos is come again, and brute force is the only force that can be uppermost; and continual civil war is the only state of society, as it was declared by Mr. Canning it would be, " every village against village, family against family, man against man ; " as it has been seen before our eyes for the last forty years in Spain; as it was in France from 1789 to 1799, and will be shortly again ; and as it is foretold in Scripture, " as it was in the day of Midian," when every man fell by the arm of his brother.

The point at issue now is, whether kings rule by God or by the people; whether God or the people be the source of power; and this asserted sovereignty of the people God will never pardon. A nation, therefore, that advisedly adopts that maxim, defies God to His face: it says in plain words, " we will not have this man to reign over us, and now let us see if His word shall be fulfilled." It is the very sin of Julian in trying to rebuild the temple, in order to contradict the words of God;

and the sin of those who conspired to set aside that royal family which God had sworn should ever remain on the throne of Jerusalem (Isaiah vii.). Let kings, and all in authority, take heed how they tamper with this principle. Let no sovereign think that his throne is safe an hour through the support of those who tell him it is founded on the will of the people, or that he has any other right to it than right divine.

Because men have ceased to recognise God as acting in kings and priests, all the essential parts of Christianity are come to be considered as speculations, good or bad, profitable or idle, according to man's natural religion, but by no means essential to the hourly interests of a nation, of a family, or of a man. Christ incarnate, — Christ come in flesh, — a present, not a merely historical absent Christ, — Christ seen in kings and priests, and in all the relationships of life, is the Christ against whom all men are now risen up. Christendom is the only place in all the universe where it is possible for God to be seen. The dwelling-place of God is not a figure of speech, but a fact; the body of Christ is not a speculation, but a reality. The incarnation of the Son of God is not a doctrine appertaining merely to an historical fact 1800 years old. God manifest in the flesh is as much a reality now as ever. One form of manifestation may be absent, but another is present. God's glory is concerned in the question of Christian monarchies: their constitution is not a thing of chance, but a thing which He has established for His purposes, and for His ends; and therefore woe be to the people who shall presume to change it for things fashioned after their own caprices, and their own notions of reforming and amending without any reference to Him, to what He wills, to what He has done, and to what He will do.

No doubt much of the difficulty of the religious aspect of politics arises from the errors so long established, even ever since the days of Constantine, respecting the alliance between the Church and the State, into which subject it is beyond the present object to enter further than to observe that since the repeal of the Test and Corporation Laws, and the passing of the Romish Relief Bill, the anomalies are increased tenfold, and the government in such a false position, as is also the Church of England, both with respect to Romanists and Dissenters, that it is impossible for things to remain as they are. All feel this: the reckless Liberals, having no scruples, would soon cut the knot; the Conservatives, aping in a small way the Tories, and so having some hereditary attachment to things as they still exist, fear to do anything. As the laws now are, there is no valid ground to compel all sects to pay tithes, rates, &c., to the priests and churches of one. The opposite conditions of the churches in England and Ireland must also produce collision. In.the former country, the bishops having three hundred years ago cast off their subjection to the bishop of Rome, remained in possession of their sees, omitted some of the ancient rites and ceremonies, read the service in the mother tongue instead of in Latin, as also some Romanists in Germany have done, but in all other respects the church, priests and people, continued as it was. The Bishop of Rome was too wise to send bishops to England for sees which were not vacant, and where he had no flocks, and from that day to this there have been no Romish bishops in England; the families which remained under the allegiance of that foreign bishop have been cared for by arch-priests, who afterwards took the name of vicars apostolic. But in Ireland all the bishops did not cast off the jurisdiction of the bishop of Rome; few of the priests, and none of the people. A lay queen, or more properly the lay usurper of kingly autho-rity, Cromwell, lay peers and commons, made a law which the bishops obeyed, but carried few of the priests, and none of the people with them; and thus arose the anomaly of a country with bishops of one faith, and priests and people of another. It would be marvellous if there were peace in that country, since the state can only be in the same condition that the church is in. The lay king and his parliament could not change ecclesiastical offices; they might command certain persons to pay certain sums to certain other persons, and they might upon their parchments call that payment tithe; but it is not tithe; tithe is the offering of a Christian man to God in return for spiritual blessings which he receives from God, and which he can only pay to God through the hands of him by whom they are conveyed, and whom he knows to be the priest of God. a ymen can neither create bishoprics nor tithes; acts by which they make and call men bishops are null and void *de facto*; acts by which they attempt to command payment of tithes are null and void *de facto.* In these days, the Liberals suppressed the archbishopric of Tuam ; the Protestant man whom the laymen appointed has ceased to exercise any functions, but the archbishopric of Tuam exists, and Dr. M'Hale is in possession of it; he may be punished for calling himself archbishop of Tuam; the payments his flock make him may not be called tithes ; but he and he alone is the archbishop, and he and he alone is entitled to the tithes.   There is little doubt that if the whole history of the different dioceses in Ireland were gone into, it would be found that the thing called the reformation there was the mere overbearing of certain bishops and maintaining them by the power of the bayonet; that their clergy and people did not follow them ; that they neither had nor have any flocks; and that they never ought to have been there, and ought not to be there now.   The Church of England was no more established amongst the people of Ireland than it is amongst those of Scotland ; its domination in that country is a palpable iniquity, and the root of all the discord that prevails in it.   This has become still more monstrous since the government has recognised all sects, the doing which, however, in another point of view, is the same as recognising none.   The case would be curious in practice if a *levée en masse,* for the defence of the realm, were to be ordered, and the clergy were to claim exemption from service.   The fact is, that the exemption of the clergy from military service stands upon as unsound a principle as their exemption from taxes, and other civil service. The king should no more recognise a priest in civil or military matters than the priests should recognise the king in ecclesiastical matters.

Many other anomalies might be pointed out, and confusion must get from bad to worse, because the politics of Christian monarchies are the greater wheels which move round the smaller inner wheels of the Church.   Any attempt, therefore, to set political matters in order without reference to the Church, is as if a man were to attempt to put a watch in order by meddling with the hands, and refuse to see what defects there were in the works within.   The most approved receipt now is just what it ever has been ; viz. "Let us kill the heir, that the inheritance may be ours ;" let us cast religion off, and then we can manage secular affairs well enough.

Every European country had a hereditary king, a body of hereditary nobles, and a selection of deputies from all classes, who ought to have consulted together for the good of the whole. But this form was never found before the establishment of Christianity, and therefore it was evidently an emanation from the Church — a development in a secular form, for the purposes of civil government, of the same principles as those which were expressed in ecclesiastical forms in the Church for the purposes of instruction in the being and nature of God, and of His due worship. The bishop and the priests, called and ordained by authority superior to their own and to that of the people, as they were in primitive times, served as a model for a king and his peers appointed irrespective of the will of the people, whilst the deacons chosen by the people, and united with the bishops and priests, not in rule, but in the deliberative council of the Church, set forth the delegates of the people in temporal matters united in council with the king and the nobles. In every European monarchy, that is, in every kingdom of baptized persons, such was the essence of its government under some modification or other. The English was the most perfect, because the Church of England, from the days when it was confined to a small district on both sides of St. George's Channel, and long before the arrival of Augustine in the time of Gregory the Great, has ever been less corrupted than the Church in other countries. It would lead to historical disquisition, too minute for the present purpose, to point out the same forms elsewhere, but everywhere the monarchy was hereditary in a single family; under it were nobles with prescriptive rights; and under them were various classes of the people, each with their respective rights. In like manner the king is under God alone, *jure divino*, and has no man, nor body of men, over him, to whom he is responsible. That such is the law every tyro in legal reading knows. The crown is placed upon his head by the Church; not by a noble, but by a priest : not by one representing a body of nobles, but by a member of an abstraction, which the Church is ; and she puts forth her act in this case by any priest, though usually, and most seemly, by the patriarch of the metropolis, or of the see in which the rite is performed. All this marks, in every way and mode by which such a transaction can be marked, that God alone appoints the king, and sets him

over the people, irrespective of their wishes or will implied in
any way.   He is king by the grace of God, and not by the grace
of the people.

In like manner as the king is king by the grace of God immediate, so are the peers peers by the grace of God, but mediately
in their origin through the king, and not by the grace of the
people; and thus, when at the coronation of the sovereign the
king puts the crown upon his head, the peers put their coronets
upon their heads, thereby marking that they hold their honours
by the same tenure that he holds his.   God's mode of government in all its essential parts has been the same in all the
members of the European family, in all Christendom, in all the
nations of baptized men.

Truth is one, and proceeds only from God; and men's dis-
putes about church government, and rites, and forms of worship,
as well as their debates about monarchies and republics, prove
only that they are ignorant of that truth.   There is but one
holy Catholic and Apostolic Church : and all its officers, and all
its rites, and all its forms, are as incapable of variation or modification as God Himself.   So there is but one form of civil
government ordained of God, and this, too, is equally incapable
of modification or variation.

This mode of government is by electing some men to privileges of which others do not partake.   The king is elected to
that office to be the immediate viceroy of the King of kings, to
whom alone the whole earth belongs; the viceroy is appointed
by the universal monarch to be His servant over a particular
country, and responsible to Him alone for his conduct.   The
office is hereditary, for all the family of the sovereign is elected
in him : no other individual, and no other family, can share the
honour.   Next to the hereditary king stands a body of hereditary
nobles, elected equally by God, but mediately through the
king, owing their first existence possibly to the king, but their
successors taking their honour by right of descent as he takes
his by right of descent.   The king was bound to take counsel
with all his people from time to time, and therefore the people
sent certain of their own number to represent, and to act
for them in all such circumstances.   All the people, however, did not choose representatives, but only such as were proprietors of land; and neither might they choose any one

they pleased, but only such as possessed an amount of property greater than the majority possessed. In the towns, also, the voters were often limited to freemen, or householders, to the exclusion of the majority of the inhabitants. Thus the king, the nobles, the representatives of the people, the electors, were all privileged classes, each, in his place and station, possessing something from which others were excluded; so that the king was the head and representative of all the privileged classes; and a kingdom is composed of such, and without them no kingdom can exist. This body of hereditary nobles, and the assembled representatives of the people, constituted jointly the council of the king, by consulting with which the king might become acquainted, from time to time, with the various necessities of all his subjects. Every country has been ill governed, because the kings would rule without consulting the nobles and people. The wisest and best king, with the wisest and best ministers, must have failed, because man is made to be dependent upon his fellows of every degree, and not to be independent of any. The necessity of keeping up standing armies to defend his territories from foreign aggression, has afforded the means of tyranny and of robbing his subjects of their rights, of which means every continental sovereign has availed himself. The insular situation of England prevented its kings from having that excuse, and God has preserved it as the model by which other countries might have corrected the errors which have crept into their institutions. Councils of the nation, which are the only means by which kings can govern well, are now become objects of terror to continental princes, and especially since the evil example of the representative assemblies of France and England has been displayed before them. The means which councils had of securing good and just government, was by retaining the purse in their own hands, and voting the necessary taxes only from year to year. If any European monarchy will yet save itself, it can only do so by adopting the substance of that form which has been seen in England, and which originally existed within itself, however long it may have lain dormant, and which would be a far better *Anglomanie*, than zeal for her manufactures or her commerce, with which so many are affected.

Unfortunately, both kings and nobles have, in every country, used whatever power they possessed for the oppression, and not for the blessing, of the people, until, being goaded past further endurance, the people rose in fearful rebellion in 1792 in France. On the preservation of their own and of each other's rights, did the common prosperity depend. But in France, the Crown destroyed the power of the nobles, and in its turn fell for want of a body sufficiently powerful to stand between it and the people. In no countries have the rights and wants of the people been duly respected. Instead of kings, nobles, and people, each respecting the rights and privileges and happiness of the other, the two former began by oppressing and tyrannising over the latter, and ultimately succeeded in denying them common justice; taxing them more heavily than they did themselves, and laying great burdens upon them, which they would not themselves assist to support. At length the king and nobles began to quarrel between themselves; and the Crown, being but one, could also make two factions amongst the others, and has thus succeeded throughout Europe in destroying all power in the nobles whatever; so that there is now nothing but an Asiatic form of government to be seen — a monarch supported by an army ruling over a people without rights. It is idle to ask the continental sovereigns to reduce their armies: they can no more do so than could the emperor of China or the shah of Persia, for it is by the army alone that their thrones exist. The only method by which they could do so, would be by re-creating the aristocracies which they have destroyed. But this they do not understand. From the time of Louis IX. to the time of Louis XIV., the kings had been trying to destroy the aristocracy, and had nearly succeeded in doing it; so that, when the people rose against the king, there was no intermediate body which was able to stand in the way. The abuse of the powers confided to kings and nobles has formed the excuse in the eyes of short-sighted men for endeavouring to pull down the strength of both, and to give power, either mediately or immediately, to the people. But such a step is fatal to all; bad government may be carried on by bad kings and by bad nobles, but no government whatever, neither good nor bad, can be carried on by any people.

It matters not, therefore, whether one set of men array themselves against the Crown, and another set wage war against the privileges of freeholders, and the qualifications of members of parliament; in all these their several oppositions they are equally opposed to a kingdom, opposed to the very essence and foundation on which alone it can subsist. Hence there never was absurdity or delusion greater than that into which the French people has fallen, in supposing that they can have a monarchy without an aristocracy; and into this absurdity Louis XVIII. and Charles X. fell also, for aught that appears from their several acts; for it was in the power of both to have created a real and efficient aristocracy, for want of which the fate of France is irremediable. A similar delusion is going on in England, for the majority of the nation, that is, all the Liberals, as they call themselves, (which name, though it may include some old Tories and Whigs, includes certainly all radicals and revolutionists of every degree, shade, and colour,) talk of loyalty to the Crown, and at the same time contend for the abolition of every privilege through the whole machinery of government, and of every peculiar qualification for every office in the State.

It is fortunate, at least, that the word monarchy is not expunged from the vocabulary of English and French politics, although the essence of monarchy has vanished from the latter, and is fast disappearing from the former. In old times Whigs have often objected to the use of the word "monarchy," as applied to the government of England, because in their opinions it resided not in one person, but in "the three estates of the realm." Convenient words these "three estates of the realm," when men would hide, behind pompous sounds, the absence of ideas. The confusion consists in not distinguishing between executive and legislative functions; for the latter constitutes no part of government. Legislation, law-making, cannot take place in England by the monarch; nor can the executive, the putting of the laws in force, be done by the joint labours of the peers and of the deputies of the people. England is as much a monarchy as Russia. Men in these days may not like to hear it, but it is so, must be so, and can be nothing else, so long as the country is not cursed by a government purely democratic. For monarchy is not merely the best form of government, it is the only possible form of government for any member of the European family of Christendom. It would be as impossible for France to be a republic, and the other countries to remain monarchies, as it would be possible for Kent to be under the monarch of England, if Yorkshire were a republic; or as it would be possible for Russia to remain as she is, with the emperor's power restricted in Poland.

All society is divided into two great parts, the one consisting of those who possess more or less of the soil of the country, and the other of those who possess none. The original acquisition was by those who had power to get hold of it, and by power must the possession be preserved. Power must be in the hands of those who hold the land, and it must not be in the hands of those who hold none of it. The implements of power are two-fold, iron and gold; the sword and pay. Privileges must belong to the one class, from which the other, and larger portion, is debarred, for it is by privileges that power is retained by the few after they have sheathed the sword. Power may be abused; nay, almost always has been; but whether abused or not, it must be maintained. Privileges were never granted to the few by the many, but acquired or taken by the few, independent of, or by means of, or in spite of, but never out of, the many as their source. The sentiment now in fashion, that " the people are the source of legitimate power," is a lie in fact; it is a historical lie; it is a theoretic lie; it is an absurdity which could never have been tolerated until men had become insensible to the accurate meaning of words. To be sure, it is principally heard at places where men are half inebriated; the fittest places for it. But the world is advancing in its own ways, which it calls improvement; and the same generation which saw George III. most properly degrade from his office the first peer in his realm for tolerating the expression of such a sentiment at a public symposium, saw also the servants of the son of that monarch publicly avow and glory in the deceitful sentiment. Such is the march of events.

Not only did power not emanate from the many, but it cannot be exercised by the many: it cannot be by the many considered as a confused mass, nor by any select body chosen by, emanating from, and responsible to them. Through the confusion of ideas, and substitution of words for things, which have been already alluded to, there is a blending in men's minds of ancient republics with the American republic, and with an imaginary republic, which is the idol of modern revolutionists in England and France. The ancient republic of Rome, and the more modern republics of Venice, Milan, Florence, and the other Italian states, were aristocracies, in which despotic power was exercised by one of two rival factions, and powerful families, always with cruelty to each other, and total contempt for, and indifference to, the wishes or wants of the body of the people. If the people ever received any boon, it was in order to court their favour, and strengthen the party which conferred it against the other. It was never as conceding rights or privileges acknowledged to be the people's due, but wholly and solely as a means of purchasing their support, and swelling the train of a powerful leader. So also it has ever been in England. In America, the immense unoccupied territory presents a continual means of drawing off the unruly and discontented spirits who disturb the public peace at home, and without which means no government there could exist. Indeed, as it is, there is scarcely a possibility of keeping the people in any subjection. The last President avowed that he had not power to prevent the people on the borders of Canada from assisting the rebels in that colony; and if America were a part of the European family, it would be impossible for her to exist as a republic, without embroiling the neighbouring states. If France had been under a republican chief in 1838, one horde would have seized on the Rhenish provinces of Prussia, and another would have passed over the Pyrenees. The Swiss republics are or were aristocracies until within these few years, and now that they are democratic, they have begun to split into endless subdivisions and fractions: the little canton of Basle, not so large as the estate of many private individuals, has fallen into two, as *Basle Ville*, and *Basle Campagne*. The Vallais is splitting into two; and Tessin has had four new constitutions in three years. Lausanne awoke one morning, and to its great surprise saw in the journals that its university and national church had ceased to exist; the professors, including some of the ablest men in Europe, who had been invited from a distance under promise of permanent provision, such as M. Vinet, and the ecclesiastics themselves, having received no other notice of what was going forward. Even this condition of republics does not suffice for the constitution-mongers; every one of them, in all his writings, speeches, &c., describes the republic he wishes to see established as an

institution in which there shall be no privileged class whatever;
no aristocracy, no hierarchy; pure equality in every possible
case and circumstance and condition, and for every possible
purpose, calling, or office.   There is consistency in this: modern
politicians imagine that the world has so far advanced in knowledge and virtue, in comparison with past ages, that they have
nothing to learn from former times except to avoid their systems;
they profess that the institutions of past ages were adapted
perhaps to the then condition of the world, but that these were
ages of infancy and nonage, while the present is the age of maturity, and of masculine understanding: they call this fancied
republic, where every one is to be equal, the condition of society
best adapted to the world as it is; and thus the examples of
former republics is as much thrown away upon them as the
example of former monarchies.

The Swiss aristocratic states were vastly superior to every
other state called republic with which history acquaints us.
Never did they rise up in rebellion against their petty tyrants
for other provocation than cruelty committed upon the persons
of the innocent and helpless; and when in their success, they
retained certain privileges which had before pertained to their
oppressors, they nobly paid the full value of that which their
courage and skill had won.   Whoever has not read the admirable
Geschichte von dem Schweitzervolke, by Schockke, should do so,
at least in the scarcely less admirable French translation by
M. Monnard.   It is a model of popular history, and shows how,
in every age, the people and nation prospered in proportion as
they merged personal and cantonal egoism in the good of the
whole confederacy.

But the moderns will make all things new: the Parisians
made a new constitution in 1830 for France, and the Liberals
made a new one for England in 1831; and they will go on, if
the privileged classes, especially the landowners, shall be absurd
enough to suffer them, destroying old things, and making all
things new, except government, for of that there shall be none.
The impossibility of any government whatever proceeding from
the people, through their deputies, is becoming more and more
manifest in France every day.   M. Thiers has written a history
of the first French revolution, in which he justifies the atrocities
then committed, under the plea of their being the necessary con-

sequences of the state of things and feelings then existing; and he is right. The absurdities broached in the National Convention used to be palliated on the ground of being the crudities of men unaccustomed to practical politics; but unfortunately for this plea of inexperience, the authors and participators of the first revolution, they who ought to have grown wise by experience, they who deplored the exuberance of early days, were the very men who in 1830 framed the "*programme* of the Hôtel de Ville," and drew up the present constitution which placed the Duke of Orleans on a baseless throne. It is not necessary to examine the various details of the lengthened act; the whole is summed up in the words of La Fayette and Lafitte, which have been often repeated by all the leading men of the party since, *un trône populaire entouré d'institutions républicaines:* a phrase with about as much meaning as a good fire kept up with logs of ice. Yet the essence of the phrase is now adopted here, and the radical journals talk of " our republican monarchy!" Ever since that time they have been quarrelling with Louis Philippe, solely because he has not kept this engagement. And most assuredly he has not kept it, because the thing is untenable; and the chamber has not kept it any better, and for the same reason : for no one can keep a fire burning by supplying it with water. A monarchy is a political body governed by a king; a republic is a political body whose affairs are conducted by persons chosen by and dismissible by the people; the institutions of the country are the forms by which the government, whether resident in a monarch, or in an elected governor, performs its functions. Louis Philippe has endeavoured to keep the only tenable part of the compact by doing his duty as king : the chamber has tried to keep the other half, to make the country a pure republic, and to disseminate its republican principles in other countries, in all which endeavours it has been necessarily opposed by the king. And now matters are come to an end: the rickety machine can go no longer: the chamber has shown, during nine years, all the power it is capable of showing, namely, that of destruction, by breaking and destroying eighteen different sets of ministers; while it has farther shown that it has not the power of forming one. Its power, like all power emanating from the people, is merely the power of resistance to all government, not the power of governing;

the power of destroying, not the power of forming; the power of dissevering, not the power of uniting anything; the power of the devil, which is to kill; not the power of God, which is to keep alive.

That blessings must flow through gradations, is not only necessary in nations, but in the smallest societies. In a family, the father, and husband, and master must have in all things the preeminence; next to him the wife, mother, and mistress; then the children; and lastly, the servants; and, if the family be large, even these in different classes. A family where all are equal could not exist. If there be one thousand acres of land to be cultivated, and one hundred persons to be supported, the greatest amount of happiness is not produced by each having ten acres, but by the whole appertaining to one, who is nevertheless unable to cultivate it for want of cattle and implements; these one thousand acres must be let to others who have the necessary means of cultivation, and to whom alone will belong the cattle, implements, and produce : these renters will employ as labourers the rest, who have neither the land, nor the cattle, nor the buildings, nor the implements. Landholders are a privileged class, and are, in fact, the only real aristocracy; and they must claim and maintain their privileges for the good of all; and the House of Lords, their great head, must resist firmly every bill which tends to reduce them to the level of mere renters.

The French struck the most truly effective blow at aristocracy when they enacted the law for the division of lands. Before that time they grew corn sufficient for themselves, and had some to export besides. Now the produce of the country has fallen one half : there is no stock, and the last contracts for the army were obliged to be supplied from Germany, for there were no beasts in France to furnish leather. When the lands of France were in the hands of the monasteries, which are corporations, and of the nobles, before the division of lands was made compulsory by the Code Napoleon, France had considerable trade as an exporter of grain. But now that country does not grow sufficient for its own consumption; and the reason of this is, that stock cannot be kept except where lands are in large masses, nor can buildings be maintained except where the succession of posterity is looked to; and where stock is not kept, the land is impoverished, so that the soil of France, which used to yield sixteen per cent, now produces but eight; and whilst the land is impoverishing every day, the number of mouths to be fed is increasing. In the interesting work of M. Rubichon, *sur le Mécanisme de la Société en France et en Angleterre*, the author has shown, from public documents, that whilst in all the towns in France the population has been increasing, the quantities of food brought into them have diminished progressively for many years past. But as he is a good Tory, the testimony of M. Balzac, *homme du mouvement*, upon the effect of the law for the partition of property equally amongst all the children, will probably be received with less suspicion : — *Le Code que l'on regarde comme la plus belle œuvre de Napoléon, est l'œuvre la plus draconienne que je sache. Le divisibilité territoriale poussée à l'infini, dont elle a consacré le principe par le partage des biens, doit engendrer l'abâtardissement de la nation, la mort des arts et celle des sciences. Le sol trop divisé se cultive en céréales, en petits végétaux, les forêts et partout les cours d'eau disparaissent ; vienne une invasion, le peuple est écrasé, car il a perdu ses grands ressorts en perdant ses chefs. Et voilà l'histoire des déserts.*

Thus there is not a single point in those things, political, agricultural, and commercial, which constitute the well-being of a nation, in which the ancients were wrong, and in which men are now right ; the ancients were right, because these things, political power, agriculture, and commerce, were in the hands of persons who had exclusive rights in each ; and men now are wrong because they imagine that the leaving of every one to do as he can for himself is the way to insure the greatest amount of happiness. Almost every law that is made, and every measure which is adopted, fails to produce the end anticipated, and promised by the promoters. Those at the head of affairs, finding themselves disappointed, get disgusted and retire, leaving their places to be filled by one loquacious pretender after another, each in his turn to devise and promise, be disappointed and fail : and the people, more and more disappointed, become more and more irritated. But if men would return to right principles, sound measures would produce again soundness in the social system. The people would have some better occupation than to strive at fabricating constitutions in which the governed are to

like to be controlled, in which men are to be blessed and
enriched by other means than by the institutions which have
been given them of God. Their happiness, all that they can
have of it, so long as the present dispensation lasts, will only be
found in doing their duty in the institution and in the state in
which God has placed them, not in breaking these down and
substituting others for them; not in escaping from them and
taking refuge in some other.

It is false to imagine that all men have an equal interest in
maintaining the institutions of society. In every society on
earth there are more men who have to gain than who have to
lose by plunder, by confiscation, by an equal partition of property among all; more people who have too little for their real
necessities than those who have too much; and, above all, there
are more whose morbid and fancied wants have reduced them to
distress and to discontent, than there are of those who are con-
tentedly living within their spheres and means. Let us hear
again what our neighbours say :—*Nous avons des réformateurs
qui, exhumant les conceptions des beaux jours de la Convention, veulent donner à pleines mains des droits politiques à
tout le monde. Cela s'appelle du progrès. Dieu nous garde
de cette perfectibilité et de ces nouveautés copiées des plus
mauvais jours de notre histoire!* (Journal des Debats, 30 Avril,
1840.) Yet this paper is of such bad principles, that in the
same number it speaks of a general lately dead as one who took
a leading part *dans notre glorieuse révolution de Juillet*, 1830.

"Order" is the word in France, and "conservatism" in
England, by which men are blinding themselves with the notion
that property can be preserved when power is placed in the
hands of the mass of the people. "A determination to preserve
order," in the mouths of the national guard, means nothing but
a desire that their shops should not be pillaged; and "conservatism" in England means that gentlemen shall keep their
estates, manufacturers their machines, and large farmers their
stock, although the power of choosing members of Parliament is
given to every one indiscriminately, and the king is to fill the
House of Peers with fresh members whenever it resists the mad
schemes of the other House. But real order is the keeping
together and preserving the respective rights of each privileged
class; and genuine conservatism is the same; and if privileges

of political power are done away with, privileges of property cannot be preserved. The rights of classes, and the properties of classes, are as sacred as the rights and properties of individuals; though not more so. The Liberals never will persuade starving Radicals that it is right to seize and dispose of one farm, because it belongs to a corporation, but wicked to take the farm adjoining, because it belongs to a rich lord. Liberal morals may be bounded by the partition hedge, but Radical morals are not: the Liberals have taught the Radicals to laugh at prescriptions, and they cannot object to the direction which the Radicals give to their own doctrine. Because classes are abstractions, a mere utilitarian, a fleshly eye, can see no use in them. In France, a bastard aristocracy has sprung up, which for the moment supplies the place of that which has been destroyed, showing that an aristocracy,—that privileged classes, in short, are an essential part of the constitution of society, and that no society can exist even for a time without at least its semblance. This bastard aristocracy is the *bourgeoisie;* in other words, they who are possessed of something; and this *bourgeoisie,* the tradesmen and manufacturers, is becoming the object of the hatred of the many who have got nothing. And so it must ever be; no power can be in the hands of the many but the power of brute force; and that power of brute force must be kept under by the privileges of the various classes above them. *Car la société est composé de deux grandes classes ; ceux qui ont plus de dîner que d'appétit, et ceux qui ont plus d'appétit que de dîner.*

Under the term "monopolies" many things which are in themselves good and indispensable are covertly attacked and undefended, because certain abuses have been committed under that name; every privilege of a class, property exclusively possessed by one class, and not shared by all, is branded as a monopoly, and as impositions, taxes, and burdens on the other classes, from which idea the transition is easy to that which seeks and calls for its destruction. But all creation is made up of monopolies; all God's government, whether of the moral or of the material universe, is carried on through them. His mercy is infinite, but nevertheless it flows only through the one channel of His incarnate Son. His Spirit, although infinite, resides only in the body of His Son, which is His church: out of these channels, bodies, and places, all concerning Him is mysticism, confusion, and incertitude. In vain do men wander and strive to find Him out of these localities, vain are all speculations about Him and His doings, whether by Socrates, by Rousseau, by La Place, or by writers of Bridgewater treatises. In the material creation the sun has the exclusive monopoly of heat and light, so that men, in railing against monopolies, are really waging war against all creation. The sea has a monopoly of fishes, and if a free-trader in animal food would have equality of production everywhere, and were to sow his land with spawn, not a herring would he reap to reward his zeal in the cause of free produce and destruction of monopolies. France has the monopoly of the best wines, and neither colder Germany nor warmer Italy can compete with her. The French are ruining themselves and their soil in vain attempts to raise sugar, which is the monopoly of the tropics, instead of being content to import it. *India mittit ebur, molles sua thura Sabæi.* Every part of the earth will not produce indiscriminately every kind of produce ; and even of two contiguous fields one will produce that which the other will not.

It is the same with the moral government of man. The Mahometans are blessed with clearer light concerning the true character of God than mere heathen. The Jews have promises and hopes peculiar to themselves, from which all other classes of mankind are exempted. Christians have the fullest revelation which has yet been made of the essential Almighty Invisible Creator, to whom He has been made manifest in His Incarnate Son : and in the Church, which is His body, He has ordained and appointed one only instrument for conferring new and spiritual life, even the sacrament of baptism, which life is conveyed by no other means; and He has appointed one other ordinance for the nourishment and sustentation of that life, namely, the Sacrament of the Eucharist, by which men feed on the very flesh and blood of His Son, and which life can be nourished in no other way; and He has ordained out of the mass of the baptized one class of men, even the priesthood, by whom alone these blessings can be administered, through whom alone He speaks the words which change the bread and wine into that flesh and blood, and through whom alone He teaches other men the knowledge of His ways, and through whom alone men can offer unto Him acceptable worship.

But the schismatics in the Church have taught their own and private opinions, which are heresy, or *αἱρεσις*, every one choosing his own fancy; and so Protestants have been for three hundred years growing more and more into the belief that every one who takes such a whim into his head is competent to teach others, and to administer the sacraments, thrusting themselves into the priest's office, and encouraging the people to choose for themselves priests whomsoever they will.

It was indeed right, at the time when all personal responsibility was destroyed by blind obedience to priests, to claim to a certain extent the right of private judgment; but that principle has now come to sanction and justify and extol the refusal of every individual man, woman, and child, to submit to anything in politics and religion save that which he approves of; the inevitable consequence of which is, interminable divisions and schisms, every one the self-sufficient king and priest to himself.

In like manner, it was right to insist upon God's purpose in man, and that He chose the instruments by which He would effect it, when man's freedom of action was taught in such a way as to make the whole moral government of the world and the salvation of man depend entirely upon man's option; but the end for which some individuals were elected to certain situations from which others were excluded, was not that the elected alone might be blessed, and others miserable, but that they might be made the instruments of, and channels for, the blessing of all. A more accurate attention to the method of God's dealings with men in His Church might have instructed them that He elected His Son, "His Elect One," to a particular work and office, not that every other might be abandoned, but in order that He might thereby become the instrument of conveying blessings to all. This might have assured them that the election of any individual to any office, whether in Church or State, was for the end of blessing, and not of neglecting or abandoning the rest; and thus of all the privileged classes. In like manner, the whole Church is elected out of the world, that she might become the means of blessing all. Yet men, finding that ignorant and wicked priests have failed in their duty, are foolishly rejecting all her institutions and offices, seeing nothing connected with them but priestcraft, superstition, persecution,

cruelty, and oppression.   The abuses of the trusts committed to
them by kings and priests are not to be defended nor palliated,
whilst, on the other hand, it is in vain to expect that any blessings can flow to mankind except through kings and priests,
through monarchies and the Church; because they are the means,
and the only means, which God has appointed for that end.   A
man may have abused his powers of eating and drinking until
he has induced every form of pain and disease which the human
body can endure; nevertheless, it is useless to rail at his stomach,
and the other organs of digestion, as the cause: so long as he
continues to live, so long must his nourishment proceed through
the very same organs whose abused powers produce his present
sufferings: he can be nourished in no other way, and if he refuse that he must die.

It is ever necessary to bear in mind, that it is the institution
which is good, and the men who are bad; that it is the men who
have to be mended, and not the institutions; and that to do
this was the especial business of the priests.   If they had made
good men, the outcry would never have been raised against the
institutions; and the fatal error of these days is the not seeing
the difference between the institutions and the men who fill
them, and thus supposing that it is the former which is defective,
and not the latter.

Throughout the whole human race we see nothing but a
system of election of a few to certain things from which the
majority is excluded.   Christendom is a small election, in comparison with the mass of mankind, the members of which are
elected to blessings, both temporal and eternal, from which
Jews, Mahometans, and Pagans, are excluded.   The trite observation, that poets are born not made, is true of all : no education can make a Shakspeare or a Newton; poets are endowed
with a combination of gifts of which the majority of men are
deprived: the same may be shown of every faculty of mind, of
genius, and of property.   Each class, each individual, has what
is peculiar to it, from which others of the species are excluded,
and which peculiarity constitutes the speciality of that class, and
of that individual.   In the formation of a community, the outward distinction of property is that which can alone be recognised,
and men must have rights and privileges corresponding to their
property ; from which rights they who have not that property

must be excluded; otherwise, although the indirect influence of property will for a time make itself be felt in resisting and protracting the day of ruin, the hour must arise when, as in France, all property shall be abolished and confiscated by a law of perpetual division, which makes a community of paupers.

Every office is intended for the blessing of others, and not for the purpose of increasing the personal gratification of him who holds it. If its duties are faithfully performed, it cannot increase the ease of the possessor, for he becomes the servant of others, and neglects himself that he may contribute to the wellbeing of others at the expense of his own enjoyment. Hence office confers responsibility, but not happiness, save in the seeing of others happy; as we are taught by the instinct of animals, mothers for example, in all cases which are undepraved by human selfishness. When men desire office, when the cry of *nolo episcopari* is not honestly in the heart, it is plain that they desire it only to abuse or misuse the power it conveys, for no one voluntarily desires to be the servant of another. The happiness of men is quite independent of the class in which they are placed, whether royal, noble, or any other; and it can only be insured by each continuing in that where he is, and neither in spirit, desire, nor act leaving it, whether by descending lower or rising higher. The same continual interference of God which keeps the beasts under the dominion of men, which makes horses and oxen subservient to man's use, is also in like manner employed to keep the masses of the people, the many, in subjection to the few. This end He effects by privileged classes, and if a nation declares that it will not have the means, it cannot have the end. The wisdom of God is necessary to be given to every one in authority, in order to rule wisely, and to bless those committed to his charge; and it is no less necessary for those who are ruled, in order that they may receive any blessing from those set over them. A bad king is a punishment upon a wicked people, and should be submitted to as to a pestilence or any other calamity with which God pleases to chastise them; but rebelling against a fever instead of being resigned to it will only increase the suffering without curing the malady; and rebelling against bad government only increases the political evil.

Two consequences have flowed from the doctrines of the schismatics; the first of which is, that radicalism has been fostered under the covert of religion, and the deceitful notion propagated that spiritual blessings ascend from below instead of descending from above: and the second is, that all God's method of government being despised and set at nought in the Church, it has come, by necessary consequence, to be despised and set at nought in the State likewise.

If the happiness of the people had increased since the sovereigns have suffered them more to interefere in the affairs of government, there might be some inducement for the people to persevere in the course which they are pursuing. But the contrary is the fact, and the best evidence is drawn from the mouths of the people themselves; the further they depart from the old principles of government, the more they distrust the fact of blessings coming to them only through the crown, and the more they believe the delusive lie that happiness and prosperity and good government can proceed from themselves, the more have they been discontented, the more loud have been their complaints, the more aggravated their clamours against their present condition. But their present condition, in so far as it is different from that which it was a century ago, is of their own making; they are more unhappy, and that unhappiness has not been caused by the additional tendency towards monarchical but towards democratical principles, at which they have been striving.

The amount of happiness in France has not been increased by all their revolutions and anarchy. There are indeed no *lettres de cachet*, but there are still long imprisonments without previous trial; and instead of the joyous, contented people, kind and courteous to all, which they were a century ago, they are moody and discontented, inflaming themselves with political theories; maddening themselves into indifference to life, both in themselves and in others; ready to kill or to be killed, and to infuse discontent and murmuring into the population of every other country; and all this in search of some imaginary perfection of government which shall make all men happy and contented. Miserable delusion! at variance with all that religion and experience have taught; and delusion incurable, because it refuses to be taught by the only masters capable of teaching, namely, religion and experience. It is in vain that M. Guizot now writes essays to tell them that they are seeking from earthly governments that which earthly governments were never intended to confer; he should have thought of that before he applauded the revolution of 1830.   The Abbé Lammenais sneers at the Austrians as a people who have only *des jouissances matérielles,* by which he means plenty to eat and drink, and plenty of amusement; and he would substitute for this an inundation of journals and pamphlets, making the people discontented and irritable by way of increasing the *jouissances intellectuelles.* It is grievously to be lamented that the English cannot eat more mutton and read fewer newspapers.   It is a common observation in France, that there is m ore general ease there than in England where there are colossal fortunes with starving millions, whilst in France wealth is more equally distributed : this is true statis tically, but not morally : there are more persons in France discontented with themselves, and with everything else, than in any other part of Europe; nothing pleases them ; neither their own government, nor that of any other country ; they grumble at the king, army, police, traders, manufacturers, and farmers : discontent has not settled down into a part of their national character, but it is fast doing so, notwithstanding this pretended general ease.

The principal great delusion under which the people labour is their idea respecting what is called " the freedom of the press." In times during which there were secret tribunals, some tyranny and injustice was no doubt exercised, and this was much modified if not corrected by the fear of exposure.   It is true that the fear of abuse from the people does operate to check improper practices, but the same judges who will be instigated to welldoing by such fear, will certainly also be tempted to ill-doing if the people are to be pleased thereby.   It is essential to the right administration of justice, that the trials be conducted in public ; more, however, in order that the innocence of those who have been accused falsely should be manifested, than that harshness towards the guilty should be checked.   As great injustice is committed now by the press in some cases, as was practised formerly by the most iniquitous judges.   The newspapers run a man down by the reiteration of charges, exaggerated and distorted, and so coloured as to make it difficult to ascertain the truth ; and in the cases of political offences, the press instigates both judge and jury to sacrifice innocence to the rage of the rabble, or to make of the delinquent a hero, and intimidates the government and the courts from the performance of their duty. ·

This power emanating from the people is seen every day to be more and more powerful to do all mischief, and powerless to do any good; it is a power of destruction, and of blasting, and of withering. Lord Farnborough told me that when he was first employed under Mr. Pitt, Mr. Burke proposed, through him, to establish a newspaper. Mr. Pitt thought the objections arising from there being an avowed organ of their sentiments greater than the advantages to be derived from it, but fully agreed with Mr. Burke in the power which the press was then beginning to exercise, observing, that it was really a fourth estate of the realm. On Mr. Long repeating this remark to Mr. Burke, he said, "Young man, you are just beginning public life, I am on the wane; but mark my words; if you live as long as I have done, you will find the press not only a fourth estate, but the government of the country." The liberty of the press is the regular subject of panegyric with orators who seek to please the common herd: "It is like the air we breathe," they exclaim: "if we have it not, we die." Every complaint of the abuse of the press is met by some of this hackneyed cant. We say a tornado, or a hurricane that sinks ships at anchor in the roads, that blows down sugar-boilers, and roots up all the plants upon an estate, is a very pernicious thing and a serious evil, and we are met by a simpering sentimentalist with an *aura veni*; · "Come, gentle air, the Æolian shepherd said;" or by a panegyric upon balmy zephyrs; or else we are plagued by a philosopher, with a lecture on the importance of air to the animal economy. The thing that is now meant, defended, and panegyrised, by the words "liberty of the press," is "an unbridled tongue that is set on fire of hell, and which setteth on fire the whole course of nature." Mr. Sheridan pandered more to the arrogance of newspaper writers than any member of the House of Commons had done up to his time. His most celebrated dictum on the subject is pure ranting: "Give them a corrupt House of Lords, give them a venal House of Commons, give them a tyrannical prince, give them a truckling court; and let me but have an unfettered press, I will defy them to encroach a half-hair's breadth upon the liberties of England." It would be far more just to say, Give us an unblemished House of

Lords,' give us an incorruptible House of Commons, give us a benevolent prince, give us a virtuous court, and let us but have an unfettered press, I will defy them all to preserve, unimpaired, the institutions of England.

In England slander is a trade. A clergyman of the Church of England told me that application was once made to him to take the direction of what was called "a religious journal." Before giving a final answer, he went to consult a brother clergyman who was editor of a review, telling him that he feared the sort of effect which the style of writing used in such works would have upon himself: his friend told him that his objection was well founded, for it was absolutely necessary for the editor of a newspaper of any kind "to have a touch of the devil in him." Upon hearing of this new agent in the concern, the clergyman declined the proposition. A journal is the joint property of a certain number of men and women ; they incur great expense in purchasing printing presses, and the rest of the stock in trade necessary for the business; and they then proceed to hire writers for different parts of the journal. Some of the ablest and best men in the country have been at times so employed, and there are no essays in the English language to be found superior to those which have adorned the columns of the principal journals. But unfortunately it is the spirit of party which alone can make a journal popular, i. e. profitable: hence the necessity either that these able men should condescend to the task of anonymous defamation of the individuals who differ from them, or some one must be found to write on any side, for or against any individual, public or private, according as the orders or the interest of the proprietors enjoin. This profligate power of detraction has become so great, that no set of ministers can long stand against it. It was this alone that overthrew Lord Melbourne's administration in May 1839, when every one wondered why he resigned, and why he returned to power : for every step which he had taken was, so far as he was able, in accordance with the principles with which he had set out; the Conservatives said he was too destructive; the Radicals said he was too conservative; but all failed to show that he had not done all that he was able to do. Nevertheless, the power of slander had alienated the confidence of members of the House of Commons, and without any apparent reason he found himself unable to carry on the government.*

· Such, and worse, will be the fate of every administration which can now be formed. The slander produces little irritation upon the subjects of it, because they are too much occupied with other business to read it. Moreover, the authors are perfectly well known to them, and their prices also. It is for their interest to keep their names as secret as possible. The secret, however, is never kept long, and, as Dr. Maginn has shown in "Frazer's Magazine," the greatest number of writers in the anonymous journals rarely, at any time, exceeds thirty; they are perfectly well known to each other, and may be, also, to any one who will take the trouble to inform himself about them. But upon the wondering multitude in the manufacturing towns who see in the word "We" an awful mystery of wisdom, at which the initiated only laugh, the effect is prodigious, and every tradesman swallows with blind faith the lie of his newspaper. There is no reform so much needed in the country as a reform of the press. Slander, when anonymous, is as much more atrocious than open and avowed slander, as a man who stabs another in the dark is a more malignant villain than he who boldly attacks his enemy in open day. *L'occasion fait le larron.*

---

* Since the above was written, the Queen's ministers have been again driven from her service by the same means; by a union of Conservatives with Radicals urging on the people against the objects of her choice, when she had no fault to find with them, and when the people could state no intelligible ground for dissatisfaction; and thus the curtain has fallen upon the first act of the Reform tragic farce. The late ministers had, indeed, become progressively unpopular, because the people have not realised the things, to obtain which they clamoured for Reform, and this the Conservatives have erroneously interpreted into a return to sounder monarchical principles, and increased love for themselves.

The question at issue is not between Whigs and Tories, but between monarchy and democracy; whether the Queen or the people should appoint their servants. The retirement of Lord Melbourne from office is a great calamity. He preserved to the country as much of government as it is capable of receiving, for he had both the Queen and the people with him. He found himself in novel and unparalleled circumstances, and he acquitted himself ably in them. To his sovereign he was not only a zealous and upright minister, but in the state of isolation in which she found herself at the commencement of her reign, from her rank, her sex, her youth, he was a father to the orphan, the guide and the friend, without forgetting that he was the servant and the subject, of the Princess, who had no one in whom she could confide: an obligation is due to him from both Sovereign and country, which the one never will, and the other never ought to, forget.

It is impossible for any one who makes a trade of anonymous writing to be as careful of what he states about others, as one who is responsible by being known. Slander should not be suffered to be a profitable trade. No journal should be permitted that is anonymous; and very heavy fines, imprisonment, or transportation, should be inflicted upon conviction of wilful evasion of the law. The government should be incessant in its prosecutions; and the more the anonymous writers cry out, the more vigorous should be the prosecution. The slanderers should be continually dragged before competent courts and competent juries; and of all men they have the least right to complain, who live and thrive by dragging men and judging them before their own incompetent, self-elected tribunals. Charles X. did not take a wise way of repressing the evil; but the report of M. de Polignac is unanswerable, which declares that it is impossible to govern any body of people where the licentiousness of the press is uncontrolled. To imprison him in Ham did not refute him; the earth did not stand still when they shut up Galileo for saying it moved; and when he got out, he said, " e pur si muove." The higher classes are not influenced by the daily press; it produces no effect on the House of Lords, chiefly because the higher classes see all the journals, and one, in some measure, counteracts the effect of the other, though all alike stimulate the appetite for detraction: but the middling and lower classes are entirely influenced by it, and votes in the House of Commons begin to change, whilst those of the wiser lords remain the same.

The sole profitable use that can be made of the press is, to ascertain from it the opinion of the mass of the people. One of the cant fallacies of the day is to call it " the best possible public instructor." It never can be the instructor of the people, for it is the expression of the mind and feelings which are already in the people; just as a man cannot teach himself by making himself a speech. A journal that would undertake to be an instructor would never sell. Readers of newspapers do not buy them in order to have a daily sermon: they take in the paper which expresses their own opinion, for the pleasure of seeing that opinion revived and enforced with better arguments than themselves can supply, as men cry " hear " when the leader of their party speaks their own sentiments. The press is the tongue of the people, and the world shows that symptom of age, garrulity; it is become like an old woman whose tongue is never still, while she claims homage for her superior experience. *Scribimus indocti doctique.*

There is one effect of the free use of the press, similar to that of the free power of the tongue, which has not been sufficiently noticed, and that is, that lying prevails in every age and country in the ratio of the multiplication of anonymous journals. Whoever will be at the pains of comparing the journals of 1840 with those of 1800, or those of 1800 with those of 1750; those of France with those of England; or those of England with those of America, can come to no other conclusion. Indeed, it would be easy, theoretically, to foresee that such must be the necessary result of anonymous and unbridled personalities, affording immunity and facility to the indulgence of public and private malevolence. Lying has become the national characteristic of the Americans, and it may become that of England also.

Yet the press is looked upon as the great means of the regeneration of mankind both morally and politically. God set up a Church to be the guide and instructor of men; and the Protestants have set up books : hence, Bibles and tracts are vainly imagined to be able to effect that which the Church should have done, which she has failed to do ; and men, instead of confessing their sins, and the sins of their fathers, in having departed from God's ways, are trying now to perform, by their machinery, that which God has not been able to accomplish by His. Fortunately, the Established Church has hitherto preserved for us one only authorised Bible; but, unhappily, Germany abounds with many versions, Luther's, De Wette's, Van Ess's, Gosner's, &c. &c. And whilst every one agrees that it is a pity so many wicked books are published, all agree to protect even these rather than suffer those which they call good books to be curtailed.

Of all the delusions of the day, that on the subject of what is called "education," is the most widely diffused. Professed critics in style, and writing, and language, the schoolmasters of schoolmasters themselves, use the words education and instruction as synonymous, in their speeches in both Houses of Parliament; and we have panegyrics upon, and plans without number for, national education by officers of the government. Instruc-

tion for all must be in those things of which all have need.
The government may cause gratuitous instruction to be given in
chemistry connected with the arts, in sugar-refining, soapmaking,
glassblowing, dyeing, mechanics, navigation, &c. &c.; but all
have not need of these things; and those who have need of one
of these have no need of the others. It would be an advantage,
doubtless, that the persons engaged in these pursuits should be
well instructed in the theories of them,— a branch of knowledge
in which English manufacturers are greatly behind their French
and German brethren. The knowledge of arts and sciences is
not useful to all; nay, it would be great waste of time for the
majority of the people to think of such things. Soapboilers,
dyers, sugar-refiners, &c., do not form the mass of the people;
they are the exceptions: an instruction cannot be for all, which
is useful only to the exceptions from the all. The mechanical
operations of reading and writing are the only things in which
the " all " can be instructed, and the boasted schemes for, and
panegyrics upon, " national education for all," when brought to
the analysis of common sense, just mean nothing more than
teaching the mechanical operation of reading some marks, and
making others upon paper. This, then, being all that is at-
tainable, if not all that is meant, what is this mechanical operation of reading and writing worth? It is just worth as much as,
and neither more nor less than, any other faculty or power with
which man is entrusted. The faculty of making poetry, the
faculty of painting pictures, of forming statues, of making
machines, &c. &c., may or may not contribute to the happiness
of the possessors, and of others, according as they are used.
They may be used to contribute to the misery of the possessor
and of all within his sphere, as did the faculty of reading and
writing to Voltaire, Volney, Paine, and others. Every faculty
which ever was, or ever can be, given to man, is a power which
must ever be exercised for purposes of good or evil, just in proportion as the possessor is or is not under the influence of sound
religious principles. The fine arts in Italy have produced more
lascivious than exalted impressions; church music in England,
more amusement and levity than devotion; whilst the Calvinistic sects, thinking to remedy these defects by banishing both
from their religious rites, have banished all praise, worship, and
devotion with them.

It was very well shown by Sir C. Bell, in his lecture at the opening of the London University, that the necessary tendency of scientific instruction is to make men sceptics. In history we are compelled to rely upon the assertions and opinions of others: but in chemistry, in anatomy, &c., the teacher must warn the pupil that he must take nothing upon the authority of another; that he must make every experiment for himself; that he cannot learn by books, and that books are only guides to show where knowledge may be obtained. Instruction in the sciences, even if it were fit for all, would necessarily produce a nation of sceptics, not only without faith but without even the faculty of believing.

The instruction which is necessary for all is instruction in the principles of religion, that is, in the duty of every man to God, commencing with the knowledge of God as He has revealed Himself; for men must learn to know Him before they can serve Him rightly; and in the duty of men towards each other in the various relationships of life, and especially in the duty of obedience to those who rule over them, whether in the state or in the church. But God has not given to kings, nor to laymen of any kind, authority to teach these things; and the king with his parliament cannot teach them themselves, and consequently cannot cause them to be taught by others. God has given the office of teaching these things to the clergy, and men must receive them from the clergy, or not receive them at all. No clergy who duly appreciate their Holy Orders, will ever permit the children of their flocks to go to other teachers: and whether the children of the sectarians, who have no faith in things of God's appointment, go or not, it matters little. It is possible that the clergy do teach falsely, or not at all, and that the people do perish for lack of knowledge; but civil governments cannot remedy this neglect, by attempting to do the priests' work. Moreover, it is not the intention of those who propose these schemes of national education, that men should be taught the knowledge of God as revealed by Himself, nor the duty of submission to those who rule over them, although these are the only points which it is equally necessary for all to know, and which therefore can alone form the proper subjects of instruction for the public. In politics, the only things essential for them to know are, that they were made to be ruled over, and not to rule;

that they are not competent to form any sound opinion upon state affairs; that God alone is the ruler of men, which act He performs by kings and nobles whom He has ordained for that end, and never by those who are not created for that purpose; and that it requires an equally powerful operation or gift of His Spirit to teach men to submit, which gift He will give to a people who fear Him, and seek to Him for it; but which He will withhold from a vain and conceited people, who think their own wisdom and philosophy better guides in politics than the rulers of His appointment; and He will let them perish miserably by rebellion. Religion is secondary in the national education both of England and France; even morality is neglected in the latter country; but whether neglected or encouraged, it makes little difference; no system of ethics is worth the name, nor indeed any system, that is not based upon Christianity.

Increased knowledge is increased power, of doing mischief, as well as of doing good. To give increased power to the people in these days is to put additional arms in the hands of those who, having broken forth from all the restraints of, and obedience to, God's Church, are doing whatever in them lies to destroy all the forms of government and religion which God has established for the control of man. A people advancing in the fear of God, and of reverence for the things of antiquity, might have been safely, perhaps profitably, entrusted with increased power, that is, knowledge; and in that case God would have given it them through the priesthood; but in the actual condition of European society, to give additional power to the people is to give increased means of circulating the poison which infects them. The great panegyrists of "national education" are newspaper writers, and the flatterers of newspaper writers: and if considered merely as a puff, by which the venders of such wares would seek to commend their articles, it might be tolerated as other puffs are, of blacking, quack medicines, &c. But it requires very different treatment, and must be opposed as a most pernicious error, when it has perverted the judgment of rulers in the state, as it has done in France, and is fast doing in England. True knowledge and government are blessings which come from God; the first by means of the priests, (either through direct instruction given in the Church, or through universities, colleges, &c., formed and conducted by them,) and

the second by means of kings. The only part which a man has
to perform is to acquaint himself with the things which are
freely given him of God, and to put himself in the way of
receiving them in order to be blessed by them. If, either
through ignorance or rebellion, he is not blessed in God's way,
h e cannot be blessed at all. A bad husband is better than the
best lover: a bad father is better than the best guardian; a bad
king is better than the best usurper; a bad priesthood is better
than all self-constituted and self-styled religious societies.
Everything in nature teaches us that there are not two ways of
doing the same thing; there are not two suns, nor two moons:
history shows that when one instrument failed to accomplish
the end for which it was designed, God did not make another
for the same work, but commenced a different work; as, for
example, when the Jewish church failed to become the blessing of
the world, God did not take another means of making the Jews
perform that office, but He took a people out of the Gentiles,
and put the Jews for the present time altogether to a side; so
having in this Gentile dispensation set up consecrated monarchy,
and ordained priests, as His means of governing and teaching
the baptized nations, He will set up no other instrument for
that end; He will not set up republics and voluntary societies;
and they who will not have the instruments of His appointment,
shall not obtain either knowledge or government, virtue or
peace, but must be puffed up with delusion, and filled with
disorder.

Another fallacy which has been inculcated by the political
economists, and with which the people are deluding themselves to
their own ruin, is, that it is better for their rulers to leave them
as far as possible to themselves, and not meddle by protection,
or interference of any kind, with their commercial projects.
This is a maxim which must, however, be received with some
limitations: if the idea intended to be conveyed, is simply that
each manufacturer and trader is best judge of his own interests,
and that all interference with his trade is prejudical to it, no objection can be made: but if the trader should argue from the
particular to the general, and say that what is best for him
must of necessity be equally good for everybody else, there he is
in error. Every manufacturer and trader would willingly sacrifice all other manufacturers and traders to his own advantage;

and the paternal government of the sovereign is necessary to see that in the pursuit of his own interests, he does not sacrifice those of other people.

In the report presented to Parliament upon the frequency and causes of shipwrecks, it is shown that these have fearfully increased in consequence of the abandonment of the former principles which used to regulate the building and manning of ships. Many ships are constructed purposely to last only a few years, and are yet, nevertheless, continued in use, until they break to pieces in bad weather, when the cargo and crew are all lost. The owners, at home, have the means of protecting themselves by insurances; but the poor ignorant sailors and boys who go on board them have no means of knowing whether they are safe or not. When the witnesses are asked what remedy they would propose for this, they all reply, that there is none but that of placing the whole under the supervision of the Queen's officers in the dock-yards. Here is a case where the people, sensible of the evil which has been committed, are themselves pointing out the only remedy, which is by the putting forth of the paternal care of the Crown, and preventing the merchants and shipbuilders from carrying on a free trade in human life.

The common fallacy by which the advocates of the *laissez faire* principle support their claims to sacrifice all other classes to their own interests is, that every class is equally able to defend itself from the aggression of its neighbour. But it is not possible for the poor sailors to know whether the vessels are seaworthy or not, whether they are built in order to go to pieces at the end of ten years, which is done in order to bring them under certain regulations of the insurance companies, or whether they are built to last as long as it is possible. It is necessary for the Crown, which is the common protector of all, to step in and protect those who cannot protect themselves from the avarice, rapacity, and power of combination of shipbuilders and merchants. It is as erroneous to urge that the mass of the people can protect themselves from all danger which may come upon them, and that therefore the Crown is justified in not watching over their interest, and interfering where it sees fit, as it would be to urge that the children and domestics of a family could protect, provide for, and defend themselves, without the continual interference and direction of the head in all the details of management. It is the duty of the Crown to afford this protection: to abandon the people to follow their own desires, is to abandon a duty towards them; it matters not whether the people, like pert and self-sufficient children, choose to imagine that they are competent to guide themselves, yea, more competent than the kings and fathers whom God has set over them: the duty of kings and fathers is still the same, and they must not slacken in their duty of supervision, and of taking care that their children injure neither themselves nor each other.

In like manner there is need of the steam-vessels being placed under proper control. Last summer, one of these running from London to Boulogne, was overtaken, on its return, by a fog, at the mouth of the Thames, and compelled to anchor. When the fog cleared away, there was not strength enough on board to weigh the anchor: the passengers at length endeavoured to assist, but there were very few men on board, although the vessel was crowded with women; the wind rose, and the whole were in imminent peril. The owners, of course, say, "Do not interfere with us; let us carry passengers at the lowest possible rate, whether a cargo of human beings goes occasionally to the bottom or not: do not meddle with the principles of free trade." But it is necessary that the government do prevent one class from doing anything that can be prejudicial to another.

Another fit of mania took these freetraders in the making of railroads: bills came into the House of Commons for their construction, to which every interest was to be sacrificed. Fortunately, the House of Lords interfered, and made a standing order, that no railroad should cross another road on the same level, but be compelled to go either under it by a tunnel, or over it by a bridge. Had it not been for this, the danger of highroads near railroads would have been so great from the fright of the horses drawing carriages, that loss of life and property must have perpetually ensued. In some cases, as near Lancaster, and near Dundee, they run parallel with the old turnpike-roads for a considerable distance. It would be curious and instructive, to give a list of the bills introduced by the Radicals into the House of Commons since it was reformed, and to point out the state in which the country would now be if these bills had passed, instead of being kicked out by the superior wisdom of the Lords, and rejected by the ministers of the Crown. Such a work would furnish a useful sample of the capacities of mob favourites, and of men lifted up from their native obscurity by the turmoil of faction, for being legislators and rulers of nations.

Trade is a means of wealth, and therefore it is necessary for trade to be encouraged. Manufactures are a means of wealth, and therefore they also must be encouraged; but there are limits to both: and under the best circumstances they generate principles which ought to be guarded against. In all ages and in all countries the ablest statesmen have perceived the demoralising tendencies of trade, and have denounced them; and if they be correct in what they allege, it follows that in proportion as a country is devoted to such pursuits, in the same proportion it is demoralised; and, moreover, that the more a country increases in trade and manufactures, the more it increases in demoralisation. Not to quote the examples of Tyre and Carthage, or to go back farther than Cicero, the following is his opinion, expressed in his treatise, *De Republica*, l. 2, iv.: *Est autem maritimis urbibus etiam corruptela ac mutatio morum; importantur non merces solum adventitiæ, sed etiam mores, ut nihil possit in patriis institutis manere integrum. Jam qui incolunt eos urbes non hærent in suis sedibus, sed volucri semper spe et cogitatione rapiuntur à domo largius, atque etiam cum manent corpore, animo tamen excurrunt, et vagantur. Nec vero ulla res magis labefactatum diu et Carthaginem et Corinthum pervertit aliquando, quam hic error ac dissipatio civium, quod mercandi cupiditate et navigandi, et agrorum et armorum cultum reliquerunt.* Lord Chatham's speech on the Falkland Isles records the opinion of that most consummate and experienced statesman: he says, "The little I know has not served to raise my opinion of what is vulgarly called the moneyed interest; I mean that bloodsucker, that muckworm, which calls itself the friend of government, that pretends to serve this or that administration, and may be purchased on the same terms by any administration; that advances money to government, and takes especial care of its own emoluments." Lord Chatham merely says that the moneyed interest will side with any party in the state; but Mr. Canning declares that it will side with any state, even with the enemy to its own. He says "We well know that at this moment there is scarcely a single

power that does not look for resources to the exchequer of our
Exchange. We are all aware that our moneyed men lend indiscriminately to all parties ; and those who are now ' the captains'
captains, the true lords of Europe,' are furnishing arms to those
who are contending against each other. Therefore let me not
be told that I may look for security to the morality of our
money-lenders. No, no ! let Ferdinand himself to-morrow show
signs of strength, and a determination to fit out an armament,
and the troops and fleets of Spain, raised by British capital, will
sail from your ports to strangle infant liberty in South America.
I defy you to prevent it ; and I defy you to show anything in
the morality of late pecuniary transactions to ensure you against
such an event." The same disregard of traders to the interest of
their native land, when anything is to be gained by betraying it,
is observed by Russell in Germany. "Frankfort," says he, "in
consequence of her commercial relations, is so thoroughly under
foreign influence, and so polluted by a mixture of all foreign
manners, that her population can hardly be said to have a character of their own. Even the multifarious connections with all
the ends of the earth, which have made her citizens in a manner
citizens of the world, have unfitted them to be German citizens,
for they judge of the happiness of mankind by the rate of exchange. Let no one hastily condemn the worthy citizens of
Frankfort for thus forgetting, in the pursuits of the merchant
and money speculator, the interest of their country; or at least,
before pronouncing his doom on their imagined selfishness, let
him study the ports of London, or Liverpool, or Bristol, and
discover, if he can, a purer foundation for English mercantile
patriotism." Vol. i. p. 52. During the last war in Canada, the
English and American armies were in sight of each other for a
considerable time, and neither could move for want of money.
The English general applied to the English merchants for some
dollars, offering an enormous interest for the loan on the part of
government. The merchants demanded a still higher interest;
the aid-de-camp, afraid to agree without fresh orders, returned
to the general. Whilst he was gone, the American general
offered to the English merchants the interest they required, and
obtained the money. The American army was the first in
motion to attack the English, by means of the money obtained
from English merchants. During the former part of the last

American war, it was well known that English money was lent to the government of the United States to carry on the war with this country.

Thus it is seen, that in every age the tendency of commerce is to destroy patriotism, and to sacrifice everything to the end of gain. As the country is now more given to trading than ever, so the manufacturing and trading classes show themselves to be more than ever demoralised. See, for example, the way in which the merchants, since free trade has been opened, have been poisoning the Chinese with opium, in violation of the laws of that land, and of all good faith between nations. See, again, the treatment of the children in the factories, and the resistance made by the manufacturers to any protection of these helpless human beings which shall interfere with their gains.

One of the chief causes of the embarrassment of the government with respect to the corn trade is the impossibility of counteracting the fraudulent practices of corn merchants in making fictitious prices of grain. The demoralisation is found descending from the great merchants and manufacturers into all the details of private life. In several of the magazines and journals there have been lengthened exposures of the corruption of domestic servants by the tradesmen in London, giving fees to them in proportion to the amount of their masters' bills; making the temptation to rob, plunder, and waste their employers' property greater than they can withstand.

Amongst the fallacies with which the age is full, one is, that commerce promotes civilisation. Here must certainly be a very wide " distribution of the middle term : " let us analyse the operation : commerce means sending cotton plush to Poland and bringing back Polish corn; who is the person civilised by the operation, the cottonman or the Pole ? or both ? or neither ? Well, but it will be said, it is not the exchange of goods, of things, but of ideas, which civilises : granted : the ideas communicated are contained on a letter of advice and a bill of lading : by which of these is Polish or Manchester civilisation promoted ? then perhaps we shall be told that it is by the intercourse of merchants with each other : first of all, merchants do not move much from home, and secondly, if, instead of writing, they send their clerks, what is to be communicated by these travelling clerks ? Intercourse between nations is advantageous to the heathen because it paves the way for missionaries to convert them : intercourse of science and art is advantageous because the professors receive mutual instruction ; but this has nothing to do with exchange of cotton for silk, or wool for wine : these exchanges are good in their way, but to speak of them as promoting civilisation is one of the impostures with which this "most thinking nation" abounds in the present day.

In ancient times in France, when a nobleman was compelled to gain his bread by trade, he was obliged to resign the emblems of his rank, which, however, he could resume whenever he was able to return to his former position in society. The custom marked the sense of all society as to the tendency of his occupation ; that it was ignoble ; that the principles and feelings it engendered were not elevating but degrading. He might, nevertheless, remain uncontaminated by the atmosphere that he breathed, and he might resist the downward tendency of everything by which he was surrounded ; but assuredly he could do so only by knowing his danger, and setting himself resolutely to contend against it. Many such examples are to be found in this country : the Right Honourable Thomas Harley was not a whit less honourable and noble when sheriff or mayor of London, than all his honourable and noble house had been before him ; he was equally every inch a nobleman in all he said, and thought, and did, in every situation of life in which he could be thrown. But such men are exceptions and contrasts, and I am not speaking of individuals, but of the tendency of a system, and this is pointed out to show the danger of any government yielding to the commercial spirit, which it is sure to do in proportion as its idol is popularity ; as the ministers look to the approbation of the mob, and not solely to that of their master : and there is cause to apprehend that from the pecuniary embarrassments of the country, the advisers of the Crown will seek to extend our trade and commercial relations, rather than to curtail and diminish that which is already prurient to rankness.

One of the evils which has flowed from the pretended Reform Bill is the infusion into the House of Commons of a greater number of economists, manufacturers, and merchants ; and consequently there is a greater difficulty in resisting the force of their evil principles in the government. But if it be bad that

the morals and maxims of traders be introduced, it is infinitely
worse that the morals and maxims of the sectaries pervade it.

The Quakers are the most absurd and offensive of all sectaries
in meddling with matters too high for them. They read in the
Bible "love your enemies," and their logic is, ergo, war is unlawful: they read "thou shalt not kill," and their logic is, ergo,
a murderer must not be hanged. Of all people they carry the
character of folly most clearly written upon their fronts; their
doctrines are, that having gotten the essentials of spiritual life
which are conveyed in baptism and the Eucharist, they do not
need the outward signs although God has appointed them, inasmuch as he who has the kernel may safely reject the husk. In
the first place, their illustration shows that they are ignorant of
the nature of a sacrament, inasmuch as it can no more be separated into two parts, so that one can exist without the other,
than can the soul and body of a man; and they might as well
say that, having a soul, they did not want a body at all. In the
next place they carry upon their backs the contradiction of their
own assertions, for if, because they have got a spiritual life, they
need not the sign of it, why, having gotten the victory over the
pride of dress, do they make it a part of their religion to wear a
particular garb? A spiritual truth apart from a corporeal manifestation of it, is mysticism; and if the Quakers had done no
more than make themselves ridiculous, they would not have
been noticed here; but they have been for a long time teazing
rulers everywhere about the unlawfulness of war, and of hanging
murderers, and have at length drawn into their vortex many
wiser men than themselves.

These mystics, and all such as they, begin invariably at the
wrong end; self is their idol, and self bounds the range of their
vision and their thoughts. Instead of putting themselves in
the place of rulers, and looking down from that elevation upon
themselves and upon all their own puny concerns, by which
they would be enabled to see things in proper proportion, and
themselves as mere units in a mass, they reduce everything to
the puny stature of their own comprehensions. Whoever is
attacked may receive the assault as he please; he may resist the
aggression, or having received a blow on one cheek he may turn
the other to receive a second on that also. But the case is
widely different where the interests of others are concerned. It

'is the duty of a parent to protect his child, and if the child be
attacked, to knock down the aggressor, or kill him if it be necessary to the safety of the child.   It is the duty of a sovereign to
protect the lives and properties of his subjects, and to order his
soldiers to fire upon all who meddle either with one or with the
other.   It is the duty of the rulers of a country to prevent the
peaceable inhabitants from being either robbed or murdered, and
to hang all robbers and murderers, if necessary for that prevention.   They who clamour against the lawfulness of war and
of putting criminals to death, are incompetent, from their position in society, to form an opinion upon the matter.   The sword
is put into the hand of the ruler for the punishment of evil
doers, and he must not bear it in vain.   "Whoso sheddeth man's
blood by man shall his blood be shed," is as christian a precept
as "love your enemies."   The question at issue is not how to
treat any enemy, but how to protect those whom it is the sovereign's duty to protect.

The right of resistance is not founded upon a right to rebel
against any authority, but upon every class of governors having
its peculiar jurisdiction.   The priests are right to resist every
interference of the king in the rites and ceremonies of the
church, and they ought in England to resist the nomination of
bishops by a pretended *congé d'élire.*   The king is right to
resist the authority of priests when they presume to say whether
or not oaths of allegiance are to be taken to him or observed,
and whether, under any circumstances whatever, he is or is not
to be obeyed.   Parents and husbands ought to resist the priests
holding indecent language to their daughters and wives under
pretence of making a good and perfect confession.   Heads of
families should resist all interference of either king or priest in
the education of their children, or management of their house-
holds.   Any individual may resist personal violence done to
himself or to those whom it is his duty to protect.   But if the
king use his soldiers to seize on the property of the church or of
any private individual, no personal resistance should be offered
to him.   The resistance of Wat Tyler was right, the resistance
of Hampden was wrong.

The question of duelling stands upon the same ground.   It is
a very evil thing for any one to risk his own life or that of other
persons for the gratification of his or their private malice and

revenge; but there are cases in which it may be as right to shoot a native as a foreigner, in private as in public war. Of such things no individual is a proper judge; his life is not his own, but belongs to God and to the king. The basis of a coroner's inquest is, that the king has been injured by being deprived of a subject, and he appoints a court to inquire by whose hands he has sustained the wrong. In former times, a court of honour determined whether the parties should have leave to fight or not, and it is to be regretted that this office of the Earl Marshal should have fallen into desuetude.

Thus have the religious vagaries of sectaries shown themselves in novel and wild political maxims, which are treated with too much contempt by statesmen, instead of being vigorously put down by inculcating sounder principles. They all tend to the same end, of showing to what absurdities men will come when, rejecting the institutions of God, for ruling and guiding them, they betake themselves to the moralities and humanities of their own invention.

Men think they can rule themselves because they think they can teach themselves. Self-teaching is the principle of Protestantism now run to seed in the sectaries in America and in England, and in the voluntary system in Scotland, whereby the people are informed that it is their province to judge of what is taught them, and to assemble in the house of God, not to be instructed by Him through His servant, but to discuss the opinions addressed to them by their servant. This is the acmé in theory of turning things upside down : the foundations of the earth that are out of course. The cause of all this is, that throughout Christendom men have quenched and resisted the Spirit, and so are become altogether fleshly. They look upon kings and priests as ordinary men, and as such they can see no reason for obeying them. Arguments of utility and general convenience are too weak to bind men for long, and in their very nature they are at all times equally open to discussion. Every pothouse politician thinks he has a better capacity for ruling and for instructing, than he who happens to fulfil these offices at the time, and consequently the mass of such people must always be in a state of discontent. They see no more of sanctity in kings and priests than they do in painters and physicians, in any professor of arts or of sciences; they see no further than the outward thing; they see flesh with fleshly eyes, but cannot see spiritual things, for they have no spiritual eyes. The Evangelical preacher tells the people not to go to their parish church, but to come to his chapel; not to mind the instruction of the Church, for that is formal and dead, but attend to him who is full of life. The demagogue tells the people that hereditary rulers and judges are absurdities; that only they who show, like himself, a capacity and talent for guiding public affairs ought to be their rulers. The *fons et origo* of all this is in having lost sight of the sacraments of the Church, which were admirably designed of God, as has been already stated, to teach men the true nature and method of His rule and direction of them. Material things, inanimate and irresponsible, could not of their own nature convey any moral or spiritual benefit. There is nothing in water more than in earth, in bread and wine more than in acorns and beer, to convey spiritual blessings, and therefore their efficacy for doing so must reside entirely in Him who has appointed them for these ends. There is therefore, of necessity, in them two principles, the one visible and the other invisible, and when one of these is lost the whole is destroyed; just as man himself is composed of a visible and invisible part: they who admit only the former are materialists; they who admit only the latter are mystics. The Romish priests began little by little to deny the material reality of the bread and wine, and ended by the climax of false doctrine and absurdity in the council held exclusively by members of their own sect at Trent, in asserting that there is no bread and wine in the sacrament at all. The Protestant sectaries began little by little to deny the real presence of Christ in the communion, and have brought their folly to a head in making it a mere commemoration of a departed friend. In like manner, the Romish priests sink their human character in their spiritual character and accuse all, who remonstrate against their wicked acts as men, of rebelling against the ordinance of God: while the Protestant sectaries deny all sanctity in orders whatever, take them up and lay them down *ad libitum*, as they would any secular employment.

But as it is only by the sacrament of water, when blessed by the priest, that God gives spiritual life, which fact men have now lost spiritual eyes to see, and faith to believe, and therefore debate upon the efficacy of water for any such end; and as it is by the sacrament of bread and wine, made the very flesh and blood of Christ, by the word spoken by Him through His priest, that the new life given in the former sacrament is continually nourished; so is it by those who are in themselves no wiser than others, and who have of themselves neither greater power nor capacity to rule over others, than any of the rest of their fellow creatures, that God does, through all those whom He makes heads, rule and bless all under them in their particular spheres, whether as kings, fathers, masters, &c. And the spiritual Christian sees God in those over him, and obeys them accordingly, and imputes whatever deficiency there may be in the fulness of the blessing which he desires, to the infirmity of the flesh in the channels of its conveyance, or in himself the recipient; but in no wise to Him who is the author, nor to the institution which has been appointed for that purpose.

The first evil act that was done in the world, was by man taking his own way in opposition to God's way: it is no matter how slight the departure, how trifling the object, how almost insensible at the first, the divergence has continually increased as man has gone forward, for the other way has remained fixed and immutable. The same tendency to independency has been in the whole race, and a training of subjection has been established from earliest infancy under parents, and continued subsequently under kings and subordinate rulers, to restrain and keep in check this tendency. Oftentimes irreligion has assumed the form of benevolence as it does now, and even the garb of piety. God has been disobeyed for the sake of offering unto Him more acceptable worship, and things devoted to destruction have been preserved "in order to sacrifice to the Lord in Gilgal." Liberals who have fostered instead of destroying rebels, appeared in all times, and would have produced the dissolution of all society long ago, if they had not been restrained; for so soon as Liberalism got a footing as a recognised principle which might be tolerated by the King, the doom of all established things was sealed. This is the only principle that is incompatible with society, incompatible with any government by God through man, incompatible with all religion, with every system or plan of bindings, ties, and dependencies which can be contrived.

No sooner were men enlarged from the small circle of family

relationships by many families being united into one great
society, and so formed into a nation under the government of
God, than it was commanded to be written in a book for the
instruction of all generations to the end of time, that God had
indignation against Amalek for ever.   (Am, *the people* ; Melek,
king.)   For sparing Amalek, for sparing the earliest type and
foreshadowing of the anti-monarchical principle, for showing
quarter to the Avatar of the idea, " the people the source of
legitimate power," did the first monarch lose his kingdom, as
shall every other monarch who will do otherwise than make
war to the knife upon all who hold similar sentiments now.

Liberalism has contrived to get itself tolerated in the state
because schism has obtained for itself a place in the sanctuary.
The people who boast that the simple Bible, without the
guidance of the church from which alone its authority is derived,
is sufficient to make them wise in all things, seem never yet, in
their reading, to have arrived at the passages that anathematise
schism, and pride themselves in Britain in sectarian names
which ought to be their shame, and shun the name of Catholic,
which ought to be their chief glory.   If God should be prevailed
with to pass by the iniquities of Christendom, it would only be
through public confession of the sin of schism by which it is
torn.   The praiseworthy endeavours of some at Oxford to return
to the " good old ways," have been assailed with the savage
virulence of the fifteenth century.   Yet these endeavours have
been but slight, and little has been attempted except a recurrence to ancient practices ; for the sound principles which led to
those practices are unknown even to those who are labouring to
revive them : and so their labours will come to nought ; and
rightly, for men are not wise to feed on shells from whence the
kernel is gone.   But the end aimed at was catholic truth, and
there is nothing true save that which has been *ubique, ab
omnibus, et in omni tempore receptum.*

Toleration has suffered morbid humours to come to maturity
and produce incurable mischief, which might have been crushed
in the bud.   Our intolerant fathers pursued a right principle,
although they pushed it to a cruel excess.   By quiet endurance,
the heterodoxy of one age becomes the orthodoxy of another,
for Word is a seed that has life, and produces fruit unless
killed betimes.   The maxims broached by the most violent

reformers were rejected by the wiser priests of the Church of England, and by the ablest nonconformists, and suppressed by all the power of the crown, so that they effected for many years afterwards no very flagrantly evil consequences. No sooner, however, was error tolerated in the church, than it began to corrode the vitals of the establishment; one sect calling itself evangelical, and claiming for its adherents all the spiritual life of the community, openly denied the plain import of words, by swearing to the belief of which they alone obtained their rank and emoluments; an act of falsehood and dishonesty without a parallel in the Christian Church; they denied the efficiency of the sacrament of baptism to make infants the children of God, and preached and published that this effect is produced through their own sermons and not through the sacrament. Now, others have gone the length of denying the divine power of the Christian priesthood, and of the presence of Christ's flesh and blood in the Eucharist. If these opinions have found entrance amongst the bishops, then, since the efficacy of every rite must be affected by the intention of him who administers it, there will have been no intention to administer regeneration, nor the flesh and blood of Christ, nor to commission priests to do the same; the Church of England will have been destroyed by its own heads; there will be no more means of feeding on the flesh of Christ in her, than in the unauthorised sects; and they who eat not His flesh and drink not His blood in the rite which He instituted for communicating the same, have no part in Him.

The improper concessions made by Constantine and Justinian to priests, brought about continual wars, and the subjection of all national, and family, and personal rights to meddling ecclesiastics; from the latter of which popish countries are not free, although the sovereigns, by their interference with the hierarchy, now trample, in their turn, on the rights of the Church. The protection sought by the Reformers from the princes at that time at war with the Emperor and the court of Rome, has at length reduced the church in Scotland, Switzerland, Prussia, and all the German States, to the lowest dependence; and in England the bishops are the creatures of the sovereign. Against this evil condition of the Church, the divine life that is in her is everywhere struggling according to its measure in each part; in Rome in one way; in Scotland in another; in England in

another: and the end will be disruption, violent, and severing
of many things that have hitherto been joined together. This
the Liberals will call purifying the church from secular defile-
ment: but it will be rather taking from things secular the salt
that alone preserves them from dissolution.

It is Liberalism alone that has been the cause of the antipathy
to the Oxford divines: wiser in this its generation than the
children of light, it perceived, though afar off, the signs of a
return also to rule and discipline in the Church: therefore was
the hypocritical cry of " no popery " raised against these able
theologians; and when the charge was denied, and proved in-
contestibly to be untrue, it was repeated in wilful falsehood by
the slanderers in the daily press. Nevertheless, it is only by
some such exertions that the purpose of God can be fulfilled,
and Himself enabled to answer the first petition which the Lord
taught man to put up, even that HIS KINGDOM SHOULD COME : a
kingdom in which church and state shall be indissolubly united;
wherein a Priest shall sit upon a throne; wherein the power
shall be absolute, and no republican or dissenter tolerated in it ;
nor any one hold authority who shall deny his mission, or the
efficacy of rites therein transacted. A hearty desire for such a
kingdom upon the earth, and the preparation for it by joyful
submission under all the bonds which the Lord has established,
is the touchstone of the genuineness of religion in these days.
It has been already observed, that the proclamation of glad
tidings now to go forth is not that of the cross but of the
kingdom : it is the kingdom that must be preached to all
nations, in order " that the end may come;" and it may be
necessary, in order to compel men to pray with earnestness and
sincerity for the establishment of this absolute monarchy, to
suffer the whole of Christendom to drink of that cup of insubordination which France, a nation not more guilty than any
other, has already drunk; a cup filled with blood mingled by
the people themselves, through the rulers of their own choosing,
in preference to those which God had given them; civil war
raging, as in Spain, in every town, in every village, in every
cottage, with such a mockery of government as France had
under the Directory. .

The heads, whom the people have now chosen for themselves
in England, are loud in the protestations of their " firmness and

fearlessness in the support of civil and religious liberty," in these days, when the only danger which threatens is from civil and religious licentiousness. Ever haunted by the ghost of the Starchamber, to them is truly applicable the sneer which some of their party cast on the last French dynasty, *imbécilles qui n'ont rien oubliés ni rien appris* from all the events which have happened within the last century. Unable to read the signs of the times in which they live, or to perceive the shaking of the heavens, or to hear the roaring of the sea, (for eyes have these idols of the people but see not, ears have they but hear not, and worse than the heathen idols, for they are not dumb;) they rave against the despotism of princes now powerless to oppress, and exert themselves to strengthen mobs which are already mighty to destroy. This metropolis was, in a former age, destroyed by fire, and in these times of high floods and inundations, the self-constituted guardians of the city cry, " To your pumps, O Israel ; " and call upon the people to overlook the deluge before their eyes, and to prepare their engines against a danger which exists no where but in an old almanac. It is a marvel, that amongst their other senile apprehensions, they have forgotten the Saracen, and do not avow themselves equally valorous to meet the paynim whenever the crescent should hover over our shores. They speak of " privileged classes," and of prescriptive rights, as of " monopolies and deeds of darkness " which are to disappear before the greater light of these improved days. Their vision, being perverted, they cannot discern the light from above irradiating the heavenly places of God's appointment, monarchies and the church ; and they rejoice in the blaze which has burst from the bottomless pit, mistaking the lurid glare of the volcano for illumination from on high. Too learned in things of matter not to smile at all endeavours to discover perpetual motion in mechanics, they are too ignorant in things of deeper import not to inculcate doctrines of " self-government," which is perpetual motion in politics, a machine acting without impulse from another — this a moral as the other is a physical paradox. Yet, truly, they themselves are acted upon by another, of whom they are not aware, even the Destroyer, whose ends they are accomplishing, and of whom they are the most efficient agents.

The self-love of the English has made them represent the horrors which marked the whole progress of the French revolu-

tion as characteristic of that nation; and in their denunciation
of them, there has been ever a secret exultation at their own
imagined exemption from natures so cruel as to be guilty of
such acts. The French revolution was nothing more than an
example upon a large scale of that which has ever stamped the
conduct of the dregs of the people, wheresoever and whensoever
they have obtained the mastery. Had not Napoleon been
mercifully permitted to seize the sovereignty, France must have
been depopulated. In that country, the cruelty of the mob is
associated with whatever is ludicrous and burlesque, as is also
their irreligion; in England the cruelty and irreligion are
associated with the solemn, long-faced mockery of the law. Be
it remembered, that it was the Parliament, which, under covert
of law, raised troops to oppose King Charles I., and it was by
the officers of the parliamentary army that the disgraceful
cruelties of those days were perpetrated. The treachery, the
faithlessness, the hypocrisies of the reformers were legalised in
their eyes by a pretended solemn league and covenant. The
histories of the legal persecutions, the impeachments which have
been carried forward by the House of Commons, show them to
have been generally foul perversions of justice, exhibiting a
ferocious thirst for blood, to obtain which, whilst forms of law
were observed, equity was set at defiance. The authors have
lacked the excuse of being carried away by momentary passion,
for these persecutions have been conducted as rancorously in
quiet as in the most violent times. The noble services of the
gallant Duke of Ormond marked him as a fit object for the
shafts of the people, who destroyed the man before whom they
had lately crouched. The disagreement amongst his enemies
alone saved the accomplished Harley from the vengeance of that
body which had recently loaded him with adulation. The
people had profited by the conduct of Warren Hastings, had received and appropriated to their own use the sums he had
cruelly extorted from the native Indians, but of which crimes
the people had made themselves partakers by enjoying the
fruits; the worst of the acts was passed over, and many years
after the deed had been transacted he was baited, like a noble
beast, for the amusement of his tormentors, until he was ruined,
and then he was unanimously found innocent by a more
righteous tribunal. In the impeachment of Lord Melville, a

man known to be a beggar was accused of embezzling money, which not an individual who made the charge believed that he had done, and one who was really guilty of whatever guilt there was, (and there was none,) was absolved by an *ex post facto* law passed expressly in order to make him available to get at the blood of the other. On the morning after the first vote on the tenth report, a venerable old member described the state of the House of Commons on the preceding evening, by saying, "The only thing that I know that it resembled, was a pack of hounds which had been a long time without tasting blood, in view of its prey at the end of the day." This is a just simile; this is a true picture of impeachments by the people; blood-thirsty cruelty and injustice under the mask of legal proceedings.

But no one who lives upon fame can exist without pandering to the delusions of the people, and offering incense at the shrine of "the spirit that now ruleth in the children of insubordination." Princes find that the power which was wielded by their ancestors comes no longer at their bidding. Men no longer guide events, but events carry away men. "They trust in armies, and their armies fail." Man, be he prince or subject, can no more stay the mad passions of the people, than the raging of the sea; yet every placeman flatters himself, until he has tried the result, with the adulation which Canute rejected. It is Almighty Power which is stretched out over the beasts, that makes them submissive to the uses for which they are adapted; and it requires nothing less than the same Almighty Power to be stretched over the brutal passions of unruly men, in order that they may be kept subject to those whom God has set over them; and this power will ever be put forth for the sake of those, who, knowing that all power comes from above, seek it in no other quarter. But princes are tempted to look to the people, as the people are tempted to look to themselves; for the tendency of all men's eyes is downward and not upward, and the principles of kingly government are as much gone out amongst them as amongst their subjects: even they are no longer Tories. It is to be feared that there is not vitality enough left in monarchy to buckle on its armour and die nobly in harness. It will slink out in one place by an *émeute*, and the overturn of an *omnibus;* and in another by a bill denouncing monopolies and privileged classes, proclaiming cheap corn, free trade, and the blessings of civil and religious liberty. Even the court of Rome is preparing to follow the advice of the Abbé Lammennais, where the priests, having used the power of kings for their own advancement in times past, are now, when kingly power is failing, ready to take the side of the rabble; and the beast which has hitherto been gorgeously attired in purple and fine linen, will now appear rising out of the bottomless pit of popular will. They too will fail. The Jesuits, who are the most learned, and the most sharp-sighted soldiers in the Roman camp, see the futility of this new attempt. The secular power of Rome has been based upon the usurpation of their subjects' rights by the sovereigns, and the same bell which tolls for kingly power will ring the funeral dirge of priestly rule.

But these observations must close for the present. The sum of the whole matter is this: Toryism is government by the crown; Whiggism is government by the aristocracy; Liberalism is a false attempt to govern by the people—a confounding of governors and governed into one—man ruling himself, not another ruling him; the only end of which is or can be, no government at all, nor anything but confusion, spoliation, and bloodshed. The proofs are found in the uniform history of mankind. The effects of Liberalism were seen in the French from 1789, to the time when Napoleon seized the dominion; they are seen again now, as the following extract from the observations of the French government upon the condition of France in June 1839 will show:—"*Les factions viennent de donner un sanglant signe de vie. Elles vivent et jamais elles n'ont cessé de vivre; elles vivent et dans leur sein se perpétuent les funestes traditions de 1832 et de 1834; elles vivent, et croissent en audace, en violence, en perversité; elles vivent, et dans l'ombre où la loi les a refoulées, elles trament à loisir leurs complots, lancent leur proclamations incendiaires, aiguisent leurs armes et se préparent à porter des coups plus sûrs et plus terribles; elles vivent, et de cent repaires inconnus où elles se retranchent, elles sont toujours prêts à fondre sur la société, à la surprendre, à la frapper au cœur, à l'attaquer avec toutes les ressources d'une organisation compacte, perfectionnée, renforcée, avec tous les avantages d'une discipline et d'une stratégie consommée, aguerrie par l'expérience de vingt échecs. Les factions vivent et se déclarent elles-mêmes immortelles. Loin d'avoir cédé du terrain, elles ont multipliés leurs moyens d'action et d'influence. Elles ont poussés cent ramifications sur tous les points du royaume, et enlacé la France comme dans un réseau fatal! Oui, c'est un triste et extraordinaire spectacle que celui que présente cette hiérarchie organisée pour le crime, le pillage, et la destruction, cette congrégation armée contre l'ordre et les lois, qui a ses chefs, ses statuts, son drapeau, ses mots d'ordre. Mais veut-on savoir quelle est la morale qui est officiellement professée au fond de ces conciliabules? on ne sera pas moins surpris ni moins effrayé. L'assassinat des rois en général et de celui que la France a mis sur le trône de Juillet en particulier, est prêché comme le plus saint des devoirs; il est écrit dans tous les ordres du jour; il est pris dans le serment que prête le néophyte à son entrée dans le sanctuaire; il est le premier dogme de catéchisme infernal. L'idéal du gouvernement que l'on reserve à la France, celui par lequel on veut remplacer les abus et les scandales de la monarchie c'est la république de 1793 et la Terreur. Voilà! l'âge d'or que l'on promet officiellement à la France! mais ce n'est pas tout; la révolution que l'on veut opérer, on déclare que c'est une révolution à la fois politique et sociale. Ce n'est pas seulement le roi, le royauté que l'on veut frapper et extirper du sol; c'est encore et surtout l'aristocratie, et les aristocrates, et la liste des aristocrates est longue. Le propriétaire foncier est aristocrate au premier chef; le capitaliste, aristocrate; le chef d'atélier, aristocrate; quiconque est convaincu de posséder un arpent de terre ou cent écus de rente, aristocrate. On portera la hâche et la torche sur ses inégalités monstrueuses! On nivellera du même coup les têtes, les rangs, et les fortunes. La double réforme que l'on veut fonder sur les ruines de la monarchie et de la société, c'est en politique la souveraineté du peuple tempérée par l'échafaud; en économie l'égalité des fortunes et la communauté des biens.—Voilà le but et voilà les moyens."*

Such is the only possible end of the French revolution of July; and such is the only possible end of the principles which were advocated by the promoters of the Reform Bill in England, unless a vigorous stand be made against them. To promote this end has been the effect, I say not the intention, of every

speech of every liberal from the beginning of the French revolution down to this hour. To promote this is the direct
tendency of every panegyric of the press; of every tirade
in favour of civil and religious liberty; of all sneers at monopolies; of all attacks upon the landed proprietors, and on other
privileged classes. To promote and forward this, is the labour
also directed of the most active, the most righteous, the most
benevolent, the most pious men in Europe. To promote this
are the operations of all that whole machinery of self-formed
societies which have risen up to do the works of government and
of teaching, instead of the regular governments and church
establishments in each country; Reform, Conservative, and
Socialist Clubs, Bible, Tract, and Missionary Societies, by whatever name they may be called, or with whatever intention they be
formed. All men see and feel the perversions of power by those
in authority in times past, and many, from a real desire to serve
God, and to be useful to man, see with satisfaction, encourage,
and even originate schemes for the supplanting of institutions
which have been unworthily filled. In the guilt and folly of
this, so far as his small means and sphere extended, the writer
of these pages has in past times had his full share; and every
just and benevolent and pious man will be found banded with
the wicked in the work of universal destruction, save in so far
as he is enlightened in the true principles of God's government
of men by kings, and of teaching them by His Church. Neither
zeal, nor benevolence, nor reading of the Bible, are sufficient to
direct men how to be " fellow-workers with God," in the work
that He is now accomplishing by these revolutions. He speaks
out of flesh and not out of paper; out of His Church, out of the
mouth of kings, and not out of Hebrew and Greek books. It
was zeal for God that caused the Lord of Life and Glory to be
put to death; it was zeal for God and reading his Bible that
made Colonel Hutchinson murder his king; it was zeal for God
that made priests in past ages light the fires of persecution all
over Europe; and zeal for God made John Knox and other
reformers declare that the people might put to death any
sovereigns whom these preachers judged to have acted contrary
to God's will. It is the *soi-disant* pious, the idolaters of the
Bible, who are in the Protestant countries as active as any in
rejecting the teaching of the priesthood; in denying the efficacy

of orders, and of all the sacraments of the Church; in despising the divine authority of kings, and the privileges of nobles and of all other classes; and the fruit of the contempt which the so-called evangelical people have inspired for the priesthood is that the mass of open infidels, who believe neither in heaven nor hell, who are wholly devoid of any principle of religion or morality, is at this moment greater in France and England than it has been at any period since the conversion of these nations to Christianity.

We have seen the fate of Louis Philippe described above by the hands of his own ministers; that of every other sovereign who shall seek to wear his crown upon a similar tenure, who shall seek strength from beneath instead of exclusively from above, who shall compromise his dignity by recognising any right than right divine to his office, cannot be mistaken.

George III. preserved his throne solely by unremitting war with levelling principles of every grade; and the most instructive page in the history of England for his successors and for all other sovereigns, is the page which records his life as long as he administered his government by the hands of Mr. Pitt. The lesson taught to Christendom by the successful struggle of England single-handed against the revolutionary power of France, with all the other states of Europe ultimately in its train, is, that the only safe, practicable, and even possible way to withstand the inroad and final success of liberal principles is by open war, by physical rather than by moral resistance.

If kings suffer themselves to be cajoled by the hypocritical adulation of seducing demagogues, which they shall receive no longer than whilst they are subservient to their purpose; if they are not suspicious of the praise of clamourers for civil and religious liberty; if they hold parley with liberalism, doubting whether it be or not the very spirit of antichrist, and whether their only safety from it be through any other means than determined uncompromising hatred, defiance, and resistance, the Spirit of God, the Ruler, is departed from them, and they are but gilded puppets, ready to be discarded on the first convenient occasion by the very mob which they have culpably sought to conciliate.

LETTER

SIR ROBERT H. INGLIS, BART. M.P.

ON THE

PAYMENT OF THE ROMAN CATHOLIC CLERGY

1845

LETTER

ETC.

DEAR SIR ROBERT,

You and I have ever been of the same opinion respecting the character of the measures called Reforms which have been adopted in ecclesiastical and political affairs. There is a large body of people who are of one mind with us, but I think the course which they follow, and which they urge you to pursue, is inconsistent with that opinion; so inconsistent, that I can only attribute their conduct to a superficial view of the subject, proving that they have not really *approfondi,* or gone to the bottom of the question.

In politics we have boasted in the name of Tories: exactly one hundred years ago, 1745, our fathers did in that of Jacobites: we may do so still; we may sing "Blue bonnets over the border," or "Wha would na' fecht for Charlie," but to attempt now to carry into practice Tory principles of government is as insane as to set up another Stuart competitor for the throne.

It is well, as a matter of history, to venerate the memories of those who fought for the ancient dynasty, and saved or lost their heads and lands as they best could; and it is well to remember that there was a time when England was a monarchy, the whole framework of which consisted of privileged classes, each exclusive, admitting no rival nor intermeddling in its affairs. But this state of things has departed never to return, unless some future Rodolph of Hapsburg, William of Normandy, or Napoleon of Ajaccio, shall regain it by the sword: nothing is now privileged, nothing is now exclusive: it may be that some parts of the ancient skin are still adhering to the new form which the animal has assumed; but it is the skin which must be entirely cast off, and not the animal which can ever reassume its former shape.

z 3

There was a time when Toryism was a reality: when the
Sovereign was the wealthiest of the hereditary landowners of
England, with his estates the most unalterably entailed : the
exclusiveness of his position accumulated until at last it reached
the point of separating him by blood from all the other natives
of England, and permitting him to ally himself only with a
foreign sovereign house.   Not only exclusive in his matrimonial
connections, but exclusive also in his faith, the sovereign of many
millions of Hindoos, of Mahomedans, of Jews, of Roman
Catholics, and of Presbyterians, he was compelled to differ in
faith from them all, and to be a member and head of the Church
of England alone : all the officers of his Court, and all his
ministers and servants throughout the country, his judges, his
councillors, his parliament, his generals and his admirals, his
magistrates, the mayors and aldermen of his cities, were compelled also to be members of the Church of England.   Moreover,
most severe laws were passed, and partially executed to punish
all dissenters from the exclusive faith of this exclusive king.
So far all was one consistent theory, carried out into a consistent
practice.   The State was united with one Christian sect, and all
others were proscribed.

The practice, however, never was fully carried out.   The
king appointed Presbyterians for his ministers ; he did not ex-
tirpate Papists ; Presbyterians and Socinians were returned as
members of his Parliament, and annual Acts of Indemnity for
this wilful violation of the laws were passed ; and ultimately the
Papists and Dissenters from the Church of England grew into a
body so numerous that he could not destroy them even if he had
been willing to do so.   At length the Test and Corporation
Acts were repealed : Roman Catholics were recognised by law;
they and Dissenters were dealt with as constituent parts of the
kingdom : exclusiveness was at an end ; and with it must perish
every reasoning which is based upon such a condition of the
English monarchy.

The changes which have been wrought in the monarchy and
in the ecclesiastical polity have not been effected by a strong
faction bearing down the wishes of the mass of the people :
rather the executive has been behind the feelings of the country,
and has adhered to the ancient exclusiveness, after the spirit of
it had evaporated alike from the breast of the sovereign, of the

nobles, of the bishops, and of all the privileged classes. You and I may lament over the present state of things, but the former is gone for ever; and it is folly of the highest kind to take other than one of two courses, — namely, either to attempt the restoration of that which is gone, and which restoration can only be effected by the sword, not by petitions, or to adapt our conduct·to the altered circumstances, however much we may dislike them.

In this latter case, however, there are still two subdivisions: we may either abstain from taking part in any public business whatever, or we must honestly carry out the laws as they are. What would you say to me, if, hating the New Poor Law with as perfect hatred as I do, in its principles and all its details, I should endeavour, when acting as a magistrate, to counteract it, instead of enforcing its provisions? Would it not be manifestly wrong and absurd so to do? and is it not the same to endeavour to carry out a principle of government founded upon exclusive privileges in a Parliament which has declared, and in times when the whole country is resolved, that there shall be no exclusive prerogatives, but absolute equality in everything?

There is no middle course between Toryism and that which the Ministers are now taking. Mr. D'Israeli has truly observed that the faction calling itself Conservative is the most silly and contemptible that the country has ever presented. It does not pretend to have a principle, and it talks of conserving nobody knows what, and nobody knows how. The county members chose to fancy, when in opposition, that if Sir Robert Peel came into office he would give them "remunerating prices," by which they meant a heavy duty on corn, and thereby leave thousands in Glasgow, Paisley, and Manchester to die of famine; now they turn round and abuse him because he has not acted up to their imaginations. The Orangemen thought that he would enable them to trample on their brethren the Roman Catholics, as they have done for these last 300 years, although Parliament has received Roman Catholics, Dissenters, and even Jews into its bosom; and are loud in their clamours because such a thing is impossible. The Ministers of the Queen have no choice; it signifies little by what name they are called, Conservatives or Liberals, Whigs or Radicals, the same measures will be adopted. Men having experience in official details will do the work better than novices; but the same work will be done, well or ill. If there is any difference between the two political parties, it merely consists in this, — that the measures recommended by the last were pursued with a view to conciliate the mob, and consequently obtained for the promoters little but contempt; whereas those advocated by the present are adopted solely from the conviction that they are the best for the country, although they create against themselves some temporary obloquy. There must be no longer exclusiveness: no one State Church; no Universities from which all but members of one Church shall be excluded; no bishops of one sect better off than the bishops of another sect. A few zealous Protestants may roar against Papists, and be joined by those who hate all religion, whenever a question of paying money is mooted; some persons of noble blood and of great possessions may endeavour to prolong the existence of a condemned aristocracy; but the doom of all privileged classes is sealed. The hereditary possessions of the Sovereign are gone, and he is only the most burdensome State pensioner, shortly to be despised, and voted too expensive, as all paid servants of the mob ever are. The owners of the lands of England are no longer the exclusive legislators of the English: manufacturers, merchants, and Jews, who have no exclusive connection with British interests, outvote in Parliament the ancient legislators. The Lords have been deprived by the present Ministers of the Crown of the right to be hereditary judges, as their right to be hereditary legislators has ever afforded subject for a sneer to Benthamites, and other concoctors of ephemeral constitutions. The Bishops no longer rule the Churches under them even in things not essential, and in essentials they publish their disagreements one with another in the face of the whole Church. One Minister of the Crown, who has kindly relieved the House of Lords from the burden of judgment, has, with equal kindness, endeavoured to relieve the clergy from the burden of teaching, and has announced himself as the Minister of Public Instruction; whilst another has had the effrontery to threaten the Bishops with expulsion altogether from the House of Lords.

In the present state of mankind it is impossible that the clergy who are dependent upon the people can do otherwise than pander to their evil passions in some way or other. This

is the condition of the clergy in America; this is the condition
of the Free Church ministers in Scotland; this is the condition
of the priests in Ireland; this is the case with the Jesuits in
France. That such is the state of the two former I will not
waste time in proving; that of the third has been shown with
irresistible wit and force by Sydney Smith in his posthumous
pamphlet; that of the last requires more details to explain than
can be easily given in this letter, and it must suffice to observe that their wicked system of lowering the requirements of
morality is cleverly pointed out by Michelet, as having been
invented, and admirably adapted, to be a means of more easily
gaining an influence over the mass of mankind, which is ever
trying to keep its sins, and yet get to heaven. It is wise to
endeavour to elevate the Irish priests out of this degraded and
dangerous condition, and this is the object proposed by the grant
to Maynooth. It is recommended, however, upon two grounds
both equally erroneous:—1st, as a means of conciliating the priests
and making them friends to the English Established Church;
and 2nd, as a means of giving better education to the clergy:
the first is impossible, and the second will not be attained.

I assume that the argument of Sydney Smith is incontrover-
tible, namely, that the Irish priests at present must be the
leaders and encouragers of the bad passions of the people.
Mr. O'Connell, in his evidence on the Catholic Relief Bill, said
plainly that such was the case; that the priests had great influence and power to lead the people to mischief, but none
whatever to restrain them from it. Instead, however, of believing a man who knew what he was talking about, and was
therefore capable of giving sound and useful counsel, the advice
was rejected from prejudice against him because he was a
Papist; some deep design was supposed to lurk under his
words, and his testimony was practically thrown aside. The
grant to Maynooth tends to increase the comforts of the students
during the time that they are being educated, and to add to
the number of scholars, but that is all: it has not any one of
the advantages which Sydney Smith says most truly would
result from paying the clergy. But even paying the clergy,
and still less merely teaching them, will never reconcile
them to the Established Church of Ireland. The education
being bad at Maynooth, the present grant simply adds to

the number of those who participate in this bad education, but does not make the education better. It is bad, because it does not eradicate, nor even moderate, the petty local animosities, faction feuds, family quarrels, sectarian bitterness, and bloodthirsty vengeance in which the inmates have been bred, but only gives them increased power of carrying these bad passions into action. When men are filled with love themselves, they see all things through a kind and loving medium; and when men are animated with a spirit of liberalism, they seem to think that all other men are fired with the same. As the House of Commons now considers all creeds alike, the members imagine that Roman Catholics have lost their consciences also; and those on the other side think that there is no real religious conscientiousness, although erroneous, at the bottom of the opposition of the Evangelicals. Every Roman Catholic, however little spiritual life he may have, holds his faith not as an opinion, but as a conviction: the Roman Catholic clergy know and teach that all the inhabitants of England are under the ban of the Pope, whose word and condemnation are as certain as any word that the Almighty can speak. "Celui qui obéit doit considérer les paroles qui sortent de la bouche de l'un des supérieurs, comme si elles sortaient de la bouche même de J. C. N. S., afin de se rendre capable de plaire à la Divine Majesté;" and that no sovereign holds his throne by any legal title save as the Pope has conferred it. These are their words: —

"The Pope has a temporal power over all princes.

"Every governor of a State holds his office in virtue of a special commission from the Pope, in such sort, that, if the latter think fit, he may *immediately* govern the former.

"The Pope can give guardians to princes, punish them, depose them for heresy, for incapacity, for negligence, or for any other cause.

"He can not only do that which secular princes have the power and right to do; but he has moreover to *dispose of their estates, and distribute them to others.*

"He is the servant of the servants of God through humility, but he is, at the same time, the Lord of lords through power; and whatsoever power there may be under heaven is a dependence upon his."

When these propositions were publicly maintained in the reign of Louis XIV., his powerful minister, Cardinal Richelieu, found they were incompatible with the existence of his master's authority; and, being more statesman than churchman, he had those who thus taught arraigned before the parliament, which demanded a categorical answer, yes or no, to the question, whether the Pope could absolve subjects from their allegiance : but this categorical answer could not be obtained; and the · utmost that the clergy would say was, " Le roi, fils aîné de l'Église, se donnerait bien garde de rien faire qui obligeat le Pape à cela : " which was, in fact, to reiterate the claim.

Most justly did Lord Beaumont sneer in the House of Lords at the assertion of those who say that any change has ever been wrought in the doctrine or opinions of the Popish clergy : they boast of holding every one now which they have ever done in former times.

There is, however, a convenient quibble by which the Papists often save themselves, which is to say, that these things, like celibacy of the clergy and praying to dead men and women, are no doctrines of the Church but only *piæ opiniones*. Technically *dogmata* are not *piæ opiniones;* but practically these *piæ opiniones* make the sum and substance of every Irish Papist's religion. He is taught to believe that it is meritorious in him to have no conscience, and to know no morals but what the priest declares to him are such. " Expedit in primis ad profectum et valde necessarium est ut omnes perfectæ obedientiæ se dedant, superiorem, quicumque ille sit, loco Christi Domini Nostri agnoscentes, et interna reverentia et amore eum prosequentes, nec solum in executione externa eorum quæ injungit, integre, prompte, fortiter, et cum humilitate debita, sine excusationibus et obmurmurationibus, obediant, licet difficilia, et secundum sensualitatem repugnantia jubeat; verum etiam conentur interius resignationem et veram abnegationem propriæ voluntatis et judicii habere, voluntatem ac judicium suum cum eo quod superior vult et sentit in omnibus rebus ubi peccatum non cerneretur, omnino conformantes, proposita sibi voluntate ac judicio superioris, pro regula suæ voluntatis ac judicii, quo exactius conformentur primæ ac summæ regulæ omnis bonæ voluntatis et judicii, quæ est æterna bonitas et sapientia."

I will not translate this myself, in order to avoid the

imputation of perverting the meaning ; but the following is the translation, made under the authority of the French Government in the reign of Louis XV. : — "Mais ce qui est par-dessus tout utile et très-nécessaire c'est que tous s'abandonnent à une parfaite obéissance, reconnaissant le Supérieur, quel qu'il soit, comme tenant la place de J. C. N. S., et l'ayant en grande vénération et amour, et que non-seulement, dans l'exécution extérieure de ses ordres, ils obéissent sans réserve, promptement, resolûment, humblement, sans excuses ni murmures, leur commandât-il des choses difficiles et repoussantes pour les sens, mais encore quils tâchent, à l'intérieur, d'avoir la résignation et la vraie abnégation de leur volonté et de leur jugement ; conformant en toute leur volonté et léur jugement avec ce qui veut et pense le supérieur ; pour cela, ils devront se proposer la volonté et le jugement de leur supérieur comme la règle des leurs, afin de se conformer plus exactement à cette prémière et souveraine règle, de tout bonne volonté, de tout bon jugement, règle qui est la bonté et la sagesse éternelle."

There seems, in the midst of this vile code of self-immolation to be a sort of salvo in the expression, " Ubi peccatum non cerneretur ; " but this is wholly taken away by the following injunction, that the faithful are to be put to trials, in proportion as they make advance in this blind obedience, until they arrive at that point that they are able to endure and obey such orders as God gave to Abraham : " Eo modo quo Dominus Abraham tentavit ; ut specimen virtutis suæ præbeant et in eadem crescant ; " that is, to kill his child, in doing of which he is to see no sin, but to obey the priest.   " Il sera bon que les supérieurs donnent quelquefois à ceux qui sont éprouvés des occasions d'exercer les vertus de pauvreté et d'obéissance, en les tentant pour leur plus grande utilité spirituelle *de la même manière que le Seigneur tenta Abraham ;* ils donneront ainsi des preuves de leur vertu et croîtront en mérite.   On gardera toutefois dans ces tentations, autant que possible, la mesure proportionnée aux forces de chacun ainsi que la discrétion le dictera."

In addition to this, their doctrine is, that the highest perfection of religious life to which any one can attain is to be as a lifeless stick, or dead corpse, in the hands of the priest, for him to handle and mould as he will : " Comme un cadavre qui se laisse tourner et manier en tous sens, ou encore comme un bâton qui sert partout et à toute fin au vieillard qui le tient à la main." M. Bouvier, bishop of Mans, is at this moment teaching in France the authority of the Church in all things over the State; and under the colour of the duty of subjects, he says, "At the voice of the legitimate prince they ought to take up arms against the usurper, to fight against him, to overcome him, to drive him away; more than this, they ought to assassinate him as a public malefactor, if the legitimate prince so command." "Immo privatim illum tanquam publicum malefactorem occidere, si legitimus princeps id expressè jubeat." Romish priests being the sole expositors of the words: legitimate princes, legitimate owners of estates, or of property, honours, ranks, &c.

Now, put this chain of instruction together, not *doctrines*, but only *pious opinions*, for the hot-headed, excitable, starving Irish rabble: — that the priests have power to say to whom estates belong; to order any usurpers to be assassinated; that the ecclesiastical superior, whoever he may be, is the interpreter to each individual of what he ought to do, even to the murder of his child. You know in how many instances murder has followed on persons being denounced from the altars in Ireland.

The Roman Catholic laymen are very little aware of what the clergy teach to the people; the Protestant laity still less. I remember once walking home from the House of Commons with our lamented friend Lord Fitzgerald, after a debate on the Catholic claims, in the course of which an acquaintance of ours had made a speech that gained for him great credit at the time. In speaking of the debate he said, "Oh how I envy ——— his speech; it showed such delightful ignorance of Catholics and of Ireland, and of Irish Catholics; it is quite delightful to see any one in such a happy condition." Truly such seems to be the condition of many Members, and certainly of all those who recommend this measure as a means of conciliation.

It is impossible to imagine an idea more absurd than that of conciliating the lower order of Irish priests. With the exception of those of Portugal, there is nothing in Western Europe to be compared with their ignorance and fanaticism. They live upon fees in kind, paid on marriages, baptisms, and deaths, and consequently they encourage the breed of Papists, as farmers do that of sheep, — the more people, the more fees. This is the cause of the rapid increase of population there, which no one has sufficiently denounced. No young persons are allowed by the priests to remain single after they are marriageable. So long as this system continues, there must be a larger number of people in Ireland on the verge of starvation than in any other country in the world, and consequently a larger number of people ready to rise in rebellion on any subject, for nothing can make their condition worse, and there is a chance of some individual being bettered. The cry for repeal can never cease; and the more absurd and the more impossible to be obtained, the more effectual will it be as a standing grievance, of which every succeeding priestly or political incendiary may take advantage. This priestly manufacture of paupers goes on, be it also remarked, in a country which, by climate and soil, is more adapted for grazing than for arable cultivation, and consequently requires fewer labourers, because less labour to make it productive. From these incendiary priests the laity have at various times endeavoured to rid themselves, and whenever they have done so, some English minister has meddled to strengthen the priests' hands. Not long ago a tariff was circulated through Ireland containing an amount of fees beyond which the laity positively refused to pay; but before it could work its effects some foolish irritation was given on this side of the water, which priests and laity united to resent, and so merged for the time their intestine troubles.

Since these words were written, observe what has occurred in confirmation of them. The Roman Catholic lay noblemen and gentlemen in Parliament have all expressed satisfaction, at least, at this grant so far as it goes, looking upon it as an earnest of something better, and at all events as a token of good-will, and well meant on the part of the Government towards the Roman Catholic Church. But the priests have expressed, through Dr. Higgins, their bishop, the most rancorous animosity. He has pretended that the English nation has risen, as one man, against the Irish, whilst it is notorious that the most violent opponents of the grant are the very parties who were equally strong advocates for the removal of the Catholic disabilities. Loud as the cry has been against the superstitions and idolatry inculcated by the *Popish priests*, not one word has been said either about *Ireland* or about *the Irish*. The clergy of the Church of England, who were strenuously opposed to the granting of the Roman Catholic claims, have been almost entirely passive on

this question; and by very far the largest number of petitions
and speakers has been from those who are as hostile to the
Established Church of Ireland as they are to the establishment
of Popery. But this view of the case did not suit the views of
the priests, and they have wilfully misstated the matter for the
sole end of keeping up a state of excitement in the people which
is necessary to their power over them; and thus the conduct of
the priests corroborates the statement here made respecting the
absurdity of supposing that Irish priests can ever be conciliated
by any measures which do not give them absolute supremacy
over the laity, or that anything short of that can content them.
Any idea of conciliation evinces extraordinary ignorance of the
doctrines and opinions, habits and character, of these men.

The evil of Maynooth is, that the system there pursued is one
of education solely for Irish priests; not for the Irish public,
gentlemen, laymen, priests, and all; nor for Roman Catholic
priests in general, to go afterwards all over the face of Christendom: but solely for the dregs of the Irish people to be made
priests exclusively in Ireland. The Roman Catholic laity and
bishops show that they hate this place and this system; they can
raise whatever money they want for repeal; but not one farthing
do they give to Maynooth. They can raise enough for the support of the bishops and clergy; but not one farthing do they
give to Maynooth. They can raise, besides, many thousands to
send abroad for foreign missions; but not one farthing will they
give to Maynooth. The English Roman Catholic noblemen
and gentlemen can supply money to build a cathedral in London,
another at Nottingham, a Jesuits' church in South Street, and
hundreds of others all over the kingdom; they can supply
abundant funds for Oscot, for Stoneyhurst, and for foreign missions; but not one of them ever gives a farthing to Maynooth.
Yet this Maynooth, the execrated, the neglected, the despised
by those who are the best judges of what is necessary for themselves, is the special thing selected as the peculiar object of
favour by the English Protestant Government!

This brings us to the second head of consideration, which is
the education of the Roman Catholic clergy. If the State
meddles with education at all, it must do so in proportions
relative to the numbers of the different sects contained within
it. If the object of giving money to Maynooth is to insure a

better education for the clergy, then is the grant not only the
very worst possible way of doing it, but wholly inoperative for
any such end.   There is scarcely any plan that could be stum-
bled upon which would not have been better.   It would have
been wiser to suppress Maynooth altogether and give the 30,000l.
a year to the English college at Rome, and send out all those
who were to be educated for the priesthood to it : or Trinity
College, Dublin, might have been reformed so as to do away
with all oaths for admission whatever, and the fellowships and
professorships opened to all sects alike ; or the money might have
been given to Oscot ; or a college in both Oxford and Cambridge
might have been exclusively devoted to Roman Catholics.   In
all these ways, the youth of all sects would have been educated
together, and the bitterness of sectarianism would have become
mollified ; as, by a similar course, the bitterness of political
partisanship, amongst the higher orders, is mitigated through
the mutual private friendships and relationships which have
bound them together from their academic days.

All these ways would have been good and efficient methods
of education, not only for the Roman Catholic priests but for
the Roman Catholic laity also, of which the latter at present
are improperly deprived ; and, if the Universities are to exist at
all (don't start yet, I pray you, for I have much more on this head
to say presently), they can only continue in existence by getting
rid of every test which excludes admission to their advantages
on the score of creed.   For rest assured of this, that the only
question which is worthy of debate is, whether you shall support
all or *none;* not whether you shall support *one* or *none.*   The
education of Roman Catholic gentlemen is inferior to that which
Protestants of the same rank and station can obtain, and they
neither will nor ought to submit to this any longer.   There
must be either a well and sufficiently endowed Roman Catholic
University side by side with Oxford, Cambridge, and Dublin,
and as efficient as these, or no Roman Catholic University, and
no Oxford, no Cambridge, no Dublin ; and, in like manner, either
a body of Roman Catholic bishops and clergy as amply and as
efficiently endowed in proportion to their numbers as the bishops
and clergy of the Church of England, or no endowment of either ;
either Roman Catholic bishops side by side with the Church of
England bishops in the House of Lords, or neither.

No Roman Catholic can ever submit to anything which shall directly or indirectly, to himself or others, put upon him the stigma of inferiority. He is perfectly and thoroughly convinced that he professes a creed superior to that of the Protestant. The degree of conscious superiority with which he looks down upon the Protestant varies immensely in degree, but there is no difference amongst them as to the thing itself. They contend, and contend truly, that the whole of the ecclesiastical revenues in Ireland which are now in the hands of the bishops and clergy of the Church of England, have been wrested forcibly from them; they maintain that they have been plundered and robbed; that in equity and before God they have a right to all the ecclesiastical property in the empire, and especially in Ireland, where the people have never been Protestants. This grant to Maynooth has been hailed by them, and admitted by some members of the House of Commons to be a partial restitution, valuable only as the earnest of more. It is amusing to a Roman Catholic to hear expressed the gracious condescension of Protestants in their declarations of liberality towards them; their willingness to admit them to perfect equality with themselves; their avowal that all creeds are alike; that it is presumptuous for any man to pronounce upon the superior truths of one above another; that it is the right of every man to worship his Creator as he pleases; and that no man ought to be subjected to civil disabilities on account of his religious faith. The Roman Catholics are very willing to bear this miserable liberal cant in all places where they are made by law the inferior class, as in Great Britain, but they utterly reject and rightly abhor such sentiments in every country in which they have the upper hand. These oily speeches in the House of Commons conciliate nobody; they are looked upon merely as first steps towards a return of the good old ways; they compromise truth on every side, and ultimately bring the speakers into deserved contempt.

The red-hot Protestant polemists, who partake much more of the fury of Orange politics than even of the *odium theologicum*, think they have settled the question with this notable syllogism —to bow down to a graven image is idolatry; Papists bow to images, *ergo*, Papists are idolaters; and the conclusion is, that Christians are bound to take the Bible for their guide and not pay Popish idolators. Now these gentlemen who talk about taking the Bible for their guide do not mean that others are to take the Bible for their guide also, but that others are to take whatever insulated half verse they choose to bring forward, and the sense in which it is quoted also. If a text cannot be found to authorise you to pay Roman Catholic priests by law, can you find one which authorises you to pay Protestant priests by law? Can you find one to pay bishops and priests of a church of which a woman is the head, and who have been nominated by her? Bowing to images is assumed to be the sum and substance of the religion inculcated and practised by the Roman Catholic Church; be it so: but is it worse than to inculcate that there are a few persons in every age elected to go to Heaven independent of, and irrespective to, all corresponding dispositions, and that all others go into hell flames? Did not the Reformers and all the Roundheads teach that sin could not hurt the child of God, no matter how much he committed, any more than mud upon his clothes, which could be washed off? If this latter statement is a perversion and caricature of Protestantism, the former is no less a caricature of Romanism. Let it even be granted that the reverence which is due to the memory of the Blessed Virgin Mary, and of others through whose labours the whole Church has been blessed, is pushed by designing priests to an idolatrous length, it betrays such an ignorance of the opinions and feelings of enlightened Catholics, or such wilful false accusation to declare that this is the sum and substance of their religion, that the persons who make these statements are totally unworthy of being reasoned with. It may, indeed, be said that the rebellious doctrines taught by the priests are more dangerous than the opposite evils taught by the reformers, because the former are embodied in a numerous and well-compacted corps, who pride themselves in never changing or modifying their opinions; whilst the latter doctrines are found now only amongst the lowest dregs of Close Communion Baptists, and Calvinistic Independents. This is true; but the common sense of mankind is sufficient to cause the opinions of both to be equally reprobated. These opinions on both sides cannot bear the light; and as you have no such rogues as Cromwell now in the House of Commons, neither have you abettors of the insolent demands of the priests.

The evangelical people, on the other hand, led by their

clergy, whose very vocation tends to make them ignorant of mankind, reason from books and know nothing of living men. Now, the business of statesmen is to deal with men and not with books. Moreover, from the books may indeed be gathered the abstract principles of the clergy, but not the practical conduct of the laity. According to the books, Papists are persons on whose oaths no reliance can be placed; but according to the practice of the men, there are no individuals in either house of Parliament on whose engagements more complete dependence can be placed than the Roman Catholics. The age in which we live is truly an infidel age; but let us take the good of it as well as the evil. The priests may, and indeed do, exact obedience as strictly as ever where they dare, but they receive it from none except from the dregs of the Irish or Portuguese. In all countries, laymen are beginning to examine for themselves the filthy books which the priests read, and the filthy things which the priests teach, and the violations of morality which they justify in the confessional, and indignation is expressed in no very measured terms. It is well as an abstract doctrine to talk about the unchangeableness of the Church; an abstraction is always unchangeable; but no class of men have changed more than Roman Catholics, not even excepting the priests. For some centuries they were married, then they forbad marriage; for some centuries they obeyed the secular power, then they assumed dominion over the secular power, and now they are under it again; for some centuries they administered the communion to the laity in both kinds, now they administer it only in one. For some centuries the Gallican clergy asserted their independence, now the French priests are at the feet of the Pope; in old times the Irish clergy were always in opposition to Rome, now the English faction has coerced them into some measure of ecclesiastical obedience. Remove your pressure, and they will deprecate union with Rome, as stupidly as they now cry out against union with England, not having sense sufficient to know that they could not exist unless upheld by both. It is the duty of all who are in the two houses of Parliament to legislate for men as they are now alive, not as they were when they wrote old books; and, however unworthy of trust Popish servants may have been by a Protestant sovereign in the reign of Elizabeth (a position, however, rather difficult to maintain, since the commander of the fleet that destroyed the Armada was a Papist), they are now fully as worthy as those of any other creed. It is evident from the smallest intercourse with them that the object of the Popish clergy is to prevent the laity from becoming·as well instructed as themselves. The end proposed by those who undertake the education of Roman Catholic children is exactly the opposite of that proposed in the education of Protestants. With the latter, the object is to cultivate and expand the reasoning powers, to invigorate the understanding, and to render every individual capable of judging upon the truth and falsehood of all propositions set before him ; to render him as wise and if possible wiser than his teacher. But the object of the former is to prevent the scholar from becoming as wise as his master. The object of the Popish teacher is to cramp ; the object of the Protestant is to enlarge. In after life, however, Roman Catholics mix with men, and feel as much inward repugnance at slavery to a priest as Protestants do, although they know not how to escape from his trammels.

If it be the fault of the age that too little deference is paid to authority, either by children towards parents, subjects towards sovereigns, servants towards masters, surely there is as little by laymen to priests. A great difficulty, on which men have made shipwreck in these latter days, is the distinguishing between that respect which is due to ancient laws and customs, and that rejection or alteration of things which should be considered as adapted only for the times in which they were ordered. The heads of the Romish Church themselves are trammelled with confused assertions on one side about the immutability of their doctrines, whilst the changes in their practices are manifest to the eyes of all. Abstract truth must ever be unchangeable ; but the forms of expressing it, either in whole or in part, must vary continually, and regulations and laws which may be necessary at one time become positively hurtful at another.

If you were not before convinced of the inevitable course on which we are bent, surely sufficient came out during the debates on this subject in the House of Commons, to open the eyes of the most dim-sighted. You pressed Sir Robert Peel to declare whether the grant to Maynooth were an insulated

Act or one of a series of measures.* It is not easy to conceive, in carrying on the business of a country, what is or what can be an insulated measure; but letting that pass, Sir Robert Peel answers very wisely, " I have not at this time, April 1845, any intention of proposing anything more; but I will not hamper future Ministers by declarations on the part of the Crown as to what it may be right to do at some future time." This answer was

---

* " My honourable friend (Sir R. H. Inglis) has asked me two questions. He called on me to state whether or no this is a part of a preconcerted system, the whole of which we have not developed, and whether this proposal in respect to Maynooth is brought forward for the purpose of facilitating hereafter the endowment of the Roman Catholic Clergy. I will answer my honourable friend explicitly. This proposal is brought forward simply and exclusively on its own abstract merits. This proposal is not part of a preconcerted scheme. It is not brought forward with a design of facilitating the endowment of the Roman Catholic Clergy by the State. We have had no communication on this subject of endowment with any authorities in Ireland or elsewhere. We have nothing on that subject in our contemplation. I have seen remarks to the effect, that though we have had no communication with Roman Catholic authorities in Ireland, yet that we have had some secret communication with higher powers at Rome. I state explicitly that those reports are altogether without foundation. I entertain the strongest conviction that we can do no good in Ireland by secret and unavowed negotiation with Rome to which the Roman Catholic Church in Ireland is not a party. I do not believe that by such negotiation, by fettering the independence of the Roman Catholic Church, or establishing any convention between the State and the Church of Rome as it exists in Ireland, of which the members of that Church were not cognisant, and to which they were not parties, we should benefit that country. I have said that this is no part of a general system; I have said that it is not brought forward designedly to facilitate some future proposal in respect to endowment. I will say also, that with reference to endowment there are very great objections. I have no reason whatever to believe that there is on the part of the Roman Catholic laity, or the Roman Catholic Church in that country, any inclination to depart from that public declaration which was recently made by the honourable member for Kildare, that the laity and clergy of the Roman Catholic Church were opposed to an endowment. It is impossible not to see, from the demonstration of public feeling in this country, that here also there would be great difficulty as to such endowment. I have stated precisely the truth with regard to the question of endowment. But my honourable friend proceeds to ask, ' Will you make a declaration that it would not be consistent with your principles that at any future time there should be an endowment of Roman Catholic ministers?' I must say I think my honourable friend has no right to require such a declaration. I have stated most explicitly the truth; but this I will not do. Now, draw no unfavourable inference from my refusal. This I will not do. I will not hamper and embarrass any future Government by a declaration now that the difficulties are altogether insuperable. I see great difficulties in the way of such a measure; but I do not think any one has a right to call upon me now to give a public opinion that those difficulties can never, at any future time, be overcome."

very wise, and such only as any one could make who desired
to be a Minister. It matters nothing to an individual beyond
his personal ease whether he be in advance of his party or not;
but for a minister *devancer son siècle* is fatal. Mr. Pitt, and
all subsequent to him, who have advocated the claims of the
Roman Catholics, have split upon this rock, and the avoiding
to do so was the single quality which enabled such ministers as
Lord Liverpool to keep their heads above water. Of all official
men Sir Robert Peel has shown himself the most practical;
that is, if you will excuse the homeliness of the phrase, the
most steady in watching which way the cat jumped; in other
words, knowing how much he could carry — how much the
country was prepared for, and would let him carry. At the
time of the granting of the Roman Catholic claims, the cause
of Protestantism had been dying out gradually; the very Dissenters, who are now loudest in clamouring against the grant
to Maynooth, were the most revolutionary in their proclamations
of liberal opinions; and it was by liberalism, that is, religious
indifference, or hatred of all that is positive in religion, that
that question was carried; the country was determined to grant
the claims, and Sir Robert Peel gave way, when the only alternative that presented itself was a re-enacting in the utmost
rigour of the penal code, and a conquering of Ireland by the
sword. In like manner with the question of free trade; all
classes in theory, save where their own personal interests are
concerned, are in favour of the removal of all possible restric-
tions, and they alone who are at the head of affairs know the
amount of deference which it is necessary to pay to the impe-
diment of selfishness in carrying out free-trade principles. It
is the same on the present occasion: every statesman is in
favour of the grant to Maynooth; there is violence to be
considered on one side in Ireland, and there is violence to be
considered on the other side in England. Sir Robert Peel
has been taunted in those "*worst* possible instructors," the
newspapers, with not doing the things which he means to do,
as measures of conciliation, at the right time, whilst they
equally sneer at him for raising a clamour by these measures
in an opposite quarter. The violence of the opposition to
such plans, when brought forward, proves that had they been
proposed at a previous time there might have been a greater

difficulty in carrying them ; and no one can be so good a judge, because no one stands on a sufficient elevation to be able to see on all sides around him, but he who is officially placed in such a position.

The true state of the case is plainly declared by Lord John Russell. "I am to judge of the effect which this measure will produce. I will not take it as if it were the last of a series, and were the crowning act of a long course of justice to the people of Ireland. No, Sir; I shall maintain, as I have hitherto maintained, that with regard to the civil and political privileges of the people of that country you have yet much to do; that those measures to which the Right Honourable Baronet the Home Secretary alluded last night, fall considerably short of that which the people of Ireland have a right to require of you, to put them on an equality with the people of England. I think, with respect to their ecclesiastical state, that that great anomaly of a large endowed church for a small minority of the people is an evil which, without entering into the ways in which it might be remedied, Parliament must consider. I will not concede that opinion. I will not deny that after this measure is passed I shall, either in support of some proposition from others, or on my own proposition, endeavour to obtain for the people of Ireland that justice which I think was long and cruelly denied to them."

Upon the same ground as that on which you tolerate Roman Catholics and Dissenters, must you cease from taxing one part of the community for the support of the priests of another. It is *now* a most flagrant injustice, an act of cruelty, even if it were right in former times, to tax the Roman Catholics of Ireland for the support of the clergy of the Church of England; but this act of injustice the gentlemen who make such pious exclamations against the proposed grant to Maynooth never complained of: now, however, that they are to be taxed to support Popery they forthwith cry out against its injustice, and say that it is very irreligious to do so because Popery is contrary to the word of God.

Whatever opinion an orator in Exeter Hall may express, he being an insulated man is not worthy of attention, and when met by a contrary opinion is neutralised ; for one man's opinion is worth no more than another man's. But you, as a Member of the House of Commons, are precluded from having an op'nion which is at variance with the reiterated and recorded opinions of that House of which you are a component part. At Exeter Hall you are a component part of nothing: in the House of Commons you are a component part of the Legislature, and that Legislature has as much right to have its opinion as any demagogue in Exeter Hall. The opinion of the Legislature is, and must be, that all exclusiveness is to be abolished; that Dissenters and Roman Catholics and even Jews may sit amongst them; and any member of that Legislature who holds the old exclusive opinion is a mere waster of the House's time, even if he be honest in retaining his seat. He may, indeed, hold his old opinion, as he may upon any other obsolete historical point, such as the criminality of Mary Queen of Scots, or the hump on the back of Richard III.; but to make such opinion the basis of his conduct therein, and attempt to induce the Legislature to act on one solitary insulated point at variance with its recorded principles and former conduct, is worse than futile.

. The opinion of a *mixed* body of Jews, Socinians, Free Church Scotchmen, Church of England men, and Roman Catholics cannot be *united* upon any system of Christianity. You have rightly said that the education proposed by this body is a system of " Godless education." The expression is happy, for it has stuck; it has been commented on, railed at, censured, but it has not evaporated as an empty sound. It is the only education that such a body can give. The Jew, the Socinian, do not — *Christum ut Deum colunt.* The Presbyterian and Independent do not eat the flesh and blood of Christ which have been offered upon His altar, and without doing which they have no part in Him; the Evangelicals do not look to the sacrament of baptism as a means of imparting to their children spiritual life; all which things real Christians do : and how, therefore, is it possible that they can unite in the Legislature on any system of religious education? They may talk of charity in living peaceably side by side with each other; but to give this the epithet of Christian charity is no more applicable than to call it Hindoo charity. They may inculcate admiration for the works of the Creator, which is very good Deism, and which Cicero and many others have done long ago, and they may recommend mutual forbearance, which all will follow who prefer a whole to a broken head.

If you want Christian education you must seek it elsewhere ; you have no right to expect it in, or demand it from, the Legislature as now constituted.

The Roman Catholics contend that you have robbed them of the whole ecclesiastical property of Ireland, and it is proposed to conciliate them by giving them a paltry 30,000*l.* a year : nay, more, it is supposed that they will be so wonderfully pleased with it, that they will never more accuse the Protestants of having robbed them, or try to get back that property which they consider their own. It would seem incredible that any men could so think and so argue, were not the fact absolutely before us. The Roman Catholics rejoice in the grant because it is an instalment of what they consider their due ; and because they will be hereafter in a better position to claim the whole. Some of them have declared in "Conciliation Hall" that they rejoice in it, because it will enable them better to contend for the dismemberment of the empire after which they are striving.

It is useless to attempt to deny or shut your eyes to the fact that 7,000,000 of rebels is too large a body to be suffered to remain without measures being taken either of appeasing or of conquering. The Duke of Wellington and Sir Robert Peel told them plainly that they gave them emancipation because they feared civil war : you now dread civil w r : these rebels have set the laws at defiance, and they have been supported in their rebellion by a large body in both Houses of Parliament. What will you do? It is idle to object to the only course which is in accordance with the principles which the Legislature has sanctioned, and not give to those 7,000,000 the ecclesiastical property of which they have been robbed. No doubt the priests will teach, under the pretext of religion, as much filth and immorality as they do now; no doubt they will be a more powerful, and therefore a more dangerous body; but our successors must deal with them as they can ; in our day we have but one course, which is to be just, and not permit the unworthiness of the objects to stand in the way of doing what is right towards them.

You, Sir Robert, and all the Evangelical party, oppose this grant because you hate the false doctrine which Popish priests teach. But the aggregate number of such opponents is not large nor very enlightened. Their ranks, however, are swelled by another class, who oppose this grant because they are of opinion, as one has avowed, " that there is too much religion in the country already ; " and by many more because they desire to see an end put to all support by the State to any one sect of Christians above another, as Mr. O'Connell has often maintained. This class is very numerous ; individuals who hold these opinions are to be found in every one of the sects ; amongst the Roman Catholics, amongst the whole body of Dissenters, amongst the Free Church Scotch Seceders, amongst many of the Church of England. It is not fair to appeal to the number of petitions which have been sent to Parliament against the grant to May-nooth, and insinuate that they support the point for which you are contending. You are contending for the Church of England against the Church of Rome ; nine-tenths of the petitions are against both equally : you are contending for the establishment of Anglicism versus the establishment of Romanism ; nine-tenths of the petitions are against both equally : you are contending for established churches against free independent churches ; the petitions are against the former and in favour of the latter : you are contending for Protestant bishops in the House of Lords to the exclusion of Romish ; the petitions are against both : you are contending for the exclusive privileges of Oxford, Cambridge, and Dublin, against the exclusive privilege of Maynooth ; the petitions are against all, and in favour only of Stinkomalee. It is not possible, consistently with the maxims of liberalism pro-fessed by the Legislature, to refuse to carry out the principle of free trade in creeds to the fullest extent ; and not simply to refuse the grant to Maynooth, leaving things elsewhere as they stand, but to come to a full understanding of the whole subject of established churches.

I proposed, some years ago, to those who had the means of effecting the plan, that the whole of the ecclesiastical property of Ireland, so far as it consists in tithes, should be redeemable in the same way that the land-tax is redeemable, with some small advantages to induce people to act upon it ; that the funds so raised should be paid into the hands of two sets of Ecclesiastical Commissioners, one Romish, the other Anglican ; that in all the parishes where there were no Protestants, the proceeds should be paid over to the Romish commissioners ; in those where there were no Papists, into the hands of the Anglican Commissioners;

and proportionally in all the other parishes. In this way, the ecclesiastical property would have been preserved for ecclesiastical uses; and in no other will it be, because the Irish laity will gladly unite with the Dissenters to plunder the Church, in order to keep possession of the tithes on their estates. All parties, too, have begun to plunder it, some for one purpose and some for another; whilst one object yet remains for which it would be more just to plunder it than for any other, an object which cannot be overlooked any longer, and for which the ecclesiastical property alone is sufficient.

But let us understand one another in the use of the terms " Church property " and " plundering the Church." The tenth part of every man's fixed income has been by God's ordinance devoted to Him ever since the creation; Christian kings gave it from the revenues of all their lands, and such was regularly paid, so long as income was derived from the produce of the land alone. Merchants and manufacturers, however, never paid it out of their revenue; they always cheated God, and do to this day. This tenth portion of the produce of the earth was given for the single object of paying priests to celebrate the worship of God; to intercede with Him continually for the prosperity of those who gave these tithes, and who had to fulfil secular duties, and for the preservation of the souls of their ancestors who were departed. To take the money away, therefore, from priests who will intercede for the souls of the departed, and give it to others who will not so plead, is a fraud and a robbery of the departed to begin with; and to take it away from the clergy who conduct the worship of God altogether, and to pay it to schoolmasters to teach boys and girls, is a flagrant robbery of God in taking from Him that which he has claimed as His due, and as great an act of sacrilege as it would be if it were taken to promote railroads, fisheries, or any other wise public measure, which might be beneficial to the majority of the people.

I suppose that no one will deny that the seizure of tithes by laymen at the time of the Reformation was a robbery of the Church, and that to take back those tithes from the laymen, who have kept them ever since, would be no more than an act of tardy justice. It is the diversion of those tithes from the purposes for which they were granted, which constitutes the robbery, not the use to which they were subsequently devoted. By suppressing bishoprics, canonries, &c., the Government has entered again upon the question of seizing upon Church property, and devoting it to purposes which it thinks more beneficial to the public good, than paying priests to carrying on the worship of God. It is necessary that men be thoroughly convinced of, and imbued with the idea of the nature and principle of the act which they have been committing; and that we do all understand that by facts and acts it is now a fixed principle with the Legislature of this country, that Church property is a fund with which the Government is at liberty to deal in whatever way it judges best for the moral benefit of the people.

Now, notwithstanding all the wise financial measures of Sir Robert Peel, the cry of distress from the lower orders is undiminished. Means for the employment of labourers cannot be multiplied as fast as labourers are begotten. The population has increased by one-half since the conclusion of the war. The one great pressure upon the country is not only unremoved, but no one step has been taken by any of the men in office since 1814 to remove it; 30,000,000l. a-year is wrung out of the labourers before one farthing is taken from them for all the exigencies of the Government. At length Lord Ashburton, who combines in himself all the theoretical knowledge of Horner, Ricardo, &c., upon the subject, with a practical knowledge of the working of the money market superior to all other persons, has spoken out in reprobation of the gross neglect of this pressure by all official men ever since the peace. The hitherto peaceful tenant-farmers, and yeomen, are beginning to combine like the manufacturers, and though less voluble are far more formidable in their insurrectionary freaks. The agricultural labourers are driven to madness by the inhuman cruelty of the New Poor Law; they are now separated by a different code of law from that which governs the rest of the community, of which the interpreters are not the Judges in the Queen's Courts, but a set of Commissioners at Somerset House. Felons in the jails are better fed than they whose only crime is to be poor; and they who are just abl to keep themselves out of the workhouse, are being driven in by being compelled for the first time to pay poor, parish, and county rates. They compose the raw material of all the militia and yeomanry corps. They have been bound together hitherto under great neighbouring leaders into the same two factions as those which have divided the House of Commons, but they complain that their confidences have been betrayed, and they will no longer be led in any such way. Party, which has ever been a clumsy and little creditable way of carrying on public business in deliberative assemblies, is crumbling to pieces: the heads of the Whigs though ashamed of, were yet urged forward into all manner of mischief by their adherents, and the heads of the Conservatives are so much in advance of theirs, that the latter are complaining of being deceived or betrayed. Henceforward such confidences will be much slighter, and the Crown may make use of the disruption to cause itself to be better served. Whoever shall dare to take hold of this debt by the throat, and be determined not to let go his hold till he has destroyed it, will carry, amidst much noise in the Stock Exchange, and amongst the Jews and their accomplices, the whole productive classes with him; and the only instrumentality by which he will be able to accomplish it will be the ecclesiastical property, which has been already diverted from ecclesiastical purposes, and is no longer devoted to the end for which it was originally given. There is no room here for a pious cry of "sacrilege;" the sacrilegious hands are those which now hold it, the owners of great tithes throughout England and Ireland, and every landholder in Scotland. The French Revolution was not more sacrilegious than the pretended Reformation in Scotland, which was a most profitable thing for the landed proprietors of the North. The tithes held now in lay hands may be extracted again from them whenever the occasion requires it; and the holders will be fortunate if arrears are not demanded also.

It is impossible that a war can be again carried on by loans, nor ought it to be. On the first breaking out of such an event, an end must be put to the annual payment of 30,000,000*l.* per annum. Many arguments might be brought forward to support this assertion, but they would lead us away from the matter more immediately in hand.

And now, my dear Sir Robert, when the ways and means of paying off the debt are seriously considered, let me ask you in sober sadness, "What is the use of the Universities?" I fear the bare suggestion of this question has made you start;

but still, prejudice apart, let me ask you again, not viewing things with our eyes, but with the eyes of the Houses of Parliament, with the eyes which see only in the utilitarian direction that things have taken of late years, what is the use of them? Of course, I omit from this consideration the use of one in sending you to the House of Commons, and long may it exist you so to send, and long may you live so to be sent; but, barring that use, of what other are they?

In good old Tory times, the departure of which you and I so fondly and so unavailingly regret, there would have been no difficulty in answering this question. There were times, now presumptuously called the dark ages, but which I look upon as more enlightened in right principles than ours, when it was a rare thing for a man to be a scholar. Reading may be the means of becoming enlightened, but that consequence does not necessarily follow. In those days men were better rooted in the principles of the worship of God, and in those of the government of mankind; from all of which they have departed, in proportion as the keys of knowledge have been placed within the reach of all. When few could read or write but those who were brought up at the public endowed schools, the Universities were indispensable to the perfection of youth in the sciences, and none could become qualified to practise medicine, or in the courts of law, but such as had been trained in those exclusive abodes of learning. But now the majority of the men who lead the general excitement have not been so trained, and none need be so. Even let it be granted that those physicians and lawyers who have been educated in the academic groves are better physicians and better lawyers than those who have not, still it is but a question of degree. In any aspect in which we can look at these ancient seats of learning the view is not favourable. I remember the son of the Archbishop of York, a student of Christchurch, saying in the debate on the Roman Catholic Relief Bill, that it was long since upon that subject he could recommend to any "inter quercos academi querere verum." They seem to be the very opposites of Popery. In Popery the evil is in the thing, in the books, and the good is in the men; in the Universities the good is in the buildings, the halls, the libraries, the colleges, and the evil in the men. Even in the management of their own internal concerns, they present the most extraordinary incapacity: they proclaim a man a heretic one year, and appoint him the next to be a teacher of theology; they tolerate in silence the most violent attacks on priesthood, and sacraments, and apostolic succession, which would, upon their own principles, unchurch them altogether; and whilst they rave against a member who speaks favourably of a sister church, whose orders they admit, and degrade him for the same, they suspend from his office a Professor who has done more to combine personal piety with sound churchmanship than all other members of the University for the last century, upon charges which they had not ability sufficient so to frame as to make intelligible, and with a defiance of equity never surpassed by Star Chambers and Church Courts in former ages. Yet the buildings are venerable, and the associations connected with them hallowed, and it will be a sorrowful day which shall see them despoiled.

The only thing which can make the existence of the Universities worth a year's purchase, is for them instantly to cease to be Universities exclusively for members of the Church of England, and become Universities for all Englishmen. If their heads have any sense commensurate to the urgency of the times in which their lot is cast, they will take steps to do this instantly, *proprio motu*, without waiting to yield to any *douce violence*, or " pressure from without," lest that shall happen to them as has happened to the House of Commons, according to the threat held out to it many years ago, that " if it would not reform itself from within, it would be reformed from without with a vengeance." But let not these heads wait till mobs of starving labourers have joined mobs of starving manufacturers, roving about the country, with a government too weak and too cowardly to repress them ; with no man of character willing to take the helm of affairs, which shall be held annually by succeeding adventurers in office, necessarily conceding to the mobs all their demands as the only means of retaining their precarious places.

You see what has already happened with regard to the Scottish Universities. A demand has been made that they shall open their gates to all the inhabitants of Scotland, and not to those of the Established Church alone. The minister of the Crown, the Secretary of State, said he was willing to do this provided the people of Scotland wished it. Now, there is no legal possibility of knowing the wishes of the people of Scotland but through the Members sent from Scotland into that House. But the Secretary of State says, " No ; let me see the opinion of the people of Scotland, expressed in public meetings, in petitions:" that is to say, " Let us have agitation in Scotland as we have had in Ireland, for that is the only way by which the people can obtain what they want, and the only index of opinion which we, the Queen's Ministers, mean to follow." It is not impossible that he may, by these indiscreet words, have drawn forth some Scotch Calvinistic agitator, who will have his Scotch Conciliation Hall and monster demonstration, where they may talk less bombast, and set a less absurd object before them than repeal of the Union, but in which they will do more efficient work. The chief ground on which this demand was urged by the promoters of the measure was, that the Free Church seceders were going to build an University for themselves, and had already subscribed 20,000l.; and this plea was admitted as valid, or at least as an important feature in the consideration of the case. The Professors in the Scotch Universities are afraid if they retain their oaths they will have to part with their fees, and therefore beg to be freed from the former that they may retain the latter. Now of all the acts of schism which have defiled and disgraced Christendom, never was one so thoroughly groundless and devoid of all pretensions to be respected as the Scotch Free Church secession ; never was any class of persons more unworthy of consideration, and to whose prejudices and whims so little deference should be paid, or where it was possible to pretend so little to scruples of conscience. Yet the threat of these people to found a college of their own has been admitted as an ingredient in the consideration of whether it is wise or not to put an end to the old system of the Scottish Universities, by which they were linked to the Established Church, or whether these Universities should lose their present standing and assume the new position of being open to all comers indiscriminately. Whatever argument can justify this change tells with immensely additional force upon the English and Irish Universities, and therefore it follows that, by conceding to the one, the days of the other are numbered also.

How can you answer such arguments? The petitions by which you are backed in opposing the payment of the Roman

Catholic clergy are of two kinds: first, the most numerous
being from Dissenters, and Dissenters in disguise within the
Church, who oppose all established churches whatever; and,
secondly, from that portion of churchmen who call themselves
the religious-world, and whose publications swarm on our friend
Hatchard's counter, endeavouring to persuade us that the
Church of England has no altar in her churches, and no sacrifice
to offer. If this be so, what is the use of priests or cathedrals?
The English people may want preachers, and preaching-houses
fitted up after the manner of philosophical lecture-rooms, such
as the Free Church Scotchmen have erected, but they can want
nothing more; and the Roman Catholics against whom you
head this unholy war are better friends to the Established
Church of England than any of the parties who compose your
forces.

The only way by which any person, with strong religious
feelings against historical Popery, and who knows nothing of
living Roman Catholics, can clear his vision sufficiently to be
able to look profitably at this question, is to remove in imagination the subject to a distant age, or to a distant land. Suppose
now that Herodotus, or Livy, had told us of a country where an
immense church establishment was maintained by law for only
one-eighth of the population, and that seven-eighths detested it,
what should we say of such a country and of such a government? Do we not read in the sacred historians also, that when
a people changed its gods it changed its ordinances of religion
also; but where did we ever hear of a church establishment
different from that of the body of the people? The charge
brought against the people is, that they have changed their
religion, not that they had priests of one kind and people of
another: this is a monster reserved for Protestantism to bring
forth. If people pretend to feel this to be a matter of conscience, how comes it that their scruples are geographical, so
active in Ireland and so dead in Scotland? Why do they not
equally insist upon Episcopalianism being the established church
of Scotland? Since they have not done this, we are justified in
saying that the excuse of their conscience is a false and hypocritical pretext.

If you are desirous to uphold an established church in
England, as I have no doubt you are, your only course is to

encourage the ministers to make the Roman Catholic the established church of Ireland. The Church of England there has not even the semblance of a justification; and in saying this I am taking the very lowest ground, that of mere political justice; and I defy you to point out such an anomaly in any other part of Europe, such a piece of pure unmixed evil as the Protestant Established Church in Ireland. I will add, also, that I am urged to the desire of seeing this by the language which that body of persons called the Religious World has lately assumed; and I do most earnestly desire, on religious grounds, to see a church within the territory of Great Britain which shall have the courage to avow and maintain, in the midst of this infidel age, that it does administer and feed its children with the flesh and blood of the Son of God, offered up by His priest upon His altar. I do long to see a clergy which knows something of that in which the true worship of God consists, and which will not degrade His house to be a mere theatre for theological mountebanks to deliver their lectures in. The *soi-disant* Protestant religious world has succeeded in presenting, as holding the pre-eminent position in the House called of God, nothing but a box with a man in it turning his back upon the altar, with his flock all round him in pens like the cattle and sheep in Smithfield-market. Apostolical authority for the man in the box they laugh at; and a bishop has publicly preached against it. All notion of an altar and sacrifices they deny; they do not, even in their common language, speak of the church as a place in which they worship, but as a place in which they sit under a man. Yet, forsooth, they are not men-worshippers! they are not idolaters! Oh, no, it is those who reverence her " whom all generations shall call blessed; " who respect and remember to pray for " all our brethren departed in the faith," by whose labours, and perhaps martyrdom, have been transmitted to us all the religious knowledge we now possess.

I long, on religious grounds, to see a church that cares for the poor. If the error of the Romish Church in Ireland has been to have only priests who were on a level with the dregs of the people, the error of the Anglican Church has been to have no priests who could even speak the language of the people: the former have sympathised with all the bad passions as well as with the virtues of the lowest orders; the latter have not had any feelings at all in common with the lowest orders. The English clergy are, or aspire to be, and to associate with nothing but gentlemen. Little religious instruction is attempted, and that little is conveyed through sermons which the lower orders, particularly in country villages, cannot understand. I have, for many years, taken great pains to examine into this point, and scarcely ever met with a labourer who could follow two sentences of a sermon : the ideas, the language, the form is beyond the level of their intellects, and they are consequently almost everywhere as ignorant as heathens. If the lower orders of Irish know nothing but tales of lying miracles of saints, the lower orders of English know less, for they do not even know that there are such things as miracles and saints at all. It is no doubt a good thing to have a well-educated priesthood, but to have a body of clergy who, as a class, are too far removed from the poor as a class, is a greater evil than to have the clergy exclusively of that same class. I repeat again, I long to see a church that cares for the poor. " By their fruits ye shall know them : " and look at the treatment of the poor by that Hyperion of Protestantism the ecclesiastical establishment of Scotland, as now brought to light by the Poor Law Commission in the report and in the evidence, and compare it with the treatment of the poor in any country in the world in which the Romish Church is dominant. No Protestant can desire a fairer criterion of the comparative merit of the two establishments, and the Scotch themselves are so proud of theirs that for five-and-forty years they have been holding up the state of the poor in Scotland as an object for admiration and imitation by the English.

It is impossible to understand the nature of that man's reasoning powers who can conceive, after the declarations which have been made in Parliament by every one who, by talents or position, can ever become a Minister of the Crown, that the Church of England, as established in Ireland, can maintain its present position. I have already stated in what way the money proposed to be given to Maynooth could be much more efficiently employed, and this Bill should be repealed next year. The next step to take is, to make the Roman Catholic the established church of Ireland, as the Presbyterians, though no church, are established in Scotland. The House of Commons should then come to a resolution, " That it is expedient that the

Universities of Oxford, Cambridge, Edinburgh, Glasgow, St. Andrews, Aberdeen, and Trinity College, Dublin, should be made available equally for all classes of the Queen's subjects: " a conference with the House of Lords should be requested to agree with this motion, and it should be laid by both Houses at the foot of the throne. This being fairly and efficiently done will be a healing measure, because it is comprehensive, and adequate to the altered condition of circumstances in which the country is now placed. Opposition cannot alter the course of events; it cannot take out any of the evil that is in it; but it may do an immensity of mischief. It prevents Sir Robert Peel from taking at once efficient steps commensurate with the greatness of the case, and compels him to wait until every measure has the appearance of being wrung from fear, instead of being granted from conviction. Whatever the other party grants is received favourably, because it is in accordance with the destructive principle on which it has acted for the last century, and therefore no one can object that the grant is inconsistent with its opinions. The only course which is possible in the altered circumstances of the country is not that which is really the best, but the best that can be followed. It can make no difference to any but the actual receivers of the profits of place, and to those who are ambitious of official importance, whether one of these factions or the other conducts the business of Government. The Crown is equally kept in the background by all, and the men in office put forth as the real rulers and rewarders of merit. The approbation of the Sovereign seems to be a matter alike indifferent to all; support is looked to from beneath, from mobs, or from mobs' delegates, whilst this most thinking people amuses itself with the pleasing idea that it is rejoicing in a monarchy. We shall certainly steer the same course whoever is at the helm of the State. One part of the crew may be more experienced seamen than the other, in which case we shall have a pleasanter passage; we shall not ship so much water; we shall not have so many thumps and bumps threatening every moment to capsize us, — but the most skilful helmsman will not alter our destiny, and we shall soon be engulfed in the bottomless pit of popular government. Let us stand for established churches whilst we can, — no one can tell in how short a time we may have none to stand for.

It has been said that there are many pious men who think that bishops should confine their labours to spiritual matters, and leave secular concerns to secular peers. There are many pious men, also, who think that secular peers should manage their own affairs, and not meddle with those of the rest of the community : that the business of the people should be managed exclusively by delegates from the people. The secular peers have no higher claims to their seats in the House of Lords than the spiritual. If prescription, if lapse of time to which the memory of man doth not reach, if the law of the land, if statute after statute are insufficient to preserve the bishops, — they are insufficient to uphold the rights of all other lords; and the day which sends the bishops to confine themselves exclusively to the cares of their dioceses will send the other peers to confine themselves exclusively to the management of their private estates. Let the restored Roman Catholic Church send her bishops over also, at least such of them as are appointed with the approbation of the Crown ; and so only will there be real justice done to Ireland, and really Conservative practices will be carried into effect.

Enough for the present, from

Yours, always faithfully,

HENRY DRUMMOND.

REASONS

FOR

REJECTING THE CLAIMS OF ROMISH PRIESTS

𝕷etter

TO

J. W. FRESHFIELD, ESQ.

HIGH SHERIFF OF THE COUNTY OF SURREY

1851

B B 4

Albury Park,
Dec. 17th, 1850.

DEAR SIR,

I regret that inability to assist at a meeting to be held in the open air, at this season of the year, will prevent my constituents having that opportunity which it is my duty to give them, of inquiring what are my opinions upon the subject which they are convened to discuss.

I always opposed the placing of Papists upon the same footing as Protestant Dissenters, because temporal supremacy over all Christendom has ever been claimed by the Pope; — because it is as essential a part of the Papacy as ecclesiastical supremacy is of the prerogative of the British Crown, — because the priests are forbidden to marry, expressly upon the ground that they may not be induced to transfer their allegiance from the popedom to their lawful prince; because therefore Papists can give, at best, only a divided allegiance; and because this claim of the Pope has in all ages been the occasion of deluging Christendom with blood. Now that this usurpation is again attempted, by sending a cardinal who, as such, has no spiritual jurisdiction, but is the paid privy councillor of a foreign sovereign, we must meet the attack, and drive it back by the mildest measures, provided only they shall be sufficient to uphold unimpaired the rights of the Queen.

In addition to this attack on the independence of the monarchy by the Pope, Dr. Wiseman commands or invites all the people of this nation to return " within the orbit of the ecclesiastical firmament," by submitting themselves to his domination, and to that of the army of priests placed at his disposal. This command or invitation must equally be resisted, because the Popish priests teach men to deny the evidence of their senses, and declare that the bread which they taste in their mouths at the communion is not bread; and this lie they teach as an act

of worship, and inculcate as a way of pleasing the God of Truth;
thus teaching lying, as a religious system — a sin committed by
no other priests, Greek, Druidical, Buddhist, or Chinese : —
because they have enslaved the greater part of the laity, and
forced them to have a priest as a director, without whose direction no layman dare read any book, nor govern his family, nor
give any vote in parliament except as the director permits him :
because they rob the laity of the right to read God's word
which He has addressed to all men, and no part of which is
exclusively addressed to priests, but all to the people ; or quibble,
by saying they will give laymen the right to read it, whilst they
deny their right to understand it : — because they teach the
laity to pray to dead men and women instead of to God alone,
through the only Mediator, Jesus Christ : — because the pretended authority of the Church is nothing more than that the
priests have decided that the priests alone have the right to
decide : — because they refuse the rites of religion to all females
unless they have previously submitted to a filthy and obscene
conversation with an unmarried priest in secret ; and because
they have reduced the husbands and fathers to such an abject
condition, that they are afraid to protect the honour and purity
of their wives and daughters : — because the priests have not
fulfilled the conditions of the Word of God, which requires that
no one shall be ordained a priest until he has given proof of his
competency for that office, by showing that he can rule well his
own wife, children, and servants ; and because the Word of God
warns us against a great apostacy, into which the Church should
fall, the sign of which should be, that men were " forbidden to
marry, and commanded to abstain from meat : " — because the
dominion of popish priests has been found, after ages of trial, so
intolerable to the laity, that it has been cast off in Italy and
France, men hating the very name of religion, and renouncing,
rather than live under it, all allegiance to the Church : — because
the Scriptures teach us to judge of men and of systems by their
fruits ; and history informs us that the crimes of the popes and
the vices of the clergy have disgraced the name of Christianity :
— because the immoral doctrines of the Jesuits, exposed by
Pascal and condemned by the pope who suppressed that order,
are now taught by Dr. Wiseman and his priests : — because the
priests have caused more human blood to be shed by persecution

of Jews, Albigenses, Protestants, &c. &c. than the priests of Moloch or of Juggernaut : — because the priests assert that the pope is infallible, and that he has a right to depose princes and to punish the magistrates, subject to such princes, who do not execute his decrees : — because the priests deny at one time the things that they maintain at another, pretending either that their principles are unchangeable, or that they have changed just as suits their purposes of deception : — because the priests teach men to defraud their relations on their death-beds, and persuade them that they will deliver their souls from punishment, by bequeathing their property to the priests : — because the priests, and the laity under their control, demand to be governed by the canon law, which is a different law from that by which other subjects of the Queen are governed, proving incontrovertibly that, though outwardly English, they are in heart attached to a foreign prince, and to a foreign law.

These are a few of the many reasons why we ought to reject the claims of Dr. Wiseman and his priests, who talk of bringing us back to allegiance to the Pope.

It is hoped that many of the popish laity in England are as bold now to reject the arrogant claims of this Italian priest (who is so execrated by those who know best the merits of his rule, that unless for the presence of ten thousand French bayonets he dare not remain twenty-four hours in his own capital,) as our Roman Catholic ancestors were, in the reigns of our Edwards, Henrys, and Elizabeth : but they who are not have no right to demand to be treated upon an equality with Protestants of all creeds, who give an undivided allegiance to the British Crown. They who have submitted to become the slaves of priests, have no right to claim the privileges of freemen; they, who dare take no oath without secretly saying *salvo jure superioris*, that is, saving the interest of the priests, are not fit to be trusted with the government of Protestants.

I am, dear Sir,

Your faithful and obedient Servant,

HENRY DRUMMOND.

PARLIAMENTARY REFORM

Substance of the Speech

DELIVERED AT A

MEETING OF THE ELECTORS OF WEST SURREY

1852

SPEECH

I AM very glad that this meeting has been called, because I think that, whether the constituents lose or gain by a more frequent intercourse with their representatives, the representatives lose immensely by not being able to discuss with their constituents various matters of public interest as they occur and proceed, instead of waiting for a septennial occasion to come to a general understanding and settlement of subjects, the details of which have long been forgotten.

Our worthy friend Mr. Barclay, who has kindly taken the chair on this occasion, has prescribed the points upon which it is desired that I should address you : these are, — 1st. The extension of the franchise ; 2nd. The relief to the agricultural interest ; and 3rdly. The state of parties. Before I enter upon these, however, I must refer to another, because I find it the one which most fills the minds of people at the present time ; and that is, the question which is commonly called the Maynooth Grant, and which is, in fact, the whole question of Popery.

I remain upon this subject of the same opinion as that which I expressed many years ago, and I am sorry to say, that, instead of finding reason to change that opinion, all subsequent observation has tended to confirm it. I do not state this for the sake of courting your favour on account of my consistency ; for I think that the boast of consistency seldom means more than that a man is as great a fool when he is old as he was when he was younger. At the time that the Duke of Wellington recommended Roman Catholic emancipation, upon the ground that he could not resist it without incurring the certainty of exciting civil war in Ireland, I joined with others in presenting a petition to the House of Commons, in which we declared our conviction that that civil war was not extinguished but only deferred. Since that time a new phase has passed over the Roman Catholic Church. The Jesuits have become its masters. I will not describe Jesuitism, nor do I call upon you to describe it, nor will I take the description of any Protestant upon the subject; but I remind you of the opinion that has been formed of the doctrines of the Jesuits by every Roman Catholic sovereign in Europe; by every Roman Catholic statesman; by all the Roman Catholic laity, and by most Roman Catholic clergy: which opinion is, that those doctrines are incompatible with the existence of liberty and the well-being of society. On this account the Jesuits were expelled from every Roman Catholic country in Europe; and finally the Order was suppressed by the Pope, because its existence was inconsistent with the rights of humanity. Since then the Jesuits have become the lords and masters of the Roman Catholic Church. They have been restored in Austria after sixty years of expulsion; they are lords over the court; and Prince Schwartzenburg declared that he was determined to put down free constitutional government in every country in Europe. He said that he did not heed republics, because nobody in the Austrian dominions cared about republics, and Kossuth ruined his cause by proclaiming a republic; but that which he would destroy was, every constitution in which the law was over and above the sovereign; in which the rights of the nobles were as sacred as those of the Crown, and the rights of the people as sacred as either. Now the Carlists in France are also ruled by the Jesuits; and these last, having full power in Rome, have determined through the priests in Ireland to send in from sixty to eighty slaves who will bring the Government of this country in the House of Commons to a dead lock. When this arrives, will you support Lord Derby? Don't now, at a time when he needs no support, boast of your proffered support; but say, will you on this day twelvemonths, which will be no sooner than I expect to see the plot fully developed, will you, I say, support him in those measures which he will deem necessary to uphold the security of the empire? Do not suppose that I am asking you to enter upon a course of religious persecution. You have no right to inquire into the religious opinions of any persons; you have no right to inquire into the theology taught at Maynooth; you have a right only to inquire into how far the moral and political doctrines there taught are opposed to the well-being of the country; and, more than that, you must not proceed upon any supposed necessary consequence of the doctrines there taught. You have no right to meddle with inferences, you must wait for overt acts. It is with overt acts alone that you have to deal, and not with propositions which, until brought out in acts, must be considered only as abstractions. As to refusing 30,000*l.* to Maynooth, it is a most trumpery way of looking at the question. I am sure that such a proposition is only irritating without producing any good. You will find that it is impossible to carry on public business in the House of Commons, partly with Protestant freemen and partly with Popish ecclesiastical slaves.

The first point to which the Chairman directed my attention is the state of the Franchise. There, again, I have to request you will pardon my obstinacy, when I declare that I remain of the same opinion that I held in 1831, when I addressed a letter to the electors of Surrey in the following terms: alluding to a former tract on that subject I wrote, " I specified as the essential details of reform: 1st. The extension of the right of voting for some one place to all resident persons of property, let that property consist in what it may." Now let me here observe, that the new bills brought in by Lord John Russell contain no such provision, any more than the last did; and none of the Whig supporters of Lord John, down to this moment, have dreamed of going beyond him in this matter. But let us proceed with my address in 1831. " 2nd. The disfranchisement of non-resident voters. 3rd. The reduction of expense of elections, by taking votes simultaneously in parishes. 4th. The shortening of the duration of Parliament from seven to three years, agreeably to the Constitution of 1688." I have changed my opinion on this point: since then we have seen the operation of the Reform Bill; and I perceive that the most popular constituencies, such as those of London, Manchester, and other great towns, are always fidgeting and changing their representatives; the consequence of which is, that they send in a parcel of raw boobies totally unfit for public business; and so soon as they get a little sense, and knowledge of what they have to do, these wise constituencies are tired of them, and return some other persons. But to proceed. " I objected to the Ballot, but probably without sufficient reason; and it might safely be granted, wherever poor voters desire it, in order to screen themselves, in the discharge of their duties, from the interference of the rich."

I retain these opinions still. The fault of my old friends the Tories was, that they would refuse the most just and universal demand of the people for some alteration in the state of the representation; they would not give a member to Manchester, nor put an end to such an unjustifiable thing as Gatton and Old Sarum. The consequence was, that the Whigs rushed in with a revolutionary measure falsely called Reform, which transferred the power in the House of Commons from the landed interest to the manufacturing interest in towns. Almost all the farmers cried, "The Bill, the whole Bill, and nothing but the Bill;" you obtained what you then wanted, and you must not complain at reaping the harvest of that which you then sowed.

I think the importance of the Ballot greatly overrated. I do not think it will prevent bribery, because I find that bribery prevailed in ancient states which had it. It seems to be a question which the electors should decide for themselves; and whenever any number asked for it, they should have it. It cannot signify anything to me whether you vote for me standing upon one leg or upon two, nor whether secretly or openly. When the Manchester people talk about tenants being driven like sheep in pens to the hustings, and needing the ballot to protect them, they talk arrant nonsense. I never saw nor heard of these pen-driven farmers in any county in which I have ever lived. Voters often need the ballot to protect them, not from their landlords, nor from their masters, but from their brother-workmen. Of whom were the mechanics afraid the other day? Were they afraid of their master, Mr. Myers? No: but when some of them wanted to return to his employment, it was their brother-workman, Newton, of whom they were afraid. Every man is afraid of what the world says; and every man's world is the little circle of his own acquaintance. I heard of a lady, expressing some opinion to a French ambassador here, say, it was that of all the world. To which he replied, "Of which world are you speaking, madam, for I know thirty?" Most people know but one. The Manchester cotton-spinners know but one.

The radical fault of the Reform Bill was, that it was framed on no permanent principle. There is no person who uses more frequently the terms, " constituent principle," " the practice of the constitution," " the best times of the constitution," than Lord John Russell ; but there is either no accurate idea behind these phrases, or else they mean some decision adopted when the Whigs were in power. There is no principle in a franchise of 10*l.* more than in one of 9*l.* 19*s.* 6*d.* The same radical fault runs through Lord John's bill just now framed ; there is no principle in 5*l.* more than in 4*l.* 19*s.* 6*d.* Lord John is totally abroad and at sea upon all such subjects : and as it is very mischievous to have such subjects always brought forward, and as they must always be agitated until settled on right principles, I will point out to you what those principles are.

Originally, in the prospect of war, the king did not summon the people at large to assist him, but he summoned his great barons. These were holders of estates called Honours, which contained many manors, and all the persons who resided within their bounds were obliged to attend those great barons when they went to attend the king's summons. But, intermingled with these honours and manors, were a few persons who held, not of the baron, but of the king ; and the lowest value at which such property was valued was forty shillings. There was no question between forty shillings and thirty-nine shillings ; forty shillings was the lowest kind of direct service to the Crown known, and so, in virtue of this, the holders were summoned by the king to attend him in his war, and also to serve him by choosing knights of the shire to meet in his parliament.

I say, then, that the true principle of the right of voting is, that every man should have that privilege who contributes direct payment by taxes or rates, or who has rendered the Crown service in his person in the army, militia, &c. ; and for this extent of suffrage I contend. I must admit, however, that this, like all other principles, when pushed to its extreme point, would be dangerous to the well-being of society, because it is obvious that if the whole population were to be voters without any limit, that the majority of electors would be paupers, and that Communism must be the result. The reason of this is obvious. Let us take any parish you please, for what is true of one parish is true of all, and is true of the whole kingdom. There is in one of our parishes a rich gentleman, ten or twenty persons less rich, and a thousand persons mere day-labourers. Is it not clear that it is the interest of these labourers to have a division of property? If all had a right of voting, as I contend they ought to have a right of voting, then, in the case supposed, 980 persons would have the disposal by law of all the property belonging to the remaining twenty. But the only use and end of civilised society is the preservation of property, and property cannot be preserved if the majority of those who make laws for it are paupers. The Constitution, therefore, has wisely provided a counterpoise, and that is by providing that all persons to be chosen members should have a certain amount of property. If this principle is done away with, Communism is the necessary consequence, and the first and most important end to be attained by all the legislative acts of civilised communities is the preservation and security of property.

Our worthy Chairman has declared that it is useless now to discuss the wisdom of the repeal of the Corn-laws, because that is a measure already accomplished, and it is impossible to revert to it. I still, however, remain of the opinion which I have often expressed to assemblies in this county, which is, that it is not wise for any country to be wholly dependent upon another for the food of the inhabitants. I did, indeed, hear a strange gentleman declare that the cause of the ruin of Tyre was that it trusted to foreigners for its food; but Tyre was a mere bare rock like Gibraltar, and if the poor Tyrians might not buy corn, they certainly never could eat any, for not a particle could be grown on a barren rock in the midst of the sea. Most of you now present signed a petition which I drew up respecting the repeal of the Malt-tax. I adhere to the opinion there expressed. If they pretend that the consumer and not the grower of malt pays the duty on malt, then let a duty be laid on printed cottons, because it is the foreign consumer who will pay the duty and not the manufacturer. But the Manchester men know that the assertion is false. It may be possible to give some relief to the occupiers of lands by the removal of the charges for gaols, police, lunatic asylums, &c., from the county rates to the consolidated fund, but that will give no permanent advantage to tenant-farmers as a class: whatever gains are obtained in this way will ultimately, so soon as the leases have expired, revert to the landlord, and all these questions of relief to the landed interest do, in fact, mean relief to the landlord, and it is he who ultimately reaps all the advantage.

Now I do not deny, nor mean to conceal from you, that I hold the landed interest to be by very far the most important interest in the country. I have expressed this on a former occasion by the phrase that "the Queen cannot sit upon a spinning-jenny." What I mean by this is, that the landed proprietors have a permanent interest in the well-being of the State, which the trading or manufacturing class has not; and if I am wrong in this particular, I at least err in concert with the greatest statesmen of all ages, from 2000 years ago down to the present time. I find that a mechanic or day-labourer seldom looks beyond the end of the week, when he is to receive his wages, and all his accounts are settled. The commercial man, the merchant, the manufacturer, the trader, looks to the end of the year when his balance is struck, and not beyond. But I see the landed proprietor continually employed in the improvement of the permanent condition of his property, making repairs, and laying out money in various ways; all tending to show that he is looking beyond his own personal interest in it. I have conversed with many able men upon the question of readjustment of the burdens of taxation, and I find that one and all say, If you try to shift a burden, the result is, that a new part is galled without a former burdened part being relieved. All such points, however, are of a very minor consideration, because the point which you have to consider, and against which, if you follow my advice, you will contend, is the avowed intention of a large party of would-be statesmen to repeal the whole of our custom duties, and raise the necessary income of the country on the excise, and inland produce, and realised property alone. It is against this that I would direct your particular energies, and when you hear men talk of repealing taxes, examine them closely as to the end which they really have in view.

I now come, in the last part, to the consideration of the present state of parties. I still adhere to the old Tory maxim, that "Measures and not men" is the point to which we ought to keep our eye fixed : but if ever there was an occasion in which we should modify that maxim, the present is that occasion. Now let us consider the facts of the case. Lord Derby told us last year that he had not a man with him fit to take office. In the autumn, however, of last year, Lord John chose to give way to that German intrigue which he had resisted two years before, and turn out Lord Palmerston from his office. As Lord

Palmerston was the right hand of the Government, every one perceived that it was impossible that Lord John's administration could continue. Accordingly, so soon as Lord John resigned, Lord Derby was compelled to accept the charge which his sovereign laid upon him, and which, by Lord John's approval, he was the fittest person to take. It has been a great advantage to Lord Derby that his opponent has cut the throat of his own party; and there is really at the present moment no party to support but that of Lord Derby. There is a class of persons in the House of Commons who think it the highest point of statesmanship to harass, and torment, and obstruct every administration that can be formed. I have a profound contempt for such a course of conduct. I support every Government. Upon the majority of subjects they alone have sufficient information to enable them to decide; and it is safest to cast my lot in with the side of information, than with the side of fidgety ignorance. I admit that I should not have cast the parts quite as they are: I should not have chained Mr. Disraeli, a man of warm and fervid imagination, to the multiplication table, for the most brilliant genius cannot make any more of twenty pence than one and eightpence. The pinching place with this administration will be next year with Ireland, on subjects with which we supported the last administration, *but on which they will not now support us.*

After Mr. Evelyn had addressed the electors present, the Hon. Francis Scott moved a resolution expressive of the determination of that Meeting to support the present representatives of the county, which was carried unanimously.

THE END.

LONDON
PRINTED BY SPOTTISWOODE AND CO.
NEW-STREET SQUARE.

RECENT WORKS

BY THE LATE

MR. HENRY DRUMMOND.

———∞∘∞———

Abstract Principles of Revealed Religion.
Post 8vo. cloth, 6s.

On Ecclesiastical Buildings and Ornaments.
Plates, 4to. cloth, 7s.

The Rationale of Liturgies and of Public Worship.
Fcp. 8vo. 6d.

Prayers arranged for the Worship of Families.
Second Edition, fcp. cloth, 2s.

Pamphlets on the Papal Question.
8vo. 2s. 6d.

The Fate of Christendom.
8vo. 1s.

A Reply to Wilberforce on Church Authority.
8vo. 3s. 6d.

The Future Destiny of the Heavenly Bodies.
8vo. 1s. 6d.

———————————

London : BOSWORTH and HARRISON, 215 Regent Street.

BOSWORTH AND HARRISON'S
NEW PUBLICATIONS.

LECTURES chiefly on SUBJECTS relating to the USE and MANAGEMENT of LITERARY, SCIENTIFIC, and MECHANICS' INSTITUTES. By H. Whitehead, M.A., Curate of Clapham; T. C. Whitehead, M.A., Incumbent of Gawcott, Bucks; and W. Driver, Superintendent of the Belvedere Crescent Reformatory, Lambeth. One Vol. fcp. 8vo. cloth, 3s. 6d.

A NEW LIST of the FLOWERING PLANTS and FERNS GROWING WILD in the COUNTY of DEVON. With their Habitats and principal Stations. By the Rev. Thomas F. Ravenshaw, M.A., formerly Curate of Ilfracombe, Devon, Rector of Pewsey, Wilts. Crown 8vo. cloth, 4s. 6d.

CAVALRY; its History and Tactics. By the late Captain L. E. Nolan. Third Edition, with Illustrations. Post 8vo. half-bound, 10s. 6d.

HANDBOOK of the GEOGRAPHY and STATISTICS of the CHURCH. By J. E. T. Wiltsch. Translated from the German, by John Leitch, Esq., with a Preface by the Rev. Frederick Denison Maurice, M.A. Vol. 1, crown 8vo. cloth, 10s. 6d. To be completed in Two Volumes.

Some MEMORIALS of RENÉE of FRANCE, DUCHESS of FERRARA. Second Edition. One Volume, crown 8vo. cloth, with Portrait and Frontispiece, 6s.

The ART of EXTEMPORE SPEAKING: Hints for the Pulpit, the Senate, and the Bar. By M. Bautain, Vicar-General, and Professor at the Sorbonne. Third Edition, fcp. 8vo. cloth, 4s. 6d.

OLD STYLES'S. By Henry Spicer, Esq., Author of "Sights and Sounds," "The Lords of Ellingham," &c. Post 8vo. cloth, 6s.

A HANDBOOK of POLITICAL ECONOMY; containing the First Principles of the Science, founded on the Works of Adam Smith, Ricardo, Mill, Malthus, M'Culloch, &c. Fcp. 8vo. cloth, 2s. 6d.

The REVIVAL of the FRENCH EMPERORSHIP ANTICIPATED from the NECESSITY of PROPHECY. By the Rev. G. S. Faber, B.D. Fifth Edition, fcp. 8vo. 1s.

The MUTINY of the BENGAL ARMY: an Historical Narrative. By One who has Served under Sir Charles Napier. Seventh Edition. One Vol. 8vo. cloth, 5s.

London: BOSWORTH and HARRISON, 215 Regent Street.

A

LIST OF BOOKS

Recently publiſhed by

BOSWORTH & HARRISON

215 REGENT STREET

LONDON

W.

List of Recent Works

I

2 vols. royal 8vo. cloth, £2. 2s.

The Works of King Alfred the Great:

Now firft collected and publifhed in the Englifh Language, with Introductory
Eſſays, Notes, Illuſtrations, &c., by ſome of the principal
Anglo-Saxon Scholars of the Day.

II

Square fcp. 8vo. cloth, gilt edges, 2s. 6d.

The Art of Ornamental Hairwork,

Containing Simple Directions for making Hair-Chains, Bracelets,
Brooches, Rings, &c.

III

Third Edition, fcp. 8vo. cloth, 4s. 6d.

The Art of Extempore Speaking:

Hints for the Pulpit, the Senate, and the Bar.

BY M. BAUTAIN,
VICAR-GENERAL, AND PROFESSOR AT THE SORBONNE.

"A book of fuggeſtions for men who would practiſe extempore ſpeaking. . . . . . . Eloquent, forcible, full of appoſite illuſtrations."
— ATHENÆUM.

"A uſeful book to the ſtudent of public ſpeaking."—SPECTATOR.

"Written by one who has thoughtfully depicted a large perſonal experience, we cordially recommend this unpretending but valuable volume, and preſs both the book and the ſubject on the attention of our readers, as worthy of their moſt careful conſideration."—RECORD.

IV

Large 4to. in ornamental binding, 5s.

The Children's Picture Gallery.

Containing 100 large Engravings from Drawings by eminent Englifh Artiſts.

v

Second Edition, fcp. 8vo. cloth, 3s. 6d. poft free.

The Book of Recitations;

A Collection of Paffages from the Works of the beft Poets and Dramatifts.

BY CHARLES WILLIAM SMITH,
PROFESSOR OF ELOCUTION.

₊ In the various "Speakers" &c. publifhed, the greater number of pieces are more adapted for reading than reciting. In the prefent collection, which is taken largely from modern writers, every paffage chofen is fpecially adapted for recitation.

"This little volume really fupplies a want. Although we have been deluged from time to time with collections of fcraps culled from various authors, we hardly recollect one in which the felection has been made with any care or judgment; one follows in the wake of another, and we have the fame worn-out paffages quoted and repeated to wearinefs. The merit of this work is in the variety and excellence of the felection. Scarcely a name is omitted which has attained any, even a paffing celebrity; and hence we have a very readable book as well as one which is peculiarly ufeful for the purpofes for which it is intended."

THE CRITIC.

"A capital collection of paffages from the works of the beft poets and dramatifts, admirably adapted for recitation. We meet here with all the fineft pieces of Englifh poetry, both old and new."—LONDON JOURNAL.

"This collection is made with great difcrimination by a moft accomplifhed elocutionift."

WEEKLY TIMES.

VI

Fifth Edition, fcp. 8vo. 1s.

The Revival of the French Emperorfhip Anticipated from the Neceffity of Prophecy.

BY THE LATE REV. G. S. FABER, B.D.

VII

Second Edition, fcp. 8vo. cloth, 2s.

The Predicted Downfall of the Turkifh Power the Preparation for the Return of the Ten Tribes.

BY THE LATE REV. G. S. FABER, B.D.

VIII

Price Sixpence.

Kingfton's Magazine for Boys.

An illuftrated Mifcellany written efpecially for Boys, and edited by

WILLIAM H. G. KINGSTON, ESQ.

Author of " Peter the Whaler," &c.

Publifhed on the Firft of every Month ; each Number containing Forty-eight Pages of interefting matter, and Illuftrations.

" ' Kingfton's Magazine for Boys' ought to be pofted monthly to every fchoolboy in England. We know that fcarcely anything would delight a boy fo much ; and older folks may depend on the ftrict morality of the tales, as well as on the purity of the ftyle and the deep intereft of the fub-jects felected by that friend to boys, Mr. Kingfton. The number for November is fully up to the average." MORNING HERALD.

" ' Kingfton's Magazine for Boys ' is as healthy and good in tone as it is poffible to be."—LITERARY GAZETTE.

" The boys ought to be thankful that they have found one fo well qualified as Mr. Kingfton to take their amufement and inftruction in hand. This little mifcellany which he edits prefents juft fuch a collection of interefting matter as every boy will be glad to pore over. There are tales with hair-breadth efcapes for the lovers of excitement, travelling ex-perience for the adventurous, fun and frolic for the laughter-loving ; biography, natural hiftory, and in-formation on various fciences for the ftudious, and, in fact, entertainment for all. What more can be offered to win the fuffrages of the young we know not."—ENGLISH CHURCHMAN.

" ' Kingfton's Magazine for Boys' grows upon us,—there is fomething fo brave and hearty in its ftories." LITERARY CHURCHMAN.

" The prefent number gives us no caufe to alter the good opinion we have formed of this periodical. There is a good variety of matter, well written, thoroughly boyifh, and full of fpirit. The illuftrations are alfo very good. If we have any boy readers, we cordially recommend them to try it ; at all events, parents who value our opinion fhould do fo." UNION.

" Mr. Kingfton will be hailed in many a fchool as a ' jolly good fel-low.' He is already a favourite among boys, and if we miftake not, his magazine will render him famous for at leaft another generation." JOURNAL OF EDUCATION.

" A new fixpenny magazine. It is full of varied and interefting matter well fuited for boys, and for girls too. It is illuftrated with fome good en-gravings."—LEEDS INTELLIGENCER.

" A wholefome, healthy, and hearty tone pervades this mifcellany, which no boy can read without be-coming better and braver, for all the incidents are caft in that peculiar mould which no Englifh boy can fail to appreciate." SHREWSBURY CHRONICLE.

" There is no magazine equal to this for boys. The very reading of it will give them a hearty, hardy fpirit —juft what one would like to fee perpetuated among our lads." HULL ADVERTISER.

⁎ This Magazine will be fupplied regularly on application to the Publifhers, or to any Bookfeller.

IX

Crown 8vo. cloth, 5s. 6d.

Kingſton's Magazine for Boys.

Volume 1, containing 500 Pages and 80 Illuſtrations.

*** The Numbers publiſhed ſince the Firſt Volume may ſtill be had.

X

New Edition, 8vo. cloth, 3s.

The Rev. Ed. Irving's Preliminary Diſcourſe to the Work of Ben Ezra,

Entitled, "The Coming of the Meſſiah in Glory and Majeſty."
Alſo his Introductory Eſſay to Biſhop Horne's "Commentary on the Pſalms."

"The preſent volume ſhews the ſeeds of all the religious movements which have diſtinguiſhed Engliſh Chriſtianity during the laſt thirty years. . . . A ſtyle chaſter than Jeremy Taylor, ſimpler than Hooker, and fuller of poetry and energy than any writer whom we can call to mind, except Berkeley."—LITERARY CHURCHMAN.

XI

Fifth Edition, crown 8vo. cloth, with Atlas of Plates, 12s.

A Treatise on Field Fortification, the Attack of Fortreſſes, Military Mining, and Reconnoitring.

Illuſtrated with 12 Plates.

BY COLONEL J. S. MACAULAY.

XII

Fcp. 8vo. 2s. 6d.

Moral Theology of Liguori the only Infallible Expoſitor of Roman Doctrine;

Or, Caſes of Conſcience.

BY PASCAL THE YOUNGER.

With a Preface by HENRY DRUMMOND.

"No antipapal work has appeared in modern times more lucid in its arguments—more logical in its concluſions—more aſtounding in its ſtatements—or more powerful in its language—than 'Caſes of Conſcience.'"—THE BULWARK.

"For powerful ſtatements, ſtartling facts, pungent wit, and that eloquence which is 'reaſoning on fire,' our day, fruitful in power, has produced nothing like 'Caſes of Conſcience.'"—ARCHDEACON GARBETT.

XIII

Second Edition, crown 8vo. cloth, 3s. 6d.

Christian Family Life.

Translated from the German of Professor Thiersch.

CONTENTS: Introduction — Marriage — Education — Filial Duty — Servants — Social Intercourse.

XIV

Seventh Edition, 1 vol. 8vo. cloth, 5s.

The Mutiny of the Bengal Army:

An Historical Narrative.

By ONE who has Served under SIR CHARLES NAPIER.

"A very spirited and instructive sketch of the revolt, which we hope to see completed. It is written by one who knows India well."

ATHENÆUM.

XV

Third Edition, post 8vo. half-bound, 10s. 6d.

Cavalry;

Its History and Tactics.

BY CAPTAIN L. E. NOLAN, 15TH HUSSARS.

With Coloured Illustrations.

"A well-written and well-digested book, full of interesting facts and valuable suggestions."—DAILY NEWS.

"The most masterly, and the most attractive book which has been written on Cavalry. It is an important contribution to military science."

MORNING POST.

"We know no book—we believe there is none—which will adequately supply the place of this. To those belonging to this arm of the service,

Captain Nolan's book is indispensable; to members of all arms it may be useful; while, from the rich fund of interesting anecdote with which it abounds, it will attract and delight the general reader."—INDIAN MAIL.

"A very seasonable work. Even to the unprofessional reader the subject of this book must be full of interest, and the soldier by profession has, we should conceive, much to learn from its pages."—TIMES.

XVI

Fcp. 8vo. cloth, 2s. 6d.

A Handbook of Political Economy;

Containing the First Principles of the Science, founded on the Works of Adam Smith, Ricardo, Mill, Malthus, M'Culloch, &c.

"This very unpretending little work contains, in a few well-written pages, the sum of the whole science of Political Economy, and lays before the reader, in succinct and lucid sections, the result of much and careful study."—GLASGOW HERALD.

XVII

Second Edition, 18mo. fewed, price 1s. poft free.

A Catechifm of Mufic,

For the Ufe of Children, in Two Parts.

To which is prefixed, a Short Dictionary of Terms ufed in Mufic.

BY GERTRUDE PLACE.

" A clear and fimple little Catechifm on the earlier portions of the grammar of mufic. It will be found really ufeful."—GLOBE.

" In a feries of queftions and anfwers all the elements of mufic are taught in a very clear and agreeable manner, and the book is further enriched by a copious dictionary of mufical terms. This is one of the fimpleft and beft books for beginners we have ever feen."

ILLUSTRATED TIMES.

XVIII

Second Edition, 1 vol. crown 8vo. cloth, with Portrait and Frontifpiece, 6s.

Some Memorials of Renée of France, Duchefs of Ferrara.

" The author has evidently been at confiderable pains in fearching out particulars of her life, and has executed a felected tafk with a zealous fidelity."—TIMES.

" The author here fubmits to the public an interefting memoir of the Princefs Renée, Duchefs of Ferrara, and youngeft daughter of Louis XII. of France. The work is admirably conceived and executed, at once fecuring the fympathies of the reader in behalf of this highly gifted but ftrangely unfortunate fcion of royalty. The reader will find much information and confiderable amufement from the perufal of this well-digefted and elegantly written volume."

LEADER.

" We cannot conclude this brief abftract of the leading events of her chequered life without expreffing our fenfe of the fervice which the author of the prefent memoir has rendered to the caufe of religious biography."

THE PRESS.

XIX

Poft 8vo. cloth, 6s.

Old Styles's.

BY HENRY SPICER, ESQ.

AUTHOR OF " SIGHTS AND SOUNDS," " THE LORDS OF ELLINGHAM," ETC.

" This capital ftory is, in a great meafure, a reprint from *Houfehold Words*, and held, in its earlier form, a defervedly high rank among the contributions to that periodical. Mr. Spicer's ftyle is the happieft imitation of Mr. Dickens's own ; the pathos is especially so. ' Old Styles's ' has merit enough of its own to eftablifh a wide popularity."

LITERARY GAZETTE.

" Mr. Spicer's fchoolboys are real boys, with all the fun, mifchief, and idlenefs of their clafs, and his fchool ftory is told as fuch ftories are and fhould be—entirely for its own fake."

xx

Third Edition, 18mo. *cloth, price* 1s. 6d. *post free.*

A Hundred Short Tales for Children.

From the German of C. Von Schmid.

BY THE REV. F. B. WELLS, M.A.,

RECTOR OF WOODCHURCH, KENT.

" Incidents, accidents, natural phenomena, thrown into the form of little narratives, designed to impress lessons upon children at the same time that interest is excited by the tale."—SPECTATOR.

" There is sufficient point, and a good moral, in most of the very brief and simple stories before us—a moral generally expressed, after the old fashion, in a proverbial couplet, tolerably impressive. We recommend the clergy to make an experiment with this volume in their parochial schools."—ENGLISH CHURCHMAN.

" This is about as pretty a book, in whatever sense we may speak of it, as could be placed in the hands of children; and we highly recommend it to parents, teachers, and all who have the care of them, as being an excellent help in developing their moral character."—LITERARY GAZETTE.

" A book with a hundred tales for little children, short, spirited, and pithy, about birds, beasts, fishes, fruits, vegetables, eatables, drinkables, jewels, clothes, watches, clocks, brothers, sisters, fathers, mothers, and every other imaginable noun-substantive, is too welcome a family guest not to be much in demand. Very justly, therefore, have Schmid's ' Tales for Children' reached a third edition. It is a common school book in Bavaria, and English parents will be glad to know that it is worth getting."

GUARDIAN.

XXI

8vo. *cloth,* 6s.

On the True Definition of the Church;

One, Holy, Catholic, Apostolic.

BY THE LATE HENRY DRUMMOND.

XXII

Post 8vo. *cloth,* 6s.

Abstract Principles of Revealed Religion.

BY THE LATE HENRY DRUMMOND.

XXIII

Fcp. 8vo. *cloth,* 2s.

Family Prayers.

BY THE LATE HENRY DRUMMOND.

XXIV

Third Edition, fcp. 8vo. boards, 1s.

Charades, Enigmas, and Riddles.

Collected by a CANTAB.

XXV

Crown 8vo. cloth, 6s.

Hiftory of the Church in the Apoftolic Age.

Tranflated from the German of Dr. THIERSCH.

BY THE LATE THOMAS CARLYLE.

" In his earlier works Dr. Thierfch had fhown powers of no ordinary kind; found fcholarfhip, a reverential tone of mind, a juft and difcriminating appreciation of doctrines and principles, and a candid fpirit and a clear ftyle. . . . . His hiftory of the ' Church in the Apoftolic Age,' which appeared in Germany in the early part of this year, is the firft divifion of a larger work on ' The Ancient Chriftian Church,' and I earneftly hope that it will be tranflated into Englifh, for it is not only a learned and inftructive work, but on nearly every important queftion connected with the conftitution of the Church, the conclufions at which the author arrives are either exactly or very nearly thofe which have always been held by the great divines of the Church of England." — Rev. T. K. ARNOLD, in the THEOLOGICAL CRITIC.

" We muft now bid farewell to Dr. Thierfch and his interefting work, which is deferving of careful reading and extenfive circulation. It brings the Church of the Apoftles very graphically and diftinctly before us."
GUARDIAN.

XXVI

Vol. 1, fmall 8vo. cloth, 10s. 6d.

Handbook of the Geography and Statiftics of the Church.

BY J. E. T. WILTSCH.

Tranflated from the German by JOHN LEITCH.

With a Preface by the Rev. F. D. MAURICE, M.A.

The SECOND VOLUME, completing the work, is in the prefs.

" Wiltsch's volume is one of vaft refearch and induftry. Without pretending to have read it through (which would be nearly as abfurd as giving out that we had perufed Forcellini's Latin, or Dr. Johnson's Englifh Lexicon), we have referred to it for explanation of feveral geographical and ftatiftical difficulties, and we find it both ample and correct."—CRITIC.

XXVII

2 vols. 8vo. cloth, 21s.

Speeches in Parliament and Miſcellaneous Writings of the late Henry Drummond, Eſq.

EDITED BY LORD LOVAINE, M.P.

"The ſpeeches, dating from Mr. Drummond's return to parliamentary life in 1847, are brilliant, original, and entirely unaffected by ordinary prejudices and conventionalities. In many inſtances they muſt have been beſide the purpoſe of the debate; but they contain more ſtriking aphoriſms, more pregnant epigrams, more pointed ſtatements of abſtract truth than the collective eloquence of a dozen miniſters and leaders of oppoſition. It might be expected that ſo acute and original a mind would provide for itſelf a ſuitable mode of expreſſion; and Mr. Drummond's language is remarkable for its idiomatic felicity and force."—SATURDAY REVIEW.

XXVIII

Fcp. 8vo. cloth, 2s. 6d.

The Early Life of Louis Napoleon.

From Authentic Sources.

" This little book is deſigned to be popular, and contains all the elements of popularity. The ſtyle is lively, the narrative conciſe, the facts are grouped together with taſte, and there is not a ſingle page in the volume which the reader will deem uninteresting."—LITERARY GAZETTE.

XXIX

1 vol. fcp. 8vo. cloth, 3s. 6d.

Lectures chiefly on Subjects relating to the Uſe and Management of Literary and Scientific and Mechanics' Inſtitutes.

BY H. WHITEHEAD, M.A.
CURATE OF CLAPHAM;

T. C. WHITEHEAD, M.A.
INCUMBENT OF GAWCOTT, BUCKS;
and
W. DRIVER.

xxx
Square crown 8vo. cloth gilt, 5s.

A Picture-book of Merry Tales.

ILLUSTRATED BY EDWARD WEHNERT.
With 40 Illuftrations.

xxxi
Third Edition, enlarged, 2s. 6d. ; by poft, 2s. 8d.

On the Right Management of the Voice in Reading and Speaking.

BY THE REV. W. W. CAZALET, A.M.

xxxii
Crown 8vo. cloth, 4s. 6d.

A New Lift of the Flowering Plants and Ferns growing wild in the County of Devon;

With their Habitats and principal Stations.

BY THOMAS F. RAVENSHAW, M.A.
FORMERLY CURATE OF ILFRACOMBE; RECTOR OF PEWSEY, WILTS.

" A copious catalogue of all ne-ceffary details, unencumbered by any fuperfluous obfervations, and will therefore be a valuable portable com-panion to the botanical tourift."
ENGLISH CHURCHMAN.

xxxiii
Crown 8vo. cloth, 5s.

Lights and Shadows in the Prefent Condition of the Church.

Nine Lectures on Chriftian Truths, peculiarly applicable to the Times we live in.

BY CHARLES J. T. BOHM.

.Tranflated from the German.

London : Printed by Spottifwoode & Co. *New-ftreet Square.*

www.ingramcontent.com/pod-product-compliance
Lightning Source LLC
Chambersburg PA
CBHW032314280326
41932CB00009B/806